To Jothi – any‘

AN ORDINARY MAN'S TRAVELS IN AN EXTRAORDINARY WORLD

JEFF BROWN

FRIENDLY ROAD PUBLISHING

Published in 2019 by Friendly Road Publishing

ISBN Paperback: 978-1-9161731-0-1
Ebook: 978-1-9161731-1-8

A CIP catalogue copy of this book can be
found in the British Library.

80% of royalties for this book will support the work of the
Meningitis Research Foundation
www.meningitis.org

Cover design by Emma Shoard

Published with the help of Indie Authors World
www.indieauthorsworld.com

IndieAuthors
World

ABOUT THE AUTHOR

Jeff Brown is ordinary. I wish I could tell you about his rugged good looks, humongous intellect and bulging biceps, but that would be a big fat lie. He was born in Melton Mowbray, works in a 9 to 5 job and grows potatoes in his garden. He hasn't even managed to write a nice novel for you, instead he has simply recalled actual events. To tell you the truth, Jeff Brown has only released this book because he is raising money for charity. What sort of reason is that! Is he not even good enough to make himself some money out of writing?

Anyway, don't read the introduction of his book; it promises a lot but who knows what mis-adventures await us in the subsequent pages.

He did ask me to confirm to you that he is donating 80% of his author royalties from this book to the Meningitis Research Foundation. There will be updates on the amount raised and pictures from the events in this book on his website www.jeffbrownauthor.com.

He also wanted to let you know that the book is written as he went along on his journeys so the tense can vary depending on the point of the day that he wrote the diary entry - sounds like a convenient excuse to me. I better go now as the book is about to start.

INTRODUCTION

There are many awe-inspiring travel books that contain the escapades of amazing people. Those that walk thousands of miles, climb down a mountain with a broken leg, discover lost cities, live in strange lands or crawl across the Sahara on a hot day in a rubber suit towing a fridge whilst eating crackers.

Well, it all sounds far too difficult for me. So the following travel diaries are of an average, ordinary, normal, standard, humble, basic man - me. English homo sapien, 1972 prototype with no added options and more than the odd imperfection. This is for us ordinary people.

'*That sounds noble*', I hear you say, '*but why would I want to read about someone average?*' Good question. Well, the book is not terrible, which is a reasonable start. In fact, I may even say it is amusing in places. It is also the sort of book that goes well with a nice glass of red wine, or a friendly pint of beer or a refreshing cup of tea.

Still not convinced? Although I can see you like the wine/beer/tea idea (delete as applicable). Well, I may be ordinary, but this world is truly remarkable. There are erupting volcanoes, deep water-filled canyons, ancient cities in the clouds, pyramids made of sand, the most beautiful mausoleum in the world with the saddest of stories, friendly cheetahs, cities that rise up from the desert, 15 pence glasses of beer, comedic elephants, vulture assassins, a pink city, mind-bending tea, sumptuous palaces, seven continents, over 200 countries, 6,500 languages and billions of wonderful people. So read it for the sake of this remarkable world that we live in, because that is what this book is all about.

The following seven diaries are from little trips in this extraordinary world. The journeys were fitted in over the years, between work, family commitments, lack of money, concerns about safety and in between all major international football championships. They take me from blundering backpacker wondering what travelling is all about, to being bitten by the travelling bug, to thinking that this travelling malarkey is the best thing in the world, to considering I might visit all the continents, and then on to the final diary.

The final diary is different. I'm unsure whether to tell you about the last diary or keep it shrouded in mystery. As the final diary is what makes this travel book different, then I think I'll explain ….. my travelling days seemed numbered and my diary writing had petered out. I think the condition that caused this is known as 'becoming a dad' (side effects include lack of sleep, lack of spare time, lack of money and, despite all these, an irrational sense of joy). When my little boy was 18 months old, he was struck down with meningitis and his life hung in the balance. At a point where we were plunging to the depths of despair, a nurse presented us with a diary. She said we should write in it to come to terms with what was happening. The irony was not lost on me. Indeed, it was like an old friend coming to support me in my time of need. So the last diary is an emotional rollercoaster including a hairy male bridesmaid, a beautiful Indian princess, a hijab-wearing eye-poking lady of inspiration, a four-year-old adviser to the gods, tears, heroes, lucky pants, Napoleon, lots of tea and a guest appearance from the eighties pop siren Belinda Carlisle.

The diaries are set out in chronological order, but in the name of travel freedom, you are welcome to read them in whatever order you fancy. Europe, India, Australia, Peru, Namibia, Mexico or the land of PICU – you can stick to the natural path or choose your own route through the book. We have a lot of ground to cover, so we better head off to ………………………

Diary 1

I'll give you a few statistics before each diary, just because I find it quite interesting and I guess it is a gentle introduction to the diary's next destination. Here it is for Europe:

	UK	Europe
Population in millions	65.6	740
Projected population in 2050 in millions	77	728
Infant mortality per 1000 live births	3.9	5
Life expectancy - male	79	75
Life expectancy - female	83	81
Gross national income in purchasing power parity divided by population (in $)	40,550	32,614
Area of country (square miles)	93,638	3,837,000

Note: I admit that I didn't count the people and measure the land but took these figures from the 2016 Population Reference Bureau. Then I looked at Nationmaster.com for the land area of countries and Enchantedlearning.com for the continent's land area. Seems odd that the population of Europe is projected to decline.

Now we are beginning to think of Europe, I need to move us to the summer of 1994. So let's put 'Four Weddings and a Funeral' on at the cinema, make John Major prime minister and Terry Venables England manager, cut the tape to open the channel tunnel and put 'Live Forever' by Oasis on the stereo. The journey is just beginning...

Day 1 - Thursday 21ˢᵀ July 1994 - Goodbye Blighty

A lexander the Great, Julius Caesar, Napoleon, Jeff Brown - it was my turn to invade Europe. But instead of battalions, I possessed a rucksack. If this was a Roald Dahl story I'm sure it would have been a magic rucksack with special powers, allowing you to travel anywhere, anytime. But it's not, and the only extraordinary feature lying within the canvas was the pukey yellow and purple colouring.

7.30am, bags packed and I was ready to spread myself all over the continent. I would be travelling with three friends who had just completed four years of study in Sheffield. Thus the group were desperate for one last flirtation with complete freedom before work arrived on the horizon bringing us all a lifetime's supply of toil and trouble.

Craig Allen arrived at 8.00am and we were promptly whisked away to the local hustle and bustle of Leicester. Despite the train tickets to Dover being safely pouched, my worry level increased when Craig began unbuttoning himself around the platform 3 area. The worries were suppressed when it was just his money belt that was pulled out, he seemed to have the groin money belt rather than the waist belt. At least I knew that if anyone got hold of his money I'd know he had made a new friend.

The journey to London was fairly mundane, with a one-hour delay whilst we waited for a lorry to be disentangled from a bridge. With Sacha (a bloke with a girl's name) Balachandran (and a surname that should be a country or at least a capital city) also turning up late at our designated St Pancras meeting point, Rich Bartlett the fourth member of the group had a lonely wait. This gave him plenty of time in which to convince himself that he had turned up on the wrong day or wrong week or wonder whether he should be waiting at Kings Cross?

Anyway, there were these four young men, they reached Dover, crossed the water and began to sort out their night's accommodation. Discussions ensued, would we go to Brussels or Bruges, Bruges or Brussels. Time was our enemy. When we reached Calais, Lille became our favoured destination. The first problem was how to escape from Calais station, a dilemma faced with 12 other Interrailers all equally confused by the foreign atmosphere. Everyone seemed hesitant in finding some useful information, like how to get out of a dodgy looking station. Instead, we were simply content to be in our little English huddle. I'm sure if any natives had approached we would have formed a circle with our rucksacks and fought them off with a stiff upper lip.

Answers were eventually sought and found. Our foursome trekked across to a different Calais station so as to continue our journey and reach Lille. Only 15 minutes more and we would have sadly had to spend our first night in Calais. For the rest of our lives, we'd have to spin a web of lies claiming Bruges was reached on the first night. The shame of '*oh you know that Jeff Brown, he went to discover the wonders of Europe but spent the first night in Calais*' would have instantaneously discredited my fledgling travelling career.

With a clean conscience, we met up with Lille at 9.00pm. At 9.01pm Sacha made his first claim to be the unluckiest man in Europe when a feathered friend suffering from loose bowels dive-bombed his bag. This was only shortly after his rucksack zip had broken. Craig was the prime suspect after loitering around the aforementioned bag shortly before the events unfolded (for the bust zip not the bird poo).

After consulting Sacha's (the bloke with a girl's name and surname of humongous proportion) guide book, for directions to the one and only hostel in Lille, we set off. 15 minutes later we were back at the station: 'we'll look at the city map kept in the station, get our bearings and find the hostel'. Off we trooped again, out the station and past a posh restaurant for the third time. 15 minutes later we passed the restaurant for the fourth time and were back in the station. The restaurant customers in the window had started smiling at us on our third excursion passed them and when we all trooped by the fourth time they could barely get their soufflés down.

The four of us studiously concentrated on the glass-cased map until each had a mental picture of exactly where to go. Then off we went, out the station and past the restaurant with the now hysterical customers. But even after all these attempts we just couldn't find the bloody hostel. These were desperate times and called for desperate measures. I volunteered to try out my French: 'Poulez Vous Anglaise?' '*Yes*'. 'Do you know where this hostel is?' I said showing him its description in the book. *'Ah yes, it got knocked down a year ago'*. As the Frenchman left me standing in the middle of the street, my mouth still open, and him with an air of French delight, the four of us reviewed our options.

We could sleep at the station or try a hotel, which would be more money than our budget could afford. The guide book did provide a selection of four hotels one of which we saw earlier. The restaurant was duly past a sixth time with Sacha almost running past it in a doomed attempt to save himself from embarrassment.

As true heroes, we did not give up and completely undaunted we selected the only accommodation from the book which had been spotted; a hotel by the name of 'Le Coq Hardi'. The name was a concern; did we really want to stay at this place? However, rooms were available and we all went to bed. Not all together you must understand, well except Rich and me. I stress this was not out of choice. Craig and Sacha took the last twin bedroom leaving only doubles. Rich told me he'd try and remember that the young attractive figure lying beside him was not his girlfriend. I crept ever closer to the edge of my side of the bed.

Day 2 - Friday 22ND July - Interesting, Belgium?

The morning brought Sacha's voice complaining of Craig waking up in the middle of the night with a loud yell, sitting up, swearing, and then going straight back to sleep. Nonetheless, his story was dismissed as Sacha going insane and we moved onwards to Bruges.

Bruges has a reputation as both the Venice of the north and the best medieval city in Europe. The beautiful canals and buildings meant that I felt obliged to agree with these statements despite having never visited Venice or being sure which years the medieval period covered. We selected a hostel from the cheap sleep guide and knocked on a closed door. A passer-by then informed us that it was the hostel as well as the door that was closed. Apparently, we were six months too late, but at least the building was still standing so we were improving. The next nearest hostel was pinpointed and we took up their offer of temporary residence in exchange for Belgian Francs.

It felt good to drop off my rucksack and actually explore somewhere.

We wandered around aimlessly in the beautiful town until we came across the Church of Our Lady. I'd never really had much time for looking at churches but I had to admit the architecture looked great. I'd also never really had much time for sculpture but there was a piece called 'Madonna and Child' that was simply exquisite. It turned out that it was a piece by Michelangelo. No wonder they still talk about him.

This seemed to satisfy our need for culture so we had a meal and then let Craig lead us on a night walk. Bruges seemed a very respectable sort of place but Craig seemed to take a couple of turns and find a dodgy looking club.

Mind you at least he'd gone a day without continually unbuttoning himself whilst claiming to be checking his money belt.

DAY 3 - SATURDAY JULY 23RD - AN ENGLISH WEREWOLF IN BRUGES

At 3.00am I was awoken by a loud cry of '*aaaaaaaaaahhhhhhh*' from Craig, then some swearing. Sacha wasn't kidding when he had mentioned Craig's strange nocturnal behaviour. I had noticed earlier that there was almost a full moon so Sacha and I wondered whether it would be wise to kill Craig just in case he was going to change into a werewolf.

The strange thing was that in the morning Craig could not recall his night-time screams and claimed to be asleep all night. In my confused state, I had a shower but left my gel in the cubicle. When I returned to the shower room some selfish git had nicked my cubicle. I was whinging about this to a bored girl waiting for a shower when it happened. The Lady from the Lake's (girl in the cubicle) slender arm majestically rose above the water (top of the cubicle) and Merlin said '*taketh the sword*' (she said '*you mean this gel*'). Arthur rowed out on to the lake and claimed the legendary blade (I said 'wow you're a star' and grabbed my gel). It's the stuff that legends are made of; maybe I am destined to be a great werewolf hunter fighting them with my magical gel or maybe the Roald Dahl in me is slipping in again. Talking of werewolves, Craig's theory for his night time antics was that he must be suffering from cramps. Although Sacha and I still favour shooting him with a silver bullet – just in case. Craig seemed quite emotive on the subject of him being killed and adamantly stuck to his cramp story throughout our journey to Amsterdam.

We made the mistake of not arriving in Amsterdam until 4.00pm. We phoned a few hostels but kept hearing '*we are full*', so the plan changed and became 'move out on a night train to Berlin and thrust our belongings into the station lockers'. It gave us seven hours to explore Amsterdam.

Our calculations informed us that it meant we had five hours to waste before going to see the really famous streets of Amsterdam. We thought Amsterdam must be famous for other things but we weren't sure for quite what. Desperate times called for desperate measures and we opened up our guidebooks: founded in the 13th century, wars against Spain in the 16th century, upheavals of reformation, followed by becoming a real trade power, then a slow decline until it became fashionable in the 1960s.

The guidebooks led us to Dam Square and the Royal Palace. Before we knew it the five hours were up and our legs took us to the maroon-ish coloured light area. There were two main streets sighted, both with canals running down the middle. On either side, there were numerous sex shops, sex shows and scary looking ladies selling their wares in the windows. The tourist guides warned us not to go down the side streets but that is where the famous booth rooms were so needed a visit (the streets not the booths). In the side streets, the booth workers looked more normal than the main street workers and it appeared you could employ whatever type of woman you desired, but my feeling is that they may not respect you in the morning.

I was hit by an array of emotions. From initial intrigue and laughter to thoughtfulness and wondering how they ended up in an Amsterdam booth touting their bodies for business while tourists like us looked on in amusement tinged with pity.

There were a lot of English accents that could be heard. One chap seemed to be bartering but was told in no uncertain terms *'no money no *ucking, no money no*ucking'* (if my mum asks they were saying 'ducking'). Another commented on the fact that one bloke was ushered into the booth by a lady on the 10.00pm shift while she was drinking her coffee. While Sacha was continually approached about drugs (selling to him, not buying from him) Rich felt a tap on his shoulder from a young female, but both were unwilling to part with their remaining guilders. Although Rich's initial reaction of *'I think she fancies me'* was met by a quick reminder of his present location.

Eventually, we tore ourselves away from the windows to go back to the station and collect our bags. Craig became increasingly frustrated as his key would not turn and the locker remained shut (that isn't a euphemism we were really back at the station). Just before he complained to a station official, the solution struck him, he should use his key to open his locker rather than the locker next to it.

Day 4 - Sunday 24ᵀᴴ July - Ich Bin Ein Berliner

The train carriages consisted of an aisle running up the side with about eight different compartments housing six seats in a 'three facing three' formation. Basically, the design associated with a victim being murdered whilst an opposing train passes by but no one believes the onlookers claim of witnessing a killing until Miss Marple pops up to unravel the mystery.

At 5.00am the train rattled on, everybody taking up different positions in hopeless attempts to get comfortable. When comfort is almost found it is the ticket inspector's job to come in and wake you up. Four and a half hours of sleep were completed before Berlin had surrounded our train.

By 7.00am each of us had examined the 'Europe By Train' handbook, and discussions were then held as to which of the two Berlin stations should host our reception. After to-ing and fro-ing the unanimous decision was to depart at Hauptbahnhof, the second stop. The train ground to a halt at the first station whereupon every backpacker in Europe seemed to jump off the train. As panic set in Messrs. Allen, Balachandran, Bartlett and Brown followed their fellow travellers in a sheep-like manner. Somewhat apt considering the stop was Zoo station, okay maybe not in terms of a proper one but what about petting zoos?

All I could think was 'I need sleep, just let me sleep, four and a half hours isn't enough'. With head submerged in hands, I fell fast asleep outside a Berlin shopping centre. Holidays weren't meant to be this tiring.

The tourist information centre finally opened at 8.30am. We teamed up with Bob and Dave, a pair of Interrailing scousers, at the information desk, then on the train (U-Bahn), on the bus (Bob successfully put on the weary traveller look and got us all on free), and then walked on to what looked like the Addam's family hostel. Worryingly our little posse seemed to be the only souls in the place and were informed by Lurch that the leaflet showing the 'evening meal included in the price' was a misprint.

Anyway, we all headed for central Berlin, directions coming from Rich's postcard which had the city layout on it, officially money being an object, unofficially no one could be bothered to purchase a map. We thought it would provide a good chance to use a little German but I had to point out to Rich that his German version of 'do you speak English'- 'Sprechen sie Deutsch' may not be very helpful, even in Germany.

It was amazing to think that Hitler conducted his violent campaigns from here. I'd been brought up on war films and Berlin had seemed the epicentre of evil. Mind you I always thought that Hitler was wrongly cast. He just seemed like a comedy caricature, being a little bloke, with greasy hair and a funny moustache, raving on about a superior Aryan race with blonde hair and blue eyes. It seems more than a little like the Emperor's New Clothes. And did he really only have one?

The postcard brought us to the endless spiral steps of the Siegessaule Victory Column. The reward for the climb was a breathtaking view of Berlin.

The journey up the steps had sent my head spinning a bit, however as the downward spiral sent my head spinning in the opposite direction the senses were scrambled half way down. This on top of the dull light led to several phantom steps being created by the bizarre shadows, as I tried not to stumble my way into a German Hospital.

Berlin and Berliners seemed to have a kind of Ready Brek glow to them that I have never seen in any other city. Maybe it is not surprising after being separated for so long or maybe it is closer to Chernobyl than I thought. After visiting the Brandenburg Gate, the Chancery and the parks we headed for Schloss Charlottenburg, which looked majestic on our postcards but not quite so good when it was all locked up by the time you arrive.

We called it a night and went to the Adams family hostel via a doner kebab shop, but being sober I had chips.

DISASTER - Courtesy of the world service it was discovered that England had lost the first test match of the series against South Africa. This did not make another hot uncomfortable night any better. The weather was great during the day but just too hot for me at night.

Day 5 - Monday 25ᵗʜ July - Sun, Sand, Sea And Wasps

The Adams family hostel still seemed fairly deserted but having seen some other mortals at breakfast, it was realised that there was a chance of escaping in one piece. I did have another thought on my mind and asked Craig, who had developed into our resident historian. He reckons there is a line of thinking (known as the 'lone nut' theory) that the ditty about Hitler was true and he only had one testicle. But some of the evidence comes from Russia, which would depend on whether you believe that they did find his body when they entered Berlin and surreptitiously whisked it away to Moscow.

After breakfast, we headed back to Zoo station, while Bob and Dave carried on to Munich. The plan had been to deposit our bags in the lockers, then travel to East Berlin and the beautiful Rhine Valley. The idea was flawed because we failed to locate any available lockers.

Thus it was just a case of setting off for our new hostel located 10 minutes walk from the beach. Berlin beach! Beach! Yes, it exists, even if it is in West West West Berlin and is a kind of lake-beach.

We reached our impeccable new hostel after travelling on a clean and effi-cient train (Germany definitely has its positives). We proceeded to spend an hour on the beach before my inability to sit still finally wore down the others. I led the way off our arses, to the station and a return to the city centre. On the way I innocently tossed an empty cola bottle into a bin, just missing a couple of wasps. Unbeknown to me I had just started the Berlin wasp riot of 1994. Wasps buzzed menacingly around me (allergic to nettles, wasp stings are as yet an unknown reaction), Craig (allergic - a real swell guy) and Rich (mum - very allergic). Whilst attempting a new anti-wasp dance, which involved the flapping of both legs and hands at high velocity, Sacha suffered an injection of wasp poison into his leg.

Report by the victim:

'After constantly annoying some wasps Jeff made a rapid escape leaving me to face the killer swarm - a decision had to be made - a personal sacrifice for the benefit of three young men. I could not let them suffer - I had to do it - a hero was born!' Sacha

After the incident, and when we'd figured out that Sacha would not die for at least a few hours, I went to tread in the footsteps of one of the greatest athletes this planet has ever seen, in a place where the spirit of Jesse Owens can never be removed. The legendary 1936 Olympic stadium stood before me but the main entrance was closed. No God, don't let this happen! Allow me to witness the spot where Hitler squirmed at the sublime performances of a supreme athlete! Then Rich spotted a side entrance. Money emigrated from pockets but who cared when we were in the Olympic stadium - well almost in the stadium. All we had to do was find where the door was in the fencing. There seemed to be a design fault. No door appeared as we followed the fencing, just a swimming pool. The truth dawned, we hadn't paid to enter the Olympic stadium but for a swim, granted in the Olympic pool, but a swim nonetheless. I didn't know whether to laugh or cry so I laughed then sulked. The Olympic stadium was closed so a very dispirited Jeff trudged to the U-Bahn. Rich went to the kiosk and used his best German to organise a refund. He said that he wasn't a swimming pool, he was an Olympic stadium. It did work though. Our underground tickets had run out of time before we reached East Berlin so we played the honourable citizens and got off a few stops before our destination.

Day 6 - Tuesday 26ᵗʰ July - A Room With A View

Bye-bye Berlin, hello Hamburg. After having an all too short affair with beautiful Berlin, we were due a quick one-night stand with Hamburg. I suppose this is a bit harsh on Hamburg but it seemed to be a big industrial city and was a come down from Bruges, Amsterdam and Berlin.

At our new hostel, Sacha took it upon himself to find our dormitory and we followed him in good faith. I put my feet up and rested on my newly claimed bed while the others wandered around the hostel looking for the showers, toilets and cola machine respectively. So there I was enjoying my easy life in Europe, with my feet up and eyelids down. Footsteps echoed in the distance and then voices could be heard getting closer and closer until they reached the room, the left eyelid slowly opened and the eye sent a message to the brain that it had recognised people of the female gender. The brain wanted confirmation of this fact, which was provided by the right eye. The left and right eye then watched as one of the three girls placed her bag on Craig's bed and another one put her bag on Rich's. The Cheap Sleep guide warned to be careful about where you stayed because some accommodation in Hamburg's Reeperbahn district provided extra services but surely we couldn't be that lucky, after all this was an International Youth Hostel. After conversing with the fellow occupants and the newly arrived Sacha it was apparent that we were not just in the wrong room but also on the wrong floor. It would have been interesting because our quartet were only spending 10 minutes in the hostel before venturing out, not to return until late in the night.

We moved our bags to the correct room then went on a tour of Hamburg that took in a large town hall and some pretty gardens. It seemed a much greener place than I expected. Like Amsterdam, it had its large port and like Amsterdam a notorious red light district which we stumbled upon. The Reeperbahn was much seedier than its Amsterdam equivalent, but while the sex-related businesses occupied one side of the street, decent respectable theatres faced them on the opposite side of the road. Burger King's decor was interesting with every window seeming to have a prostitute outside it, a bit different to Amsterdam where they were all on the inside of the windows. I decided that however hungry I became I wasn't going to ask for a whopper.

The hostel was reached by midnight but myself and Rich stayed in the lounging area of the hostel for a bit longer. Rich departed after another 10 minutes only to return several minutes later telling me that he had innocently entered our dormitory and switched on the light only to see the German lad in the room had invited his girlfriend along. Rich thought they must be cold because they were hugging each other very tightly.

I heeded his words, then headed to the dormitory and switched on the light.

Day 7 - Wednesday 27th July - An Innocent Man?

In the morning the four of us caught a train to Copenhagen. We tried to work out the best time to jump off the train and board the ferry, but all this mental energy was wasted when to our astonishment the train itself boarded the ferry. The ferry had train lines inside it, which I'd never even considered. When we landed in Denmark the train simply drove off the ferry and continued on its merry way.

The first impression of Copenhagen proved positive and I thought we could get an even greater feel for the city by walking to the hostel. One and a half very hot hours later and this seemed to have been a bad idea, especially with our rucksacks sweatily stuck to our backs. The hostel is positioned by a small lake and being quite secluded, we only found it after asking directions from the friendly locals. Unlike in the UK where if you don't know the correct directions to a destination the correct response is 'don't know mate', in Denmark if you don't know the correct directions you grab somebody else who does know the correct route. Well, I think that is what happened and that they were not saying *'these stupid British can't even find that hostel!'* My Danish is still limited to Kobenhavn so I could not quite interpret exactly what they said between themselves.

On reaching the hostel we selected Sacha to find our dormitory in the hope of him again leading us into a female dorm. He let us down badly and found the right all-male room. There were four bunk beds crammed in the room and lockers for your valuables in the corridor near the male and female bathrooms.

On one visit to his locker, Craig glanced up to see a half-naked female in the women's bathroom. He said with conviction that he averted his eyes to save the young lady any embarrassment and also he is short-sighted so unless he stopped to put his glasses on he could not see properly.

Report by Mr Allen on the alleged incident:

'I was INNOCENTLY walking along a corridor when a young woman opened the door to the women's toilet/showers. I inadvertently glanced across and saw a very attractive naked young woman rubbing herself

down with a towel. This may have been done to dry herself. I "quickly" glanced away to save the young woman's honour (being the gallant guy I am) and stumbled to the dorm.' Craig.

Our attempts to leave the hostel were then hampered by an inexplicable number of trips to the lockers as Barry, Reg and Godfrey claimed that they kept changing their mind about what we should take from the lockers into our day bags (names changed to protect the guilty).

When we finally reached Copenhagen city centre it was really lively with several excellent buskers, especially one from Northern Ireland who entertained a large crowd, which included the four of us. The temptation of a bar finally became too much, but at £16 for three beers and an orange juice, one round lasted most of the night (quick note from me, the 2018 Jeff, to say that the £16 drinks round is worth £31 in today's money – I knew we shouldn't have ordered that orange juice).

Day 8 - Thursday 28ᵗʰ July –
Football, Beer And A Little Mermaid

I enjoyed a long sleep and felt suitably refreshed. A visit to the supermarket left us with our regular low budget meal of yoghurt and bread although the others did not appreciate my strawberry yoghurt sandwiches. I think the taste for strange food must have gradually festered within me from the fairly sensible egg and salad cream sandwich, to the corned beef and tomato sauce bap, to the fish fingers and tomato sauce butty, to yoghurt and ice cream pudding and then yoghurt sandwiches. Well either that or I am pregnant.

We had a lazy day in Copenhagen and treated ourselves to the cheapest boat trip available that would visit the Little Mermaid. I am not sure whether it is traditional that when the boat passes a big fat scruffy old bloke he is obliged to drop his trousers, but one chap displayed this peculiar ritual. This precluded four English voices fighting to be the first to say 'I didn't know your dad lived in Copenhagen'.

When we arrived at the Little Mermaid she was covered in Mr Bean tapes. I was sure that it was nothing that the Little Mermaid couldn't handle. Over the last 30 years she has had a bra and knickers painted on her, been decapitated and had her right arm chopped off, but still she sits contentedly on her rock.

Now I knew her first name may be 'Little', but she was tiny. However, she must have inspired Craig because he thought we should go and see Hans

Christian Andersen's grave, and this I confess, did not seem a bad idea at the time. The graveyard was located and there were even maps of where certain gravestones were resting. We searched for Hans Christian Andersen's grave; we searched, searched, still searched, whinged, searched, whinged, gave up and went home.

At night time a beer was sipped in our regular bar (well we'd been there twice, but I was still working on everybody shouting *Jeff!* as I walked in). Chat went in an 'old college days' direction as we reminisced; 22 years young and already reminiscing.

We arrived at the train platform ready for a return to the hostel and were met by the sight of a Danish man in a shell suit pacing up and down, sweating profusely and blatantly feeling himself in front of some ladies. The train arrived and he entered our carriage. On the realisation that we were English his face lit up and a conversation started.

Danish Bloke to me : Where are you from?
Jeff: Leicester .
Danish Bloke With Smile : Ah Leicester City.
Danish Bloke to Craig: Where are you from?
Craig : Nottingham.
Danish Bloke With Smile : Ah Nottingham Forest.
Danish Bloke to Rich : Where are you from?
Rich : Bristol.
Danish Bloke With Smile : Ah Bristol Rovers.
Danish Bloke to Sacha : Where are you from?
Sacha : Milton Keynes.
Danish Bloke With Frown : Ah Oh.
Sacha : Near, Luton.
Danish Bloke With Smile : Ah Luton Town.

At least we made somebody happy.

Day 9 - Friday 29ᵀᴴ July - Yabba Dabba Do

Day 9 would be when Copenhagen would be left to fend for itself but we planned to return. The Danes had been very friendly and if I was forced to live outside the UK, I decided that Scandinavia would be home, especially as they show live English football on their televisions.

A train from Copenhagen to Gothenburg was caught. Why Gothenburg? Well, despite being about to become an accountant, Sacha had chanced upon a young Swedish female in London and we were due to meet up with her.

The trip to Gothenburg was fairly uneventful, but a problem arose due to an oversight i.e. we let Sacha book it. The hostel was not actually in Gothenburg but lay 16 km away from the city. This involved a train journey and 4 km walk. It wasn't all bad because living 16 km away gave us plenty of time to practice our skills in verbal abuse on Sacha.

Before we left the city Sacha and Rich nipped off to spend a chunk of money at a burger joint. Meanwhile, myself and Craig enjoyed Pizza, free chips and salad accompanied by Beavis & Butthead on MTV for about £2.80 which seemed a miraculous price in Sweden.

When we walked the 45 minutes from our local station to the hostel I was to be hit with a bombshell. It emerged I was the only mentally stable one in our party. Craig and Sacha revealed the imbalance in their contorted minds when a Red Dwarf discussion led to the revelation that they preferred Betty Rubble to Wilma Flintstone. How could any sane man prefer Betty over Wilma? Rich did not make a selection, instead mumbling something about they're only cartoon characters or something. I put that down as a vote for Wilma.

Day 10 - Saturday 30th July - Psycho The Return

I had quickly realised that Gothenburg was the most dangerous city I had ever visited. I would be innocently walking along when yet another beautiful blonde would glide by transfixing my eyes and rooting my feet to the floor. Meanwhile the oh so silent trams would be bearing down on me.

I managed to dodge the trams to meet Ingelar, Sacha's Swedish contact, in the shopping centre. This was despite the fact that they had both confessed that neither of them could remember what the other one looked like. Ingelar was blonde, friendly, 20 years of age and strangely worked at a London branch of Burger King.

We all went on a pleasant boat trip around the Gothenburg canal and harbour. That was followed by a visit to the park, which also had a zoo with wild animals such as cows, goats, horses, seals and sheep. A zoo with sheep, brilliant, my Berlin station joke works after all. The park was ideal for a lazy afternoon and we realised its potential to the full. Seldom am I ever ashamed of being English but on hearing how Ingelar was actually hit by an England football thug after the 1992 European Championship game I was not impressed. How could they hit a girl?

It appeared that Swedes have a very low opinion of themselves, despite being very successful for a country with a relatively small population. I have great respect for the Swedes, we give them our pollution and they give us a friendly disposition and a clutch of top sports stars. Life seemed much easier by having a Swedish guide and we could just go with the flow. No thinking about the language or the best sights to visit, simply follow the pretty Swedish girl.

We went for a meal, which cost us money day 17 and 18; the budget was stretched, to say the least. The British thing was done and we paid for her meal. Brits may be thugs, but we are polite thugs, as proved by invading various nations to create the British Empire whilst trying to teach them about cricket, drinking tea and queue etiquette. The journey continued to a bar where several beers were consumed, while, like a few other groups, we sat on the floor. I had a conversation with Ingelar about Swedish football which was interrupted by yelling coming from Sacha. Poor old Sacha, it appeared that a drunken Swede had accidentally stumbled on to his outstretched hands as they walked by. The trampling experience continued to feature on his hands throughout the night much to the amusement of everyone, with possibly one exception.

In fact, Sacha was beginning to metamorphosise into his alter ego 'Psycho Backhander'. The alter ego, as with most people, arrives after numerous beers and is a loud happy-go-lucky version of Sacha. The 'Psycho Backhander' alias was derived from an alternative offered by a computer spell check in response to Sacha Balachandran. Insanity was creeping through his mind when he suddenly made an addition to his family and gained a brother. No sweaty doings were involved in his brother's conception; it simply took his mouth to go into overdrive with a flood of amusing drivel coming out. The story was then accepted by most of the group. Craig and Rich who had even lived with Sacha for a year even started to believe he had a brother. I think he should have gone for 'I was a trainee astronaut' rather than 'I've got a brother'. I put it down to the wild imagination he had developed after studying accountancy for 4 years.

Day 10 was edging towards day 11 when four brave British lads were walked to their bus by a lone Swedish girl. Hey das (goodbyes) were exchanged and the hostel beckoned. We were greeted by a moose on the loose, a real live moose, in the dark it looked kind of 'mystical'. Sacha had been shat on by a bird, stung by a wasp, what would the moose do to him? Luckily for him, it just looked up and walked away.

Day 11 - Sunday 31st July - Heaven Is A Place In Sweden

Sacha woke up with a speech impediment; all he could muster was *'Git, Git, Git, Craig, Git, Git'*. Apparently what had happened was that Craig had revealed details of his or rather Psycho Backhander's murky past to Miss Ingelar Andersson. Craig was so shocked and deeply upset by this accusation that he burst into laughter. 'Murky Past' is actually too strong a phrase; basically, Craig gave details of Sacha's drunken escapades but what are friends for? Well in most countries it's a trusting overtly friendly relationship, in Britain real friendship is obviously trying to embarrass, insult and take the piss as much as possible.

We had originally hatched a plan to spend the day in Gothenburg and take a night train to Stockholm. This would save us some more money because our train ticket gave us free travel on most trains. It was just certain trains that we weren't allowed on or had to pay an additional surcharge. However, we fancied more time in Stockholm than Gothenburg and managed to book a hostel in Stockholm that was only £5 per night – although we needed to be there before 6.00pm. And anyway Gothenburg was not quite the same without our guide; we were kind of sheep without a shepherd (I hoped Craig with his suspicious werewolf behaviour did not have a similar thought).

We arrived at the station to wait for our prospective train which was due to reach Stockholm at 5.00pm. Perfect. It was then that Sacha started leafing through the Thomas Cook Book. This was our book that showed all the train timetables for Europe and allowed us to plot a course across the continent. Anyway, Sacha spotted a little asterisk which we hadn't noticed before which confirmed that we couldn't take the train without a reservation. With no time for a reservation, Sacha worked out an alternative train which was a little slower but would get us to Stockholm about on time.

The train was peaceful and the land majestic, although it was disappointing not to see any Viking ships on the lakes and rivers because it would have set the scene perfectly. The long journey had neared its conclusion but the train was particularly old and slow which enabled the sands of time to completely cover our hostel reservation. It was 6.01pm as I leapt (well made two little steps) from the train, I wanted a phone to re-reserve our reservation and I wanted it immediately. Surging Christie-like (that's Linford, not Agatha) through the station, I spotted some phones. Unfortunately, all of them had people attached to the receivers. Still, a phone was needed to stop us from becoming the homeless of Stockholm. I sprinted out of the station and then back in via the higher section, still phoneless. As we rode the escalator Rich managed to pluck the address book from my bag thus saving a couple of potentially vital seconds.

A mental note was made that if I ever went to any superhero conventions, to have a word with Clark Kent and tell him not to visit Stockholm Central as he would have difficulty changing. 'A phone, please a phone' and then within the space of 30 seconds it was all over and the hostel was still ours.

The hostel was absolutely superb, set on an island next to the old town and by another hostel, which was actually a sailing boat. A chatty receptionist greeted us and sent us on our way to a 20-bed dormitory.

Later we explored the old town, which is a small island with beautifully preserved cobbled streets. It is not a place for an asthma sufferer like me as it takes your breath away.

We aimlessly wandered agape with admiration. If you had to kiss a city centre then my choice would be Stockholm and my tongue would be slipping into the mouth of the distinguished Royal Palace (sorry, you and the Royal Palace think I got a little carried away there).

Day 12 - Monday 1ST August – The Hitch Hikers Guide To Stockholm

I love Stockholm. I suppose it is difficult to elope with a city but I tried to think of ways in which it might be accomplished. We did the Stockholm walk, which mainly covered the area around the old city. Craig and I even nipped into the cathedral to see the statue of St George. It was an act of patriotism even though I thought before going in that he probably never existed and maybe it was time for England to change over to St. Lineker. However, I learnt that he might have existed. The story goes that he may have been a soldier in Palestine around 300 AD who protested against the bad treatment of Christians. As a result of this, he was beheaded and became one of the earliest Christian martyrs. Typical though isn't it, the story wasn't selling very well so they added a bit of sex (fair maiden) and violence (a dragon) and suddenly everyone laps it up.

My historical knowledge was improving by the day, as was my ability to eat yoghurt sandwiches. I thought I'd make my first million marketing them. I could tell the others were impressed by the strange looks cast in my direction.

Sacha led a hike in the evening to the restaurant of his choice from the guidebook. After booking the 'miles out the way' Gothenburg hostel he had now found us the 'restaurant at the end of Stockholm', but after our three mile hike we decided, to Sacha's disgust, to eat at the restaurant next door to the 'restaurant at the end of Stockholm'. It was very cheap and I dispatched a large portion of much-needed pasta.

Craig and Sacha headed back to the hostel, the pressure of having an alter ego must have been making them tired. Rich and I wandered the streets and somehow into the Stockholm nightlife. It was a shame we couldn't stop for a beer but it was too expensive for my bank manager's liking. I also looked a mess after being attacked by a Calippo lollipop. I was trying to eat it when it lurched menacingly. It escaped from its wrapper and I just managed to fight it off, but a large brown mark was left on my shirt – yes, shirt. Earlier I teamed up with Sacha to enjoy better luck with the art of ice cream consumption, taking account of banana, cherry, rum & raisin and Irish coffee varieties. We were left happy, poor and pot-bellied.

Anyway, the nightlife looked good, the harbour looked great and I was a contented man.

Day 13 - Tuesday 2ⁿᵈ August - Bored

Rich and Craig both confessed to entering the hostel's female toilet, allegedly by mistake. Craig and the incident at the female toilet/changing room were becoming a regular event.

Rich had come up in a rash; maybe it was something to do with him using the wrong toilet or it could have been a reaction to the salmon he ate, who knows?

We left the hostel and headed for the station to dump our bags in their lockers ready for our night train exit later in the day. The 'dumping the bags' ceremony was becoming a regular ritual as hostel checkout times didn't allow for a lie in and the body refused to cart a large rucksack about for an entire day.

A walk along the harbour led us to a park where according to the tourist bumf *'in one afternoon you will learn more about Sweden than if you travelled for a week'*. What should have been said was that in one afternoon you will learn more about Sweden than if you travelled around Outer Mongolia for a week. I learnt nothing about Sweden except not to go to Skanson Park again. It was full of little kids, old Swedish cottages and a zoo. The zoo had all kinds of strange animals such as rabbits and cats. There were also wolves etc. but they all looked like they had the Monday morning blues. In fact, they looked more bored and frustrated than me.

My personal feelings about most zoos outside the top ones like London are not favourable. I know I get agitated if I am stuck in one room for too long, although it is probably worse for anyone stuck in the room with me. If all the animals were allowed to go to the pub for a quick bevvy and on for a kickabout afterwards then all well and good, but it doesn't work like that.

Boredom grew, thirst grew, boredom grew, thirst grew, boredom, thirst, boredom, thirst Aaaaaaaaaaaahhhhhhhh! I had to escape and a suitable plan needed to be hatched, a tunnel, climb the wall or just walk out the exit. All people have an Achilles heel; for Superman, it's kryptonite; for me, it's boredom; and for Achilles, it was a dainty ankle or something. I walked off around a track leaving the others on a bench. I thought they'd follow me; they thought I'd come back. No one got the right answer. I wandered around the path and finally came to one of the exits, I could go back and find the others or leave. On the other side of the exit, there was a cafe and I ordered a jumbo size Pepsi in an effort to quench my equally giant thirst. I watched and supped as the world went by, all fairly relaxing but at the same time hoping that the others would find me at some point. About three-quarters of an hour later the fab four, as no one called us, had regrouped.

Day 14 - Wednesday 3ʳᵈ August - Pride & Prejudice

The night train carried us in a Copenhagen direction. Although I slept through the ferry journey, Craig had the essential night ferry experience. As the train neared the ferry Rich, Sacha and I slept like the proverbial baby whilst Craig's conscious and unconscious were battling for control of his mind. The train chugged towards the ferry, jolted, stopped, reversed; Craig's conscious dominated his mind once more. The train tried to board the ferry again; it chugged forward, jolted, stopped and reversed. A faction of Craig's conscious calling themselves 'paranoia' began canvassing for support. The train chugged forward and onwards, paranoia went back into the closet and Craig could rest easy once more on the train on the ferry. Then a ferry alarm sounded, which led to paranoia returning bigger and stronger, with the manifesto 'we are going to sink'. The alarm was switched off and Craig survived. The rest of us took the better option of sleeping through the chaos and waking up on the other side of the water, feeling better for a bit of shuteye.

We reached Copenhagen still weary from the journey and eager to secure more sleep. Copenhagen station had a two-floored Interrailer centre that allowed you to lie around or even take a shower, but not at the same time. Shower tokens were purchased which provided 5 minutes of deliciously hot water and then cold water when the shampoo was in your hair and the 5 minutes was up.

We left the centre in the late morning and had another lazy day in Copenhagen. The best lazy days involve a couple of beers so what better place to go than the Carlsberg brewery. The grand tour was completed, which was quite interesting and I was impressed to learn of some British-related facts:

- The first barrel of beer that Carlsberg exported was to Scotland (for some reason this doesn't seem a big surprise)

- In 1939 - 55% of all beer imported to the UK was from Carlsberg (really?)

- In order to celebrate a visit from Winston Churchill, Carlsberg commissioned a new beer, which they named Special Brew (that is amazing although it kind of adds up)

The finale of the tour consisted of drinking several bottles of various Carlsberg beers, although our table quickly ran out of bottles. Meanwhile, the people on the next table left so we nagged Sacha to jump up and grab their bottles. Whilst he was thinking, someone else from another table put the idea into action. If only he had been a bit quicker more free alcohol would have been mine, I mean ours (after the excessive prices we had been paying, anything free was to be savoured, it was not totally the craving for beer, honest!).

However, we would not let such defeats due to Sacha's lack of pace put a downer on proceedings and chatted merrily away with the Slovenian and Spanish girls at our table. They were obviously very impressed with our command of the English language. Mid-conversation there was a pregnant pause and a giggle (as in a long pause and a laugh) as the people at the next table who had left re-emerged with cigarette packets clutched in hands. A minute later they were involved in a blazing argument with the table who had swiped their bottles. Sacha instantly claimed credit for his amazing insight.

The remaining beverages were duly tucked away and we started to walk away when the guide shouted at us to stop. We looked at each other wondering which one of us had slipped a couple of bottles into their bag. She came over to us with a camera in her hand and I sort of thought 'ah she must want to take a photo of us, these Danes just can't get enough of us Brits'. It was then I realised that her camera was the same make and type as mine. She handed it to me and laughed. I had left my new expensive camera sitting by itself in a brewery. After several renditions of 'thank you, Danish people are so nice, oh thank you', the happy couple of myself and the camera were reunited.

We headed back to the station with Barbara from Slovenia who was also having one last decent holiday before venturing into the world of work. The four of us posed for pictures with her before bidding farewell and going on the Copenhagen maps official walks number two and three. The walks were basically around the parks of Copenhagen but these were not entirely successful as a couple of them were closed. At one point, when we were on the edge of the pavement looking to cross the road, a couple of Danish lads on bikes passed by. One of them veered across directly at Sacha before pulling away at the last second. My red mist descended but he had all but gone before my mouth was into gear to let rip at him. I was none too impressed with the 'racistik svin' (pardon my Danish) and was still chuntering a volley of abuse before Sacha calmed me down. It seemed ironic that the black bloke was calming down the white bloke about the racial abuse but I suppose he was more accustomed to dealing with it than me.

We returned to the Interrail centre but overdid the relaxing because by the time we left there our train was already at the platform and had filled itself with people. The last thing you needed on a hot night was a compartment full of people, especially with my smelly feet, therefore with great foresight, we had reserved four places in a compartment. The only problem was that we hadn't been in place to frighten off other potential inhabitants to our compartment and the two other places were occupied. Our cohabitees were a couple of Australian girls, from Australia strangely enough.

Day 15 - Thursday 4TH August - Prague & Prejudice

It went something like:

00.01am - can't sleep.

00.03am - it's hot.

00.05am - can't sleep.

00.07am - I don't believe it! Sacha, Craig and one of the Australian girls have fallen asleep.

00.09am - can't sleep it's just too hot.

00.11am - my feet are melting I've got to get my trainers off.

Gradually mind you. I've got to let people slowly acclimatise to the smell.

00.13am - heaven, my feet are released.

00.15am - I just can't sleep it's far too stuffy.

00.17am - much to my amusement and Craig's pain he head-butted the window in his sleep. A confused Craig woke up wondering what on earth had just happened.

00.19am - oh that's taking the piss Craig's gone back to sleep.

Can't sleep Too hot Can't sleep Too hot Can't sleep Too hot
Can't sleep Too hot Can't sleep Too hot Can't sleep Too hot
Can't sleep Too hot Can't sleep Too hot Can't sleep Too hot

The train boarded the ferry and within 10 minutes myself, Rich and Natasha (one-half of the Australian girls) escaped this Interrailer's version of the Chinese water torture. In total there must have been four people on the deck, which was sparsely lit by a mixture of dim lights and the stars. It was about another hour before we dared to venture back below deck into the 'oh so hot' train. It was a simple matter of finding the right door to take us back to the deck where the train lay. The darkness and tiredness seemed to have concealed the door that we had originally popped up from. We knew it couldn't have disappeared but our search lacked a certain door when the realisation dawned that it was a long walk from the port to Berlin. This spurred us on to open any door we saw. The approach worked because after five more minutes the door, followed by our train and even the correct carriage all came into view. We sat back down and tried to find a sleeping position. The mistake that Rich and I had made was that we were in the middle seats and had nothing to lean against, hence comfort was but a dream.

I finally managed a couple of hours sleep but the body was still crying out for rest and recuperation when the platform sign showed Berlin. The train pulled into the station and after discussions between just about everyone in the carriage, just about everyone from the carriage figured out that this was the Berlin stop that they wanted and got out.

We grabbed a bite to eat, which involved one person being left with the four rucksacks whilst the other three headed to opposite ends of the station. It was here that I spotted a newspaper headline stating that Jurgen Klinsmann had joined Tottenham.

My bravado in reading the back page of English newspapers rather than paying £1.50 for the whole paper had increased substantially. All I wanted was a 20-second glance at the main sports headlines. What I really needed was a mobile remote control with a teletext screen. The two elements had already combined so that I could never watch a TV program from start to finish, often convincing myself that two shows could be watched at the same time. If it was a program I really wanted to watch, then I would continuously keep the same channel on, but obviously teletext would flitter about on the screen. My ideal cinema would provide me with a remote control so I can switch to the other films and bring up the latest sports news. Thus if the boffins couldn't invent a remote control with a teletext screen what about a remote that can control any television set so I can use it wherever I am.

I digress. Hunger had set in; an unsuccessful rummage through my pockets had led me to find just enough German money for a drink and a lump of stale bread. Rich and I were still particularly tired and everything seemed a bit bleary as we headed for our platform to Prague (or is it train to Prague, I don't know I said I was all blearied up).

The train wasn't particularly packed out but many seats were reserved, so we knew that our knees might only be bent on a temporary basis. The guess was accurate as me and Rich soon had to find another cabin. We were joined by two Germans, one male, one female and many tattoos. As Rich and I occupied the window seats, trying to catch the elusive experience known as sleep, they folded the remaining four seats into two sleeping bed/seats and laid down. After getting bored with this they folded them back up. The bloke and Rich attempted conversation but the guy favoured the words '*fuck it*' and '*I hate the English*'. Other than that he was quite friendly. I could not be bothered to argue with him, for one I was shattered and for two he was bigger than me. Although my official line was option C - you do not argue with him as you do not respect his opinion.

It wasn't my imagination that the journey was going slowly; on reaching the Czech Republic the train had slowed down to a canter, apparently due to the state of the track. This was by no means disastrous as the views were wonderful.

10 miles out of Prague an old lady came into our carriage wanting us to stay in one of her apartments, we politely declined but admired her enthusiasm.

Rich and I re-joined the Czech Landscape Admiration Society. The peace was shattered when we stepped off the train and were immediately hassled by a guy wanting us to sleep at his hostel. If they were dragging people off trains in order to fill the beds of their 'guest house' did we really have the desire to reside in their residence? We politely declined.

The four of us tried to wake up our weary and sleepy minds to assess the problem of being homeless in a foreign country. We were hindered by having no local currency as it could not be bought outside the Czech Republic. It would have been easy to have accepted the lad's offer of a hostel and changed some travellers' cheques at the station, but both options had a 'being ripped off' feel to them. Instead, we sat down to rest and look through a guidebook or two.

10 minutes later the hostel tout found us again as the hostel was so good and lively he didn't want us to miss out, how thoughtful and to think I thought it was due to him being paid on commission. We politely declined.

Another five minutes passed, he was back, wanting to show us his wonderful hostel. We declined.

Another two minutes and our pesterer's return was greeted with a firm confirmation that we had no intention to sleep in his hostel. The steam coming off Sacha should have given him a clue to the fact that if he asked one more time someone's rucksack may end up in someone else's face, the only problem being that with Sacha's aim it could have been mine.

We hung around the station for another 15 minutes trying not to look overly pathetic but unsure where to go or how to get there. Prague was not looking good. The strain of the train journey from Stockholm to Prague began to take its toll; sleep deprivation didn't seem to assist the decision-making process.

The plunge was finally taken and a search commenced for the American Express office. It was not an easy stroll, especially with the rucksack and sweltering heat partnership. While we sat on the steps of American Express, a Dutch lad approached us to see if we wanted to stay at the hostel where he lived. He had the honesty to say that there would be a couple of free nights at the hostel in it for him and said it was just a short walk away. It was a tempting offer for our battered bodies and as he'd been up front with us it was accepted.

The hostel lay about three-quarters of a mile away, reasonably clean and very cheap. They had three spaces in one very crowded dormitory and one place left for me in a merely crowded room. I experienced Paradise when my rucksack slunk off my back and my feet emerged from the unholy stench that was the inside of my trainers. There were five sets of bunk beds in the murky room. A bed, even the sound of it felt good after not sleeping in one for the last couple of days. A bed, bed, bed, bbbbeeeedddd. The other room was just a muddle of about 30 beds, beds, bbbbeeeeddddssss.

Prague waited for us outside and I wanted to Columbus around. That initial feeling after dumping your bag was of a real buzz, who needed beer and sex when you can take off a rucksack? Well, obviously me, but it was a good feeling. On our minds besides sweat and hair was a desire to find the University accommodation recommended by a couple of friends.

The clues led us up the side of Petrin hill, which overlooks the city. The tracks wound their way up the steep slope, but the quicker ascent was to try and negotiate the gravelly face. This was attempted successfully, although we reached the summit hot and sweaty in the fading light.

There were about nine hostels on the top, which we assumed to be either present or old Halls of Residence. After chatting to a couple of English people staying there we decided on a change of home for tomorrow but a meal was a more pressing issue.

We picked our restaurant and ordered, delighted that the waitress could speak some English. Three stomachs took on a satisfied slumber but Sacha's decided there was still room for some pudding. However, the dessert he ordered was not forthcoming, instead, a cappuccino appeared. When he protested, the waitress forgot all the English she knew and reverted to Czech. He paid for it but enjoyed a good moan.

DAY 16 - FRIDAY 5ᵗʰ AUGUST - MAYDAY

The novelty of sleeping in a bed was appreciated by my whole body from head to toe. Suitably refreshed we departed from our hostel and with rucksacks in place headed up the hill to find our new home. The new home was about £6 a night, £1 more than the previous hostel but proved a class above our previous domain. The rooms were for two people but were relatively spacious and we spent much of the day lazing about doing nothing.

Another sultry day seemed in store as the temperatures rose through the eighties. Strangely I'd always thought that because Czechoslovakia was behind the iron curtain it must be cold. Another childhood illusion shattered.

Sacha decided that despite the fact that he wasn't going to take a shower at that time he would find out where it was for future reference. Sacha had not brushed up on his foreign languages and as the showers were only marked with male or female in Czech, Sacha being Sacha ended up in the wrong one. Unfortunately/Fortunately (depending on your point of view) there was nobody there so his alleged mistake was recognised and addressed by an about turn.

Before we headed into the city I decided to use his information and take a shower. On completion of the towelling down process and the introduction of boxer shorts, a couple of visitors arrived. The English girls had made the same mistake as Sacha but as I knew where the other showers were I happily gave them directions, while they writhed with embarrassment. This was probably to do with them being in the wrong set of showers rather than the sight of my body, but it is debatable.

By the time we were ready to go out, it was Friday evening and Rich thought it would be quicker to go straight down the hillside rather than using the winding path. The side was quite stony and relatively steep but it did not faze our brave heroes. The trick was to weave from one side to the other rather than straight down at a suicidal pace. Halfway down one particular slope, Craig and I were bringing up the rear; Rich was some distance ahead followed by Sacha. The Balachandran machine then strived for another gear (second), but the increased speed was compensated by a loss of control causing him to go hurtling down the slope. Rich was stunned to find a yelping Sacha flying by him with little room to spare. However, Sacha's body was just not ready for such excesses and the legs gave way, the body crashed to the floor and the next 15 yards of the slope were undertaken on the Balachandran undercarriage before he ground to a halt.

The fall left one broken watch, several cuts and bruises, a poorly leg and a moaning Balachandran. The journey was completed down the paths and all was forgotten for a while when we found an excellent downstairs restaurant and tucked into some delicious food. This allowed Sacha time to develop his injured but brave soldier repertoire in time for our walk across to the hillside cable lift. It was far easier than trudging up the hill and, for Sacha, far less dangerous.

The hostel complex had several bars, so our foursome headed for the main one. A couple of 15p pints disappeared before the conversation hotted up with Sacha accusing me of lacking stamina. This hypothesis was based on my habit of trying to sleep anywhere, anytime. The gauntlet had been thrown down and the duel commenced. Both parties agreed to run around the outside of the nearby stadium to decide who had stamina. Well everyone agreed on it except for Sacha who preferred a kind of 'sitting still in a chair' sort of stamina contest. Thus the gauntlet ended up lonely and cold on the floor, which was a good thing as I didn't have any intention of doing a run. It was the non-runners, Craig and Rich who were keen on the race.

Day 17 - Saturday 6th August - Fight Night

Overnight, Sacha's leg swelled up to a worrying level, although everybody else had a good night's sleep so life wasn't all bad. The leg had etched concern right across his face and he decided to rest his leg today. We combined our medical resources to search out various types of antiseptic. The leg had bled a little and had scraped layers of skin from various areas, but hopefully, it was just the bruising that had caused the swelling.

Sacha had developed an uncanny knack of being at one with nature especially pigeons, wasps and hills. Suddenly the thought of Sacha, Pompeii and Vesuvius did not appear a tempting cocktail. We were due to reach Pompeii at some stage although Sacha had received a letter just before he left requesting his presence on a pre-work training day scheduled for the 18th August, so being the conscientious chap he was, a curtailed trip was already on his cards.

The rest of us descended on the old town, but glimpses of sheer greatness were often distorted by layers of bird faeces and general disrepair. We traipsed along the magical Charles Bridge and then ascended the bridge's tower via the steep and twisting steps. It proved to be a good decision, as it lifted us above the crowd and into a grandstand view of life. On one side stood the castle and cathedral astride the hill, whilst on the other is the old town where most of the city seems to lie. Wherever you are the cathedral seems to dominate the skyline of this place, once the capital of Bohemia, once the capital of the old Holy Roman Empire, not so long ago in Russian hands but free once more. Laying in the midfield of Europe means you're in the thick of the action.

My eyes were drawn to a man with a python; he was charging other people to have it around their neck. Everybody seemed interested in looking at the snake instead of being tempted into any physical contact. I pointed this out to Rich and we observed this pattern of behaviour for a minute. Suddenly the form book was turned upside down as one brave punter had it placed around his neck. 10 seconds later there was another and then another and another until people had to queue. I thought we had just witnessed an economic cycle or at least half of one.

Our wanderings brought us to the old market square. Rich and I decided to test our legs once more by going up to the top of the clock tower. In our attempts to find the entrance we mistakenly wandered into the main Tourist Information Centre, which we had been looking for earlier. Well, we get there in the end. On the hour the clock chimes and the mechanical apostles were unsheathed to jiggle around to the delight of the tourists below.

Although Prague seemed to be inexpensive, a top up of funds was needed. As Rich and I stood outside American Express waiting for Craig, hunger began to nag away. In order to defeat it, I went to buy a hamburger and was closely followed in the queue by Rich. I bit into my hamburger, longing for the feeling of food and stomach as one. As I was chewing an American approached wanting to know where I had purchased the burger. I swallowed my mouthful and pointed to the burger stall; he shook his head and unravelled a story of how he had eaten a hamburger from the same stall. It had been undercooked and he spent 5 days in bed with gastroenteritis. Realising gastroenteritis wasn't the name of a pretty Czech girl I stood in horror and thanked him for his warning. My gaze turned to the bitten burger and I was shocked to see how red it was on the inside. First Sacha left 'incapacitated' at the hostel, next me? The burger was duly binned and similar advice was relayed to Rich who dispatched his burger in the same bin. I enjoyed the bread anyway.

By 6.00pm we had arrived back at the hostel to check on the afflicted. He seemed to have enjoyed a nice quiet day. Another bread-dominated meal was completed before wandering across to the bar; the stomach seemed unflustered despite the burger concern.

All seemed peaceful as Sacha whinged about his leg at the hostel bar and recounted his story about contemplating going home within a couple of days because of his injury. I then glanced up to see about six lads in a heated argument; we all turned hoping to see a bit of fisticuffs. A spot of shoving started, then suddenly one lad drew a can of mace out of his pocket and sprayed it into another's face. All hell broke loose as fists flew and glasses shattered all over the bar. As the first glass broke it was the signal for Sacha to metamorphosise from 'the incapacitated' to Colin Jackson as he leapt across our table and over the small fence. He stormed to a gold medal but was quickly followed by everybody in the bar as the first showers of glass rained down. About 12 lads were now involved in the scuffle which seemed to be quietening down as I nipped back to get my beer. No young hooligans were going to keep me from my pint, after all, I had spent 15p on it. This coincided with the participant's violence levels increasing again. I retreated back to where everybody else was although I seemed to be one of the few with a drink as no one else had been pig-headed enough to venture back to the bar mid-fight. The police arrived after a few more minutes followed by an ambulance which was patching up the wounded. One lad had taken a full glass on the head which did not seem to do too much damage, but others did get glassed.

As the glass was cleared up, people returned to their seats. One English lad had fled in terror when the fight broke out, leaving his wallet which then vanished in the chaos.

The fight made everybody in the bar much more friendly and chatty although Rich could have started another scrap when he asked a couple of Australian girls *'Which part of the States do you come from?'*

Sacha then departed for bed and the rest of us sat on the steps of the hostel nipping to the upstairs bar every so often to increase our alcohol content. We chatted with some Americans and Brits in an interesting night, as the conversation went from Asterix the Gaul to felching. In my naivety, I had to ask exactly what felching was? I was told *you don't want to know*. When they did finally explain I found out they were right, some things are better left unknown.

Day 18 - Sunday 7ᵀᴴ August - The Calm After The Storm

3.30am - rumble … RUMBLE…CRACK

The early morning alarm sounded from the Czech sky courtesy of Mr Thunder and Miss Lightning. The storm was absolutely magnificent and showed off breath-taking power as a sheer torrent of thunder, lightning and rain hit Prague. I had never seen or heard anything like it. Our hostel, near the top of the hill, took a grandstand view and the lightning seemed to strike at the same time as the thunder sounded. It was relentless in its assault and I watched from the window for about 20 minutes, relishing the sight. Craig and I decided that when morning came we would have to see where the lightning landed because it seemed to have all but knocked at our door.

The power was eventually sapped from the storm and a dull morning greeted us. Nowhere looked to have been electrically scorched but 300 yards from the hostel lay a mast that's purpose seemed to be either radio/television transmission or a lightning conductor. Either way, it must have taken the electrical hits, but rather it than me.

A decision was taken to stay in Prague until Tuesday the 9th, because of a lack of funds, a bit of lethargy and the fact that much of Prague had been left untouched by our grubby little hands. As a cost-cutting measure, we thought that instead of having two rooms we would book one and a couple of us could sleep on the floor. Unsurprisingly volunteers were slow to step forward for the floor-sleeping exercise. Lots were drawn, well a coin was tossed leaving Rich and Sacha bedless. It was shortly afterwards that they decided we would get caught and thrown out the hostel so two rooms was a good idea after all.

What better place to go in Prague than the castle that overlooks the city. We had delayed going to visit the castle until Sacha felt better and I am pleased to report that today he managed to pass his own fitness test. I led the way, without the constraints of a map, but a miscalculation led to us overshooting our target and finishing up on the far side of the Jewish town. Prague is based on four towns; the Old town, the Jewish quarter, the Lesser town and the New town. Unfortunately, the castle was definitely not in the Jewish quarter and Sacha's leg did not seem to appreciate the extra 3km walk.

While Sacha's luck was still bad (in that he had me navigating the way to the castle), Rich was mistakenly handed a 1000-Koruna note. But being the honest chap he is, the decent thing was done and he pointed out the mistake to the shop assistant.

Eventually, our foursome arrived at the Charles Bridge and started to weave a way up the pathways to the castle. The castle entrance was guarded, however, Sacha managed to pass them without being arrested so his luck was improving. It provided a splendid view of Prague but the cathedral was closed so we could only marvel from the outside.

On the way down from the castle, we reached the Charles Bridge then stopped, sat and listened. An Irish busker entertained about 150 people on the bridge, to such an extent that other people couldn't pass the crowd. A couple of times the police appeared in order to move people along. We must have stayed for about half an hour feasting on the atmosphere before relocating to the hostel bar.

Day 19 - Monday 8th August - Dirty Laundry

It had been noted that the hostel complex offered a laundry service, a temptation far too great to be resisted; finally, our clothes would receive a proper wash rather than a quick handjob in a sink, as it were. On Sunday everyone had dropped off a small bag of dirty clothes which were due for collection today. The laundrette consisted of a tiny damp room decorated in drying clothes from top to bottom, manned by a single Czech woman who operated two washing machines. She warned us that the clothes might still be a little damp, but I wasn't too worried as they would soon dry. I took my clothes back to our room and emptied them out of the bag only to be disappointed that they displayed an interesting array of stains, most of which hadn't been there before their excursion to the laundry. I also discovered a pair of old underpants that I had never set eyes on before and concluded that they must have been exchanged for a couple of my socks that bravely left for a wash and then went missing in action. Having witnessed the clothing mayhem of the laundry room I knew there would be no chance of a reunion with my socks, besides there was enough life in them to escape of their own accord rather than suffer at the hands of soap and water. Already my AWOL socks were probably contemplating their own European tour (possibly Sockholm, the Sockre Coeur and Athens – as in the home of philosopher Sockrates). The others did not suffer as badly but some of their 'washed' clothes had also acquired interesting stains.

A visit was planned, in our freshly washed and stained clothes, to the Jewish town and tickets were purchased which enabled us to see several of the most notable sites. The first stop was the Jewish cemetery, which was an unbelievable montage of 12,000 gravestones that were literally built on top of each other. The Jewish town had been a ghetto area and during the final burials, in the late 18th century, there were some 100,000 graves. The concentration of the gravestones gives the impression that the ground must be several bodies deep. A tourist group passed with an American guide so we tagged along and heard about several of the more famous people buried here, but we didn't recognise any of them. A small church stood nearby; inside there were some decorators at work. They were no ordinary decorators. The artists were meticulously painting the names of Jews from Prague who had died in the Holocaust. Each one took five minutes and as apparently over 18,000 died there was still a lot of work remaining. It seemed incredible that so many people from one city could have been murdered but then even that paled into insignificance when we were told that the total number of Jews who died in the Holocaust was six million. I can not even come close to comprehending six million people being killed.

When we left the graveyard we were greeted by torrential rain, so upped the pace to a jog and headed to a synagogue. The synagogue proved to be quite interesting but attention to all items was lengthened because no one fancied facing the rain outside. We waited on the porch for a while waiting for it to die down, others lost patience and were soaking within seconds. The weather couldn't take a hint so eventually we could wait no longer and sprinted to our next port of call, but the next synagogue was in the process of closing so we were abandoned flapping about in the water. The journey continued around another corner where a number of empty market stalls stood. They were about the same size as a Punch and Judy tent but only had the roof bit of material. We took one stall each and after a couple of minutes had edged our way down the line of 24 stalls, employing the cartoon 'tree to tree' creeping up method. It looked silly, but proved effective until reaching the roofless foundations of the 25th stall and receiving another soaking.

The only feasible solution to this wet problem was to find a restaurant, achieve moisture-lessness and eat some food. We ran from one restaurant menu board to another until finding one that was reasonably priced, in fact quite cheap even by Prague standards.

The restaurant was fairly empty but orders were made and we happily ate our food. Rich and Sacha took the opportunity of cheap food to have a three-course meal. All was well until the bill arrived. The prices that appeared on the price list were well below those on the bill. On our request, the slightly smarmy waiter brought across a menu. It still in no way reflected the charges on the bill. The increasingly smarmy waiter came over again and explained the damage in broken English. There was a compulsory service charge that had not been included in the menu prices and there was VAT or some other tax, which had also been added. The bill was paid to the very smarmy waiter with our grumbles falling on deaf ears. It had taken about three weeks for Europe to figure out a ploy to rip us off but it had finally succeeded. This led to a unanimous vote to only eat dinner in Prague at the friendly down-stairs restaurant where we had previously eaten two delicious meals. The only drawback to the place was that the bill had been completely wrong both times but they just went away and found the correct one.

It was to be our last proper night in Prague so we made a conscious effort to savour the cheap beer. This could have pre-occupied my mind as we rose in the hillside lift and I held Sacha's camera in my hand, a second later I was rising in the hillside lift without Sacha's camera in my hand. It had slipped my grasp and crashed Sacha-style to the floor. Although, unlike Sacha, it survived its hillside crash without any suffering and it didn't once whinge about its injuries.

Luckily for me, the camera was still in working order, so I bought Sacha a beer in lieu of his further mental torment and we considered what Italy had in store for him.

Day 20 - Tuesday 9th August - Doctors & Nurses

Bags packed, keys handed in, all that remained on my list was to have a good nose around the stadium that lay just beyond our accommodation. The stadium would have once housed big football and athletic events but was in a sad state of decay. However, behind the first stadium was a more impressive stadium that also housed the headquarters of the Czech Football Association. Then a few more paces on was a third stadium. This stadium version of the Russian doll phenomenon was finally brought to an abrupt halt by a disappointingly big car plant. No route was unearthed which would easily lead anybody to circumnavigate the stadiums so it was lucky that Sacha and I never managed our race around the stadium, especially with his dodgy leg.

We traipsed back, rucksack clad, through the hostel complex. It was kind of disappointing to leave but that was tinged with excitement about the cities that lay ahead. We descended Sacha's hill for the last time, walked across the bridge, along the street laid with tram lines, past the British Consulate, past our hostel of the first night and on to the main street.

While Craig and Sacha headed for Thomas Cook and American Express respectively, Rich and I tried to find the correct railway station to book our seats to Vienna. The first part of the train mission was successful but it was a strange old station with almost all the facilities below the street.

The second part was to actually reserve seats for our forthcoming visit to Vienna. The difficulty of the task was increased because the lady on the reservation desk spoke little English, although admittedly her English was far better than our Czech. She wanted to know what day we wished to reserve our seats for, a question that would be easy to answer unless your train left at midnight. I tried to think it through logically, it would be Day 20's midnight so it would be the 9th August but the time on any clocks would stand at 00.00 so it could actually be the 10th August. After several unsuccessful attempts to explain, the Czech man behind us kindly intervened on our behalf and the four reservations were booked for a total of about 80p rather than the typical £3 each that had been paid on other trains. However, Rich and I decided to inflate this figure to £12 when Craig arrived - which he happily accepted. By the time Sacha had finished in the American Express office inflation had taken the figure to £20 which Sacha grudgingly accepted after I explained how shocked I was at the high price. Craig had long since figured out the deception and Sacha's suspicions were soon aroused especially when we added a 25% VAT charge and a compulsory service charge.

Sacha had been dreading the next bit of the day because we were due to visit the doctor. His leg was still swollen and looked a little septic in places, although Craig insisted to Sacha that he'd always looked a bit septic. He bravely entered the medical building, which looked like a normal eight-storey office block. We gathered from the signs that Sacha would meet his destiny on floor 4. The worry level would not have been so high but an American girl from the hostel had told Rich and I some Czech doctor horror stories. Obviously, these were gleefully regurgitated for Sacha's benefit.

The 4th-floor stairs led to a big empty waiting room. Greetings were exchanged with a Czech nurse who didn't speak any English but when Sacha got his leg out she soon got the message. He was then led away.

We waited a couple of minutes and convinced ourselves that we would never see Sacha Balachandran again. At that very moment, he was probably strapped down having his leg amputated. They would then realise that it was the wrong one and take the other leg off, the doctors would not want anyone to know about the mistake so Sacha would be locked in a deep dark dungeon away from prying eyes, for the rest of his earthly existence.

As Sacha's dungeon was being contemplated he returned with both legs miraculously intact and a relieved smile on his face. He had experienced Czech medicine and survived to tell the tale. This put him in a better disposition to be convinced that it was too early for the dodgy leg to force his hand in returning his feet and arms straight home.

The afternoon was spent in the Czech National Museum which had many different displays involving planets, dinosaurs, minerals, ancient villages and sculptures, including one of a male with a certain snapped phallic object. Every woman that passed it smiled while every man let out a quiet wince.

The museum provided a good view of Wenceslas Square, where a fine statue of the good king stands. I hadn't realised King Wenceslas ruled Prague and is the patron saint of the Czech Republic.

The last cheap quality supper was eaten at our usual, the Black Baron restaurant, before food stocks were increased by a visit to the local supermarket. Little Czech money remained and what I had was invested in four different flavours of the delicious Prague ice creams. Rich took first prize in the ice cream stakes though, licking his way through six different varieties.

The clock moved remorselessly towards 11.00pm as the final curtain drew on the Prague adventure and we headed to the station for the train to Vienna. I always think of Austria, hence Vienna, being in Western Europe and the Czech Republic being in Eastern Europe, so how come Vienna is further east than Prague?

A separate thought grew in the back of my mind. In fact, it always seemed to appear whenever my bag had been dumped in a station locker. It was that I'd return to find an empty locker. Czech stations had a reputation for such events, but there was the added concern that I would forget the self-selected four-digit code required to open the locker. As ever everyone got their bag back, there were no problems and my paranoia subsided.

The train arrived so we found our reserved seats and settled down for the night.

Day 21 - Wednesday 10ᵗʰ August - Psychological Thriller

00.01am - the train moved away and goodbyes were said to Prague.

Our carriage was due in Vienna at 6.00am so it was important to get some sleep. I achieved three hours' worth, which wasn't too bad although I was still pretty dozy and grumpy when we reached our destination.

We stayed at the station for a bit, waiting for our senses to wake up and in turn used a sink for a quick wash and brush up. Then it was into Vienna to find the nearby underground station, and consult the Interrail book as to whether it was free on our ticket or not. It stated that the 'schnell zug' is free for Interrailers. I thought this was good as the same 'fast train' was our selected form of transport. Somewhere along the line, the translation must have misfired for we were actually on the 'tediously slow' train. Our cause was not helped when the map showing the different stops, inside the train, did not correspond with the stops that the train was actually making. Everyone was too tired to worry and somehow or other we arrived at the correct station.

There was still no sight of a tourist information centre despite our best efforts. Instructions to the nearest one, about a mile away, were slowly forthcoming and with bags safely tucked away in the station lockers, the Austrian adventure began.

Success continued to tread our path when as if by magic the Tourist Information Centre appeared. With a map in my sweaty little hand, Vienna was my oyster and the succulent dish that I desired was Sigmund Freud's house. After having to study his work during A-level Psychology the least he could do was to let me into his house. The only trouble being that it was just off the edge of the map; however, it did offer instructions so we set out on our psychological quest.

The journey appeared doomed to failure as our bearings seemed to have linked up with a needle in the proverbial haystack. Then a native walked up to us and asked if he could be of any help. My faith in human nature was renewed. With a new lease of life breathed into the quest I stood on the great Sigmund Freud's doorstep within another five minutes. It still looked like a consulting office and a doorbell had to be rung before we gained entry. Craig and Rich quickly decided to let themselves out again, not willing to dig further into their budgets to see Sigmund's house.

Sacha and I paid the price, receiving a folder in return, which documented Freud's life and work. I could not believe it, I was standing where one of the world's great minds had stood previously and I didn't mean Sacha. I even found out where he was buried in London (again Freud not Sacha). The book recounted many of his famous studies and I thought back to those past Psychology lessons where I had laughed at some of his theories such as 'Every boy finds his mother physically attractive and every girl fancies her father'. But to visit his house and meander through his former practice was truly an honour. We finally left down the stairs and out the door.

What had felt little more than an hour in the house had, tardis-like, proved to be nearer two hours. Craig and Rich had continued to wait outside for the entire time. As had been proved on the last day in Stockholm a high boredom threshold is not a quality I possess and if I had been waiting for myself I would have missed myself by about an hour, if that makes any sense.

The injury to Sacha's watch, in the Balachandran v. Prague Hill clash, had been fatal so a cheap and cheerful replacement was sought and found on the way. It was not an ideal substitution by any stretch of the imagination because the original was passed on to him when his dad died. For all the remarks about Sacha's relationship with nature, his presence on earth was a feat in itself. His mum and dad were both from Sri Lanka but his mum was a Catholic and his dad a Tamil. They were a pilot and stewardess respectively so chose to live away from Sri Lanka and I suspect to stay away from any Sri Lankan hostilities. Although, somewhat typically for Sacha, the initial place they chose to settle in was Belfast in the 1970s.

Our tour continued around the big buildings of Vienna including quite a smart Parliament and a decent palace. Rich frantically led the way whilst complaining about lost time waiting outside Freud's house – he was normally quite laid back so it was somewhat of an achievement to have temporarily annoyed him. It was around this period that Craig announced that time may be a problem because the world would end in 1998, well according to the predictions of Nostradamus. This seemed a real shame, but still, it left us with four years to enjoy.

Anyway, it was on to see the Habsburg's house, an Austrian family whose hobbies were apparently ruling an empire for 600 years and inbreeding. Their name cropped up in various places including as part-time owners of Prague and it took the First World War to finish them off. I'd never quite understood the First World War but our history man said the Austrian Archduke got assassinated by a Serb, thus Austria declared war on Serbia, Russia as the protector of Serbia started moving its troops, matched by the Germans on the Austria-Hungarian side. Then Germany invaded Luxembourg giving them a better position to invade poor old Belgium, before declaring war on France and actually invading Belgium. As Britain said it had agreed to protect Belgium some 60 years previously we entered the war. It all seemed a bit confusing but I did take in the simpler idea that the palace was big and impressive.

A slightly 'off the beaten track' Viennese street housed a supermarket which led to bread, cola and biscuit stocks being replenished. While the remaining party frequented the inside of a restaurant in the underground shopping centre my budgetary cutbacks took me to a seat on a solitary table outside, where I tucked into my cola and bread. This lasted for about five minutes until a waitress noticed me on 'their' table and decided that I was not consistent with the image they wished to portray so moved me on. I left the underground mall and sat on the ground near the top of an escalator swigging my bottle of cola and picking at a loaf of bread. The clothes draped around me were not exactly looking smart by this stage. In fact, my impression of a down and out was pretty impressive. From this position I watched the world go by and was quite contented. I would see people come up the escalator and others who would slowly disappear down with only a few buying a paper from the ever-enthusiastic vendor at the top. After about half an hour I too disappeared down the escalator. They still hadn't finished their meal so I pretended to look interested in the surrounding shops until the bill was paid.

The travel tide was sweeping us back towards the station despite our best efforts as the required turn was missed and Plan Two (let's go another way) was successfully swung into operation. Sacha's leg had lasted the day and several miles without any ill effects, so he announced that his journey would continue, cue loud groans and Sacha finishing the sentence with '*gits*'.

Goodnight Vienna.

DAY 22 - THURSDAY 11ᵀᴴ AUGUST – AN INCH IS BETTER THAN A MILE IN THE RIGHT DIRECTION

The train provided a comfortable night's sleep partly due to it being me and Rich's turn to have the window seats. They are always the prime sleeping area and far superior to the middle seats of the six-person train compartments, due to the level of head support.

The train pulled in and Ciao's were said to Italy, in particular, the classic city of Venice. The idea was simple, we would steam into Venice, go to American Express, get some money, go to the cheaper nearby town of Mestre and find some accommodation, but the execution had flaws in its flaws.

We steamed into Venice but found out that the American Express office was on the other side of the island, thus with my prompting, we headed back towards Mestre to sort out the accommodation. Mestre station had an accommodation desk and the Italian girl helped us to find the cheapest roof available via her computer. The hotel was apparently 40 minutes' walk away or a quick bus ride.

Off we trooped followed by our rucksacks. The need to find an American Express centre had become obsolete as Mestre possessed a Thomas Cook office so Rich could cash in his traveller's cheques commission free. After subjecting ourselves to the baking late 80's mid-day sun, it was located. Rich went in and quickly came out because it only did holidays. No problem, we would catch the bus to the hotel. Everybody knew in which direction the hotel was meant to lie so we waited for a number 22 bus, which was heading that way and boarded. All was well for five minutes and then the bus turned around and headed in the opposite direction. The driver's English was as good as my Italian so we could swap footballers' names but nothing else. What had become fairly obvious was that the distance between us and the hotel was increasing by the minute. The English got off their backsides, picked up their bags and clambered off at the next stop; another 15 minutes passed and another number 22 bus was caught. This took us to the station and then started to travel away from the hotel direction before veering back again. The only problem now was that nobody had any clue to the whereabouts of the hotel, or to call it by its proper name: 'Johnny's Motel'. Attempts were made to interrogate the friendly locals but try as they might, they didn't seem to understand a word. Despite this big disadvantage we understood through their signs and pointing that this bus would not take us to the motel, the next stop would be the best one to get off at and then we should board another bus. It was quite amazing to find out the amount of communication that can be accomplished despite the lack of a common language.

The bus tickets were bought for a certain time period and with all the fannying about our limit had been breached so a decision was reached to walk the surely short distance to the prospective hotel even though it meant facing the searing heat with our rucksacks. 20 minutes later we had walked to the outskirts of Mestre. Still there was no sign of the motel but we were on the right road and just needed the right house number. Another 20 minutes passed along with a couple of buckets of sweat, the Italian countryside, the odd house, numerous choruses of 'always look on the bright side of life' and a torrent of cheerful verbal abuse to me for suggesting staying in Mestre. The torrent continued as we reached a garage alongside the country lane we were traipsing about on.

Whilst Sacha considered collapsing as an alternative to walking another step Rich approached a man at the garage who gestured that our destination was around the corner. The corner was duly rounded and a building came into view. A blast of 'Mad Dogs & Englishmen' would have been suitable for the next scene. With my brain slightly affected by the heat, I started to sprint the 400 metres towards the big yellow building, determined to reach Johnny's motel as quickly as possible. Rich took up the cerebrally-challenged gauntlet and just edged by me before we collapsed in a hysterical heap outside the motel entrance. Sacha and Craig looked on bemused.

After recuperating in our room, we caught a bus directly to the 118 islets, 400 bridges and 150 canals that make up Venice. Whenever I thought of Venice I thought of Italy but Venice was an independent state for about 1,000 years and it took a mighty emperor in the shape of Napoleon to take the Venetians' freedom away. Instead of going on any of the guided tours we took the water bus most of the way around Venice which provided a cheap method of seeing the sights. We disembarked near the St. Mark's Square stop. It's not every day you can say '...then I caught a bus to St. Mark's Square'. Bloody brilliant! All four of us stood amazed at the sight of St. Mark's Basilica, the Moors' clock tower and the vertigo causing coffee prices. Apparently, it is known as Saint Mark's because back in 828, two Venetian merchants stole what remained of his body from Alexandra and brought it back to Venice, where it still lays in the basilica. If you have to spend 1,200 years somewhere then there are far worse places than Venice. It definitely had a unique ambience and was not the foul-smelling place others had suggested.

We stopped at a restaurant for a meal and ordered a very reasonably priced spaghetti bolognaise without realising that in Italy this is often just a small starter and not the main course. That was the reason it was so cheap.

We called time on our day in Venice and went to wait for our bus. This still allowed us time to try and unravel the mysteries of the bus ticket machine — eventually we worked it out — it was broken. The bus journey took place in the pitch black which was not ideal when you are travelling on country roads moving past a number of large buildings, looking for a hotel you had only ever seen once in your life. The thought of ending up in the middle of Mestre at the dead of night did not endear itself but thanks to a bit of guesswork and some good luck the bus took us to the correct stop in a journey that amazingly only lasted 15 minutes. Our hotel proved to be closer to Venice than Mestre after all.

The motel was lacking in the beer department but we compensated for it with a round of lollipops. Granted they weren't an ideal substitute but they were suitably refreshing. So we had a second round.

Day 23 - Friday 12ᵀᴴ August - The Trains To Nowhere

We made an early start to make up for the previous day's tale of wasted time. The bus into Venice was a bit late which left us with a sprint to the train, much to Sacha's disgust. However, everybody managed to clamber aboard the train with a minute to spare. It would only take us to Mestre but it would then connect with the Florence bound train. We jumped off the train with six minutes before our connection was due to leave and jogged off to another platform. There were sighs of relief all round when we saw the Florence train at the platform waiting patiently for us. Finally, things were beginning to go right for us in Italy.

It was then that a strange little asterisk was noticed on the departure board by the word Florence. The Thomas Cook timetable book decoded that a heavy supplement would have to be paid to travel on the train. Alternatively, a small supplement could be paid but only if you had a reserved seat and two minutes wasn't enough time to book a reservation. Goodbyes were waved to the train.

Oh well, no problem, we'd go to Rome instead. A wait of an hour would have to be experienced but that was no hardship; it was up there on the departure board with no asterisk in sight. Who needed Florence when you could go to the legendary city of Rome? After a while the train flashed up on the next departure screen; it had some writing beside it, which concerned us. A conductor explained succinctly *'first class only, Interrail not valid'*. Goodbyes were waved to the train.

Who wanted to go to Rome anyway? A backpacker huddle formed and the outcome was that we would wait another hour for the train to Bologna and then get a connection to Florence. Goodbyes were finally waved to Mestre.

A pleasant journey took us to Bologna where there was another 20-minute wait for the train to Florence. The signs were all there before stepping on the train. The number of bodies on the platform swelled until it was virtually covered. An already packed train arrived and everybody squeezed on board in a similar manner to a Monty Python cartoon. The carriages were packed to the rafters with what must have been enough for three people per seat (including the toilet). I separated from the others in the desperate search for space, but it was doomed: the best I could manage was to be jammed between two Italians with my head supported by a window whilst semi-sitting on my rucksack. When people attempted the toilet trek (comprising a journey up and down the corridor, which, considering the number of people, happened with regularity) I had to fully stand up to let them pass. This was also a necessity every so often because of the recurring pins and needles in my legs; comfort did not come from the exceptionally hot weather. I vowed never to complain about British Rail again. The only entertainment provided was when I arched my neck and then pressed the side of my head against the window thus gaining a view of the landscape. Failing that I would try and catch Rich's eye that floated around at the opposite end of the carriage; then we would have a flabbergasted face-pulling contest (this ended in an honourable but ugly draw).

At 2.00pm we eventually arrived in Florence and our main concern was accommodation. The fund level was low but our books had mentioned a large roofed area that was in the open air but designated for travellers to pay next to nothing; just lay the old sleeping bag down and stay for a night. Unfortunately, the information desk informed us that it closed down last year, so we phoned all the hostels in our combined books (well the ones in Florence). There was no room at the inn, not even a stable. This left us with the expensive option of having to book into a hotel. After filling in a hotel form at the accommodation desk and queuing for processing, Rich, who had been wandering around the station, rushed in, grabbed us and led the three downtrodden travellers to a pretty Italian girl. She represented a large campsite complex that was offering tents, so it would be cheap, but she warned us that it lay 12 km out of Florence. This comprised of a small train journey and a free bus trip. Our finances could not cope with the cheapest of hotels so it proved an irresistible offer.

The next train was two hours away; this left us scope for a quick tour of Florence. The weather remained scorching so no one was keen on touring whilst burdened with a rucksack and we weren't prepared to pay a day's rate for just two hours' worth of a locker. Thus lots were drawn which resulted in Sacha and I touring for the first three-quarters of an hour while the others stayed with the bags, then vice-versa. So that was that, the greatest Renaissance city in the world with wall to wall works of art and we had 45 minutes to see it. The only silver lining was that this left plenty of time to ensure that the train didn't leave without us.

Sacha and I completed a whistle-stop 'there is the cathedral' tour of what looked like a very good-looking city, then handed over the baton. Five minutes later, with me and Sacha sat on the station floor, which had become an all too familiar experience, I spotted it. My eyes quivered at the wonderful sight. How I longed to sit beside her. She had what I desired. Oh surely she could share it with me, after all, I was an athletic red-blooded male, I should not be denied. She had The Times newspaper and what's more, the sports supplement was sitting there, lonely looking, just beside her. Luckily she was a friendly English girl who worked as an au-pair in Italy and had nipped to Florence with her Times to see a friend. My chance to catch up on a little sport was not wasted and news of the European Athletics Championship filtered through to my sports news-starved brain.

At 5.00pm we headed towards our train which was scheduled to leave at 5.15pm. It sat there waiting for us. Finally, things were beginning to go right for us in Italy. We sat patiently in our carriage for about 20 minutes, waiting for the train to depart and were beginning to wonder why it was being delayed, I mean the train next to us had gone five minutes ago so why couldn't our train leave? Five minutes ago, that's strange having two trains due to leave at the same time. Uh oh, I poked my head out the window, 'QUICK GET OFF THE TRAIN!' Bags and people flew until they touched down on the platform; our train was indeed the one which had left five minutes ago. For no apparent reason, we had climbed aboard the Rome train. The platforms were clearly marked as were the trains' destinations. Four reputedly intelligent people, each with a degree behind them, had somehow followed each other on to the wrong train.

We even had to trudge past the pretty Italian girl who worked for the campsite. She stopped us and was very apologetic when we told her that we missed the train. She assumed that it was her who told us the wrong platform, but we confessed that she had said the correct platform, that we were stupid and it had just been one of those days. An hour later we caught the right train and were joined on it by the Italian girl and a couple of English lads, one of whom had just been robbed of his Interrail pass, money and travellers cheques. He had been approached by several young children begging for money; one of them thrust a piece of cardboard horizontally at his waist which the lad assumed was to put money on. However, under the cover of the cardboard another kid slashed his money belt and made off into the crowds with the booty. He would have to depart for home two weeks early. Bloody hell, it sounded like something out of Oliver Twist.

The bus journey that followed was about three miles and curtailed any hope of us returning to Florence at night as the bus was the last one of the day. The complex was quite large and included a small lake, supermarket, swimming pool, restaurant and bar. It was very family-oriented and we had arrived about four years too late or a few years too early. Despite this Craig convinced himself that all the older daughters and some of their mothers could not keep their eyes off him. I think he preferred life on his own little planet rather than the real world and I don't blame him.

The tents that were meant to receive our bodies had been billed as luxury tents but as they were all occupied, home would be the scruffy two-man tents at the end of the campsite. Rich and I entered the first tent and unpacked. Disturbingly, a pair of Rich's Y-fronts had entered the Jeff occupied half, so I prodded the off-white item back across the tent.

The supermarket managed to provide our staple diet of yoghurt and bread. Cheap tuna was also purchased but even I couldn't face yoghurt and tuna sandwiches. Meanwhile back at the tent Rich's Y-fronts had once more strayed across to my side. Oh the pleasures of camping.

DAY 24 - SATURDAY 13TH AUGUST - OLIVER TWIST

5.45am - Rich: *'Rise and shine'*.

5.45.01am - Jeff: 'X!%!X# off! It's the middle of the night!'

The only trouble being that Rich was right, an early start had been planned so we could meet and greet Rome at a reasonable time. With this in mind, Sacha had switched into organised mode and booked a taxi to the station for an ungodly hour. The showers and bathrooms were all in one large building at the campsite, with no proper sit-down toilets. Thus the 'squat and poo down the hole in the floor' facilities were very much in operation. When Sacha arrived back from the shower he reported brown footsteps from one of the aforementioned amenities. I decided that I wouldn't be taking a shower this morning and instead completed my packing. Rich called me back into the tent saying that I'd forgotten something but all I could see that was left on my side of the tent was that pair of Rich's grotty Y-fronts. *'Jeff, you must be joking they're not mine, I thought they were yours'*. The realisation dawned that we'd both been prodding the Y-fronts back and forth across the tent like it was some form of 'pant tennis'. We decided to leave them there for the next occupant (and for all we know they will still be there for many years getting older, grottier and eventually moving across the tent by their own accord).

The taxi collected us from the front gate and drove us down to the station, between us the fare was cheap but when it came round to paying I couldn't find my stash of Lira so the others had to cover my share. Amazingly the train arrived; there were no supplements, it was the right one and to top it all off I even found my Lira.

It was a peaceful journey and we entertained ourselves by accusing Craig of being a cheap Italian whore in a previous life due to his uncanny knack of spreading his legs as far apart as possible whenever he sat down. He wasn't that bothered about the 'whore' part of the accusation, the 'Italian' bit he wasn't keen on, but he wasn't having 'cheap'! If he had been an Italian whore, he was damn sure that he was an expensive one.

Craig's finances were about as healthy as an anteater with a broken nose and he considered going straight home. We tried to change his mind and he agreed to spend one night in Rome but would only accept a £20 donation to the 'Keep Craig in Europe' campaign.

The Cheap Sleep Guide and Interrail book were examined. It was discovered that there were quite a few hostels in the city centre plus the International Youth Hostel six km from the centre, opposite the Olympic stadium where Roma and Lazio play football. I was subsequently banned from telephoning the hostels to make a reservation because they thought I'd be selfish enough to reserve the Olympic hostel; alas they knew me too well.

They telephoned a number of different hostels without any success, at one point telephoning the same one three times as turns were taken at trying to understand whether the Italian guy on the other end of the line was saying that there were vacancies or they were full. We were approached by about three different people offering accommodation, although the difference from Prague was that they were not pushy and seemed more than happy to answer any questions about the eternal city. In the end, we decided to accept the offer of a bed (each) from one of them, who then phoned through and made a reservation. Meanwhile, Craig queued for three-quarters of an hour to organise a train back to Blighty.

In total, we had hung around the station for two hours, but that seemed perfectly natural after the previous couple of days. With the hostel booked there was just the Metro underground that lay between us and our new home. We descended two flights of stairs and were met by a number of little kids pleading for money. After the experience of the English lad in Florence, there was no way anyone would be getting attached to my belongings. Thus football tactics were engaged and I became all arms, legs and pointy elbows.

Another ploy was to carry your rucksack in front of you rather than on the back, where someone could easily slash the bottom spilling everything on the ground. The train arrived and everybody descended upon it, including 15 people heading for the same door as our little party. Sacha was a person and a bit in front of me when suddenly an Italian man's hand slipped into Sacha's pocket (he always did make friends easily). In the split second that I moved forward to push him, his quick hand had already emerged empty from the pocket. In the train, I spoke to Craig: 'watch this bloke', who proceeded to walk up and down the carriage touting for business. While his two English spectators stared at him his friend cast an evil look into our path, thus a happy balance was achieved. It lasted until the first stop whereupon they left to ply their trade elsewhere, good riddance!

I then told the details to Sacha who had been totally oblivious to the event despite his starring role. His face filled with horror because in the trespassed pocket were his beloved sunglasses; the holiday may have come to an abrupt halt without this essential fashion accessory.

The hostel was only 100 yards away from the mighty Vatican. After ringing the hostel doorbell the door opened and we walked up to the 2nd floor of the building, which was the only level occupied by the hostel. The hostel was very small, consisting of about four dormitory/ bedrooms, two showers and a reception area. The English receptionist took great delight in showing off my abysmal passport photograph to anyone vaguely interested, ah ze English sense of humour. Our bags were despatched in the reception area and she said that our beds would be put up by about 6.00pm. No time could be wasted as our first (and last for Craig) tour of Rome began in earnest.

The first port of call was the Vatican. As we walked towards it Sacha bought some holy beads for his very Catholic grandmother from the honest-ish looking bloke on the corner of the street. We then proceeded to enter the Vatican itself and the church of St. Peter. I'm not a religious man but I felt like I may be visiting God's house or if not the main man (or woman) himself then a good friend. The place was an incredible work of art, from the floor to the pillars, the giant dome and exquisite sculptures. Even children were reduced to wide-eyed, jaw-dropping silence. Unfortunately, the renowned Sistine Chapel was closed to the public for the next three days because of the forthcoming Italian bank holiday, so we had to content ourselves with the other 1001 things to do in Rome.

Like any other tourist attraction, the Vatican had a souvenir shop. In there, patiently waiting for Sacha, were the official Vatican holy beads, which were reasonably priced but lacked the tackiness of Sacha's previous investment. In the midst of a deep quandary, he screwed his features all across his face before deciding to buy the official beads. This probably spared both his and his gran's blushes when the tacky beads caused a rash or simply fell apart on their maiden neck voyage. Sacha's chances of getting a refund from the honest-ish bloke were rated as likely as the Pope scoring the winner for Poland in the 1998 World Cup Final (and as he was a goalkeeper, rather than an attacker I felt the odds were pretty high).

The journey continued on to the Trevi fountain, where many people would sit just to hang out, enjoy the water and oven-like temperature. Rome is full of fountains but surely the others can't compare to this beauty. There are about five streets that lead to the fountain, all of them cobbled and more or less pedestrianised, but whichever one you take the fountain seems to appear from nowhere. Its centrepiece is an impressive 300-year-old statue of Neptune riding a chariot out of the water. The custom is to throw a coin into the fountain to guarantee a return visit to Rome.

Onwards we trekked to the Victor Emmanuel II monument; it looked very prominent and strangely new, just 100 or so years old. It was another good photographic opportunity, although we had to cross the busy road and join some others on a grassy traffic island to fulfil its pictorial potential. Everybody safely crossed the road and took up their respective camera positions. It was at this point I heard a whistle; luckily it did not disturb my David Bailey like concentration. The whistle then sounded again and was accompanied by some shouting. A policeman dismounted from his motorbike and indicated, quite strongly, that in his humble opinion our grassy position was not favourable. We respected his view but were dismayed and confused to see him ignore the Italians on the same traffic island.

The setback was shrugged off and we trooped away to the Coliseum. It was both imposing and slightly eerie, as here was a sight that you had seen on television and pictured 100 times but there it stood within my grasp. Our arrival had coincided with its closing time thus glimpses were limited to the outside of what must be one of the five most famous buildings in the world. There would be the Coliseum, Taj Mahal, Sydney Opera House, Pyramids of Giza and um one other. Call me biased but I'd select the Houses of Parliament at number 5. I'm not selecting the Eiffel Tower because I'm confused whether it's a building or not.

The heat dictated that a drink would be needed to quench a growing thirst. A drink in most cases on this tour has meant Fanta. It has been our standard thirst quencher and with a trace of vitamin C we have convinced ourselves that it has supplemented our poor diet caused by our budgetary restraints. Another addiction that has been developing within my body is to Calippo lollipops. My dependency has risen to three Fanta cans and three Calippo's a day.

If this wasn't enough I then had to play a game to try to secure my continued presence in mainland Europe. Money funds were low and the options had been whittled down to one. I had to try an Italian cash machine with my cash card; if I lost then I would be joining Craig on the Interrailer scrap heap. I slotted the card in the machine, the features came up and I selected the Union Jack, the rest, as they say, is history. My fingers dazzled as they sped from button to button the correct combination in their tips, followed by my card and cash, lovely cash.

To celebrate Craig's forthcoming departure a round of milkshakes slipped down our throats at the local McDonald's. This rounded off the witching hours and we headed back to the hostel only to find that there was only one bed in our room. The first thought was I'm not sleeping in the same bed as Rich for a second time. A second glimpse showed that even that bed was occupied by a lump in the shape of a fast asleep bloke. The receptionist arrived, four beds went up and sleep was found.

DAY 25 - SUNDAY 14TH AUGUST - THEN THERE WERE THREE

Four little Interrailers in Italy,
One ran out of money,
Then there were three…

The only way to guarantee a hot shower in the hostel was to be the first in, but despite rising from my slumber at 7.15am I did not take the gold medal and believe me the shower that greeted my nervous body in no way, shape or form resembled anything like a warm shower. The only silver lining being that cold showers encourage a fast moving queue.

Although Craig's train wasn't due to leave until the afternoon, he had decided against lugging his baggage around Rome. Instead, he was content to take up residence at the station for several hours and wait.

The underground delivered us all to Craig's station, where another search for lockers proved ineffective. There were, however, numerous telephones and I took advantage of one to phone our friend John. He was on holiday in Naples, so we thought it would be great to meet up. My attempt to dial his number was met with a dead line, as were my second and third efforts. I realised that the number he had given me still included the code from England. However, John wasn't going to escape that easily and finally the correct digits connected me with Naples. I even got him out of bed to answer it, so success was complete and the plan conceived was for John to meet us off the Rome to Naples train in a couple of days' time.

Our final farewells were bid to Craig, who started a long sit-in before the arrival of his 30-hour train to Paris. The three survivors headed to the Coliseum although it immediately felt strange that the numbers were depleted by one Brummie. The Coliseum was ready for us with open gates and we finally entered the legendary sporting arena. The surface had given way to reveal the maze of underground tunnels where slaves or animals were held. In its pomp, it had been a 55,000 seater with gladiator fights, mock sea battles and wild animals, but as I stood there the only wild thing at work was my imagination.

It was Sacha's last full day in Rome because he is heading home tomorrow to start work on Thursday. He was determined to make the most of the day. That was the aim; the result was the Coliseum, church, church, Rome Cathedral, railway station (one reservation to Paris), church, church and Pantheon (old church). Each and every church was beautiful, even the ones that looked shabby on the outside were simply unbelievable on the inside.

The Pantheon is the oldest standing structure in Rome. It was also the oldest standing structure in Rome that we could not enter. It was closed and the only glimpse of its inner sanctum was via a crack in the door. Not only is it 2,100 years old but it is the final resting place of Raphael and the first Kings and Queens of Italy. I never used to be that interested in Italy but the guidebooks took an absolute battering from the moment I stepped into Rome.

Evening descended so we turned our attention from the Pantheon to a restaurant, which must have boasted some of the grumpiest waiters in Europe. It was next to an ice cream shop, which Rich just could not resist. His mission in life seems to be to taste as many varieties of ice cream as possible. There are worse missions.

Night-time all too quickly arrived and another McDonald's milkshake toasted Sacha's imminent departure. Our financial restrictions meant that the milkshakes had taken over from the Venetian lollipops as the new beer substitute. Finally, arses were wearily placed on the Spanish Steps, below yet another church. So many steps but all of them seemed to have people sitting on them basking in the moonlight backed by the sound of chatter. Comedy was provided by a pushy rose 'retailer' who couldn't sell his product despite continuously thrusting them into people's hands. The sands of Sacha's Rome were low when the four walls of the dormitory surrounded us once more.

Although Craig had left, the bed count stood at six. A South African chap (awaiting the arrival of a visa so he could leave Europe) informed us that a couple of American girls had arrived. Rich's bed had therefore been moved towards the door and a bed for one of the girls placed in its previous position. This was apparently so she didn't get trampled on when people came through the door because '*she is only a little girl, practically a dwarf and probably about 12 years old*'.

I removed my shirt which had been scarred by another lost battle with a lollipop and slipped under my sheets to prepare for another day in the Eternal City.

Day 26 - Monday 15ᵗʰ August - Two Down One To Go

Three little Interrailers in Italy,
One had work to do,
But two were still free…

7.15am - I woke up, my eyes wandered around the room assessing the situation; five other people remained asleep under their respective covers.

7.20am - I made a dash for the showers. Although I was the first to emerge from our dormitory I was third into the shower (not all at the same time) and the hot water lasted a mere 15 seconds. But I was definitely getting closer to that legendary hot shower because the silver medallist swore the water temperature was fine for him.

Sacha checked out before the 8.30am deadline and we headed to the station once again. It was kind of weird walking along with Sacha being the only one with a rucksack. The station was reached, Sacha having made the same cautious decision as Craig to wait at the station for several hours. The main worry was that he had been a walking jinx throughout Europe, his destination may be England but on hearing that he was travelling by himself there were rumours that even the Mongolians were patrolling their borders to ensure a Sacha-free zone. Genghis was nervously twitching in his grave, wherever that may be.

And then there were two.

It was a very strange feeling to be reduced from a group of four to just two. The thing was that the vocal cords moved into overdrive, I suppose I felt more compelled to talk. We began to walk from Sacha's station to the main 'Rome Termini' but got bored and Metro'd it. The plan was for a day trip to either Florence, Pisa or the Mediterranean. Two seats at the station were occupied studying all manner of train times but none of them fell our way so it was Rome for a third day. However the master plan for the next few days was hatched, Naples, Milan, Monte Carlo, Nice and home.

There was still much of Rome to explore and we made a start on the parks. They seemed to last forever and were full of water fountains which were greeted by swallowing mouths. At first, just the strong stomach of Rich had been keen on using the numerous drinking fountains but the heat had been so intense I quickly followed his lead. As much liquid as possible had to be taken on board to combat the fierce heat.

Finally, one of the hills of Rome was clambered and a magnificent view of Rome was ours. There was only one thing to do after that, which was to walk across to the other side of the city to see what the view was like from the opposite hill. The journey was quite easy to start off with, all downhill and bust upon bust (it is not as good as it sounds) of famous Italians along the paths, well I thought they must be famous Italians.

The long haul was worth the effort and provided another breath-taking view of the city, but somehow breath-taking had become the norm and you didn't really expect much less. Another large fountain met us at the top of the hill and Rich joined others by being shoeless and sockless with feet dangling in the water. It seemed to be common practice for Europeans to greet a fountain with their naked feet but it didn't seem natural for my prudent English demeanour.

For the first time, I realised that not everybody was on holiday. It may be a strange thing to say but it had felt like when we were on holiday, the rest of Europe was also taking a break. Daft eh?

As expected, night fell again and we drifted from fountain to fountain breathing in the Roman atmosphere. Although it could be argued that the Roman atmosphere is actually a touristy atmosphere around this time of year. We crossed the Tiber and headed for our Vatican home. I was experiencing a strong desire to watch Ben Hur or some other classic Roman film.

Day 27 - Tuesday 16th August - California Dreaming

6.50am - on hearing movement I woke up to see the South African guy getting up, so a quick hello was exchanged before returning to the world of the half dead. It would be the last I saw of him; hopefully, he got his visa for Austria which allowed him to catch his flight back to South Africa. His travel tip was to speak Afrikaans when trying to get information from people. They would not understand him, so he would then speak English. Believing he was making an effort in a second language they would then go out of their way to help him. Interesting, but not much help to a typical one language Englishman like me.

My body and mind resurfaced to find that of the six beds in the room only one was occupied: mine, and it was still only 7.15am. I headed towards the shower, which was not quite as freezing as usual, well, for about 20 seconds anyway.

I returned to the dormitory and discovered that 'the 12-year-old dwarf' report was somewhat inaccurate. I am not sure whether the South African had been living with Amazonians but the '12-year-old' turned out to be Jen a Californian girl of 21 years, who stood at about 5 foot 3 inches and would not let down the Beach Boys song. She and her friends joined us on the Metro. We arrived at the main station stop and started to get off. I was the penultimate person leaving the carriage from the Anglo-American party but noticed that the '12-year-old dwarf' had tangled up her rucksack with a seat and was struggling in her quest for freedom. Every time she got up her rucksack pinged her back into her seat. If I moved away from the door then it would probably close and take us to the next station leaving the others very confused because they had all walked away oblivious to the state of affairs. However, if I stayed in the doorway it may shut automatically anyway. Mind you if I wanted to get lost in Rome with anyone then Jen would be quite high up the list. As I considered the pros and cons of the situation she released herself from the clutches of the seat, the door remained open and the platform was reached safe and sound.

Rich and I then boarded the Naples bound train, which proceeded to sit still well past the scheduled departure time. The Florence butterflies flapped but a quick glance out the window confirmed it was the right train.

The train finally left 20 minutes late; typical, when somebody was due to meet you off a train it's bound to be late. Luckily Rich and I had caught an earlier train than scheduled, so despite the train becoming 40 minutes late, we were only a quarter of an hour late meeting John. He was a bizarre sight, the man that we had always seen in Sheffield had been transplanted to Naples, it was as if some sort of space-time continuum had been breached.

John was on his second holiday to Naples and showed us the main sites, many of which he hadn't seen before because he was staying with friends just outside the city. Initially, we went to the youth hostel to dump our baggage. The Cheap Sleep guide reputed it to be one of the best hostels in Europe, but despite us having made a reservation there didn't appear to be an unlocked entrance on show. All the doors were locked up and no one could be seen or heard. After five minutes of constant banging on the doors, a figure appeared in the shadows and slowly came across to let us in. Apparently and annoyingly the hostel was closed each afternoon so it could be cleaned. Eventually, they allowed us to drop off our bags so we could start touring around Naples.

The mighty Vesuvius volcano cuts a very imposing figure over the city. We learnt that the phrase 'See Naples and die' didn't refer to its crime-ridden reputation but the spectacular view of Vesuvius and the bay. Our attempt to walk along the bay was halted when we were stopped in the grounds of a private yacht club and asked to leave. John pleaded our ignorance which was accepted and the best directions to reach the other side of the club were taken. The tour continued in a vague sort of direction although we tried to stay out of the highlighted area on John's map. His friends told him that this is the designated top-level pickpocket area and as none of us felt like doing any pickpocketing we maintained our distance.

The time reached evening and the stomachs were rumbling, so food came up on our menu of the day. When in Naples it is surely illegal not to sample a pizza from this the birthplace of the cheese and tomato food item. I had already sampled a genuine Italian pizza earlier in the trip, but the taste buds were ecstatic with the Neapolitan version.

John headed back to the army base, where his friends lived, whilst Rich and I caught the Garibaldi line to the hostel. Unfortunately, mention of the Garibaldi line set us off on a course of do we change on to the Hob Nob line or do we head up the Jammy Dodger? Is the brown line the Bourbon line? Is a Jaffa Cake an underground or overground line? Nice line? Is the orange line the ginger line? etc. etc. This also allowed me time to work out how much money I had lent Rich in the last couple of days. The figure agreed on was 78,400. I thought rather than Rich having to change more money I would accept him paying me back with 78,400 pounds rather than lira. He declined on the dubious grounds that just because £1 pound was worth 2,450 lira he preferred to pay £32.

The hostel facilities were quite good and well worth £9 a night even if they don't put any Californian girls in your room. However, the hostel was fairly dull and evidence for this came from the fact that we watched Italian television for part of the night. The closest thing to entertainment was an

Italian bloke selling drinks and making bad jokes, some worse than mine. He seemed convinced that a German chap was my brother; I laughed and the German scowled.

Day 28 - Wednesday 17th August - Up Pompeii

Now for Day 28's prologue: I had a good long sleep, put on my final clean T-shirt and my just washed but still damp England football shorts. Clean T-shirts were not a priority with only three days left. One T-shirt is normally lasting about three days and I am sure I still have a semi-dirty one left in my bag. Boxer shorts are tending to last two days but no more; they seem to become a bit stale by the third day, in fact, the only clothing that wouldn't last more than a day were my socks which had to house my notoriously smelly feet. From Naples to home we planned to have three overnight trains so it wasn't feasible to complete any more washing. Our portable washing machines consisted of concentrated washing liquid and a pair of hands, usually the sinks would have no plug so a sock would be stuffed in as a replacement. My mum in that inimitable motherly way had suggested that I took some Persil powder in a plastic bag. I pointed out the interest a bag of white powder would receive from customs officers and then the subsequent search of my cavities.

After our clean clothes audit, Rich and I left the hostel for the main station to reserve a Milan bound night train. The train we wanted was the 11.40pm but it was 'couchette only' so the finances would not stretch for such a luxury. Therefore two seats on the 7.47pm were booked, the difference being that Milan would be reached at a ridiculously early time.

But that was for Thursday; today it was time to go 'Up Pompeii'. A very hot and crammed train was endured for 45 minutes before we arrived at Pompeii. Money then changed hands and we were in the legendary city.

The panorama of Pompeii is dominated by the proud and solitary cone of Vesuvius, the arbiter and witness of its life and death. Laid out at its feet, the silent remains of the long-buried city are charged with the vivid fascination of history and conjure up, with extraordinary immediacy, a distant past. That's what the guidebook said anyway.

It was strange to walk through the streets of this old Roman city whose remains have been preserved for 2,000 years, the amphitheatre, in particular, was most impressive and virtually in one piece. Yesterday, John had mentioned a ruined brothel in Pompeii which had 'artistic' pictures of a normal business day on the walls but our search for art ended in vain. Rich and I slid all over the slippy stony streets and legs, shorts and last clean T-shirt finished up covered in sandy dust. Here I am moaning about the streets but it is incredible to consider that they are 2,000 years old and there is much of the old town still to be excavated. The size of the town meant that despite the numerous tourists it was possible to find a quiet area to look and imagine the streets bustling with Romans.

After several hours getting happily lost in Pompeii's ancient streets, the train was caught to the Naples station where we trudged wearily to the bag collection area. Naples was different from many other major stations in that there were no lockers. Instead, our rucksacks were given to baggage handlers who gave you a ticket in return. I looked for my ticket and Rich looked for his ticket. I found my ticket, Rich looked for his ticket. I handed over the ticket for my rucksack, Rich looked for his ticket. He was only carrying a small bag, which was consequently emptied without a sniff of a ticket. All pockets were emptied, still no sign. Rich's sirens were ringing as everything was re-examined. It took four long minutes before the ticket made an appearance. Four minutes may not sound long but believe me when your rucksack is on the line and an examination of pockets and bag only takes a minute, the stress levels are well past worrying. Relief flooded across his face and a big smile appeared in anxiety's place.

There was still time for Rich to phone his girlfriend and find out that she had sorted out a flat for them to move in together. Rich returned in another state of shock as I ushered him to the platform.

The train was boarded, left on time and we enjoyed the scenery. The most spectacular of which was a blazing hillside which seemed to be wearing an out of control fire. Looks were exchanged and attempts were made to convince ourselves that Sacha had left the country rather than playing with matches deep in the Italian countryside.

Day 29 - Thursday 18ᵗʰ August - Easy Life

There was only Rich and I in the six-person cabin, so with three seats each, the luxury of stretching had to be tasted. The result was a very good sleep. We reached Milan at about 6.30am and as ever breakfast consisted of yoghurt and bread. The time was too early to do much so bottoms were placed firmly on the station floor, only interrupted by a trip to the toilets for a quick wash and brush up.

Milan may be well below the peaks of Rome and Stockholm but it was fine for a lazy day and that was exactly what we had planned. Hanging about the main square by the magnificent cathedral became the main occupation of the day. It was, without doubt, an incredible building but I'd never known anything to take so long to build. They began work on it in 1386 when Gian Galeazzo Visconti took control of the city. He sounded an interesting character because he came to power after imprisoning his uncle, was married by the age of 9, had his first son by 14 and apparently, there is a statue of him disguised as Saint George somewhere in the cathedral. Anyway, work carried on through the years as figures from history lent a helping hand. Leonardo da Vinci was employed as a consultant at one stage and in 1805 Napoleon who had taken command of the city tried to increase the pace of work. Finally, in 1965 the last major piece of the cathedral was finished, bringing to an end an incredible 579 years of construction.

The pigeons seemed to appreciate all the work because they covered both the cathedral piazza and the people in the piazza. Professional photographers carried round bags of birdseed which were passed to tourists, who would quickly have a flock aboard their shoulders. Then the photographers whipped out their cameras and offered to take a picture for a price. The rest of the day was spent gently walking around the Milan fortress and falling asleep in the main park.

The sands of time had reduced from a dune to a pit by the time we left the park for the station and there was still a three-hour wait before the train was due to leave. The Euro trek had that 'winding down' feeling to it, but we were both content to be on the journey home, back to a comfortable bed, clean clothes and regular meals. It seemed unbelievable that Sacha and Craig would already be back into their normal routines.

The train arrived but appeared to be heading in the wrong direction for Monaco. It turned out to be one of those special European trains where the carriages break up and go their separate ways. One set travelling to Switzerland; another back to Rome; another bound for Germany etc. There were about two carriages allegedly destined for Monaco and despite a conductor indicating which ones, she didn't convince us that we wouldn't end up in Germany. Thus a unanimous decision was taken to chicken out and wait another couple of hours for a sensible train.

The platform number from which the train would depart had not appeared so the departure board was watched intensely. We knew it would be important to jump on the train quickly to find an empty cabin.

11.45pm - the platform number came up and a dash was made for a cabin.

11.48pm - there must have been a sprinters convention in Monte Carlo because all the carriages were full of people who had managed to get ahead of us. Eventually, a compartment was located with just two people to the six seats. The strange thing was that there were three jackets hanging up.

Three jackets plus Rich and I soon meant five people in the compartment. This suspicion proved accurate when the third man walked in. If there are four people then everybody has access to a corner which can be lent against and a bit of room for stretching. Five people equalled no stretching, the temperature being intolerably hot and no sleep.

Day 30 - Friday 19ᵗʰ August - Nice Day

00.00 - 2.00am: No sleep for Jeff.

2.05am - someone departed at Genoa; not just anybody but somebody from our compartment. In a mixture of Italian, Greek and English it was decided to pull the seats down so that they stretched bed like across the cabin. Sleep could then be contemplated although everyone was squashed up against at least one other person. However, sleep is sleep is sleep.

We reached the French border town of Ventgliani and jumped out to locate the local Monte Carlo train. The departure board showed that it would leave from platform 2 but when we reached platform 2 the only train that was leaving from there was Italy bound. This caused a rubbing of brain cells until a solution could be found.

A solution was found.

It turned out that there were two completely different platform 2's, one was on the Italian side of the station and another was on the French side of the station. All the French platforms were on the other side of a tunnel that had to be walked with passport stretched out ready for inspection. The night train we were due to catch about 12 hours later would leave from Nice so strangely enough, the Monaco stop was ignored and the journey continued onwards to Nice.

The Nice station facilities were impressive, especially the showers where francs were exchanged for a clean body. This was to be the last time that I saw my toilet bag and its contents of creams, ointments and toothbrush. I don't know whether I left it there or it got swiped out my bag, but all that remained was a solitary string cord. Thieving continental gits or thicko Jeff, I will never know. As I whinged Rich led me to the Monaco train.

By about 10.30am Monaco surrounded us and we wandered around the principality working up yet another sweat in the unrelenting heat. Having had enough of walking we lazed around on Monte Carlo beach in our scruffy and semi-dirty clothes. Everyone around us smelled of money, whilst me and Rich just smelled.

The Monaco tour continued along the coastline through the superb Japanese gardens and up the hill to see Princess Stephanie. Her family have ruled the Monte Carlo roost for 700 years but if the royal line comes to an end Monaco will revert to being a part of France. Rich and I were keen to offer our services to Stephanie in order to avert such a gruesome fate.

The climb up to the palace was steep but offered a splendid view of the bay. However, the Princess missed out because the prices for palace entry were too steep for our shallow pockets.

Treasure of a different kind did get discovered; cheap food. An almost hidden supermarket with a complete garden on its roof and with prices similar to your local Tesco's.

After filling our day bag with food we waved bon voyage to our hopes of winning a million in the casino or becoming a kept man. The short trip down the rails to Nice was taken in preparation for the last leg of our tour.

If Milan had been a lazy day, today constituted a walking holiday as we tried to tour round two cities. After all those great historic cities, here was Nice with its sun, sand and sea; we were lapping it up. The TV cameras had even arrived. Some old American guy with two French models on his arm was introducing a show; as subtly as ever Rich and I merged into the background on several different takes.

Another half mile down the coast a big crowd had gathered. After mingling in we discovered that somebody appeared to be missing in the sea; within no time a helicopter hovered above and frogmen dived into the water. It always seems to be human nature to look at an accident scene, but such a scenario with helicopter and frogmen was irresistible. With so many people gathered it became difficult to keep in touch with events but the frogmen emerged to applause and we thought that meant everything was okay.

We turned in a station direction and took in the last of the day's sunshine. The involuntary, month-long competition between Rich and I to see who could stay the whitest had finished as a contest several days ago with my victory assured. The colour of my skin, especially my legs, refused to change away from pale white whatever factor cream I spread. Therefore I had a cunning plan not to use any cream on my legs, this led to them beginning to blister and in response they were coated in high factor cream once again. I think this proves I'm traditionally British and a bit simple.

The walk to the station was similar to that of a child returning to school after the summer holiday. The holiday as a holiday was over.

Day 31 - Saturday 20TH August - The Final Word

3.00am: - the last sleep on mainland Europe was disturbed. We had safely boarded the train hours ago and the carriages were of the normal English style with an aisle in the middle splitting two pairs of seats. When Rich and I had made the reservations we managed to get seats in different parts of the carriage. However, we had talked to each other for 30 days and were starting to run out of original insults so no great harm was done.

3.01am - the most likely reason for my early morning consciousness was a close-to-bursting bladder. The problem was that the lad between me and the aisle was fast asleep leaving me somewhat boxed in. The aim was to get over his legs without waking him up. In trying to achieve this goal I came close to equalling Dalton Grant's British high jump record. The double pike twist and lunge (known commonly as a big step) proved successful. The crowd roared, grown men cried, women threw underwear, well one bloke nearly woke up.

3.02am - an emptying bladder is a happy bladder.

From the hot climate of Italy, it was a shock to head towards the plummeting temperatures of Northern Europe. My trouser-less legs (I had shorts on) were absolutely freezing and my search for some ice cubes to warm them up resulted in failure.

Paris and its Metro were then conquered leaving us to work out the trains to Calais and those connecting with the ferry at Dover. In order to contemplate such matters, the Thomas Cook book was once more unsheathed. A local pigeon took a distaste to this idea and vented its bowel contents all over the book and my hand. For the next 15 seconds, Rich howled with laughter. I then pointed out that it was his book. Cue Rich to stop laughing and me to laugh. Rich pointed out that I still had bird crap on my hand. I stopped laughing and Rich started laughing again. The Euro trek that started with bird poo dripping off it faded out with another fresh creamy helping.

DIARY 2

I'd adored the sheer freedom of Interrailing around Europe. It seemed incredible that I could have a train ticket that would take me across so many countries and that we could decide on a whim what country to be in the next day. The time spent travelling on the train had given me the chance to keep the diary as I went along and then when I returned home I wrote it up. I loved writing the diary and realised that it reminded me of the small things that made me chuckle but which I would have quickly forgotten.

I followed up my first Interrailing trip with a second and then a third. Although they'd both been for just over two weeks because that was the maximum time I could get off work. Following those holidays I was ready for something different. My friend Stu mentioned a world trip for a year. It really appealed – I could do it. I resigned from my job. One week later my company had offered me more money, a better position and extra holiday. I weakened and accepted their offer. Stu was a braver man than me and I took some holiday to meet him in India at the start of his trip. This means it is time for a table:

	UK	India	Asia
Population in millions	65.6	1,328	4,437
Projected population in 2050 in millions	77	1,708	5,327
Infant mortality per 1000 live births	3.9	40	31
Life expectancy – male	79	67	71
Life expectancy – female	83	70	74
Gross national income in purchasing power parity divided by population (in $)	40,550	6,020	11,969
Area of country (square miles)	93,638	1,240,000	17,212,000

NOTE: In fact, the information in all the tables comes from the 2016 Population Reference Bureau, Nationmaster and Enchanted Learning. Tell you what, I thought the UK was full of people per square mile so how full is India?

Stu was beginning his trip in January 1997 and I flew out just before him. January 1997 was one of my saddest ever months but I will explain about that in a minute. In the meantime let's enjoy the journey through 1996 and on to 1997 by changing cinema screen 1 to 'Trainspotting' and cinema screen 2 to 'Jerry Maguire'. We can keep John Major as prime minister for a bit longer but we need to replace Terry Venables with Glenn Hoddle and as for the stereo well I can't really turn to 1997 as it had only just begun but 1996 had led the Spice Girls to breakthrough with 'Wannabe', then there was Beautiful South's 'Rotterdam' and Baddiel & Skinner's 'Three Lions', but I guess I am still in Trainspotting mode so I'm throwing on the Trainspotting soundtrack and playing 'Born Slippy' by Underworld.

12 times in Skegness, three times Interrailing around Europe, once to each of Yugoslavia, Spain, Austria, Scarborough, Sheringham, Criccieth, Exmouth, Chapel Point and Cromer but I had never been so unexcited about a holiday as I was that Thursday. Two weeks previously my grandad had died. As well as being my grandad he was also my hero – he was strong, very loving, never complained and was always ready to talk sport or provide another gem from his seemingly bottomless anecdote well. Ignoring all logic I had always figured that he was indestructible, so he may get older but not die; surely he would be far too stubborn for that. However, on the 14th January 1997 at the age of 87, he took his last breath and I was absolutely devastated. After shedding many tears over the last couple of weeks my body felt like a sad empty shell devoid of happiness and energy.

It was only on the Friday morning that the adrenaline acknowledged I was travelling to India. I left Frisby-on-the-Wreake with little purpose, a rucksack and a brother.

Day 1 - Friday 31ST January 1997 – Alone Into The Big Wide World

'*See you after we check in*' said Graham at Heathrow. Graham had split up with his girlfriend a few weeks earlier and then thought he would join me in India for a couple of weeks. However, he was on a different flight to me so I had to wait another hour before I could check-in. It then took me two hours to get through the check-in queue, the passport control queue and the 'check you haven't got a concealed machine gun queue.' I finally reached the departure lounge at the same time as my brother's flight was due to leave. I had passed much of the queueing time bantering with a lad who was going to Australia but when he left for his flight I was alone. There was no safety net of having somebody else around, I was by myself, so I did what any decent chap would do and bought a packet of wine gums.

I then boarded my Gulf-Air flight and sat next to a flight supervisor travelling back to Bahrain after being on a month's snorkelling holiday. The plane was a 767 but because of a technical fault, it was a 767 with its wheels firmly on the ground for the next one and a half hours. The televisions were flickering, there were arguments over the amount of hand luggage allowed but my companion assured me it would be a safe journey. Although she asked me what I was going to do about the two-hour delay that would mean me missing my connection from Bahrain to Delhi. I laughed, fairly certain that she was joking then fell asleep, woke up, slept, woke, slept, woke…

Day 2 - Saturday 1st February - Oh Brother!

The historic island of Bahrain provided the scene of Asia and I meeting for the very first time. I just hoped that my baggage was also meeting Bahrain but was not too confident, especially as, like me, it would also have to change planes. I was also a bit confused because some passengers stayed on board my plane and were continuing their journey to Abu Dhabi. I was 'in transit' in Bahrain for about an hour and had no one obvious to talk to while I waited for the now-delayed Delhi plane.

I boarded the Delhi plane and slept, woke, slept, woke … before touching down in Abu Dhabi where among other passengers a British couple boarded. I had queued with them at Heathrow, flew with them to Bahrain whereupon I departed but they stayed on board until Abu Dhabi. The even stranger detail is that on the way back, in three weeks' time, I'm changing at Abu Dhabi and they are changing at Bahrain.

My brother had taken a direct Air India flight to Delhi whilst I'd taken the £150 cheaper indirect option. As he would be arriving seven hours before me his great plan was to leave instructions at the airport saying where he would be staying. Mentally I prepared myself; the easiest scenario would be for him to be at the airport (10% chance I calculated) but basically, that's not going to happen. The more likely case would be that there would be no Graham but a message stating at which hostel he was encamped, and then I would resign myself to being ripped off by a taxi driver for the several miles trip (40% chance). There may be no message I thought to myself (50% chance), I mean my flight supervisor friend had said how useless they were at getting messages through. In that case, I would try to book in at one of the hostels that I had suggested to Graham. If he wasn't there the back-up plan was to meet him at 10.30am tomorrow in Wimpy on Connaught Place. It seemed a bit frightening to be heading to a strange country by myself. So I had another wine gum and said to myself 'tonight I am not going to see my brother; it will be a strange environment but I will not be fazed, I will simply meet up with him tomorrow'.

Suitably toughened up I touched down in Delhi. The moment we hit the ground it seemed as though all the Indians undid their seat belts and went for their hand luggage with the 'please keep your seatbelts on until we stop moving' sign flashing in the background. A few minutes later the plane ground to a halt. The tannoy sounded *'Gulf-Air would like to thank everybody for flying with us and could Mr Brown please see the ground staff'*. Either Graham had successfully left a message or I was going to be prose-cuted for illegally importing wine gums. Before I had a chance to swallow my stash of wine gums the ground staff told me that Graham would be waiting outside the airport. Well, at least if my luggage had got lost somewhere in the Middle East I had my brother. When I reached the conveyor belt of luggage it brought the usual mix of suitcases and bags and then it arrived; my purple and pukey yellow backpack. Despite undergoing 50 stitches from my fair hands and persistent rumours that after three European trips a new younger backpack would be recruited, my bag had indeed been selected for this tour of duty and, being as loyal as ever, successfully navigated her way to Delhi. I walked off with her on my back, whilst many of my fellow passengers, who had prematurely undone their seatbelts to hurry off the plane, still waited for their bags. Yes, I was a little smug.

I rounded a corner about 100 metres from the exit and could see hundreds of friendly looking brown faces and one solitary white face. The white face was surprisingly that of my brother and he seemed to tower over most of the locals. He stood out like a haystack in a needle. As I got closer, and much to my amusement, the haystack started to frantically wave its arms to try and show he was there. I had never been so glad to see his familiar features; he'd even got a taxi ready and waiting for us to drive straight to the hostel. The only problem being that he didn't know where it was waiting. As Graham searched around he told me to sit still. So there I sat, on the roadside, happily taking in the alien environment. It was about 6.00pm, it was dusk, the sky was an incredible orange colour, the roads were full of impatient cars with busy horns and the air thick with pollution. Welcome to India – this should be interesting.

As I sat on a kerb trying not to get run over, Graham found our Scarlet Pimpernel of a driver and we set off on the taxi ride of a lifetime. How we escaped not having an accident I'm still unsure. I'm not certain but I think in India green means go and red means go even faster else a car from the other direction might hit you. For a good half a mile we were fighting for road space with a lorry. I wouldn't have been too bothered but the lorry had a skull and crossbones on the back with the letters T O X I C and we were never more than 10 inches away whilst travelling at 50 mph. Our taxi had all but hit a motorcycle before its passenger gave us a rugby style hand-off. I loved every minute!

After half an hour or more, the taxi headed down a back street and arrived at Sunny's Guest House. I spent a few minutes in our room before we left for some food with a couple of Danish girls who had invited us out. The restaurant was a very friendly Chinese place; the food was good and the company, Meter and Clitera (she said to try and remember her name because it sounded like a disease but we had our own method and had a feeling that we had been searching for her for a while), was entertaining.

The night was very chilly and I was thankful for my jacket in the open air. Graham confessed in the room that if he had missed me at the airport he couldn't remember what time he was meant to meet me at Wimpy; lucky we met up then. I crashed out shortly before midnight but not before tuning into the World Service football commentary and classified results.

DAY 3 - SUNDAY 2ND FEBRUARY - DELHI BY BUS

I woke up several times in the night. I'm not sure if this was to do with the ongoing commotion of life outside the hostel. There were street dogs barking, cars peeping, street kids shouting and more dogs barking. I finally woke up at 8.30am to the sound of pouring rain. Both Graham and I slept fairly well, in the circumstances, and were happy that we seemed unaffected by jet lag.

We had been made aware that the traditional method of wiping your bottom in India was with your left hand and a jug of water. Therefore, toilet rolls should not be expected to be found in many toilets and consequently, we had brought our own supply. Minutes after getting out of bed I realised that Graham was at my mercy when a voice from the bathroom uttered those immortal words '*Jeff, can you bung me the bog paper please?*' 'Maybe, maybe not, what is it worth to you?' I don't think I should write down my elder brother's response.

Graham had booked us on a tour around the city. We were under the impression that it was some sort of all-day taxi drive, mainly due to yester-day's driver continuously repeating that he would see us tomorrow to drive us around Delhi. However, it turned out he was after a full day's fare from us and our tour was on a dilapidated old bus or 'luxury coach' as the locals put it.

In the daylight, Delhi seemed to be even more daunting than last night. The poverty came at you from all sides but this was not like any poverty I had ever seen before. The beggars looked terrible with various concoctions of ragged clothes, missing limbs and ugly growths. There were 'estates' of family homes on the pavement consisting of plastic sheets kept up by a couple of sticks. But it was the little kids that broke my heart. I could see their meshed hair, grubby little faces and rag-covered bodies playing in rubbish, but still they smiled and waved. I don't think they realise that the Indian caste system has made them the untouchables and they may be dead before they are ten.

The city was a sprawling mass of life with cars, rickshaws, bikes, mopeds and people desperately vying for space amid air thick with pollution and a cacophony of sound. I found it totally bemusing and bewitching. I have never witnessed anything like it in my life.

I didn't really know much about the history of Delhi or even India come to that. So I looked it up in my guide book. Apparently, Delhi came into being around 700 AD although there are claims it could date back as far as 1000 BC. Initially, it was established by the Rajputs before being invaded by an Afghani-led army that established a succession of Delhi Sultans. The names of the sultans conjure up amazing images in my head - Iltumish,

Ala-ud-din-Khalji, Firuz Shah. By 1526 Babur, a descendant of Genghis Khan (but aren't we all) had seized Delhi and established the Moghul Empire. They hung on to power until 1803 when the British moved in and then India received its independence in 1947.

The first stop on the tour of this historic city was at a temple where to our astonishment all shoes and socks had to be removed. Only parts of the temple were sheltered, so there we were in our bare feet whilst the rain poured down on us. It reminded me of our family holidays in Skegness. I was amazed to see swastikas decorating the temple. Our guide said that the swastika is an ancient symbol and has been used by many cultures to represent life, strength, and good luck. Even during World War I, the swastika could be found on the shoulder patches of an American Division and on the Finnish air force until after World War II. There we go, it represented good for 2,931 years but because of some Austrian painter and decorator, many people think of it as a symbol of hate, anti-Semitism, violence, death, and murder.

A more expected sight in India was a cobra. I don't like snakes but to my surprise, on the walk back to the bus I calmly passed a cobra that was dancing in its basket. Well, on the outside relatively calmly but on the inside quite nervously; in fact, I was just glad I didn't scream in terror and jump into my brother's arms. The bus was full and ready to go when we arrived back at it. By the time I jumped on, it had started to move and by the time one of the Israeli lads had jumped aboard it was moving even quicker. We then had to yell at the bus driver to stop to give two more of our fellow passengers the chance to board. The 'trying to get on the bus before it left' proved to be a theme of the day. The tour went on to: Indira Gandhi's preserved home and the spot where she was assassinated; Bahai Temple, Qutb Minar Complex (tower thing which has been closed for a few years due to a spate of people jumping off it); Raj Ghat and the Red Fort. A fair bit of Delhi was seen but the feeling was that we were being rushed from one site to another and eventually a couple of our Israeli friends were left behind by the hurrying bus.

Arriving back at the hostel my chief priority was to have a word with Stu Blood, who was still back in England. I needed to tell him exactly which hostel we were holed up in and that Graham had booked us on a bus trip to Agra at 7.00am on Tuesday, the same Tuesday morning that he should arrive in Delhi. There was a telephone exchange about 15 minutes' walk away, so I managed to leave a message at Stu's mum's house for him to phone the hostel as soon as possible. Unfortunately, by the time Stu arrived at his mum's, Graham and I had gone out for some food.

DAY 4 - MONDAY 3ᴿᴰ FEBRUARY - CLEANED OUT & STITCHED UP

Shortly after midnight, I was woken up by a knock at the door. Stu was on the phone so I sleepily transmitted my message to him. I returned to the room to get to sleep. At 1.30am I still could not sleep, as the jet lag paid a visit, the also wide-awake Graham and I embarked on a football game we played as kids. Starting with 'A' for Arsenal, he would name one of their players, then I would name another, then him again etc., until one of us cracked and couldn't name anyone else, thus making him the loser (normally Jeff the younger brother) and the survivor (Graham the elder brother) the winner. As we had been kids when the game was originally played each footballer had to be from the 1977-78 Panini football sticker album, which the five-year-old and eight-year old brothers had so eagerly invested all available pocket money in. I think it is thanks to Mr Panini that neither of us has ever had a filling, as our teeth weren't decimated by pocket money purchased sweets from an early age. I digress; the game stopped and started its way past 4.00am to the backdrop of constant noise. Noise from street dogs, cars, street kids and more street dogs. Even my remaining stash of wine gums, which I had been rationing, had run out by the time sleep arrived.

At 10.00am I woke in a half-awake state but I didn't make the big push to surface until 11.30am, beating Graham by one and a half hours.

We then wandered around Delhi and finished up at a park in the middle of a big roundabout at Connaught Place to relax. Instead, the moment one foot was placed in the park it was hassle, hassle, hassle. '*Can I clean your shoes?*', No, '*Can I clean your shoes?*', No, '*Can I mend your shoes?*', No, '*Can I mend your shoes?*', No, '*Your shoes need mending I will clean them*', No. Relentlessly it continued on from one side of the park to just past the middle and then finally they gave up. So we sat down. Big mistake, it's much easier to attack a stationary target and off they went again. '*Okay*' he said, '*I will glue down the ends of your trainers for free*'. Well my trainers were splitting in places; where could the harm be in having them stuck down at the ends. He again asked to mend the split in my trainers; well he had done the other for free so I relented and he began stitching up the side. '*These will now last you another 3 years*'.

Meanwhile, Graham had weakened and was having his ears cleaned out! Basically, the bloke was saying how clean we were on the outside but on the inside '*very dirty*', then to prove his point he inserted a long metal implement into Graham's ear and pulled out loads of gunk for want of a better word. How the amount he pulled out compared to the amount he put in I'm not sure, but Graham was more open than me to these new experiences, so off he went to sit on the grass and have his ears cleaned.

As my trainers were being mended another ear cleaner sat nearby continually stating how much Graham was enjoying it and that it would be good for me. This diverged from my opinion and I turned to discuss this with him. On turning back the shoe man had started whacking some terrible bright whitener on my shoes; having just about finished the right boot I allowed him to paint the other as well. Whenever I mentioned the price he said '*yes standard price, I show you my book*'. His book was a montage of comments from allegedly delighted customers who had all been completely ripped off; now I was to follow in their footsteps. He demanded £14 for his work; I couldn't even remember how I had reached this predicament, I negotiated the price down to £7 but it should have been more like 25p. I gave him the money and he even had the cheek to say '*now the price for cleaning your shoes sir*'. My first proper experience of bartering had ended in a crushing defeat but an important lesson had been learned; always set the price before the transaction.

Graham had fared little better, handing over £9 to his wax remover and making the further mistake of saying 'I'll pay the same as my brother' (without knowing what I'd paid) when being hassled over his shoes. So we were properly cleaned out and stitched up. The only thing I did receive for free was a hand massage while watching the end of the ear cleaning operation, from one of the crowd of traders gathered around us. The massage was fairly relaxing but as he continued to hassle me about a back massage I became increasingly stressed.

We finally broke free and noticed a couple of Indian lads wryly grinning about our plight. They were a couple of sympathetic University students and the banter started to flow. They joined us for a cup of tea and a chat in the nearby Wimpy. After 10 minutes the Wimpy security guard hovered across to our table and then started to talk seriously to the lads in Hindi. At one point they produced some ID and then the security guard looked satisfied and headed off. They laughed and then told us that the security guard had accused them of being Kashmiris negotiating an arms deal with the white men. In order to convince the over-enthusiastic security man, the lads showed that they were not from Kashmir. Brilliant – I have never been accused of doing an arms deal before.

In the evening the two Brown brothers relaxed back at the hostel hearing many a different tale. Including one from a Canadian, who said that when he was in Venezuela he started talking to a local man who claimed he was going to University in Ottawa, the lads home town. After having a pleasant enough chat they had a spot of lunch whereupon the Venezuelan claimed to have no money for the bill; as the Canadian handed some money over to him the police charged in and grabbed the Venezuelan, dragging him off saying he was a terrorist. They then told the Canadian that it was a criminal offence to give money to a terrorist and he could either go to the police station or pay an on the spot fine. On choosing the fine he walked to the bank to get the money, but strangely the 'police' wouldn't go in with him. This prompted him to realise he was in the midst of a scam so he made a couple of allies in the bank who let him flee out the back of the bank.

Stu is due to arrive tomorrow at 1.30am in Delhi airport and stay there until first light then get a taxi to arrive at the hostel for about 6.00am. The man from the hostel advised me to be waiting outside the hostel 15 minutes before that to make sure the taxi can find the place. There will also be a knock at the door at 6.00am from the receptionist to make sure that we are up for our trip to Agra; somebody else is then meant to be calling round to get us at 6.30am and take us to the bus. The question is: will Stu manage to get to the hostel before we are due to leave for Agra? Anyway, it's now or never for a bit of sleep.

Day 5 - Tuesday 4ᵗʰ February - Beer, Blood And The Taj Mahal

'Knock Knock' went the door, 'oh god, it must be 6.00am already, I've slept through my alarm'. In a sleepy daze I staggered to the door, opened it and was greeted by a beaming Stuart Blood, *'Alright Jeff'* said the wide-awake figure. A quick glance at my watch showed the time to be 3.30am precisely, 'you're early Stu'. *'Yeah, fancy a beer?'* he said producing a couple of cans of Directors bitter. In my sleepy state, I opened a can and watched helplessly as its contents sprayed in each and every direction of our room in this 'alcohol banned' hostel.

He had originally planned to stay at the airport until daybreak and then make his way to the hostel. However, when he had collected his luggage he glanced around, saw a couple who looked as though they knew what they were doing, went over and asked them where they were heading. By pure chance, the answer was '*it's a place called Sunny's hostel*', so he caught a taxi with them.

All in all, Stu had managed to disturb two nights sleep on the trot. The three of us put the two single beds together and tried to fit the three of us on top without Stu falling down the middle. Within a couple of hours, it was getting up time again.

Although the bus started off at 7.00am it didn't leave the outskirts of Delhi for another two hours due to various stoppages and the ever-sprawling nature of the city. After enduring a haphazard back road, which was just about one and a half bus widths (we still managed to pass about five buses going the other way with the use of various embankments whilst scraping trees and hovering precariously above ditches while vultures looked on) Agra was reached at 1.30pm. That was two hours late and we were compensated by way of a free rickshaw for the day. Our new found friend, Tina the Geordie, joined us as we headed to the Taj Mahal. For Tina this was her second day trip to Agra, having been yesterday but suffered the problem of the Taj Mahal being closed every Monday!

There were swarms of people but just between hundreds of heads I glimpsed something beautiful. It was stunning. How can a building be so beautiful? And how had I reached this point without knowing why the Taj Mahal had been built. A quick look at a booklet confirmed that the Taj was built by Shah Jahan over a 20-year period until its completion in 1653. It is, in fact, a mausoleum for his favourite wife Mumtaz Mahal who had died while giving birth to their 14th child. He must have had a child too many because one of his sons seized power in 1658 and imprisoned him in Agra Fort. He had a view of the Taj from his room in the fort but remained a prisoner until his death in 1666, when his body was laid beside his beloved Mumtaz.

Other local stories are that a black Taj Mahal was going to be built on the opposite bank except it would have been made in black marble and provided a separate tomb for Shah Jahan. Also the British started to number blocks of the Taj with the aim of taking it apart and rebuilding it elsewhere. I don't know how true the local stories are but I know I could sit there all day just staring at this legacy of Mumtaz Mahal. I thought that out of all the places on this planet of ours I could not wish to be in a better location. Claudia Schiffer's bedroom would be nice but I'm sure after she'd prosecuted me for trespassing I would think that I should have gone to the Taj Mahal instead.

The four of us moved on to the Red Fort, which was built by Shah Jahan's grandfather Akber the Great who had moved his Moghul capital from Delhi to Agra. We then moved on to a marble shop where they train youngsters to become craftsmen who will assist in the continuing restoration of the Taj Mahal. Graham decided he wanted a piece of crafted marble and would be bartering for it. He was led away to a private room and upon his return had bartered the price down from £65 to £50. Well, at least I think he got the price down by a good barter.

Tina collected her train back to Delhi while we headed on to our Agra hostel via a slap-up curry feast. Stu by this stage had managed just two hours sleep in the last 28 hours and after cleaning his teeth he laid down on his bed to read and immediately fell asleep.

Day 6 - Wednesday 5ᵗʰ February - Alone With The Taj

At 5.40am I left the confines of our room to find a view; I looked up at the sky where the moon and stars were shining without a cloud in sight. The conclusion of this astronomy was that it was getting up time to witness sunrise at the Taj Mahal. We stumbled sleepily out the hostel and were half hoping the rickshaw driver wasn't there so we had an excuse to return to bed. However, he was waiting for us and looked far more awake than us. The streets of Agra were relatively deserted and we quickly pulled up at one of the Taj's gates. About 25 pence later we were in.

We made our way through the deserted and tranquil gardens in the gloomy light. Where yesterday we had to fight through hundreds of people; for a glimpse of the Taj Mahal, today we had it to ourselves. If it was obviously beautiful yesterday it was beyond my words today. I sat on a stone bench in front of the Taj Mahal knowing that myself, my brother and my great friend were the only people, at that moment, gazing at the most beautiful building in the world. I looked at this monument to love, soaked up the moment and tried to take it all in. It was just so beautiful.

Slowly the sun started to rise to change greys to oranges, to bright yellow and then the beautiful white of the marble was revealed. As I was engrossed in the moment, Stu had been convinced by a local guide to take a picture from one angle, then another slightly different, then another; I hoped Stu realised that he was going to be asked for a lot of money in a moment. Slowly more people arrived and my intimate moment with the Taj Mahal was gone.

It was another couple of hours before we left. Walking away it was a case of 'right, one more look then I turn and leave forever': in reality, it was the look, the turn and then I've just got to have one more look. After having five last looks the Taj and I separated.

Our rickshaw man drove us to the baby Taj, which had been built about 30 years before the Taj Mahal and was for some prime minister or other. Then it was on to a carpet making place and a silver shop. The rickshaw drivers are always keen to take you to a shop because they receive commission on whatever you buy. The shopkeepers are happy to chat away and provide a cup of chai with the aim of selling you one item or other. It all seemed so friendly and civilised that I forgot that I was simultaneously fighting off the advances of these master salesmen.

Our bus was due out of Agra at 4.30pm so at 3.00pm we were taken to a ticket operator's back street office to pick up our tickets. We chatted along whilst drinking some chai and waited for our tickets to arrive. The carpet makers next door were mentioned, where we were offered beautiful handmade carpets for £270; he took us to another room and said the actual price should be £180. Graham wanted a carpet and agreed on the £180 price. The bloke even mentioned that if we paid about £300 each for a couple of carpets then he'd send them across to us but would not have to pay the 100% import tax and one of his men would meet us in England and pay us £450 each. It sounded a great deal and made some sense but I was still reluctant. I think I am just learning to differentiate the master salesman from the master scammer.

The bus journey consisted of a six-hour voyage to Jaipur which allowed us a bit of time to put the feet up in our usual dilapidated 'deluxe' bus. We sat near four Canadians who had just completed arranged marriages and were in India for four months. One of the Indian Canadians was the most beautiful Asian girl I've ever seen, but it was all two weeks and one arrangement too late for me!

We all decided to walk to the Jaipur Inn, which didn't seem far from the bus terminal on the map. The problem was that the bus hadn't dropped us off at the terminal, so we were heading to nowhere before a rickshaw driver offered us a lift for five rupees (about 10p). *'My name is Piquet, Nelson Piquet'* he chirpily announced to us before helping us reach the Jaipur Inn just before midnight.

There were a couple of free rooms remaining and a dormitory. Graham rightfully left the rooms for the newlyweds and we headed down to the basement where we had a dormitory to ourselves. This was the dungeon dormitory; damp, dreary and grey it possessed all the features of a dungeon except for the chains. However I was tired, there were six beds each and I fell fast asleep.

DAY 7 - THURSDAY 6ᵀᴴ FEBRUARY - PANDORA'S BOX

The first and only visitor to our dungeon arrived at 10.30am. After being turned away from two other hostels last night Tina the Geordie had been accepted by the Jaipur Inn. She then joined us for a walk to the old city which coincided with the time a local school was breaking for lunch. The four of us were mobbed by the school kids all wanting to shake our hands and have a quick word. In fact, all Indian kids seem desperate to say hello to us. I am staggered how friendly everyone is to visitors. I feel like a superstar.

On reaching the old city there was the familiar collection of locals wanting to chat. '*Nationality? City? Name? Age? Occupation? First time in India?*' And, oh yes, '*Would you like to see my shop?*' The number of Indian business cards that have been passed in my direction is ever growing. A little girl aged no more than four, followed us for a mile. Whatever speed we walked she was there with '*hello, money?*' Even as we forced our way across the busy roads and figured she would have to wait for the traffic she was still just behind us. In a country full of persistent people she had the talent to be a national champion.

Jaipur is known as the pink city because of the colour of the buildings. Apparently, they were turned pink in readiness for the visit of Prince Albert in 1856. They weren't making any comment about Albert but in this area pink is the colour of hospitality. Anyway, ever since then the buildings in the old city have been regularly doused pink. I said 'old city', but Jaipur did not exist until 1727. At that time they had a Rajput ruler called Jai Singh who decided to move his capital from nearby Amber. Jai Singh ruled for 43 years but, after his death, there was a big fight over who should succeed him between the children from his 28 wives and four concubines.

After touring the city palace where the Maharaja still resides we walked up to the fort. In order to reach the fort, our path took us around the back streets where the number of 'hellos' increased to a 'one every 30 seconds' level. Most tourists obtain transport to climb the hill so there was a certain novelty value attached to our presence along the hill. As we started to struggle a bit up the increasingly steep and windy path the odd cow passed us on the reverse journey. It now seemed normal for cows to pass us on the street, but a hillside path? Mind you Tina told us she saw one on a railway platform.

The view from the Tiger fort was pretty good without being spectacular. The sun started to set but by the time our cameras had been unsheathed the sun had dropped, such is the speed of it in these parts. It signalled that we should head back to the hostel.

The hostel had a nice courtyard and served bottles of beer. It proved perfect for relaxed banter with Caroline the American, Carol, Lucy, Shaun, Lake District lad and us lot. Caroline had just visited the dentist to sort out a filling. After completing her filling he had turned to her and asked whether she was suffering from her wisdom tooth. She had struggled, with the tooth, for a couple of years but as it was so expensive to sort out in America had not bothered having it extracted. The dentist offered to take it out and tried to instil her with confidence by showing her his American textbooks, his 1964 and 1967 editions respectfully. Anyway, she is going back to him tomorrow to have the wisdom tooth taken out. Rather her than me! In other news, Carol of Anglesey and Lucy of London had uncovered a Pizza Hut in Jaipur, whilst Lake District lad was suffering his fifth consecutive day of Delhi belly (but was confident that tomorrow he would be okay).

The time in the courtyard drifted pleasantly away until about midnight. It was at that point that an uncomfortable feeling became painful. Ahhh - terrible cramps meant that I needed to lie down. I announced my reluctant retirement and then headed off, not to the dungeon but the better 16-bed dorm where we had been transferred. Whilst I sat on the dormitory bed getting my toothbrush and toothpaste out, the body's alarm bells rang. I needed a toilet and I needed it quick. I was lucky; in a country where toilet rolls are seemingly only used by tourists someone had left a bit of toilet roll in one of the two bathrooms, so I jumped on the throne then released the ghastly and vast contents of my bowels. What relief. It was a bit strange in that while I sat there the window of the bathroom was still close enough to faintly hear the courtyard chatter. Feeling much better I couldn't resist a Frank Sinatra style comeback (in a 'returning again' sense rather than blasting out 'I did it my way') and re-joined the group.

Everyone retired at about 12.30am.

Day 8 - Friday 7th February - A Helping Hand

3.00am - My cramps started again; the only way I could sleep was to curl up with my knees near my chest. The cramps were bad Ahhhhh! It was dark; I was in a large dormitory and in pain. Oh god, I just wanted to be back home,

England seemed so far away. The cramps were getting unbearably worse. Then a message was received by my brain from the afflicted area. 'Red alert captain, I'm losing control of the bowels, I canna hold her much longer'. With no time to reach my personal toilet roll, located in the locker, I scrambled out of my sleeping bag, headed to the bathroom where I thought the bit of toilet roll was, switched on the light and switched on the light. The switch would not work, so with no light and little time I grabbed the toilet roll and went to the other bathroom, light on, boxers down, sit down, pure liquid release and simple blissful relief.

The stomach cramps eased and I went back to sleep in my now familiar tuck position. At 6.00am the cramps returned with their friend called vengeance. Someone was getting up and I could hear them in a bathroom, but I had satisfied myself that I didn't need the toilet just yet. I did feel a bit nauseous though, in fact very nauseous, I needed to be sick. Up I jumped and headed to the lightless bathroom. Luckily I didn't need a poo because I had moved the toilet roll on my previous excursion. However, as I threw up my now possessed bowels started to move. Every time I threw up I was edging closer to re-decorating my boxer shorts. So when the last of the sick came up, my boxers flew down and a second later brown liquid flowed into the toilet. In England, the state of this Western-style toilet would have been a disgrace, even before I touched it, but at that moment it felt like it had been heaven sent, despite the stained seat, the peeling walls and the dirty floor. Although I was now in a bathroom with no toilet roll. My only option was to clean my bottom in a manner that I had never before seriously contemplated. As per Indian custom, I used my left hand. With every wipe, I washed my hand in a bowl. Mission completed I headed back to bed, finding a wet wipe to perform an additional clean of my hand. It hadn't been pleasant but it had been worth it just to dampen the searing pain.

I lived off crackers for most of a quiet day, relaxing out on the hostel roof talking football and cricket with a couple of Birmingham and Middlesbrough fans. Caroline joined us after she returned from the dentist. Her operation was completed smoothly, much to our surprise.

In the evening we visited the Palace of the Winds with Tina. The four of us piled into one rickshaw which involved Graham sitting partly on my knee and partly on Stu's. The Palace of the Winds is an amazing place with about 500 decorated windows with balconies designed hundreds of years ago to allow women to watch the processions below without being seen. As I moved below the palace I wondered whether the eyes of every beautiful eligible princess were excitedly watching my every movement (well obviously the answer was no but allow me to dream a little longer). Then on to what would have been my non-spicy food highlight of the day, a meal at Pizza Hut; but my stomach was not feeling healthy, so I managed about half a small plain pizza.

After the meal, Tina caught the night bus to Udaipur while Graham decided to journey on ahead to Jaisalmer. With him only being in India for a couple of weeks he wanted to do as much as possible. I decided that I was not fit enough for a 13-hour bus journey so Stu and I stayed in Jaipur for another night.

Day 9 - Saturday 8ᵗʰ February - Fort In, Good View

My three brown liquid visits to the toilet this morning led me to try and cork myself by taking a diarrhoea tablet. I hoped I could naturally come to a halt but with the journey to Jaisalmer beckoning a quick fix seemed preferable.

Stu and I then caught the local bus for the nine-kilometre ride to Amber, the old Rajput capital. The Rajputs were renowned for their fighting abilities, so the Moghul leader Akber seemed to have the right idea in 1570 as according to our books he married a princess from Amber and formed an alliance. As for the local buses, everything appears to be made of metal including the seat covers and when they are driving along the bumpy roads it is a bottom bruising experience. There is also no such thing as an Indian bus that is full because there is always room for one more. In fact, what you would say is full in England is barely half full in India. We decided to climb up to the big fort on the hill, meeting Ray and Mark, a couple of blokes from Nuneaton on the way up. The fort was huge and we spent three hours walking around the place. The view on offer was quite spectacular.

On seeing Ray and Mark, a Japanese lad's face lit up and he ran over to acknowledge them despite only speaking very limited English. Evidently, when Ray and Mark had arrived in Jaipur on the train there was the usual scrum of rickshaw drivers clambering all over the tourists. The Japanese lad stood still while being hounded by them and was too nice to tell them politely where to stick their rickshaws. He looked lonely, frightened and on the point of tears when Ray and Mark grabbed him, put him in their taxi and on to a hotel where he recomposed himself and managed to organise his own hostel.

So much time was spent wandering around the fort that we didn't have enough time to properly look around the palace below. On our brief visit to the palace, we bumped into a couple of Portsmouth girls from our hostel, who had become the idols of a group of Indian schoolchildren to such an extent that the teachers insisted that they were on the official group photograph of the trip. We lost Ray and Mark somewhere and ended up on a balcony of a shop with a local craftsman who said that we could go on his private balcony with its wonderful view without him insisting we visit his shop, but if we'd like to see his shop…

The local bus took us back to Jaipur and to the Palace of Winds where Stu wanted to take some more photographs. He disappeared to do that while I haggled my way to a good price for the rickshaw back to the hostel. After five minutes or so Stu still hadn't returned so I formed my own one-man search party and was quickly set upon by the usual set of shopkeepers. 'No, I don't want to go into your shop, I'm looking for my friend'. '*Ah yes, friend in my shop.*' 'How do you mean, you don't even know what my friend looks like'. Another shopkeeper added '*You're looking for friends, three girls?*' 'Well, I wouldn't mind three girls but my friend is a man'. Back at the rickshaw, there was still no sign of Stu and as a few more minutes passed I figured he must have lost his bearings and gone back to the hostel. A minute after I reached the hostel Stu turned up. He had gone to the Palace of the Winds, got talked into visiting a shop and then agreed to buy two pairs of Indian trousers and a shirt.

At the hostel the girls' verdict on the extension to his wardrobe ranged from '*the camel patterned trousers would look good on a girl*', '*I like them but I admit to having bad taste*' and then the plain old '*they're terrible*'.

We carried on to Pizza Hut to meet up with Carol and Lucy. My stomach had significantly improved and I managed to finish two-thirds of my medium sized pizza, saving the remainder for our bus trip. Carol and Lucy didn't seem to have picked up the 'just scraping by' mood of the typical backpacker, having flown over to India on British Airways and eaten the last three nights at Pizza Hut. But they were friendly, good-humoured company and I enjoyed every minute.

On returning to the hostel I completed my packing and joined a couple of Aussies plus the Portsmouth girls at a table. '*We're just talking about gay clubs and S&M*' they told me; I laughed, but it turned out that was precisely what they were talking about!

The friendly Jaipur Inn had to be deserted for the bus station, where we were still hassled by people wanting us to stay at their hostel. Having arrived early for the bus with time to spare, I tried to phone home but ended up speaking to Graham's voice on the answering machine. I make a 4,000 mile call and talk to my brother who is just 300 miles away; there is definitely something odd about that.

Day 10 - Sunday 9ᵀᴴ February - Jeff Of The Desert

Sleep was on and off during the bus journey but I was just glad that the diarrhoea tablets seemed to have worked wonders. In one of my longer sleeping spells I dreamt that I was back in England for the weekend and was trying to figure out how to return to India. On waking up I was relieved to find that I was still in India but confused that there was hardly anybody on the coach, not even any sign of Stu. Was this reality or was I still in the dream? It turned out that it was just a break in the journey and most people were enjoying a cup of chai by the roadside, so I tucked into the remnants of the cold pizza from Pizza Hut. We had grown used to these stop-offs which were basically shacks on the verge that were the centre of attention. You would sit there with hands firmly wrapped around a metal cup full of sweet brown liquid, the cold night air blowing and the pitch black sky dotted with bright stars. More for the romantic than the hygienic but I loved it. Chai is the standard Indian tea but I'd read, before I left England, that it is best to think of it as a completely different drink. It was good advice because if I'd expected my normal English tea I'd have been sadly disappointed but as Indian Chai, I thought it was wonderful.

The landscape gradually became more arid and, well, for want of a better word, it became more deserty by which I mean browner and sandier looking. Although that wasn't a surprise as we had entered the Great Indian Desert.

Jaisalmer fort was still many kilometres away when we spotted it, sitting majestically above the surrounding landscape. It looked like a mythical fort with its walls naturally blending with the landscape giving it the appearance of having risen out of the desert floor. Jaisalmer is renowned for tourists being hassled immediately on leaving a bus or train, with touts trying to drag you to their hostel. Then unless you agree to go on the hostel's camel trek they will sometimes throw you out! The hassling started one kilometre out of town when a couple of guys jumped on the bus. It continued as we stepped off the bus. After a night on an Indian bus, the last thing you want is more hassling, but a mirage seemed to appear on the roadside. Away from the three-deep crowd of touts, gathered around the steps of the bus, a familiar brotherly figure sat in a jeep with a beaming smile. Coincidentally, the same

Japanese guy that Ray and Mark had saved, travelled on the coach and as the touts turned their attention to him, their main tactic being to grab his bag, he desperately blurted '*go with you*' so we grabbed him and bundled him into our jeep.

Our hostel lay just outside the fort and provided a grand view. I grabbed a brilliant shower, not the usual dribble of cold water but hot liquid bursting in all directions. I got dressed but my head needed a cover from the fierce desert sun. The friendly hostel people said they would lend me a turban or a baseball cap. I tried on the turban for a laugh before asking for the cap. It wasn't exactly a typical baseball cap, being made of a felt-like substance with a metal button stuck on the small brim so it could be buttoned up to the top of the hat. I chose the turban.

By then it was about midday so we had a quick look around the fort with my turban causing much hilarity amongst the locals and the call of '*Maharaja*' ringing in my ears. I even got stopped for a picture by some Indian tourists. The continuous attention lost its appeal after a while with the final straw coming with the 100th cry of Maharaja and an attempt to yank me up on to a camel. I purchased a new hat whilst telling Graham how relieved I was that the Delhi belly had not threatened an accident on last night's bus, but then Graham revealed a slightly different tale. On his Jaipur to Jaisalmer night bus he was feeling a bit dodgy and felt something accidentally slip out from the bowel area. He was certain that he had made a solid release and typically when you need the bus to stop, which they regularly tend to, it was another couple of hours before he could jump off the bus, run into the desert and pull his trousers down. Luckily for him, it had merely been a little gas coupled with paranoia that had slipped out.

At 2.00pm we left our hostel to go camel trekking; three days and two nights of camel trekking to be precise. A jeep drove us on a one-hour journey, via a local village, out into the desert and to our beasts. I had never ridden a horse before, never mind a camel, so a couple of butterflies fluttered in the stomach region. There were four camels between the three Brits, Ken the Japanese lad and a couple of guides, who would spend the first day walking. To the Brits' horror, one of the camels was foaming at the mouth, thus we quickly concluded that it had rabies. I noticed Graham subtly shuffling away from it and towards the other camels. Stu and I quickly followed suit. This meant that when the guides turned round to allocate each of us a camel, Ken was closest to the foaming beast and the guides naturally put him on it (sorry Ken).

All riding nerves were dispelled as I jumped up on to my camel; it was brilliant. Jeff of the Desert was born as I rode my ship of the desert into the sunset of the Great Indian Desert.

It was so relaxing moving across great expanses of the desert. Lovely peace and quiet after the hustle, bustle and general chaos of Delhi, Agra and Jaipur. The camp for the night was assembled in the sand dunes, so cool. Not just the camp, the weather as well, from the hot sun beating down on us the state of the temperature had plummeted to what the Russians would term 'freezyourbolluxov'. Anyway our guides, Jandia and Sadiq, made chilli and chapattis by the campfire, which proved to be very filling, and the stomach began sending signals that the Delhi belly had passed. The chilli was eaten out of small metal dishes to which Stu asked '*So what do we eat it with?*' This was far out in India's back garden, no knives and forks here. The right hand is not only for shaking hands but useful for stuffing food in one's mouth. The left hand is for wiping, as we realised where the coloured bits in the 'both of Jandia's hands made' chapattis came from. Hope that's just a joke.

The darkness fell quickly in the evening and the sky gradually filled up with stars, until the whole ceiling started to twinkle. Stu reckoned he could see a satellite above us; it was like a star but moving or so we convinced ourselves. Graham countered that if you stared at any star long enough it looks as though it is moving. His argument was pretty solid and we eventually agreed that it was just a star… unless there were no stars and they were all satellites. I knew for sure that I had never seen so many stars and I happily lay there looking up at nature's masterpiece.

I went to bed in my sleeping bag, on the mattress known as sand and the roof known as sky, ready for whatever dared to crawl over me.

Day 11 - Monday 10th February - Camels With A Hump

The hour was extremely early and nothing stirred, but it was bloody freezing. Being fully clothed in my two season sleeping bag with another blanket on top provided little protection in keeping out the bitter cold, so I went back to sleep and tried to think of warmer times.

Once more I dreamt of being back in England; this time I had crashed a car before playing Frisbee with a metal bin top in a field just outside Melton Mowbray. My grandad was watching whilst leaning on a fence and I was trying to figure out how to get back to India when I threw it to Stu and realised he would also be attempting to return to Asia. I'm sure there must be some meaning somewhere in there.

I rose at about 7.30am when the campfire burned and a whiff of the first chai of the day wafted in my direction. I sat by the fire, hands around a cup with a blanket wrapped around my shoulders, waiting for the sun to warm me into action.

There were plenty of scurrying marks scattered around the campsite. They were likely to be desert rats but Stu was the only one to report anything running over the top of him. In conclusion, it had been my best night's sleep in India so far with the dunes proving very comfortable. Back at the fire, breakfast consisted of toast, jam and eggs. The wild dogs that were spotted yesterday moved ever closer due to the smell of food, but maintained a polite distance.

At 9.30am the trek started up again but this time I was joined on my camel by Jandia whilst Sadiq accompanied Ken. The camels walked on for about two hours before we stopped for lunch. As the food was being prepared Graham batted against Stu and me. The pitch consisted of a dry riverbed, the stumps were sticks, the bat a bigger stick and the ball a lump of dried camel turd. After Stu bowled Graham, big brother took his bat away and sulked/slept on the side, refusing to bowl the camel turd. The 'if it's good enough for you to bat with, it's good enough for you to bowl with' had little effect on him. I had a quick innings before Mr Blood rattled me with his bodyline then bowled me with a full toss. Stu batted majestically striking everything that headed towards the stumps and belting three blowbacks. Blowbacks being the term we coined when the ball is struck so hard it shatters and dry camel turd rains in every direction, including the batsman's face.

Lunch completed, another camel trekking group arrived, talks were held and Ken's camel went to the side for a shag and not of the carpet variety. It turned out that he wasn't suffering from rabies but happened to be feeling horny or 'in season' or something like that. Anyway, when he was introduced to a lady friend he had trouble getting it up and eventually received a helping hand from a guide, appropriately named job title I thought. I have to admit camel sex is not something I had ever contemplated before. The camel couple went happily about their business despite nine tourists busily snapping away at them with their cameras. It proved interesting for the first five minutes or so but then a bit boring. So Stu asked a guide how long it normally lasted; *one and a half hours* he replied. We were suitably impressed. Unfortunately for the camel, the pressure of the audience must have affected him because after half an hour he had emptied his sacks.

The afternoon consisted of a three-hour trek and I eventually got my camel back to myself for the final half hour. Mind you, when Jandia was there we were always in front and all I could see was desert; who needs so-called civilisation? Most buildings just spoil the view anyway. Graham possessed a slow animal between his legs and despite setting off first would have to reluctantly hit it with a stick to provoke a response (just say no to innuendo). Dismounting from the camel after three hours provided some welcome relief to the legs, thigh and groin regions. We settled by some bushes and were warned that the night would be even colder than Sunday. With this thought planted in our minds, we were offered the chance of buying some home-brewed whisky from a local village. What better way to keep the cold out? It arrived in a re-used James Bond rum bottle, smelt strong, tasted extremely strong, kept the cold out, but the taste buds successfully protested against a further intake.

The guides badgered the teetotal Ken to partake and eventually he succumbed to a full glass. He was no drinker, but he was Japanese, so down it went in one, with a drunken Ken disappearing into the bushes a few minutes later.

I have noted that our position is swarming with rat holes so I don't think we'll be alone tonight.

Day 12 - Tuesday 11ᵀᴴ February - Sleeping With The Enemy

I guess the time had hit 4.00am when something first arrived on my sleeping bag. It then moved up to my hip/ bum sort of area and started to settle. If I knew it was a mouse I would have turned and thrown it off but I couldn't distinguish its shape from inside my bag. The possibility that it could be a snake meant that I planned to stay absolutely still and with the help of the freezing temperatures frozen still I stayed. I tried to sleep but it's not easy when all you're thinking is 'there's a snake lying on top of me'. After a few minutes it moved, I felt it try to seemingly snuggle up beside me and then off it went into the night. Thank God!

The cold had become so bitter that for the first time in my life, snuggling up to my brother seemed a very attractive proposition. The main sound I could hear in the starlit desert was Stu's snoring which sounded like some sort of camel mating call; he better watch out for that horny camel else it will be calling for the guide's help again.

My peace was short-lived; I awoke to find another settler on the prime estate hip/bum area. I was beginning to get the feeling that there was a To-let sign sticking out my arse. The animals I fear the most in the world are snakes. The thought one could be lying on top of me filled my body with dread.

'Just leave, please'. 'It's a rat, oh god, please let it be a rat'. 'But what if it is a snake?' Thoughts just tumbled from my brain. The side I was sleeping on was becoming numb, so oh so slowly, making no sudden movements, I turned on to my front. I closed my eyes, tried to sleep and desperately hoped to see sunrise soon.

The morning was very similar to yesterday, the guides rising about 7.00am to start the campfire, Stu and Japanese (as the Indians called Ken) rising at about 7.20am. With the passing of another 20 minutes, the Chai was brewed which coincided with my appearance. 10 minutes after the Chai had been served Graham arrived on the scene.

To our amusement, the daylight showed that Stu had slept beside a particularly large camel turd. It was either that or he'd shat himself in his sleeping bag and had sneakily shovelled it out.

Talking turds; when you have to squat in the desert (or with a traditional Indian toilet), success is probably 50% technique. The other 50% is having faith that your pants around your ankles won't catch the falling poo. I made numerous calculations, involving the trajectory of release, before my faith was up to an appropriate level for my first desert poo. The mission was a success as I gave birth to a hot steaming one that thankfully missed my pants. I triumphantly contemplated taking a picture but decided that was a little over the top.

Feeling a little lighter I told Stu about my night-time experience and he commented that yesterday he asked the guide what animals lived out in the desert. The guide said *dogs, scorpions, mice/ rats and cobra, but there is no need to worry*; glad Stu didn't tell me that last night.

By mid-afternoon the camels had taken us to Jaisalmer; the total trek had been 40 kilometres over three days. From being a blip on the landscape, Jaisalmer's 'Arabian Nights' fortress beared down upon us and it was soon time to enjoy the comforts of our hostel. Jandia the guide kindly invited us back to his hut for some dinner in the evening. He had proved a useful cook and we were interested to see what an Indian home looked like, so his invitation was gratefully accepted.

On our arrival, Jandia's hut was locked up and his little brother was sitting outside. He proceeded to make us chai and relayed that Jandia had gone off to the market, but would be back soon. This continued to be the main line of the night as we were made sandy chapattis, a bit of disgusting bright red hot chilli and a half-cooked, un-scrubbed potato still in the shape God intended, all done by some bloke Jandia's brother had grabbed. His brother then told us how poor the bloke was and asked us to pay for the food. Graham had smelt a rat (not literally) when the brother had started asking how much food cost at the hostel; as Stu started to answer Graham interrupted to give a suitably low figure. Then when he did ask for the money complete with his sad face we were ready with easily enough rupees each to cover the cost of the food. Then off we went for some food that our stomachs dared to digest.

After the meal, I went to sleep on a bed with no freezing cold wind rattling through my body and nothing crawling over the top of me. Bliss!

Day 13 - Wednesday 12ᵀᴴ February - Sleeping Beauty

A brilliant night's sleep was only interrupted by the loud peep of car horns outside, signalling another crash narrowly averted. Suitably refreshed we took a wander around the fort.

Jaisalmer was originally established by the Rajputs but there were numerous regional Rajput wars and it was eventually conquered by its Muslim attackers in 1294. This caused many defeated warriors and their wives to Jauhar. My understanding of this act is that they commit suicide by throwing themselves on their swords or a fire. If they were prepared to do that, no wonder they had a reputation for being fierce warriors.

This city changed hands several times but the Rajputs had re-established themselves again in time for the ruler of Jaisalmer to marry-off a daughter to Akber who must have been employing his usual diplomatic tactic. The town within resembled scenes from an Indiana Jones film, with narrow desert streets leading to ancient temples and exquisitely sculptured palaces and mansions. There is even a well, which in the past was used to plunge criminals to their death. The town was bustling with life and as cars are too wide for the streets it is motorbikes that zip about.

As 3.00pm approached we found a bus for the 14 hour journey to Udaipur, with a change at Jodhpur. At 3.15pm the bus started to move, the only problem being that Stu wasn't on it; he'd gone to take a picture of a travel agent shop with a friend's name on it and then disappeared. I looked around in vain for him and guessed he'd gone in search of some fruit. The bus had only moved 50 yards to change stops but on spotting Stu walking merrily along to the original bus stop a yell was cast in his direction.

The bus was the most uncomfortable so far, which was some achievement. Whenever I opened my window it would gradually rattle shut within five minutes. Every time the person behind me opened their window it would slide past hitting my elbow or head and when I bent forward or back the seat could be heard to bend like a piece of cardboard. Having said that I still managed to get a bit of sleep.

We passed through Jodhpur, which apparently has an impressive hilltop fort but the darkness hid its location. The bus journey had provided a good opportunity to catch up on my history and I noticed that the Moghuls wanted to invade the city but didn't have the necessary forces to oust the Rajput clan in control. So instead of fighting, an alliance was formed by the ruler's sister marrying Akber. No wonder he was called Akber the Great.

We changed buses at 9.00pm, which thankfully provided a more comfortable seat, but strangely tiredness wasn't high on my agenda as we bumped our way into Udaipur at 5.00am

Day 14 - Thursday 13ᵀᴴ February - Perfect Pictures

By 5.20am I was in the hostel and asleep.

I slithered out my sleeping bag at about 10.00am to enjoy a very cold shower, despite flicking a switch, which was meant to produce warm water. Stu was next into the shower by which time the switch had started working and I had seemingly ran off the cold water making way for the hot stuff. Stu completed his shower after finishing off what hot liquid there had been and Graham was left with another cold shower.

As the others sorted themselves out I traipsed up the hostel steps to the rooftop cafe for a glimpse of Udaipur in the light. She was beautiful; a glimmering lake, surrounded by rugged hills and three palaces - that was just the first glimpse. I sat there enjoying the sunshine and the sublime view and again wouldn't wish that I was anywhere else in the world. It was a good way to get over the devastating news, brought by the BBC World Service, that England had lost 1-0 to Italy at Wembley in the World Cup qualifier.

It took Graham a while to surface so I checked my book to see if my new found hero Akber had been around this area as well. Apparently, Udaipur was established in 1537 as a new Rajput clan capital when the old capital seemed destined to be sacked by the Moghuls. They would not recognise Akber as emperor and Pratap the ruler couldn't have had a pretty daughter because a battle ensued. Pratap led his men to victory and the present ruler is an amazing 76th in an unbroken dynasty.

When Graham popped up we headed out on to the Udaipur streets for all of 20 yards, to a travel shop where he arranged his bus to Bombay, for his flight on Sunday. My flights home have to be confirmed at least three days in advance, else they cancel the booking. As I am in India, phoning up to re-confirm a flight is never straightforward so I asked the travel shop to re-confirm for me. They tried but said that the Gulf-Air computers were down so this wasn't possible, instead they took my details and told me to return tomorrow.

Walking along with our express aim being to put food in our mouths, a lad waltzed up to chat. He was travelling to Birmingham in a couple of weeks for an art exhibition and would we like to see his art school? Graham, Stu and I all knew that this would wind up in a shop, but what the hell, he seemed a nice enough bloke and Udaipur was renowned for its miniature art. They talked us through the different painting techniques and the finished products, which were absolutely superb. The bartering started and we finished with about 20% off the original price. The problem with the bartering is that while you are attempting to buy something that you desperately want, you have no idea of its true value. What you do know is that in England you would pay a lot more for it and that the Indian salesmen will expertly use every trick in the book to extract rupees out of your pocket. On the negative side Graham left £100 poorer, I left £60 poorer and Stu left £50 poorer; on the positive side the trio were all delighted with their respective acquisitions.

While one man continued to pester Stu into parting with more money, a few of the artists took Graham and I into the courtyard for a Pepsi. In common with many conversations in India, the topic drifted to cricket. The next thing you knew we were playing cricket in their little courtyard; I suppose with all the money that had just been passed their way they wouldn't have to work that afternoon. Stu enjoyed a swashbuckling little innings, then a lad from Nepal batted and settled in thanks to a diet of full tosses, which I provided. Later I trapped him plumb LBW but with no umpire, not even Mother Theresa was going to walk (in fact when she was in next she even claimed that when she was caught that she had never hit the ball). Eventually, he got caught and a couple more wickets fell, so I was ready to chance my luck with the willow. After a steady opening, a bouncer at head height was sent my way, which was duly despatched, on to a first-floor terrace with a tennis smash shot. I was no longer Jeff Brown, I had been transformed into a right-handed Graham Thorpe and started to despatch the ball all over the eight-metre square courtyard. Plumb LBW once, I resorted to the no walk rule and eventually succumbed to the world played 'six and out' rule when hooking a full toss over the second floor terrace, out the courtyard and never to be seen again. The English party finally departed about one and a half hours after entering, the Nepalese lad showing us a brilliant but cheap place for Indian cuisine.

The late afternoon took us up to the Monsoon Palace on the hill for a breath-taking view of the city. The place is now home to Udaipur's radio station and is officially closed to the public, but if you give the little old Indian bloke at the gates ten rupees he will let you in and allow a snoop around the disused part. The palace was in desperate need of repair. It had been built in 1880 but the royal family had abandoned it soon after because water couldn't be pumped up the hill. Its other claim to fame was that it was where the baddies were based in the James Bond film Octopussy. I was content just sitting on the hilltop staring out as the city continued about its business in its perfect valley setting. A flutter of excitement occurred coming down the hill as a leopard had been spotted in a roadside gully. All the rickshaws pulled up and the crowd gathered for a glimpse but the leopard remained deep in the undergrowth waiting for the unwanted audience to disperse.

When we reached the hotel the only course of night-time action open to us was to consume a meal whilst watching Octopussy. Udaipur is proud that Octopussy was based here and seemingly half the restaurants show the video each night. A lad from Warrington who sat on the table next to us amazingly had relatives from Melton Mowbray who we knew. On telling him about our desert adventures, he also told us about a batch of home-brewed whisky from an Indian village that killed three people a couple of weeks ago. Wow, that is deadlier than my student house homebrew that gave you a hangover before you got drunk.

He also said that he had entered a nearby restaurant and was greeted by the owner who explained the presence of numerous James Bond photographs on the wall. *'James Bond and his wife come here for a meal'.* 'You mean Roger Moore'. *'No, James Bond'.*

Day 15 - Friday 14th February - One Brown Down

The morning was fairly laid back with a decent breakfast consumed on the rooftop cafe. A stroll around the City Palace was followed by a search for a vessel to take us around the lake. Eventually, we found one, but not before running into a fashion shoot and mistakenly walking to the far end of Udaipur. Whenever the camera is slipped out of its case the local Indian kids are desperate to get in on the pictures, not to just appear on your photographs but to charge you for the pleasure! Even at the fashion shoot when Graham unveiled his camera the little girls figured he wanted a picture of them and not the drop dead gorgeous model.

The Indian sands of time were running low for Graham, whose bus to Bombay was due to leave at 4.00pm. He is then flying to London early on Sunday morning. At 2.00pm and still in need of a boat and a meal, the three of us hired a motorboat and driver to glide us around the lake palaces. The photo finger got a bit twitchy again. The palace on the lake looks beautiful even if it is just a posh hotel these days.

We jumped ship at 2.30pm and ordered our curries from yesterday's roof-top restaurant; Graham then nipped off to pack his bag, returning briefly to shovel down his food and then in a blur he was gone. I sat there continuing to eat my curry. Whilst my brother had been about, it was a bit too easy to take a back seat, let him lead the way with his previous Asian travelling experience, so it will be interesting to see how Mr Blood and I cope without our leader!

The plan had been to stay another night in Udaipur, but on discovering that the bus to Kota would leave at 11.00pm, the first post-Graham decision was to pack our bags. I called in at the travel agents shop again and was informed that they had re-confirmed the place on the planes for me and to my surprise didn't even charge me for the service, which was very good of them.

A wander round the streets saw us bumping into the cricketing art shop lads. So we hung around with them on a street corner, chatting and drinking chai.

With the last drop of chai suitably drained another game of cricket beckoned. Wickets fell with regularity, especially mine; having faced 10 deliveries my wicket had fallen three times. Then I launched into a marathon innings; I ended up playing aka Sri Lanka by trying to clout every delivery and my eyes were registering the ball being the size of a football. In the heat, I began to tire and my hands had got very sweaty. With a large back lift, the arms swung for another mighty hit and it flew perfectly to the first-floor terrace. But it was not the ball, which had nestled on the terrace, the ball lay at my feet after hitting the wicket, it was the bat, which had squirmed out of my sweaty palms and flown up into the air hitting a spot where minutes before a little girl had stood. I was shocked and we thought it was a sign to leave, although you couldn't fault my follow through.

As the evening descended we watched the sunset from the opposite side of the lake. There was nobody else about and it was so peaceful watching the sun go down on this beautiful city. I hadn't expected to find a city in India where I could sincerely say 'I'd love to live here' but Udaipur had cast her spell on my senses.

Following the familiar bag packing ceremony, large amounts of food were ordered at the rooftop restaurant. After taking an age to arrive the realisation dawned, it was not a meal that had arrived but a feast. The clock showed 9.00pm and the bus was due to leave at 10.00pm from the station a couple of miles away. We speedily stuffed as much food down our necks as possible and twice the belt around my trousers had to be let out another notch.

After a spot of hard bargaining, a rickshaw driver agreed to deliver us to the bus station for 15 rupees. However, after returning from the hostel with our bags, the rickshaw driver must have had a better offer because he had disappeared into the night. We had 30 minutes to come face to face with our bus, but for once there was not a rickshaw in sight. After a five minute wait, a German lad came past in a rickshaw and invited us on to split the fare. A price of 20 rupees had been agreed with the driver but by the time Stu had finished bartering he had somehow managed to increase the price to 30. I think Stu either needs to spend time honing his bargaining skills or he is on commission from the rickshaw drivers.

The bus station was safely reached and all that remained was to find the right stop. Six different Indians were questioned and we chose the four-to-two majority of where to stand. There does seem to be a tendency for locals to prefer to give you an answer, however wrong, rather than saying that they don't know the location of a bus stop, palace or whatever you are looking for. We stood next to three English girls; two of them were going to Jodhpur and the third was returning to a mattress in Jaisalmer, under which she had safely hidden her air ticket before forgetting it. Among other typical hassles, the bus had been delayed and attempts to find someone to open up the luggage compartment proved challenging. While everyone else including the driver sat on the bus, Stu looked around for the inspector and I kept one foot on earth and the other on the bus in an attempt to stop the thing going without us. With the bags safely dispatched we took our places on the back seat. The back seat is the worst seat to have on an Indian bus because every single one of the numerous road bumps is exaggerated for your benefit. Not ideal when a large curry meal with extras has been bolted down and the belly's response was indigestion.

Day 16 - Saturday 15ᵗʜ February - White Men In A Black World

I hardly managed a wink of sleep as I performed my pancake impression of being tossed and turned all over the bus, but luckily did not get stuck on the ceiling. On the bus journey my shoes, which I had meticulously tied together to stop them moving too far when I took them off, had completely disappeared. The phenomenon of shoes being bumped to the front of the bus had been experienced a couple of times, although in this context the pizza box which rattled to near the driver on the previous Jaipur to Jaisalmer bus was still my most impressive achievement (and the contents were still eagerly eaten). My shoes were eventually located near the front having travelled under 12 sets of seats of which I looked under every single one in an attempt to reclaim them. The bus's suspension must have suffered on the bumpy road because I know my personal suspension was numb. Despite the fact that there was just Stu and I on the back seat, comfort was impossible when you are catapulted in the air every other minute.

We arrived at Kota, a place described by the guidebook as '*one of Rajasthan's dirtier and less stimulating cities, foreign visitors are sufficiently unusual to attract stares in the street*'. It seemed an accurate summary to us as the bus arrived at dawn. Stu and I wanted to reach Sawai Madhopur to go on safari and were scrambling around in the terminal trying to find out where our bus left from. The light was still non-existent; the bus terminal was packed out and I'm not talking English packed out, multiply English packed out by three and you get Indian packed out. Besides us two, there was not another white person in sight and no one seemed to speak any English that we could understand. After being pointed in a couple of different directions an official sat us down in a couple of chairs beside him and provided us with a cup of chai each. The man was heaven sent, but it was typical of the Indian hospitality – they are such wonderfully friendly people.

When our bus arrived he despatched us. No 'deluxe' coach for the journey to Sawai Madhopur, it was a chaotic and as expected bumpy public trans-port for us. If there was a spare seat next to a local or a spare seat next to an Englishman a good percentage of Indians seem to pick the Englishman option. After another uncomfortable four-hour journey, split up only by play-ing cards and talking to curious locals, our destination lay around us.

Twenty-seven hours without any sleep and 14 hours without any food left the energy tanks running on empty so we just headed for the nearest hotel. Even its name, 'The Pink Palace' could not put us off. The quandary of whether to have food or sleep first was decided when on sight of a bed I crashed out.

On waking up I investigated the television in the room but it was more of an ornament rather than a working device, unless you enjoy looking at a small white dot on a screen.

In the evening and after a hearty meal from our deserted hotel, we booked our £1.20 safari at the Project Tiger headquarters before wandering around town for a couple of hours. The walk brought many '*hellos*' and even more stares from the townsfolk. Stu and I were the centre of attention wherever we walked and the feeling was quite bizarre, even eerie. We had seen one white person all day and they had raced by, totally ignoring us.

The town proved to be pretty dead so we returned to the hotel and listened to the Saturday afternoon sport on the World Service, with the real treat being live coverage of England beating Ireland in the five nations rugby. The second half was played to the backdrop of Stu's snoring, however, his cold is improving and he doesn't seem to be making his camel mating noises anymore. The only other items worthy of note are that our dirty dishes from dinner still lay upstairs in the dining room, (the hotel must be run by students) and still not a single other guest has been spotted in the place.

Day 17 - Sunday 16ᵗʜ February - Tiger Hunt

Unwashed and dressed at 6.00am, why so early? To go on safari at the Ranthambore National Park. There are only about 20 tigers in the park, but it represents the best chance of seeing one of these magnificent beasts in the state of Rajasthan. After stepping over the sleeping receptionist and assuring him that we were going on safari rather than doing a runner, we went to the Project Tiger office. Our canter, which is a truck with seats in the open top back (20 in our case), left Sawai Madhopur at 6.45am and picked up the only other participants, who were a family of Indians, from a local hotel. Being an Indian family that meant there were 10 of them covering three generations and that they adopted us.

The National Park was picturesque with a fort on a hill overlooking lakes and beautiful landscape. The wildlife sighted included peacocks, monkeys, white-breasted kingfishers, numerous other birds, deer, deer, more deer and sunbathing crocodiles. The family kept us stocked up with their biscuits and familiarly friendly Indian manner. All too soon the two hour adventure had reached its end and our eyes hadn't climaxed at the sight of a tiger; the nearest we came to a tiger were one's tracks in the road. I think it had been driving a Land Rover.

The canter was taking us back to town when we decided to stop off for breakfast. I didn't want to face yesterday's plates in our hotel dining room again. Along the Ranthambore road lay numerous posh hotels so one was randomly picked for a relaxing garden breakfast that consisted of an omelette and giant pile of toast basked, along with ourselves, in the bright sunshine. Stu and I reflected on the fact that we still hadn't seen anyone English in this town; the only other Westerners being middle-aged Germans, when we heard '*it is them!*' With that Mark and Ray, the Jaipur fort men, popped out of the hotel. They had arrived, via their chauffeur driven car, in Sawai Madhopur last night and were staying in the plush hotel. The car and driver had been hired for five days at a cost of £100.

Their previous stop had been the religious city of Varanasi. The Hindu's holy river of the Ganges flows through the ancient city and it is believed that if you die in Varanasi then you will attain enlightenment. If there is one place to have your funeral process it is there, where the ashes or the corpse of the deceased are thrown into the Ganges. Apparently a year ago the authorities were worried about all the limbs floating down-river, polluting the place, so introduced thousands of small turtles that would eat the dead flesh; unfortunately, after three months, all the locals had eaten the flesh-eating turtles. Mark and Ray told us they were shown around and talked through the funeral process by a guide. The guide mentioned that for religious reasons no photographs of the working ghats could be taken. However, Ray was desperate for a picture of the amazing scenes below them so Mark paid the guide off to get rid of him. They watched carefully to ensure there were no onlookers, Ray lined up his shot and clicked. 30 seconds later three Indians had run up the stairs to the roof where they stood claiming to be the police and that Ray would have to accompany them to the station where it was an automatic three-month prison sentence, or alternatively, he could pay an on the spot fine. The on the spot fine was £1,000 and they added the further threat of telling the grieving family about Ray taking pictures. He bartered the fine down to £14 and left quickly. They suspected that the guide had been in on it all and that they had been set up, but on the other hand, they shouldn't have taken the pictures.

A snake caught in the hotel grounds was gleefully brought over to us by the gardener as we quickly tried to establish 'poisonous or non-poisonous?' '*Yes.*' 'What?' '*No-poisonous*'. My cool exterior had hidden an involuntary need to bring on another bout of Delhi belly until the non-poisonous fact was ascertained.

Breakfast which had started at 10.00am, finished at 1.30pm with a glass of water. Easy life. We finally left to head back to our hotel, realising that check-out was midday, oops. Goodbyes were exchanged although coincidentally we are heading to Pushkar today while Ray and Mark are going there tomorrow.

At our hotel reception the bill was requested and unsurprisingly two nights had been included because we hadn't checked out on time. I argued that we were stupid and hadn't realised there was a set check out time. After a bit of persuasion, they relented and just one night appeared on the bill.

Our next destination of Pushkar meant catching a train up to Jaipur then another to Ajmer, before grabbing a bus to the town. It hadn't been possible to make a reservation on the 5.15pm train so we cautiously turned up at 4.15pm to obtain a good 'grid position' and we sat down on the platform. A few kids followed us and crouched down by our side, staring at these strangely pale specimens; only one of them ever talking to us, at that only intermittently. Stu and I started a game of cards; come 4.30pm a crowd of 20 to 30 people had gathered just to watch us. Few words were spoken to us they just stared. It was a bit intimidating, but mainly bizarre, oh so bizarre, especially as attempts we made to start conversations were mainly met with blank faces. We just tried to laugh and joke our way through the scene. The Jaipur bound train turned up at 4.45pm and we were more than happy to leave the spectators behind by boarding the train, only to be told that it was the express train and our ticket was only valid for the normal passenger train; to get on it a switch of tickets would be required. We got off the train again, much to the remaining spectators' delight. Stu nipped off to organise the tickets while I stood on the platform with the bags, even this event attracted a crowd of 10 people around me. I had no qualm with the people that would attempt a conversation but most of them stood or sat near me just staring. The behaviour wasn't malicious, they were just interested in the white boys, but it felt very odd. Shouldn't Stu be back by now I thought?

The tickets were successfully switched to allow Stu and I to make our way back to the beaten track. We sat in the carriage glad to be away from the crowd. We just had the odd beggar coming to pester us by knocking on the windows and a couple of kids from the crowd who kept coming on the train to talk to us. As a gesture of friendship I gave the talkative lad and his friend a couple of English 50 pence pieces. The next thing you know he'd brought along another friend who wanted a coin. Oh no, what had I started? They then came back with more friends. 'Sorry, there are no more coins'. They went away. But were back a couple of minutes later, again asking for coins. 'There are no more coins'. And again. And again. Finally, Stu's increasingly frustrated and aggressive manner gradually got the point home that a touch of peace and quiet would be appreciated. Although I don't think peace and quiet translates into any Indian dialect. It sounds cynical but tourists have created their own problem in India. By giving out money they, or should I say we, perpetuate the amount of begging other tourists face. If I ever come back I'll arrive with a supply of pens because if kids aren't asking for money it's pens for school and to me that's more constructive (unless they're selling them on). Before the train had left the station a woman sat down opposite us and dumped a cloth-roofed bag a couple of seats away. After a couple of minutes, the bag started to move a little; there was definitely an animal contained within its walls. It may have been a dog but the movement seemed very snake-like to me, as I edged those vital inches towards the window.

The night came down followed by Jaipur at 8.15pm. The train to Ajmer would be 10.00pm and packed to the rafters, so with time to spare a plan was hatched to see if a bus could drive us there quicker. We headed off to get a rickshaw to the bus station. This led us to meet a driver who was already taking a couple of Indians to a bus heading for Ajmer. 120 rupees were handed over at the travel shop where we were deposited by the rickshaw man. The time had struck 8.25pm when the tickets for the 8.30pm bus were in our sticky mitts so the rickshaw driver put us all back in his contraption and flew off in a hurry for about half a mile. He then stopped in the middle of nowhere for a minute before flying off in a completely different direction again, stopping for a minute and off again. He dropped us off at 8.35pm by a few buses and pointed out which one was ours. I had been a bit worried that the bus may have gone but at last, it stood before us.

Tickets out for the conductor before we boarded was not an entirely successful process. '*The bus is full, your tickets are not valid*' did not appear to be the hoped-for 'here are your seats' sort of response. Turning around there was now a space where the rickshaw had once stood. So there the Englishmen stood uselessly waving their worthless tickets in the air, feeling completely ripped off and still in need of some transport back to the station. Luckily there were a number of Indians in the same boat as us; unfortunately, the boat wasn't going to Ajmer either. However, we stuck by them; they did the talking and eventually, a man turned up with a refund for us all. A bus ticket refund in India, now there's a claim to fame.

On the return to the station all the reservations in second class had been purchased and even our attempt to obtain a first class reservation was thwarted. The second meal of the day, a loaf of bread, was bought and consumed as we waited for the train, which as expected turned out to be full, mainly with people in reserved sleeping accommodation. 98% of people were winding their way to Udaipur, which was a 10 hour journey; our tortuous little trip was meant to take three to four hours so the train would arrive at somewhere between 1.00am and 2.00am.

Stu and I sat on our rucksacks in a gangway simply trying to stay awake. Only saved from going stir crazy by a one-hour game of cards, which kept the senses ticking over, and the mind off the fact that all we wanted to do was sleep. A couple of conductors unsuccessfully tried to move us and our rucksacks but stubborn mode had been engaged. Whenever there was a sprinkling of lights outside I would look out one side and Stu the other, desperately trying to figure out whether we were in Ajmer. Towns came, towns went, I didn't know where the train was but confidence seemed fairly high that Ajmer had not been left in our wake. I didn't think I'd fallen asleep at any time despite the 10 stone weights that seemed to be my eyelids. A big tired sigh of relief spouted from my mouth as a station sign recorded A J M E R.

A hostel had been selected from Stu's Lonely Planet book that was fairly close to the station. We headed there despite the standard insistence of the rickshaw driver that it was full and he knew a better hotel. He took us to our selected building and instead it was the receptionist who discouraged us with his asking price of 400 rupees. The driver showed me a price list for his suggested hotel and for a few others. I thought this suggested he wasn't on commission from the hotel so went along with his recommendation. It looked an okay sort of place and the requested 275 rupees for a room with a shower was given to the receptionist who we woke from his slumber on a camp bed behind the desk. All I could think of at this stage was just show me my bed and let me sleep.

There was a television in the room so I thought that it would be rude not to test the mechanism. I began tuning into various stations and then, well surely it must be a mirage or could I be dreaming. There were extended highlights of Barcelona v. Real Madrid on some Indian satellite station that sparked me into life. I lay there a contented man. Stu laid there an unconscious man.

Day 18 - Monday 17ᵀᴴ February - Pushkered

After breakfast and a morning squat ('it won't land in my pants, it won't land in my pants – bullseye!') we surveyed the town.

It brought about an interesting visit to the bank to simply cash a traveller's cheque. I filled in a form, gave it to a bloke who checked the details for five minutes, passed it on to another bloke who looked at it and stamped it, then gave me a wooden token and I was sent to the main office. I went up to the counter with the wooden token in my outstretched palm but got told to wait; 10 minutes later I was called up and the bloke had a copy of the form I signed in his hand and happily gave me the money. The bizarre thing was that those forms were always in my sight in the first office and they never moved. When I changed offices the cashier was never handed a piece of paper during the time I was there but yet he still had a copy of my form. How can this be?

India is a country in a state of organised confusion, where everything gets done eventually, but you're not quite sure how.

A half hour bus trip later and Pushkar had arrived. According to legend, at the dawn of time, the God Brahma dropped a lotus leaf from the sky and Pushkar was formed. With no rickshaws, it is a very peaceful and laid back little town. At 2.00pm Stu and I booked into a hotel, followed by a bit of washing and a nap, then it was on to the rooftop restaurant for an all-you-can-eat buffet. This provided us with the best food of the trip so far and our seats were not left vacant for another one and a half hours.

After all this eating, a bit of exercise to waddle off the food seemed to be a logical step. 100 yards down the lakeside and an '*oi!*' sped towards us. It was Claire and Louise, the Portsmouth girls, who we had met in Jaipur, with some Aussies. They went on to tell us that the Australian lad they were with had a famous relative and the clue was that the lad's surname was Venables. We obviously guessed former England manager Terry Venables, but this was a purposefully dropped red herring. It turned out that his sister was married to Sid James's son. We asked him a question and he replied '*yes, everybody does ask that question but I've never heard Sid James laugh, so I don't know whether he has the same laugh*'. I'm assuming that the answer would be no because if his brother-in-law had that classic Sid James laugh he would have commented about his amazing laugh.

Later on, I again won the 'worst passport photo' contest. I seem to be the champion of this game in both Europe and Asia. I think it is the fact that I look about 10 years old in the photograph that tends to clinch my victories.

For years on end, I have hated looking younger than the evidence on my birth certificate. I was always one of the smallest in my school year. It was difficult to get into pubs as an underage drinker and it was difficult to get into pubs as an overage drinker. Now I'm not bothered and am just beginning to like the fact that people think I'm still 21. It could be one of those things that I appreciate more and more as I get older.

We had sat down at 5.45pm at the sunset cafe, aptly named as it was a cafe and gave a brilliant view of the sunset in this beautiful little town. A couple of hours later the others left to pack for their bus to Jaisalmer and a couple of English blokes joined us. All anybody seemed capable of doing in Pushkar was relaxing; it's one of those places where people come for a couple of days and leave a month later. The time was 10.00pm before we even managed to leave the cafe and head for the Chai shop with the English lads. I was still in my shorts as I had washed my sole pair of jeans in the morning and it was distinctly chilly on my goose-pimpled legs.

The tea or chai shops serve a large variety of drinks and most have a special chai which can mean anything at all but usually contains the legal 'bhang' which is a substance derived from marijuana leaves. All other drugs are forbidden in India and there is a minimum sentence of 10 years in prison for possession but you may only have to serve two years if you can prove it was just for your own use. This is with the exception of the holy men who are allowed to smoke ganja to show their devotion to Shiva. The Portsmouth girls had said that for the main Pushkar chai shop, *'don't finish the cup'* 'Why?' *'Just don't finish it, Jeff'*. When we ordered the increasingly mysterious special chai an English lad I'd spoken to earlier turned around and said *'I had some special tea yesterday, don't finish the cup'*. I decided not to finish my cup.

Unfortunately, Stu finished his chai, every last drop.

I'm not sure whether he believed the tea man when he said that he'd make it weak for us or if he'd not taken in some of the stories. Especially as the common theme was that people said that they felt like they were going to die before gradually feeling better.

Anyway, on returning from the Chai shop (300 yards away from the hostel), we felt great. We pretty much hovered back to the hostel at 11.15pm but there was a problem. The hostel curfew was set at 11.00pm. However, a loud knock on the door later and we were on the inside saying 'thank you so much for letting us in'. We had drunk the tea (well me three-quarters of a cup) and survived.

A bit later Stu felt terribly ill and desperately wanted to be sick but just couldn't bring anything up. He felt worse and worse before reaching a '*get me a doctor'* sort of stage. God knows where I could get a doctor at midnight. Meanwhile, Stu was on all fours on the floor trying to retch but nothing would come up. 'I feel terrible'. *'I feel like I'm going to die'*. Bloody hell, I didn't know what to do. Then there was a knock at the door. An Indian chap poked his head around the door and asked whether he could use our shower. I was so taken aback that I said 'um, yeah'. Stu was still in an awful state and we scrambled through our kit looking for something to help him puke up. Eventually, a mix of rehydration salts and water was concocted. Stu eventually succeeded in making himself puke up and slowly began to feel better. As I stayed up with him there was a background noise of someone else in the hostel also throwing their guts up.

Even a couple of hours later I could still hear the sound of guts coming up from the depths of the hotel. What a horrific night.

Day 19 - Tuesday 18ᵗʰ February -
The Calm After The Storm

The carnage of last night passed and the hotel was once more a tranquil place. Hence the eat-as-much-as-you-can breakfast was enjoyed.

We then sat down for a relaxing read before a 20 minute stroll around the town which was interrupted for lunch at a place recommended by everyone for its superb chips. It was another eat-as-much-as-you-can place, with two plates of food, banana custard and a chocolate disappearing down my neck. I was completely bloated.

Thus we waddled back to the hostel and I fell asleep. There is definitely something about Pushkar that makes you want to do nothing. A walk around the sedate little lake was completed, but after exerting all that energy we chilled out by the lakeside for another hour, then it was about time for dinner. We had been keeping an eye out for Mark and Ray but there were no reported sightings. We spoke to other people about the mysterious tea and people thinking they are going to die from the tea or being paralysed is a very common theme. One lad was convinced the extra ingredient was opium.

There was an opium reference in my guidebook but it related to Britain's East India Company. Apparently, it had failed in trade negotiations with China so they created a clandestine market for Western goods. Instead of silver, they began to pay the Chinese for tea and silk with opium, cheaply imported from India. Silver drained out of China as opium addicts and opium demand increased. It became such a devastating problem for China that they made opium illegal in 1836.

This then opened up the issue of there being no treaty between Britain and China. This was because the British would not hand over British citizens to a Chinese legal system that was deemed barbaric. Whilst the Chinese demanded that all foreigners who were accused of committing crimes on Chinese soil had to be dealt with by Chinese officials. The lack of agreement on such matters and Britain's refusal to stop supplying opium led to the first Opium War. War was something we were very good at during this time so a treaty was eventually agreed to end the war and all trade restrictions were lifted. This increased the opium trade. By 1860 there had been a second Opium War, which again China lost and another treaty was signed which actually legalised the use of opium. It isn't Britain's proudest moment but was fascinating.

Well, whatever the substance in the chai was, food was today's main substance. I stuffed my face for the third time in the day and then decided it was time for a rest. A quick rest and then we would be fresh to relax in the Pushkar night air.

The only problem was that I went to sleep at 8.30pm and didn't wake up until midnight. Stu had not been able to wake me up, being asleep himself. We had turned into the incredible eating and sleeping men.

Day 20 - Wednesday 19ᵀᴴ February - Hello Brahma

It was my final proper day of the holiday, as my bus was due to leave at night. After going to sleep so early both Stu and I were as bright as buttons. That meant an early stroll up the hill for sunrise. Despite much pointing by locals, in varying directions, the hidden path up to the summit remained hidden. Eventually, a young girl left her donkeys around the back of the hill to show us the path at the side. The path was just a collection of stones and fairly treacherous on the way down because, with every step you took, the path seemed to move with you. But sitting at the top watching the sun come up was just so nice. I didn't seem to have a worry in the world.

All this exercise was rewarded with a healthy breakfast and the company of a lovely Norwegian girl and her mum. She was travelling around India for three months and her mum has joined her for five weeks. It is very sweet.

Before submitting ourselves to the Pushkar air again, Stu and I created our forged Pushkar passports, which we thought consisted of a strand of coloured thread wrapped around the wrist and then another thread meticulously coiled around it. It looked bloody professional even if I said so myself. If you didn't have a 'passport' numerous locals would nag you to undergo the ceremony. We learnt about it from other travellers in Udaipur and the Nepalese lad from our Udaipur art shop provided us with the required coloured cotton. Now should it be worn on the right or left wrist? The unanimous vote was for the left.

However, as soon as the hotel was vacated the hassle started; it turned out our forgeries were both over-elaborate and on the wrong wrist. We were approached by a local with a 'free' flower. Aussie Rod who we met yesterday got caught for the ritual by the lake and was well into the prayers, repeating the 'priest's' words, until the Indian said '*and I will make a donation of 200 rupees*', at which point Rod realised this wasn't for free and let out an '*Oh fuck*', followed by a quick rebuff about swearing from the priest/salesman.

I digress, I knew that by accepting the flower the course of events would lead to the ritual, Stu's feeling being it was just mumbo-jumbo, but I grasped the flower and off we all trooped to the nearest ghat. There we sat on a 12 inch wide bit of pavement in the outline of half a rectangle, with the lake in every direction. I sat cross-legged for the ceremony repeating in Hindi whatever the chap said, whilst holding a coconut, throwing flowers, sugar and various other substances into the lake. The main bits I picked up in English were wishing Brahma for a good life for 'father', 'mother', 'brother', 'sister', 'friend' etc. You had to be careful not to move as the path was so narrow and surrounded by water that there would be a distinct possibility of toppling into the water. After five minutes each, of saying the prayers, Stu and I were presented with our official Pushkar passports and the red Hindu dot on our foreheads. I had wisely stipulated at the outset that I intended paying 20 rupees for the ritual but enjoyed it so much that I gave 40 rupees, which allegedly goes to the temple and then is dispersed amongst the poor.

Ajmer was on the day's agenda, but only for a quick flirtation to collect a couple of Stu's films that had been developed. We were soon back in Pushkar tucking into a late lunch, with a couple of serving guys intrigued by the photographs. Especially that of the humping camels; which also did the rounds in their kitchen before returning 10 minutes later (the photograph rather than the humping camels).

One last lazy walk around idyllic Pushkar finished with us sitting and relaxing on the holy bridge. We talked to a couple of English lads who were on a two week holiday and were being chauffeur driven around India at a cost of £100 per week. They had stayed in a five star hotel in Jaipur, were moaning about Indians continually approaching them, the flies (of which there were relatively few at this time of year) and couldn't believe that we were having a great time on little more than £5 a day (and were even more staggered that this included accommodation).

I made our excuses and the walk continued, but before we were off the bridge a shout sounded from a couple of reprobates, in the shape of Ray and Mark. We had been keeping an eye out for them ever since we arrived in Pushkar and there they were, larger than life on a hotel balcony. We chatted in a shouting manner as you do in a bridge-to-third-floor conversation. They arranged to meet Stu tomorrow for a chai, whilst simultaneously taking the piss out of me because I had to head home.

Stu and I sat down at the Sunset Cafe overlooking the lake as I savoured every moment in Pushkar.

It was an absolute wrench to leave this serene little town and I wished I'd quit my job to go travelling instead of taking this extended holiday. Stu had before him Nepal, Thailand, Malaysia, Indonesia, New Zealand and Australia. But whatever I do at home I know that there will be a roof over my head and food on the table which is more than can be said for many people I have seen in India.

Stu saw me to the bus stop. I would be by myself again but was not in the least bit bothered; the confidence had come on in leaping and bounding movements since Heathrow. The bus appeared and I shook Stu by the hand, told him to try and keep in touch; with that I was off, but not really alone. The Norwegian girl and her mum sat near me and the bus was packed with travellers.

The journey wasn't smooth because I developed stomach cramps. They increased in severity as we went along. I was in absolute agony. Common sense told me it was similar to that Delhi belly night in Jaipur; the uncommon sense told me I was going to die of a burst appendix in India. I just wished that I was back in England. The searing pain just kept on coming. The only relief from the long drawn out journey came from farting and the occasional conversation with the Norwegian girl. The farting seemed to reduce the pressure in my stomach and convinced me it was bowel problems rather than appendicitis. At that moment what sounded like a good time would be farting whilst talking to the Norwegian girl, but I don't think she'd appreciate it as much as me. Farting also brought the threat of follow through so I just carried on dying. I brought my knees up to my chest, which seemed to ease the pain a bit. This must be one of the worst nights of my life; I just want to see the morning.

Day 21 - Thursday 20ᵀᴴ February - Hostelised

The stomach pains eased a bit and I managed some sleep for an hour or so before we reached the outskirts of Delhi, then the bus stopped. Not only was it the outskirts and in the middle of nowhere, but strangely there were a group of about six auto-rickshaw drivers waiting in the lay-by. Everyone whinged that it was nowhere near where they wanted to be but nonetheless half the bus party got out. I heard a rickshaw driver quote 100 rupees to go to the railway station. Considering the bus journey from Pushkar was 140 rupees, the bus company must have some sort of agreement with the rickshaw drivers to stitch us all up. If anyone asked whether they should get off here for the railway station, bus station, Connaught Place (where I wanted to go) or the pot of gold underneath the rainbow the bus conductor would answer '*yes*' and they do this at 7.00am when everybody is in a susceptible sleep-deprived state.

I was far too stubborn to be ripped-off like that and stayed on. The bus travelled on for about another 30 minutes before stopping with the call '*last stop, everybody off*'. I knew we were in old Delhi but beyond that, I, and come to that everybody else, had no idea where we had been despatched. After a couple of minutes, the bus had been spotted and the rickshaw vultures descended, smelling tourist blood. As they swooped in trying to grab your bag, to put them in their rickshaw, we stood firm.

I wanted to get to Sunny's Guest House near Connaught Place, which is across town in New Delhi, but had no idea of the distance involved. The rickshaw driver said '80 *rupees*'. I put my totally astonished face on and said '40 rupees'. He put his totally astonished face on and said '*long way, 70 rupees*'. 'It's not that far'. '*Okay good price, 60 rupees*'. 'No, 40 rupees is a good price'. '*No, 60 rupees is Indian price, good price*' he said. I turned and started to walk in what I hoped was the right direction, he came after me '*Okay 50 rupees*', 'No thank you'. I carried on walking. After another minute or so he came riding after me. '*Okay, forty rupees*'. I slung my bag into his rickshaw and we headed off to Sunny's guesthouse. He tried to pick up a fellow passenger, who was the archetypal middle-aged hippie, with his plan to charge him 40 rupees for going on the same journey but failed miserably. Whilst I argued the price should still be 40 rupees in total and not 80 for the two of us. The old hippie gave him instructions that entailed an act that I do not believe is physically possible for a man and his rickshaw to perform.

The driver had loose sleeves and I expected that there would be a number of tricks still to be revealed. I was not disappointed. '*Sunny Guest House is very expensive and likely to be fully booked I know a better, cheaper hotel*' (and I knew he'd be on commission for taking me there). My turn. 'No, I've been to Sunny's before and I'm going again, besides it's a really good atmosphere'. He rambled on for a bit then seemed to give up and start to chat normally. After 10 to 15 minutes he pulled over at an accommodation office saying I could phone to see if Sunny's was booked-up. Then a bloke came out of the office to see me saying he would phone up on my behalf. I smiled knowingly, thanked him and claimed that I was meeting a friend at Sunny's. The rickshaw driver finally gave me up as a lost cause. I knew that if the man phoned Sunny's they would definitely be booked up even if Sunny's receptionist said that all the beds were empty. As the driver eventually pulled up at Sunny's he said that if they were booked up to come straight back. I pointed out that it was still only 8.00am and even if it was booked-up now, people would be leaving later. I pulled my wallet out, the driver greeted this by saying '50 *rupees*', I smiled at his cheek and gave him 40. I walked up the stairs having got a buzz out of feeling in complete control all the way through the shenanigans.

Sunny's dormitory was full but they were waiting for people to check-out. I sat in the seated area for a couple of hours talking sport to anyone that would listen, including Kevin from Bradford who is going home tomorrow after having been away for 16 months. The owner who I presume to be Sunny saw me sitting there and immediately came over for a chat and asked after Graham; I didn't even think he'd recognise me. We were still anticipating news on the dormitory front when Kevin and I discovered that there would be a double room available at midday, so we booked the room and headed off for an Indian style pizza.

I came back after that, got the room and crashed out for the next four hours, which provided a couple of hours' actual sleep. I emerged again in the late afternoon and sat on the roof with Heral, a Danish lad who had been mercilessly ripped-off. On his second day in India he had gone to an Indian travel agent who suggested that he should go and stay with his family in Kashmir, thus the accommodation would be free and they would take him mountain trekking, show him all the sights etc. He paid about $500 for this, then when he got up there the expenses that the family asked him to pay for started to add up: food, taxis, clothes, dodgy souvenirs, a donkey for carrying trekking equipment, actually trekking (only two days were completed) and the free accommodation (at $20 a night). In 24 days he forked out $1,400 and had a terrible time. I told him his problem was that he was far too nice a bloke and then clarified that I would be charging him $10 for listening to him (unfortunately, he realised I was joking).

Anyway, a few of us relaxed on the roof. Heral gave me a bottle of beer and by 10.30pm myself, Heral and another Danish lad were scrambling around the back streets in an unsuccessful quest for another beer. I can't envisage having this many problems trying to get a beer tomorrow. I passed my diarrhoea tablets to yet another Danish lad who had been suffering for a couple of weeks (maybe 'I passed' aren't the best words with diarrhoea tablets but you know what I mean).

After I drained the last dregs of my beer I said my goodbyes and went to catch the last bus to the airport, armed with a couple of croissants from a local bakery, courtesy of Kevin.

Day 22 - Friday 21st February - Escape From Delhi

There were four others on the bus and we were all sleepy backpackers. Shortly after midnight, we reached the airport. The waiting room was separated by a road from the main body of the airport and they even charged me to enter. After grumbling about this to the security guards, I went in and found an Aussie girl who had been on the airport bus.

She taught me how to play backgammon on her Indian made wooden travel set. After beating her three games to nil I decided that it was a very good game and she decided it was time for her flight. She left me sitting with a Scouse lad she knew and I chatted with him for the next two hours while Inspector Morse played detective on the nearby television screen. Basically, he had been doing bar work in Hong Kong for the last one and a half years and decided to go to India for three weeks, which had turned into two months (the Scouser, not Inspector Morse – although it could make a good episode). Air India had switched his ticket without any problem and said he could get a flight back whenever he wished. As soon as he got to Delhi it would be organised, they promised. When he actually arrived in Delhi they could only guarantee a flight after 10 more days. He had been on waiting lists for three days and had come to the airport for the first time tonight to try and force his way on by whatever desperate means he could. After the peace of Pushkar, I could sympathise with him and was keen to leave Delhi myself. On the first visit to Delhi it had the novelty value of a different culture but after Pushkar it just seemed smelly, crowded, noisy and busy.

When my check-in time of 4.00am arrived tiredness had caught up with me. The disposal of the croissants into the pit of my stomach hadn't even helped rejuvenate the senses. The previous night's bus journey had provided only about an hours sleep plus the couple I got in the afternoon, then staying awake all night meant that in the last 46 hours I had experienced a total of three hours' sleep. At least I could get some rest and recuperation on the plane. After waiting for half an hour, at check-in, I arrived at the front of the queue. Then to my horror, the flight attendant informed me that they had not got a record of my flight confirmation so my ticket was void. I would have to wait to see whether there were any spaces as the flight was currently full. I stood there arguing; the flight had been confirmed one week ago! One! Week! Ago! How could they do this to me! They told me that I would be top of the waiting list and they expected spaces so to relax and come back at 6.15am. Relax, after barely any sleep for two days? I flung my rucksack three yards away from the desk and sat on it for the next one and three-quarter hours, getting increasingly agitated with the whole process.

When the checking-in queue finished at 6.30am, there were four others who had tickets but had not confirmed their places and were equally pissed off. Things were starting to go from bad to worse as no seats seemed to be available; then the news came, full flight - no seats. I let them know exactly what I thought of the situation. They said that we could go on a waiting list for tomorrow's flight; just bloody brilliant! Here I was struggling to stay awake and these incompetents couldn't even sort my seat out. Even if it had been the travel shop in Udaipur that had cocked up and not confirmed my flight I was not letting up with my insistence that I phoned myself to re-confirm and that I shouldn't be suffering for their mistake. I just felt that I couldn't face another day in Delhi. Let me go home! I saw Kevin checking-in for his flight and was delighted to see a friendly face; he was with another couple of English folk and they all gave me a gee up to tear another strip off the Gulf Air staff. I was desperate to get out of Delhi and would be quite willing to pay for another flight to get back home and then charge it to Gulf Bloody Air. I headed back to the officials for another moan. Then another official came across with five extra boarding cards. Yes!!!!!!!!!! Thank you Jesus, Grandad, Desmond Lynam or whoever is looking over me. Thinking about it, maybe after my prayer in Pushkar it was Brahma who arranged the extra boarding cards.

We were rushed through customs and boarded the plane in time to hear an announcement apologising for the delay '*which was due to passengers having problems with their visas and passports*'. What a pack of lies, it was because they couldn't work their computers to know if seats were available. We took off and I let out a big sigh of relief before exchanging smiles with the lucky five.

The plane landed in Oman, then flew off to Abu Dhabi where I was due to wait for a couple of hours for the flight to London. That was 11.00am, I was still waiting for the plane at 3.00pm. I hung around chatting with a Sikh lad from Wales who rated highly in the popularity stakes after telling me that free meals were being provided in the restaurant because of the delay. The waiting was a bit frustrating but the truth was that I was pleased to be away from Delhi. I had adored India and wanted to stay longer but my mind had got used to the idea of returning and with no sleep I had become desperate.

The flight took off at 4.30pm and arrived in London at 8.45pm, an eight and a quarter hour flight and 19 hours after leaving Delhi. The underground was followed by an hour and a half wait at St Pancras for my train, which gave me plenty of time to sit in the nearby pub and sup a good old English ale.

Diary 3

I 'd loved India (well except for the times that I was hating it) and was amazed by the sheer life of the place. The poverty was appalling but I was equally surprised that people were like me; smiling, joking and just trying to make their way in life.

I had returned to work whilst Stu carried on travelling and discovering new worlds, but it was time to catch up with him. Let's check the table below. Oh yes, Australia is the next destination.

	UK	Australia	Oceania
Population in millions	65.6	24.1	40
Projected population in 2050 in millions	77	41.3	66
Infant mortality per 1000 live births	3.9	3.4	20
Life expectancy - male	79	80	75
Life expectancy - female	83	84	80
Gross national income in purchasing power parity divided by population (in $)	40,550	44,570	32,456
Area of country (square miles)	93,638	2,900,000	2,968,000

NOTE: the internet is amazing for getting information like this. Although typical Aussies, we started well on the population numbers and then they go on to beat us at nearly every other statistic in the table.

We are only moving on to October 1997 so shall we bother to change the music? Well since the last trip Tony Blair had replaced John Major as Prime Minister and Princess Diana had tragically died in a car crash. In short, the world had moved on so we better change the films and songs. So please move to Screen 1 for 'Men in Black' or Screen 2 if you fancy 'The Full Monty'. In the world of music it is worth writing (or reading) these diaries just to hear the 'Bitter Sweet Symphony' album by the Verve. I haven't listened to that for ages. I've got the CD just here...

A rucksack lay between my legs as my body was parked on a bench with Melton Mowbray Railway Station surrounding me, all two platforms worth. The destination was Darwin, but there wasn't a direct connection from Melton Mowbray. Instead, I would have to change at Leicester, Kings Cross, Heathrow and Kuala Lumpur.

I travelled by myself, not even a brother in sight but if I could survive going back and forth to India then how difficult can getting to Australia be?

With a bit of luck, I'll meet up with Stu in Darwin which is the smallest and most northerly of the Australian state capitals. The only clouds on a bright and sunny horizon are that I only have two weeks and I don't know where he is staying. I'd spoken to Stu about seven weeks ago to organise meeting up with him at which point he was in Indonesia. A date of mid-October was set and the next week I looked at flights but before I could book a flight I tore a calf muscle. This preceded one and a half weeks shuffling about in the style of an old man whose zimmer frame had been kidnapped, followed by two and a half weeks actually being able to swing around on crutches. My leg was in such a state that I phoned Stu's dad and informed him that if he spoke to his travelling son to tell him that I was in no fit state for a journey to Clacton let alone Australia. This seemed to start a seemingly miraculous recovery of the muscle whose medical name I still can't pronounce.

The miraculous recovery meant that a week and a half before mid-October and with still no one having spoken to Stu I decided I could make it after all. But I couldn't find a spare plane seat to Australia, not for love or money, and I offered both. Then followed a fax from Stu saying he was looking forward to us travelling together again, I faxed back saying I couldn't make it, De Montfort University Travel then phoned offering a seat. I said 'I want a flight to Australia, not some old seat', tell a lie (and a bad joke), my reaction was more related to somersaults and whooping. A fax was cast in an Indonesian direction stating that Mr Brown would be travelling after all and finally the tickets arrived 13 hours before the plane's scheduled departure time. Although flights back were limited and with six months two weeks and a couple of days left on my passport I had to be due to leave Australia before

I entered the last six months else I wouldn't receive a visa, hence the flying visit. Only two weeks in Australia '*you must be mad*' was the reaction of most people and I couldn't think of a good answer. To be honest, I didn't really care, I was free, no getting up for work or being cooped up in the house because of my dodgy leg. Even my stomach felt satisfied after a pub meal with Bob and Matt to celebrate Paul's 26th birthday (Bob being Paul in the strange world of nicknames).

Melton, Leicester, Kings Cross, Heathrow and it was still only about 7.00pm. I say 'about' 7.00pm because I was watchless. My old travelling watch had gone AWOL, but it was a cheap bulky thing and I could never quite figure out how to turn that bloody annoying hour chime on or off. It seemed to be set on some sort of random play. I suppose I could have read the instructions but that would have been as good as admitting defeat.

Talking of annoying beeping, I've always been slightly bemused by the metal detecting machines at airports. Sometimes they go off, sometimes they don't and it doesn't really seem to make that much difference as to whether I've emptied my pockets or not. Anyway, on this occasion, I emptied all coins, keys, knives and guns on to the tray and walked through the doorway. BUZZ! A search found my ventolin about my person, well in my pocket. How did I miss that? Okay, this time I was a bit daft but normally these machines can buzz for no apparent reason.

I then met and joined up with Rebecca, in the seeking gate 8 sense. We had made the assumption that gate 8 would be found between gate 7 and gate 9, how stupid of us. Obviously, gate 8 was before gate 7 and gate 9.

Day 2 - Thursday 16ᵗʰ October - The Day That Time Forgot

The flight felt a bit strange in that my seat was in the middle of the plane, so I couldn't see anything. This coincided with a very smooth night time journey during which I slept through the three in-flight films and reached Malaysia with the feeling that I hadn't really travelled very far.

10 hours into the day and it was already 6.00pm. I had three hours to kill at the airport so completed the usual exploration and then took a seat for a relaxing read. Never being one who is capable of sitting still for long I wandered off again and bumped into Rebecca who had momentously decided to give up smoking. All she wanted to do was enjoy her last cigarette, but was experiencing difficulty locating anywhere that allowed smoking. The Brown

Kuala Lumpur airport exploration 1997 had charted a room that legend told allowed humans to inhale burnt tobacco for brief pleasure. The airport was by no means small but the smoking room was the size of your average living room, with its own permanent smog hanging in the air. The last cigarette burnt, withered and fell.

She was catching a flight to Sydney that was due to fly in three-quarters of an hour but the passengers had not been called. Had she got time for a drink? Predictably as soon as she received her vodka the flight call went up so she knocked it back and headed off to start a new chapter in her life. I gradually supped my beer and read my guide book. I was fairly certain Captain Cook discovered Australia in 1770 but my book points out that the aborigines had been living there for about 50,000 years so discover wasn't quite the right word. From 1770 it took us 18 years to start transporting prisoners to Australia. Then it took another 106 years for them to beat us at cricket, 139 years to beat us at rugby and 233 years to beat us at football (editorial update and 246 years to beat us in the Eurovision song contest).

My flight call finally sounded and I headed to customs carefully removing my coins and ventolin on to the plate. 'BUZZ!' went the machine and a pair of hands went up and down my body again. I just had the feeling that the operators were saying *'well I don't know why it buzzes but I'm damned if I'm going to admit defeat and read the instructions'*.

Day 3 – Friday 17th October - Sleep Lag

I flew beside Miriam, an Australian, fresh from working for a couple of years in Vienna. She was carrying on to Cairns but suggested I declared something on the immigration form so I'd get through customs quicker i.e. join the short queue rather than the long queue. The question that asked whether I'd been on a farm in the last month was chosen, Miriam told me that it would just be a case of them making sure I wasn't bringing any soil into the country. I just had to say no and I'd be straight through.

The customs officers examined my form, but instead of letting me straight through, started asking me questions. *'Are you wearing any of the clothes that you wore on the farm?'* 'Um, er, no'. *'What about your shoes?'* 'Um, er, no'. *'Are you sure there is no soil on your shoes from the farm?'* 'Um, er, yes'. *'When were you last on a farm?'* 'Um, er, a couple of weeks ago'. I wasn't prepared for questions and was on the verge of confessing to smuggling top grade Colombian soil when they said *'go straight through'*.

The plane had been due in at 4.55am but there I was at 4.50am through customs, even having claimed my rucksack and was ready to go round the corner to be greeted by Stu. I headed around the corner but unless Stu had turned into a 14 stone middle-aged Australian woman he wasn't there. Never mind, I was early and was confident that he would turn up any minute, of course, if he didn't there was the administration hiccup that I didn't have his address or telephone number. I carried on thinking this as seemingly everyone else from the flight filtered through to meet people or carry on to their destination. Eventually, everyone dispersed and an hour later I was the only one left at the airport from the Malaysian Airlines flight. It wasn't looking good so I started to form a plan of action. I'd phone my parents and Stu's dad to see if there was a message, like Stu had lost his left leg crocodile wrestling and would be late because he wanted to hop to the airport with some kangaroo friends (I figured that would be a typical Australian day). If there was no message then I would find somewhere to stay and leave messages with Stu's dad. The plans were useless though because Stu turned up five minutes later, with a smile on his face and both legs still firmly in place.

After dropping my bags off at the house we had a big cooked breakfast, reminisced about India and Stu recounted his travelling exploits after Pushkar. It was great to see Stu, nice to have a cooked breakfast and good to have the Australian sunshine rather than the British chill on my face.

It was then back to the house which Stu had occupied for the last few days. It was a kind of an exaggerated student house with the floor carpeted in a litter montage and eight of us staying in the three bedroomed bungalow. Five of us squeezed into the small living room to watch 'The Bill'. My poor travel-weary brain was further confused by seeing a British program on television. In fact, it added to the theory that I hadn't left England and all airlines were involved in a conspiracy, the earth was really only the size of France. Although that's a self-defeating argument, so I left it there and put it down to jet lag.

I decided that what I needed to conquer the jet lag would be a quick afternoon sleep of say 15 minutes then go out for a spot of food and possibly a beer before returning about 9.00pm for a good long sleep, thus feeling fresh for the morning. I went to sleep at 4.00pm and woke up at 7.00pm, it then took another 15 minutes for me to summon the energy to stand up. Slightly behind schedule me and Stu headed off for some food at a pub called 'Rattle & Hum'. They had an offer on which meant that when you bought your first beer at just £1.25 they also provided you with a free meal.

The only logic behind it must be that they thought that everyone would stay there for numerous more beers. Well, we had a couple more beers but that was me about finished because all I wanted to do was sleep. So off we went. Shenanigans Irish pub marked the route back to bed and as a couple of our fellow house sharers were working there it seemed rude not to nip in for a beer, besides the time had only reached 9.30pm so I had made inroads into the schedule, one solitary beer would do me no harm.

One pint of Caffreys later and I was wide awake as we chatted away to some Australian girls who were quite entertaining and twice our age. Then in came Stu's friends from Indonesia; Dave the Scotsman, Miriam the pretty Dutch girl and Amanda the pretty English girl but everything had become blurry by that stage and everyone was beginning to look pretty. I remember talking a fair bit about football and different countries, probably. The time had hit 2.30am before we got back to the house. Stu pointed me into the direction of a bedroom; I opened the door and could make out three bodies on mattresses and another six-foot space which I carefully collapsed into.

Day 4 – Saturday 18th October – I Love It When A Plan Comes Together

Would my jet lag cure of living a conscious 23 hour day and dispatching numerous beverages be successful? Well, the sun shone brightly outside and I felt wide awake. There were still three bodies around me but that wasn't surprising because the time only read 7.30am. Either I had found the miracle solution for jet lag or my body clock had lost track of what, where and when.

The thought had struck me that I was different from every other traveller, I'd be in Australia for just two weeks and they're nearly all travelling for at least six months. I felt a little uncomfortable, as other people ushered the conversation towards travelling I'd start to send it down another path because either I just couldn't compete or maybe it was jealousy. But all things considered, it was still sunny outside.

Up early, Stu and I decided to make the most of the day by working out our options. In relative terms, Kakadu National Park, where Crocodile Dundee was filmed, was relatively close but would basically be a three-day trip leaving no time to see Ayers Rock. Although common sense would also rule out Ayers Rock, or Uluru as it is now called, because it would mean a 4,500 kilometre round trip. The problem with trips to Kakadu was the price, $250 for three days being about the cheapest.

I felt a burning sensation emanating from the heart region, it was a desire, I wanted to see Uluru whatever the distance. I mean what was a few thousand more kilometres after travelling from England. We unsuccessfully did the rounds of various hostel notice boards to see if anyone was offering a lift down to Alice Springs. Then carried out an inspection of the 'backpacker car yard' (where big beat up old cars were bought and sold by backpackers). Further disappointment led us to the Greyhound Bus office and on a bit of a whim I purchased a 5,000 kilometre pass and Stu bought a 3,000 kilometre pass. A plan emerged, catch the bus down to Katherine then to Alice Springs on to Uluru, Kings Canyon back to Alice Springs where Stu would stay and I'd head back to Darwin Airport. I'd prefer to travel by car with a couple of others but Father Time had me by the proverbial balls and for once I had to follow a plan.

That was that, by lunchtime, we were on the bus to Katherine, a small journey in Australian terms. After four hours travel the Kookaburra Lodge, in Katherine, welcomed us into their old motel units. Our unit consisted of a fairly large room with five bunk beds and a bit of a kitchen.

Katherine is renowned for its series of 13 gorges which stretch for about 12 kilometres. There was a lot of bumph in the reception about the various ways of seeing the gorge such as helicopter, boat, walking and canoe. Canoe sounded the most interesting for our budget and I expressed a genuine interest for more information, even joking about whether there were any crocodiles. The receptionist was not meant to reply *Yeah, but they're just freshies*. Suddenly the canoe idea didn't sound quite so enticing. 'So what does only freshies mean?' I enquired. '*Oh the freshies are harmless, nothing to worry about*', 'Okay um two for the canoeing'. Stu seemed fairly confident and said '*yeah, the freshies are okay*', but I still looked them up in the guide book for some sort of reassurance. '*Freshwater Crocodiles have narrower snouts and rarely exceed 3 metres in length, are harmless to people unless provoked*' (well should be okay because I have no intention of provoking them), '..unlikely to seek human prey, have been known to bite, and children, in particular, should be kept away from them'. I don't feel as reassured as I hoped to be.

I decided to retire to my bunk bed at 6.00pm for a quick snooze but woke up at 9.00pm. Stu was in charge of cooking dinner and this ensured that there would be a pasta mountain. It took about half an hour to cook and about three-quarters of an hour to eat, but that gave us a chance to meet some of the others in the dorm including Dan the Canadian who had experienced the canoeing that day and not only lived to tell the tale but enjoyed it.

Day 5 – Sunday 19th October -
Up The Gorge With 'Crocodile Brown' & A Paddle

I had an uncomfortable night dreaming about crocodiles tipping up canoes and eating their contents with a swirling frenzy topping. My head thought crocodiles, crocodiles, crocodiles, no Jeff don't do it! No!

I think it was just a further consequence of the jet lag as I woke up extremely excited about the prospect of the gorge, crocodiles and a canoe (not necessarily in that order). The bus drove us the 15 kilometres to the gorge and we went past what our driver described as the biggest classroom in the world. But no matter how hard I tried, my eyes couldn't fix on any gigantic building. He then explained that it was the school of the air which broadcasts lessons to children in remote parts of the outback. It was a classroom without walls.

We arrived at 9.00am and received the relevant equipment consisting of paddles, life jackets, a semi-waterproof tub and a two-man canoe. Of the 13 gorges, we were told that we could canoe up the first three but not the fourth and *you'll see why*. What? A waterfall? Saltwater crocodiles? Loch Ness Monster on holiday? The water hasn't been heated up yet? He wouldn't say. One of his mates piped up *'Bill can you go out with some chickens to gorge two, the crocodiles haven't been fed yet, okay everyone, no swimming in gorge two until 11.00am because the crocodiles haven't been fed yet'*. I for one nodded thinking it made good sense to take in the advice, but it was followed by an *'only joking you'll be fine'*.

The water calmly lay before us, the life jackets were safely put on our seats, the rule being you don't have to wear them but you have to take them out with you. The canoe had to be returned before 4.45pm else an extra charge would be made and more importantly we'd miss the minibus. The large cliff-like walls of the gorge seemed to catapult us into a different world some-where between Deliverance and The Lost World. Although the calm water, beautiful scenery and lack of rednecks or dinosaurs (well unless crocodiles count) meant the world seemed a fairly serene place. I never imagined doing anything like this in my life, or anyone else's come to that. Stu was the first to crack and come out with the surely mandatory *'It is Gorge-ous'*.

After 45 minutes canoeing, the end of the first gorge had been reached. The only thing we had to figure out was how to pull the canoe out the water. It was too heavy to simply jump out the canoe then pull it up, more of a case of jumping into the wet stuff and lifting the increasingly heavy canoe out. The problem of how to get the canoe to gorge two still had to be figured out.

We watched a couple in front of us struggle; putting the canoe down every so often to ensure their arms didn't fall off, then giving it another pull. After looking at the rock paintings to put off the inevitable, we walked with the canoe for 10 minutes, then underwent a little paddle, back out of the water, another 10 minute walk across rocks of all various sizes and finally me, Stu and the canoe were at the start of gorge two. We sat down on a rock to join a Scottish couple in whinging that we were never told about having to cart around a bloody one tonne canoe across rocks for 20 minutes. The second gorge took a good half hour of rowing for my now aching arms. It always seemed so easy when Redgrave and Pinsent were shown on television. The third gorge only took another 20 minutes of rowing and at the end of it, tucked around a rocky corner, were four other empty canoes. We followed their lead and tried to block our canoe in the rocks to make sure it didn't take its own little journey. After a swim in the water at the end of gorge three, Stu and I headed off to see exactly why the fourth gorge couldn't be canoed.

Rocks. The water level was too low, in fact hardly existent. We must have walked about a mile before coming across some more water so promptly went back in for another swim. Its times like this you think you should have brought that water resistant sun tan cream. Or at least your crocodile resistant sun tan cream, for I couldn't help but keep an eye out for the leathery beasts. Whilst Stu swam anywhere he pleased I stayed in close proximity to the shallow bank.

After passing another group going back to the canoes and being left swimming by a couple of Danish girls it meant that out of the 60 canoes available to people, Stu and I were now the 60th furthest away from the canoe hut, with no watch or clock between us. I studied the sun and decided it was bright and hot but it would not tell me the time. On catching up with the Danish girls they informed us that it was 1.15pm, which by our calculations left us three and a half hours to return the canoe.

The heat was on a setting of ferocious and as I'd forgotten to bring a hat, my head began to roast nicely, so I tied a spare T-shirt around it. Boy did I look cool, illustrated by the fact it never appeared on my head when other canoes were nearby. Frantic canoeing, meandering canoeing and a stop off at a butterfly bank later and we were still in 60th place, with arms now trying to convince the brain that there has been some terrible mistake and they are really legs and as such should be laying down in the canoe. Stu's solution was to think that we were earning our beer and to think of that reward. We kept going and by the return of gorge one even started overtaking other canoes.

Okay, so they had stopped for a breather, but we were still overtaking as our boat spurted (well at least drifted quickly) through the water. We docked at 4.40pm, not bad for two blokes without a watch. The only disappointment was not having canoed past any crocodiles. A number of 'crocodile nesting area keep out' signs were on view but they were no substitute for actually canoeing with a croc. Having stated that, as one lad put it *'well I wanted to see a croc, but if I'd actually seen one I think I'd have wished it wasn't there'*, strange words but it made complete sense.

Weary bodies were rounded up and put into the back of the mini-bus. An hour later we were seated at a pizza restaurant contemplating the 'all you can eat for $5' offer. Large slices were served up but I surrendered after five slices, leaving Stu to defend the British honour. The man's stomach expanded in front of my very eyes, seven slices, eight slices, nine slices and yes, no, yes a tenth slice and the equivalent of a large family pizza. The explanation, *'well they didn't have any proper cheese in Indonesia'*.

I fell into a deep sleep at 9.00pm.

Day 6 – Monday 20TH October -
Pleasure On A Bed Of Peanut Butter

I awoke at 8.00am, 11 hours of pure recuperation which should have finished off any lingering jet lag, unless I had developed some sort of canoe lag (we were going pretty quick by that last canyon).

A lazy day lay ahead with the main event being a 15 hour bus journey from Katherine to Alice Springs. In the meantime, some peanut butter sandwiches were consumed before heading into town where after much debate Stu purchased a tent. A $40 investment in the short term would hopefully reduce dormitory bills in the long term. Stu decided that the extra cost of a fly sheet at $30 would be a needless luxury and praying for no rain would be a far more cost-effective alternative.

I had never really eaten peanut butter sandwiches before this tour of duty, but with normal butter in a hot rucksack not being a viable option, peanut butter had become a substitute with the additional advantage that it could also be the main filling.

After returning from the shops I assisted chef Stu in preparing a noodle feast that despite just the two of us covered three large plates. As I struggled to make an impression on a seemingly growing noodle feast Stu ploughed through. Whatever weight he'd lost in Indonesia was returning in Australia.

Some of our fellow canoeists faced a lack of funds so had to organise work as mango pickers for the next couple of weeks. Fruit picking is one thing, but fruit picking in blistering temperatures with god knows what venomous spiders and snakes for company just didn't sound like my idea of fun. One of the few advantages of being a part-time traveller is that I don't have to take any blisteringly hot and sweaty job. Talking of fun, we boarded our packed-out 15 hour bus, with a large, smelly, all burping all farting Aussie across the aisle from Stu. Our mood was not helped by the film on the bus. Some Cybill Shepherd offering where Robert Downey Junior, who is her husband, dies but then is reincarnated and becomes friends with her daughter. He then realises who he was and goes out with Cybill Shepherd before finishing the film going out with her daughter who in effect is still his daughter. Enough said! In fact, probably too much has already been said.

The only pleasure to be enjoyed was our pre-prepared sandwiches of mushrooms, tomatoes and cucumber, obviously on a bed of peanut butter. It may not get the taste buds whistling in normal circumstances but it tasted delightful at that moment.

The night bus finally ground to a halt at a small town where we had a 20 minute break before the bus was due to leave again at 10.15pm. Stu and I had a coffee and returned to the coach at about 10.10pm, well Stu was just behind me when we left the cafe but we somehow separated. A few minutes passed and a couple more, still no sign of Stu. The bus driver did a quick count up and then another, before looking satisfied that everyone was present. I grabbed his attention with a quick 'wait a minute, someone's missing I'll get him'. '*Well quick it's 10.20pm*'. The only problem was that I didn't know where Stu had wandered off to. I nipped into the cafe, but no sign, then I turned and spotted him happily chatting away on the telephone. 'Stu, the bus is going!' '*Dad, got to go the bus is leaving, bye*'. The bus waited for us and started up as we boarded.

Day 7 – Tuesday 21ˢᵗ October - A Town Like Alice

The bus trundled on, sometimes stopping in the middle of nowhere to pick up another passenger or drop off a sack of post, but as the sun rose the outback came in to view. The wildlife seemed to be in hiding with only the occasional sighting of a kangaroo, but what struck me was the vast wide open spaces, no buildings, no people, just the countryside.

The main advantage of Australian buses, over Indian buses, besides the massive increase in comfort, was that they had a toilet and I thought it would be jolly rude not to use the facility. As I stood there having a wee, trying to keep my balance and accuracy as the bus wobbled about on the road, I looked out the window and saw the outback flanked by a mountain range. That without a shadow of a doubt is the best view I have ever witnessed whilst taking a pee. Mind you as most of the competition is the four walls of home or standing in a scruffy pub urinal next to some hairy bloke then it may not be that surprising.

It was still fairly early when we reached Alice Springs, a famous town but with a population that only numbers 22,000. The reason a town was formed in the middle of Australia was for the telegraph line in the 1870s and then it continued to develop with a view to the railway passing through. Although the railway does go south from Alice there still isn't a line connecting North Australia to South Australia. Alice is built where the Todd river meets the Charles River, but both normally run dry. Once a year they have a regatta where the rowing boats are hollowed out and the rowers run Fred Flintstone style with their boat. Although, it had to be cancelled the other year because there was water in the river! The town had a really good friendly feel to it and I instantly felt at home.

We headed off to the Stuart caravan park where the tent could be pitched. After a couple of minutes in the tent trying to figure out where the poles should be stuck, it was figured out that they should go on the outside. I never was a very good scout. The heat bore down on us and with the weariness caused by the 15 hour journey, a rest and lunch in a bit of shade seemed a good idea. Lunch consisted of Peanut Butter and crisp sandwiches. I don't think any further comment on that is necessary.

With the energy bank restored, a five hour meander around Alice Springs ensued. You could tell that we were in the middle of the desert because as darkness fell it became very chilly on my legs and arms which were merely covered by a T-shirt and shorts. Cold and hungry, there was only one thing for it, Barramundi and chips (without peanut butter). Nicer than your normal cod and chips if the truth be told.

Stu and I headed back on the two mile walk to the campsite which followed a rendezvous with the local supermarket and brought us a couple of bottles of beer each. The lager proved just too gassy for my constitution and brought about a bout (bizarre, two words that make up one in succession and it still makes sense) of hiccupping burps as I struggled to finish my second bottle. After the last drop was drunk my head hit the bottom of the tent and I was out for the count with Stu still in mid-conversation.

DAY 8 – WEDNESDAY 22ND OCTOBER -THE ROCK

I woke up in the middle of the night, fully clothed but on top of my sleeping bag, not a clever move during a cold night. Anyway, it was an early start to walk down to the bus station for another bus trip, although this one did make me tingle a bit because when the bus reached its destination I would be at Uluru, one of the most famous places on earth. It was a three day, two night trip to Uluru, the Olgas and Kings Canyon, all we had to do was get on the bus for 9.00am. Having arrived at 8.45am this would not be a problem, until Stu disappeared at 8.55am. 9.00am came and went as I stood on the steps of the bus telling the driver 'he can't be far away, he'll be here any minute'. I went in search of Stu, the bookies favourite, at evens, was in the toilet. I headed into the gents and realised that someone was in the cubicle. I could look like a complete prat (amongst other things) by talking to a stranger in a toilet cubicle. However, as the bus driver had threatened to leave any minute I had to speak up. 'Stu are you in here?' *'Yeah.'* 'The bus driver is about to go, hurry up, if you can'. A slightly lighter Stu emerged a couple of minutes later and claimed his bus seat.

Our jovial driver was Hans who encouraged passengers to talk to each other and told everyone to introduce themselves to the people near them. This prompted Stu to stand up and declare *'I'm Stu from England'*, I followed this with 'I'm Jeff from England', and then a deathly silence hit the air. In fact, at one point I was sure some tumbleweed blew down the aisle. We squirmed with embarrassment, but as the hours passed people did begin to talk and at least they knew who we were.

I still couldn't believe that I was actually in Australia. I mean, Australia is around the other side of the world. Whilst contemplating this concept in my head, the bus ground to a halt at a camel farm. We were informed that there were over 250,000 camels in Australia and that they produce the healthiest ones in the world and actually export them to the Middle East. I'd heard there were camels in Australia but didn't realise the extent of the breeding.

It took about five hours to reach Yulara, a purpose-built holiday resort just a few kilometres from Uluru. The resort catered for most needs and was a real oasis in the desert for any luxury seeking tourist. There were about 20 people on the coach, mainly our sort of age and most of them got off the bus at the resort hostel. There were just three of us who braved the resort campsite and a few others who scattered themselves at other hotels. The resort consisted of about four different hotels, a hostel, a campsite, various shops and restaurants all meticulously built into the landscape so as to be unnoticeable as possible, but it's not easy to hide four large hotels.

The third camper turned out to be Dan the Canadian who slept in the bunk below me in Katherine. He decided to take things easy whilst Stu and I rushed about to get back to the campsite bus stop. Obviously, it was no ordinary bus stop for it would be the place to stand if you wished to be taken to Ayers Rock. Although Ayers Rock is not really Ayers Rock. It was always known to the aborigines as Uluru but when the first Europeans saw it in 1872 they named it Ayers Rock. It was only a few years ago that it officially reverted back to being generally called Uluru. When Uluru came into sight it just looked brilliant. I had made it to Ayers Rock I was there (my brain is still thinking Ayers Rock), this thing of incredible natural beauty was not some picture in a book it was in front of my eyes, incredible, just incredible, this is what travelling is about; 'getting somewhere'. Hans drove us right up to its base before letting us walk around a bit, then drove for a bit longer and let us walk for another stretch. He gave us a run-down of interesting facts and showed us the two waterholes at the rock.

There are about five aboriginal religious sites around the rock where you can't take pictures and although Hans could tell us some details, the main religious significance of the sites is held close to the Aborigines chest. Some of the stories did not match up to the Victorian morals of the time so the stories would get altered on their way to England, which annoyed the aborigines because part of the meaning was lost. Henceforth they only told the stories to people of their religion. They used to tell a couple of tales about serpents in the waterholes. This was for practical reasons more than anything else, because if their children played in the waterholes they could dirty the water and cause a valuable water supply to be of limited use.

The other significant thing about the rock was the number of bloody flies not giving you a moment's peace. I remember as a kid watching television pictures of Africa and wondering why the people didn't just knock away the flies that were on their face. However, after you have knocked away the 1,000th fly, the choice is that you can give up and let the fly land wherever it damn well pleases or go stark raving mad continuously slapping your own face.

Hans also mentioned that the rock is actually rusting, I think it is to do with the iron ore or some such chemical explanation. Fantastic fact number two, two-thirds of the rock is believed to be underground.

Before arriving in Australia I had made a decision not to climb Uluru, on the basis of watching an episode of the Lonely Planet that said it was an insult to the aborigines to climb it. Hans reckoned that it was an insult to about 25% of the aborigines to climb Uluru, another 25% said people could climb it and the other 50% were unsure. This complicated things in my mind because I quite fancied the steep trek, although in recent times 33 people had died trying to reach the top, 25 by heart attack and eight fallers. But considering the number of people ascending and descending that wasn't such a surprising figure. My conscience told me not to climb and Stu said that he had done so many climbs in Indonesia he wasn't bothered and quite fancied a tour around the cultural centre. So despite having the opportunity I have decided not to climb Uluru tomorrow.

The bus took us on to the sunset viewing area which was a mile long section that weaved its way around the numerous bushes. The problem is that some of the weaving paths went in front of other weaving paths. So someone could have placed themselves in a prime position to photograph Uluru only for a head to pop up 20 yards in front of them. Hans said he'd seen some brilliant punch ups over the years as everybody vied for the best possible camera positions. Over a half-hour period, the colour of the rock slipped from orange to very orange to bright orange and then dull brown, all fairly stunning, the sunset orange being spectacular. A constant camera clicking stream flowed in all directions. I chatted away to Nathan from Hawaii and said that if this was America the rock would go back underground after sunset and there would also be the facility to twist the rock around to see the other side plus there would be three sunsets a day to pack in the punters.

Day 9 – Thursday 23ʳᵈ October – What A Wonderful World

Dan the Canadian had not come on the previous day's Uluru trip because on the Greyhound passes you were allowed to jump on and off the buses as you liked. Dan lacked a watch or a clock (sounded familiar) so he asked us to give him a knock at 6.30am to make sure he was alive for the 7.00am start. At 6.30am I went over to his tent and knocked on it, being material this wasn't entirely effective, so I followed it with a 'Dan', 'Dan', but to no avail. I waited a few minutes and tried again, still no success, Stu followed it from outside our 10 yards away tent by shouting '*WAKE UP!*' The New Zealanders on a ground mat 15 yards away responded with a '*we are awake*', but there was still no sound from Dan's tent. What was wrong with the bloke? I unzipped his tent and found out the truth. He wasn't in there. Had he been dragged away by a dingo in the night? Or kidnapped by a pack of rampant Kangaroos? Or led astray by a duck-billed platypus? A minute later he returned from the washroom, explaining he had woken up early and did not want to disturb us.

As the bus approached Uluru I agonised. Okay so I'd insult some Aborigines and I didn't have any water for the two hour trek but I really wanted to climb it and I felt like a big girl's blouse by not climbing it, everyone else from our group seemed to be climbing it, I wanted to climb! But I couldn't insult them! But I wanted to climb! After much soul searching my morals relieved themselves on my desires flame and I stuck to my original decision.

The culture centre proved most illuminating and in typical fashion, Stu and I were late for the bus despite having one and a half hours to look around the small buildings. The learning curve included that you should not take a photograph of an Aborigine unless they give you their express permission. Basically, when an Aborigine dies their family acts as if nothing has happened to start off with, soon after they believe that the dead person's spirit leaves the body and walks in any remaining footprints of the person. However, as they do not wish to meet a bad spirit they stay away until the footprints are no longer visible. The situation is further complicated because a good person can still produce a bad spirit on death. Anyway, they then have a funeral which lasts about 24 hours in which they both start and stop the mourning process. In this time the mourners can wail and scream as much as is necessary. However, when the 24 hours is up they must act as if the person never existed so most possessions are burnt and they don't talk about that person ever again. Even to the extent that dead people are sometimes blackened out of photographs. It seemed harsh, but it was practical when they lived in small groups. If someone was mourning for months then the rest of the group would suffer because they relied on each other. I also felt vindicated in my early morning decision-making because the culture centre said 'Don't climb'.

The climbers were also late for the bus but I think Hans was getting used to it. Next, it was on to the bizarre 'Olgas' or 'Kata Tjuta' as it has now reverted to. It's difficult to describe, 'some strange rounded red mounds' doesn't seem to do it justice, the aboriginal name means 'many heads', if you take the two together then it probably still doesn't help anyone, all I can say is 'bloody impressive'. Although it covers an area of some six kilometres we were only given an hour and a half to see, photograph and make sense of these strange rocks. It gave us enough time for the main walk, although the other longer but equally popular 'valley of the winds' area had to remain untouched.

Apparently, in recent times a tourist lost his party on this walk and died within four hours, because of the heat and lack of water.

Predictably, Stu and I were in a group of four walkers who were late for the bus. This included the Tasmanian Denise who I learnt had also not climbed Uluru out of principle, instead doing the base walk. It still amazed me how many Australians were touring around their own country, I suppose it shouldn't really, but these are the perspectives you get coming from a small island.

The bus left the Yulara resort after lunch for a four hour trip to Kings Canyon, so the tent had to be packed up again and we wished the staying Dan a good life. Kings Canyon also had its own resort and was not cheap at $33 for a bed and $15 each to camp. I realised that we had a tent and Nathan had a tent, but was surprised when a number of our fellow passengers also headed to the campsite. They had decided that the beds were a rip-off and were going to camp without a tent.

After watching Kings Canyon at sunset and another 'home-made' pasta meal had gone down the hatch, everyone huddled around the campfire to keep warm. Jed the 'confident Manc', Mel the 'I may have been away for eight months but what's happening in the soaps', Miriam the 'sleeping bag less', Linda & Evelyn the 'amusing Dutch girls', Nathan the 'Hawaii Boy' and Bob the 'well I've heard of a dry sense of humour but he was in the midst of a 10 year drought'. Anyway, we enjoyed a beer or two and had a good laugh. Nathan, Stu and I especially enjoyed the 'we have a tent you don't' related conversations.

This helped my personal torment of losing my last film; all the Ayers Rock photographs and everything before had been recorded on that film and I couldn't find it. I must have put it in my shirt pocket and it had come out, I figure that the only hope would be if it had fallen out on the bus. I couldn't believe I was stupid enough to put it into such an open pocket where it could so easily drop out. Stupid! Stupid Stupid! Oh, why hadn't I put it somewhere else? All those photographs lost.

Poor old Miriam had to face the cold desert night without even a sleeping bag, so Stu offered her a blanket and I offered her my jacket. At first, she refused but Mel insisted it was only because she was shy so I told her to take it and to make whatever use of it she wanted, as long as it wasn't to burn on the fire. I reached for my jacket and felt something in its pocket, it was my lost film, I wasn't that stupid after all, still fairly stupid but not that stupid. I jubilantly tossed my jacket to Mel reflecting that a moment of kindness had seemingly been rewarded with the reappearance of my film. What a wonderful world!

Day 10 – Friday 24ᵀᴴ October –
Beer, The Lost City And A Jedi Knight

Hans had allowed us an extra hour in bed, or in sleeping bags as it was, so we left to trek around Kings Canyon at 6.00am. Some lie in! Due to the bitter cold, Miriam had hardly managed a minute's sleep, but thanked us immensely for the blanket and jacket without which she would have adopted a cold blue colour. She and Linda had spent all of the night huddled beside the remains of the campfire.

Kings Canyon is an ancient red coloured canyon with 100 metre walls and a rocky plateau that looks out on a fairly desolate landscape.

The trek around Kings Canyon took five hours and it was five hours of my life that will forever live in the memory. The scenery was stunning, I had come to Australia thinking of it as a relatively new country, but Kings Canyon helped me realise that it was an old country with a new marketing team. The views were incredible and I was never sure whether to keep my eyes peeled to my feet to make sure of my footing on the rocky paths or just keep looking up saying 'wow'. I put in an impressive impression of Noddy with my head moving from feet to scenery in regular movements. Looking down at one point gave us a view of 'the lost city', so called because of the many honeycomb shaped rocks that combine to look like an ancient city. Just standing on the canyon gave you that feeling of being somewhere incredible, I think the phrase that came to mind was 'I'm not worthy'. In the middle of this was an area they called the 'Garden of Eden' which was a waterhole and vegetation in this rocky paradise. A few people went for a swim. Stu and Nathan returned quickly with their blood showing on the outside rather than just the inside of their bodies, both having dived into a seemingly deep area only to hit some rocks.

All too soon the trekkers were back at the Kings Canyon resort and bags were packed but not before a fellow passenger was enticed into taking a picture of the nine camp-siters and another picture and another until he had used everybody's camera. Then we headed back to Alice Springs.

At the bus terminal, which was more of a bus stop, there was a massive hostel called Melanka's. We'd been warned off it by a Dutch lad in Katherine who said it was just too big and impersonal. However it was handy, allegedly had a good bar and when they realised that Nathan, Stu and I had tents they offered a special discount with a space in a three-man room costing $10 each rather than $15. My and Stu's main rucksacks were still at our original Alice campsite but after trekking for 5 hours in the morning I didn't really fancy a two kilometre walk back to the campsite only to return to town for food and beer and then head back to the hostel again. So Melanka's it was.

By 8.30pm Stu, Nathan and I had changed our attire and were ready to consume some food and drink. We were told that Legends was a good place for a beer, but the doors were still locked. 8.30pm on a Friday night and the place was still locked, what was the Commonwealth coming to? We met the campsite girls at a Mexican but the prices were a bit too steep for the boys, so it was back to the hostel for a cheap meal which also provided a free beer. Then it was back out to see if Legends had opened. 9.15pm and still closed, a local came by and told us that it didn't open until 10.00pm, I guessed last orders weren't at 11.00pm. A second beer was wearily consumed in a different pub, but it had been a long day and the three of us were all very sleepy when the last drops drained away. A unanimous decision was reached. We'd head back to the hostel for one last beer before hitting the sack. Exhausted, our trio trudged to the large hostel bar for a night-cap. Return of the Jedi was playing on a large screen, its sound deafened by the disco music. So watching the film another beer was had and then one more as we kept an eye on the dance floor. Nathan thought there was not much point in buying another glass of beer when you could buy a pitcher and save some money. A couple of Australian girls came across to talk to us. They had travelled some 120 kilometres to reach Alice for the weekend so it would have been rude not to carry on chatting to them. It's a bit of a blur but they were both teachers and the hyperactive one of them was Rowan Atkinson's cousin or second cousin or something.

Stu thought the pitcher idea was so good that when the Nathan bought jug dried up he purchased another one. Nathan put our names down on a long list to get involved in the seriously fought pool games. Another pitcher of beer and a dance later we finally got on to a table. The pair we played seemed to have been on for most of the night and obviously fancied themselves as pool players, although when one miscued badly we said 'ah, don't worry about it take it again'. Although they played far better than us, somehow our drunken efforts got us down to one yellow versus their one remaining red, at which point I played a snooker. This prompted a big protest from the other pair; *'you can't do that we've been here three months and no one's ever played a snooker, you can't play that shot'*. Nathan laughed, beerily I said 'it's an easy one, even Nathan's Gran could get out of it … although she is an international pool player'. They missed the snooker, but a pitcher or two too many had been consumed to take advantage and they won the game, but we took great pleasure in having made them squirm. Another pitcher of beer seemed to arrive, I couldn't figure where they were all coming from but I knew where they were going.

By about 2.00am there was hardly anyone left at the bar and they wouldn't give us any more pitchers so we headed outside to find a club. This is where it gets even patchier, but after pulling the combined memories of Stu, Nathan and myself it goes something like this: for some reason we never got to a club, instead Stu was going to phone home but we think he decided he was too drunk, so decided it wasn't a good idea. But we wanted to use this amazing speaking device so I decided to phone home, 'dad won't mind'. Therefore I ended up speaking to dad for five minutes, or so, as everyone kept piling change into the phone. Then for some reason, we headed to the chairs at the side of the pool for a game of cards. It was around this time an Aussie girl, the name Claire rings a bell, asked where I was from. As no one's ever heard of Leicester I used my standard answer of Nottingham. She said '*I used to live near Nottingham, a place called Melton Mowbray*' 'Wow I live in Melton Mowbray'. '*Wow!*', Wow! To quote Steven Wright 'It's a small world, but I wouldn't like to paint it'.

We played cards for about an hour, in which time me and Nathan just couldn't figure out what and whether there were any rules to these games that Stu and Claire kept making us play. It all got confusing and we turned in for the night, but not before I had lost my room key and with it a $10 deposit.

DAY 11 – SATURDAY 25ᵀᴴ OCTOBER -FOR A FEW DOLLARS MORE

I was dressed at 7.30am, quite impressive when you consider the amount of ale despatched and the time of going to bed. Not so impressive when it is revealed that I had never managed to get under the sheets never mind take any clothes off. I took full advantage of the situation to get up and have a quick look around for the lost key. This brought no success so I asked whether any had been found in the bar. Apparently, another reception looked after the bar but they had not discovered any keys. I headed back to the main reception to find out what time check-out was and spotted a key for number 203, our room, hanging on the hook. Someone must have handed it in after all so the receptionist passed me the key. Happy, I returned to bed.

A couple of hours later I got up properly to the mumbling of Nathan that he was never going to drink again. Meanwhile, Stu had found a room key in his pocket, Nathan also had one, if my mathematics skills haven't deserted me that adds up to three keys in total. We only had two keys to start with; the one from reception must have been a genuine spare key.

Each key was handed in and each time a $10 deposit was returned. Now should I mention the mistake or keep the extra $10? The thought pattern ran something like it's a massive impersonal hostel where we have invested heavily to keep up their beer profits, I don't think there is any reason to return the deposit. If it had been a small friendly place I would have returned the money at once, but not a place where I'm just a number. I reached a compromise whereby I accepted the money and then felt bad about it for the rest of the day.

The Alice tourist operators should be impressed with the way me and Stu have been fairly distributing ourselves around the available accommodation. We left Melanka's for the Alice Lodge and after booking in there went back to the Stuart Caravan Park to pick up our rucksacks which they had stored. On returning to the Alice Lodge in the midday sun, which was a hot and sweaty three kilometre walk, a busy days schedule involving the flying doctor base, School of the Air and the Old Telegraph station was mapped out. However, the relaxed and shady areas of the Alice Lodge proved too tempting and from 1.30pm to 6.00pm precisely we did nothing. Finally, after four and a half hours of inactivity, the legs rebelled and took us to the nearby ANZAC hill for sunset. A mellow time ensued on the hill as my film quickly ran out so I just sat there enjoying the moment. It was kind of apt really as the Aborigine's say that they don't know why people take photographs because you miss the essential experience; you're so busy looking into a camera you can't appreciate what's happening in front of your eyes. I think they have a point.

Stu was adamant that while I was in Australia a big barbecue would be enjoyed, the hostel had the facilities, we had the raw barbecue food and Nathan developed a familiar pasta and sauce mountain to go with it. The Alice Lodge not only had that laid back feeling, but was really welcoming and you felt that you were part of the Alice Lodge family which is totally the opposite to Melanka's (he says still trying to make himself feel better over the $10). That laid back feeling left me when I was minding my own business sitting by a table near the barbecue and felt something thud on to my shoulder. I could see some sort of big black brooch type thing and tried repeatedly to flick it away in a panicky sort of manner, not helped that I could feel it, but not really see it. To be fair to the beetle it must have fallen out of the overhanging tree and was more startled than me, I never thought I'd be jittery about a bug though.

The night petered out with a couple of bottles of beer, Nathan accepting half a glass, but refusing any more.

Day 12 - Sunday 26ᵀᴴ October - Plenty of 'Humph'

I had a, well would you call it a vision? No, a vision sounds like some mystical glimpse into the future, but I was dreaming and could see a plane covered in bright fiery red light. I hoped it wasn't my plane. How strange, it wasn't as if I felt consciously worried about the flight, although that could change.

After the previous day's inactivity, Stu and I struck out towards the old Telegraph Station, the reason Alice Springs was originally built. The woman at the hostel said that there was a path up to it but she wasn't exactly sure where, but if we basically followed the dry river bed it would lead us to it. After a couple of kilometres a barbed wire fence stretched across the river bed, so we thought that we couldn't be too far away and we were even closer after ducking under it. We weren't sure what it was there for - maybe to keep some animals away from town? You have your saltwater crocodiles, your freshwater crocodiles maybe there is the lesser known dry water crocodiles that they were trying to keep out, or maybe not.

When we eventually arrived at the telegraph station, a free guided tour was offered. There were other tourists about but none interested in the tour, so luckily we had the guide to ourselves. The guide looked about 60 years of age and had a knowledgeable sort of face. The tour started in the main building and consisted of a 20 yard walk down the main corridor, this lasted one and a quarter hours. The first 15 minutes were interesting, the next 15 minutes were okay, I struggled for the next 15 minutes and then for the remaining 30 minutes tried to edge towards the end of the corridor and freedom. The guide just rambled on and on, repeating himself intermittently as he eased into a monotone voice. At the end, I knew everything you ever needed to know about the Alice Springs Telegraph Station and a whole load more. My mastermind specialist subject had been found.

Then it was back to the hostel in the heat of the day to pack my bag for Darwin and leave Stu to continue his world meander. We thought that we'd follow the local customs in saying goodbyes, so enjoyed a last beer together and then I nipped off for the bus. It was genuinely sad to leave Stu. Not only did it mean the start of the end of my holiday but he's a great friend and ideal to travel with, in that we have never remotely argued, I think we're both too easy going to bother expending energy on arguing with each other. My main criticism of him as a travelling companion was that he wasn't a pretty blonde female, but maybe that's being picky. After a few more days looking around Alice, he planned to look for work. A cattle station cook vacancy had already attracted his attention. If my experience of his cooking is anything to go by, there were going to be some fat cattle hands in the Alice Springs area.

Nathan was on his way to Katherine and had booked on the same bus, by pure coincidence we ended up sitting next to each other, which gave us plenty of time to have a dig at the other that we couldn't get rid of them. 15 hours' worth of time to be precise, and that was only the time Nathan would be on the bus, after that I would still have another four hours remaining. Instead of the normal joking bus driver, we got the grumpy version. At the first pit stop everyone got out, Nathan and I nipped into the shop and looked at the lollipops. The bus driver came across and said '*you can't have one of those, we only have a couple of minutes here and you are not bringing one of those things on my bus*'. 'Well, we'll just look then'. '*Humph*'. At the next stop we again got out and still fancying a lollipop I saw him in the shop and asked 'how long have we got here?' '*I told you on the bus*'. 'Well we're down the back you can't hear anything there'. '*Well you should have said* (in a very grumpy tone). Most drivers used the PA system but I thought his must have been broken because he just used his normal voice, so we had no idea what he was saying or who he was talking to. Nice bloke, nice and grumpy. On the next leg of the journey he turned on the stereo, only the speakers at the back worked so he decided to turn those right up so that he could hear properly. Those of us at the back were blasted out of our seats and an Aussie girl went to the front to request that he turned the volume down '*Humph, right I'll turn it off*'.

A new driver appeared on the bus, giving Mr Grumpy time to go to sleep; he seemed to be able to use the PA system without any problems. He even gave us the chance to go and look at the Devils Marbles, which is a pile of large reddish photogenic spherical boulders. As the sun had already set they became a sort of murky red unphotogenic pile of rocks. The devil has big marbles, I'll tell you that for nothing.

The journey dragged on until about 10.00pm when we were allowed a half an hour break. After making our way through various takeaway price lists and cooking times I purchased some sort of chicken drumsticks in barbecue sauce, and some biscuits from the bus terminal. The grumpy bus driver saw me, '*You only have 10 minutes and you're not bringing those chicken things on my bus.*' 'I know'. '*Humph*'.

Day 13 – Monday 27th October - Damp Darwin

4.00am - The bus gradually ground to a halt at the familiar town of Katherine where we were due for another half hour break. This was Nathan's stop so it was a 'cheerio' from me and a '*it was good for you to meet me*' from him. I'd lost a friend but gained a seat which seemed a pretty good swap at that time in the morning. I was relatively comfortable curled up across the seats, the only thing keeping me awake was trying to figure out exactly what the couple in front of me were up to and where had her head disappeared to?

I rolled in and out of unconsciousness in typical overnight bus fashion but the previous night's dreamy picture seemed to recur except in more vivid detail. The scene from my head showed me looking out a small window and seeing a plane land in a blaze of fiery red light. Very peculiar.

By 8.00am my 19 hour marathon journey had nearly ended and I was suitably impressed with myself for surviving. Although the girl sleeping opposite me, in the bus sense, had come from Cairns and had now hit her 43rd consecutive hour of bus travel (two different buses), there's always somebody ready to outdo you.

When I finally took my stiff limbs off the bus, I booked into the hostel across the street, which I vaguely knew because Stu had originally stayed there. I even bumped into Stu's friend Miriam who had bought a car with her Scottish boyfriend Dave. The people they bought it from took their deposit then claimed the engine had been stolen, they finally sorted out the car by which time they were no longer boyfriend and girlfriend. They are now in the process of trying to sell the jinxed vehicle. My dorm, which consisted of four bunk beds, was still sleeping as I showered, changed and headed out to the streets of Darwin for the day.

I had set my sights on getting to the out of town crocodile farm but for some reason, the trip wasn't running, instead, the day was spent walking along the waterfront, then on to the Northern Territory Museum. In my best mad dog and Englishmen impression the mid-day sun bore down on my increasingly hot head as the apparently four kilometre walk to the museum lasted 6,000 metres. It was a relief to reach the museum for a sit-down, good drink and just to see some other souls. The museum seemed really interesting as I learned about how the town was destroyed by Cyclone Tracy and all about the animals in Australia, plus how they could kill you. It was a good decision to come here at the end rather than the start of the holiday.

I finally returned to the hostel where I met some of my fellow 'dormees'. There was Rich (an absolutely hammered 35-year-old American) and his friend Les, Ben the Australian, a couple of long-haired English blokes and a Swedish lad (who Les said he found in an alcohol-induced unconsciousness in the shower last night). 40 winks later and I headed to Rattle & Hum for the $2.50 beer with the free meal deal. After a couple of lonely laps of Darwin town centre, I retreated back to the hostel. Rich and Ben were in the dorm, but Ben left quickly, leaving me with the very drunk Rich who talked and talked, embroiling me in a boxing conversation. Every time I edged to the door he would spice up the conversation with some controversial statement which I seemed compelled to respond to. How do you mean Naseem Hamed isn't that good? How do you mean you've never heard of Steve Collins?

Finally, the Swedish lad came into the room, got involved in the conversation and I made my escape. I headed down to the pool where Ben sat and revealed he'd been glad to see me come into the dormitory because he hadn't been able to get away and before him, Les had left soon after he had entered. Well, the Swedish lad had the Rich baton now. It made it even more difficult to speak to Rich, in that every so often his left testicle would drop out of his shorts and it would take him a couple of minutes to realise and bring it home again. What does a polite Englishman say? 'One of your Hairy Ollock's has escaped and needs returning to its enclosure' - to be honest I think he would still have just carried on talking.

I relaxed by the pool and laughed at the group nearby, as one of the girls pushed one of the lads into the pool while he spoke to his swimming mate, then she got pushed in. Then the last lad of the group, then another girl and then the final girl was caught and duly wetted. I thought that the original lad was Miriam's Dave who I had met after a few beers on my first night in Darwin, but that wasn't the thought that concerned me. The thought that worried me was that the swimming vultures were looking for new prey. As we laughed at them, from the third wetted person onwards we felt that predatory eyes were turning our way. For the time being, we were saved as new victims innocently opened the hostel gate to be met with three Scottish lads desperate to throw them into the pool. Three times complete strangers opening the gate were greeted with a friendly 'hello' and were duly dispatched into the wet stuff. Surely the Scots would not want to throw an Englishman into the pool? Yes, I was definitely on swimming pool row and started to feel a bit edgy as my passport and ticket were in my money belt and my wallet in my pocket. The options were:

a. wait to be thrown in

b. hide under my seat

c. try and edge away back to the dorm

or

… Ben had the idea and I followed. I took off my money belt, shirt, shoes, watch and wallet before I jumped in, pre-empting the inevitable. It was much more comfortable in the water watching the greeting party throw hosteller after hosteller into the water, often in farcical fashion after victims either pleaded to be let off, pleaded for their wallet to be let off or took our lead and jumped in. There were several people who tried to wriggle away from their captors but after a soaking joined the dark side and led the way in rounding people up. The scene climaxed at 11.00pm with three people drying off, about eight of us in the water and another six running around trying to pounce on the dry people. By then the pool was circled by a ring of wallets and valuables.

A shower and pool-side return later I thought about turning in for the night, however, the thought that the only person present in the dorm was a stark naked Rich lying seemingly asleep on top of his bed encouraged me to stay by the pool a bit longer.

Day 14 – Tuesday 28th October - The Killing Hours

After a good sleep, I woke up to find my last day in Australia greeting me. It would just be a case of killing a few hours before heading to the airport. I didn't want to just hang around the hostel with people who had another six months of travelling left, so following breakfast, it was out into the bright hot sunshine. After a brief walk, the body decided sitting in the shade was a far better proposition.

I did venture along the seafront and reached a narrow walkway which cut through the undergrowth and overhanging trees to the empty beach. The beach and harbour are popular with jellyfish and the odd crocodile at this time of year. After seeing a metre long lizard near the path the previous day I didn't have much incentive to head down the walkway. However, a few steps past it and the path became a personal challenge. There's nothing down there, if you can't simply walk down the pathway to the beach what are you ever going to achieve in life. I went down the path purely because I didn't want to go down it. I trundled along to the deserted beach, took a picture to record the moment and happily trundled back to the road.

Next on the list was to gaze upon the $30 million state government building (strangely the government only sits 11 days a year), but even after that it was still only 11.00am and my bus to the airport wasn't due to go until 1.30pm. Luckily I chanced upon the old telegraph house, an engaging little building, which really caught my eye with the sign 'free entry'. In the three-quarters of an hour I was in the house there was only one other visitor, but it was surprisingly interesting. I still had time to kill and wandered into an aboriginal shop actually owned by aborigines. A couple of hand-crafted pieces were sought and found, the attendant telling me all manner of interesting details. From the special paper the pieces are wrapped in to stop them sweating to the details of the last Cannonball Run. I thought it was just a film but no it was alive and kicking in Australia with cars racing on a 5,000 kilometre route of Darwin, Alice Springs, Uluru and back. Although he said that the first race had only been held a couple of years ago. I must have spent 20 minutes chatting to him, by which time the clock had struck 1.10pm and I still had to re-pack my bags which had been hastily thrown into the hostel's luggage room.

All packed, I headed across the main road for my bus from the airport shuttle office, meanwhile, the bus passed me. The driver must have recognised my airport destined looking face, as he stopped, picked me up and told me I should have booked. I truthfully said that I had booked. Strangely the time was still only 1.25pm.

After my Indian led paranoia about not being confirmed on the flight list came to nothing, I chatted away to Jurgen the German and then on the plane to Bruce the Australian. Okay, those names were kind of made up, but as is common you speak to these people for ages without knowing their name. The thing is, do these people actually have names? Since I was a kid, this conspiracy theory developed in my head that there are television cameras permanently on me, showing my life to a worldwide audience and that everyone I meet is really an actor or actress. When I'm not there the world doesn't operate properly, it's all a big conspiracy. Just before I reach the corner of a street people are dawdling about waiting for a signal from the director to play people in the street. This theory is fuelled when I meet someone and think I'm sure I've met you before, it's because they're an actor and they've been an extra in 'Jeff – a social experiment' more than once. Now 99.99% of me realises it isn't true but it is a nice theory nonetheless. (Editorial note: An idea I obviously shared with whoever dreamed up the film 'The Truman Show'. Unless that film was created just to throw me off the scent).

When the plane hung over Kuala Lumpur I could see the occasional flash of bright light from the city below. I looked down and could see 18 floodlit golf holes. I'd never considered a floodlit golf course before let alone seen one. As we came into land I realised that the light flashes weren't all coming from the city below but the lightning storm around us. After landing safely we taxied across the runway. Then as I looked across from my small window I could see a big plane land with a clatter of white lightning in the background. Exactly the same picture I had seen in my dreams but white lights not red. Surely everyone has dreams and every so often they can be linked into a real event, although it was very spooky.

I spent a couple of weary hours in the main hub of Kuala Lumpur airport and then went to get my plane. But before that, I had to pass through those metal detector machines. I took all the money out of my pockets, placed my ventolin on the plate and even remembered to take off my St. Christopher medallion. I was sure there was no metal on me. 'BEEP!' Had it just slipped mum and dad's mind to mention to me that I'm not their flesh and blood, instead I'm an android experiment that strived for physical and mental perfection but went sadly wrong? I was too tired to worry about it. I just concentrated on staying awake until seat 35C had been allocated to my body.

DIARY 4

Stu stayed in Australia for 6 months, before moving on to Borneo, Vietnam, Cambodia and China. Meanwhile, I continued to live in Frisby-on-the-Wreake and work in the nearby town of Melton Mowbray. What can I say about Melton Mowbray? Home of the pork pie and alleged originator of the term 'painting the town red' (thanks to the Marquis of Waterford, some pots of paint and copious amounts of alcohol). Melton is a nice town, but in 1999 I felt I knew nearly every bit of it and would see the same faces every lunchtime and each Saturday night. I needed a bit of an adventure, to see new faces and maybe find lost cities in the Andes.

	UK	Peru	South America
Population in millions	65.6	31.5	419
Projected population in 2050 in millions	77	40.1	494
Infant mortality per 1000 live births	3.9	17	17
Life expectancy - male	79	72	72
Life expectancy - female	83	77	79
Gross national income in purchasing power parity divided by population (in $)	40,550	11,960	14,628
Area of country (square miles)	93,638	496,225	6,880,000

NOTE: Peru seems like a normal South American country

It is 1999 so please fasten your seat belts as we head towards the end of the 20th century. It is the time when people worried that the Millennium Bug would be causing chaos, the London eye was erected, Jill Dando was murdered, Kevin Keegan took over the England manager job from Glenn Hoddle and, in response to the atrocities in Yugoslavia, the bombing of Belgrade was carried out by NATO. As for films, well if you take the red pill you will watch 'The Matrix' and if you take the blue pill you will see 'Notting Hill'. Can I play Prince's '1999'? You're right that is cheating, but what if I make it Peruvian by playing a pan-pipe version? Oh okay, let's listen to 'Californication' by the Red Hot Chilli Peppers.

DAY 1 - SATURDAY 10ᵀᴴ JULY 1999 - VIVA SOUTH AMERICA

It was midday when I perched on a Heathrow Airport toilet. The remnants of several pints of bitter from the previous night's party topped up by the morning's malaria tablets had caused a somewhat disgruntled stomach. I sat as I travelled, by myself. Well, that's not entirely true as there were people at the sinks a few feet away but on the outside of my cubicle (I would say within touching distance but it seems somewhat inappropriate in a public convenience).

The peace of the cubicle proved an ideal place to contemplate how I ended up on the verge of travelling to Colombia of all places. I have recovered from hangovers in strange places but Bogota, probably the most dangerous city in the world, was a strange choice. To make matters even worse, last Thursday there had been an uprising there and at least 50 people were shot dead, as one of my friends took perverse delight in informing me. Well, to be honest, I'm only going to Colombia on my way to Peru, which brings the question, why Peru?

I think it started in India when a traveller told me that in two years of backpacking his best memory was the first glimpse of Machu Picchu in Peru. I'd also worked out that my numerous jabs were wearing out so I would have to be stabbed several more times unless I got a move on. Having said all that it may have been my feelings of boredom with Melton Mowbray that drove me over the edge; pork pies can only cause a sense of excitement for so long.

Travelling alone to Peru sounds impressive but I'm one of a group of 20 who will meet up in Lima for an organised tour, so I have effectively sub-contracted the plotting and planning. I'd not been on an organised trip before but thought it was my best chance to see as much as possible, in a limited amount of time, in a country that didn't speak English. I spotted one chap who could be on the same trip. He looked about 65, bearded, with a big 'Exodus' holdall. As the trip I'm on is run by Exodus that seemed a bit of a clue to his destination. If he is typical of the trip I could be the youngest by about 30 years, but maybe the bingo nights will be good.

After much pondering, I left the sanctuary of the cubicle and headed towards the departure lounge. The flight was with Avianca who are the

Columbian national airline. Their organisational skills did not impress me when it turned out that my seat was between a husband and wife. I switched seats and made conversation with the young couple. A young couple going to Peru, were they part of the Exodus trip? No, they were on the rival 'Explore' tour. Although, they said the three-week schedules were very similar and it was likely that our paths would cross in Peru. Avianca started the in-flight entertainment, after three hours, with a Brazilian film; I think they should stick to football. My understanding of the film was not helped by the heads in front of me blocking out the English subtitles. The second and final film was Shakespeare in Love, which the headphones provided in either English or Spanish. I was eager to build up my Spanish vocabulary, which was based on several episodes of Fawlty Towers, but plumped for the mother tongue.

Eleven hours after leaving Heathrow the plane reached Bogota. I had purposefully kept awake for the flight because my theory was that if I kept awake for the whole journey I would be shattered on arrival at the Lima hotel. Then I thought I'd sleep really well at the hotel and at the proper local time, thus becoming accustomed to the six-hour time difference quite quickly.

My dubious plan was stretched in Bogota when the scheduled two-hour wait gained an extra hour without any explanation. I chatted away to a Scottish lad on a two-week Explore trip, he was meant to have met a friend at Heathrow airport. However, his friend seemed to have missed the Edinburgh to London connection. The suspected reason was a hangover caused by an ill-timed work outing. I don't know, these people that go out the night before travelling. I also met a couple from Seagrave, which is only a few miles from my village, who were on the three-week Explore trip. Is it just me and the bearded chap on the Exodus holiday? Is he even on the same Exodus trip?

We landed in Lima at 1.00am local time, 7.00am my body's time. Finally, at Passport Control, I met a number of Exodus travellers so we set about trying to find the guides. I wandered off and found a guide but she was from Explore. Rob from Exodus then quickly appeared, rounded up the stragglers and off we set through the streets of Lima in a minibus. The first impressions of Lima were scrambled by the thought of bed and sleep, sleep and bed. I was quite pleased that the bingo nights now only seemed a faint possibility as nearly everyone seemed to be in their thirties.

On arrival at our hotel, the Pasada Del Inca, there was a lonely figure huddled in a coat who had been awaiting our presence for a couple of hours. Although an Irishman, he was working in the Bahamas where the night time temperature would have been in the seventies so he didn't appreciate the cool Lima night. The group were divided up and I headed towards the room to be shared with Mark, the huddled figure, and Russell, the bearded 65-year-old with the Exodus holdall.

After a quick scan of the room, I headed to the reception for a reunion with my rucksack via the lift. It was obvious I was on the fourth floor but the other options were fifth, third, second, first and something in Spanish. I was fairly confident that the something in Spanish was ground floor. I pressed the button. Moments later the door slid open and a confused Jeff was greeted by a car park. I narrowed the options down to: I had just entered the twilight zone (I listened out for a deep American voice announcing 'A MAN ON VACATION IN PERU ENTERS THE LIFT OF DESTINY'), I had been slipped a mind-bending drug (such as a malaria tablet) or it was an American lift. I had just become the first of 12 British victims to reach the car park rather than the ground floor (which apparently is the first floor in American).

Day 2 - Sunday 11th July - Amigos

I slept intermittently, not helped by some loud snoring from Russell which I whinged to Mark about in the morning, although he didn't hear anything. Two minutes later Russell whinged about the snoring he heard in the night, so it was either Mark or a group effort.

The morning brought our inaugural official meeting with the leaders Rob and Jenny. The group of 20 set eyes on each other and everybody seemed fairly lively and very friendly. The first briefing had barely finished when I earned a nickname from Jen and Fiona, the English-born Australian citizens. In Peru, it can be very difficult to change travellers' cheques, so instead most people carry bundles of American dollars. These are easily exchanged for the local currency of sols or you can sometimes just pay for items in dollars. There were about three sols to the dollar and five sols to the pound. I had paid my 30 dollars for the afternoon's trip but Fiona had a 50 dollar bill so I offered the smaller notes in my hand to help. However, I had innocently, yes innocently, mixed my green 10 dollar bills with the 10 sol notes leading to the outcome of a nice healthy profit. Albeit a 20 second healthy profit because Fiona exchanged notes again and re-named me Dodgy.

The bus tour in the afternoon introduced us to the sights and sounds of Lima. The dull grey sky caused by the sea mist is apparently a fixture from

May to November and means that, if what I have seen is typical, most months pass by without even a sight of the sun. The first stop was a pretty square surrounded by colonial buildings. As soon as we stepped off the bus for a five-minute photograph stop we were approached by hawkers selling their wares. The most compelling of these was a little lad of about 10 years who desperately wanted to clean Phil the Canadian's boots. It was true that his walking boots were in desperate need of a polish, but this was only a quick break and as Phil pointed out to him there just was not time. This did not stop the lad producing a desperately sad face and a forlorn '*Amigo, I clean your shoes, Amigo*'. He relentlessly stuck by Phil's side from the moment a big Canadian foot landed on the pavement, throughout the walk on the square, before following him to the bus still saying a desperately sad '*Amigo*' as if Phil had badly let him down.

Phil sat on the departing bus with the lad staring up at him with the saddest puppy dog eyes you could ever see.

The bus travelled on for another half mile to the Plaza De Armas where Lima cathedral is situated. The guide had expected it to be closed but luckily for us, its doors were open and welcoming visitors. A chapel inside the cathedral housed the remains of Francisco Pizarro, the Spaniard who conquered Peru. He had just 170 men but met up with the Inca leader and massacred thousands of warriors. Then to control the Incas he held their emperor, Atahualpa, as a hostage. Atahualpa pleaded for freedom and claimed he would fill his cell with gold if he was set free. After about six months the room was covered in gold but the Spanish still feared his power so killed him and crowned an emperor that they controlled. The Spanish had a couple of major advantages in their brutal conquest. The Inca's initially thought they were gods because they came from the sea and were scared of the horses that the Spanish cavalry charged them with, as they had never seen such strange beasts. Oh, and guns – that helped.

Anyway, after our first Peruvian history lesson, we left the cathedral and the first sound Phil heard as he passed the doors was '*Amigo*'. His shoeshine boy had magically switched squares and wore a delighted smile at the sight of Phil's six foot four-inch frame with accompanying dirty boots. Phil had time on his hands, his boots needed a clean and he couldn't bear to see the lad wear that sad face again. A price of two sols was agreed and the shoeshine boy enthusiastically went to work. The laces even came out as the lad performed an immaculate job. When he finished, the boots dazzled even in the dull Lima atmosphere and he asked Phil for his 10 sols. Phil reminded him that two sols was the agreed price, which brought on the sad face again, so gave him five for doing such a good job.

The next port of call was the Franciscan Monastery and its amazing catacombs. The crypt, which apparently holds the remains of 70,000 people, was only re-discovered about 50 years ago. I can't say we saw much of the vast crypt but there were skulls and bones laid out in synchronised patterns. The group nearly added a couple more skulls to the collection by taking it in turns to clatter into the low stone doorframes. All 18 of the group clambered back on to the bus. That's right we had already lost two people, if we carry on at this rate there should be about five people left to visit Machu Picchu. Anyone lost in the catacombs could be down there for hours as it is effectively a maze, but no one could remember our missing duo entering the monastery. The main school of thought was that we must have lost Andrea and Mary outside the cathedral.

The final stop of the tour was at the gold museum where we not only found an abundance of the precious metal but also Andrea and Mary. The museum provided our first glimpse of mummified Indians and ancient skulls with holes in the top. The original owners of the skulls had been operated on and even lived to tell the tale because the skulls often showed signs of healing.

Our dinner was then forthcoming at an Italian restaurant where Rob the guide confirmed his vocations had included being an opera writer, a marine and a music teacher. The conversation moved on to tropical diseases where I was made to feel inadequate as others listed typhoid and malaria among their past ailments, plus stories of friends who had parasites crawling out of their feet. Mumps in a caravan at Sheringham when I was 10 was the best I could muster.

The only people who didn't make it to the meal were Roger and Anna (the fruitarians), and Russell. Roger and Anna were vegans at home in Cambridge but as the Peruvians were unsure of such a term they had made the decision to just eat fruit thus affectionately became known as the fruities. Meanwhile, Russell had spent much of the day logging down in his book the exact sequence of events from dawn to dusk, and because he didn't feel hungry, decided to write up a neat copy.

I was still struck that everybody on the trip seemed intelligent, interesting, funny and friendly, which brought a couple of questions. Why the hell had I been allowed to join this trip? And did the Peruvians still require human sacrifices?

Day 3 - Monday 12ᵀᴴ July - Bird or Bloke?

Depending on whom you asked, the night had gunshots, frequent car alarms and an earth tremor. I can confirm that in my room the earth never moved for me, Mark and Russell.

The morning brought about our introduction to the truck that would be our home for the next couple of weeks. It was a big Mercedes vehicle with a cab at the front for Jenny and Rob, then 24 seats in the back. Rather than comprising of the typical two seats - isle - two seats design, it had a sort of open plan set up. There was a back row of four seats, on both sides there were another four seats which faced each other, then two sets of two seats facing forward which faced another two sets of two seats which looked backwards. Then there were a few steps up to a set of four seats that faced the front and overlooked the cab, giving a good view of the road ahead. The open plan design meant it was easy to chat with several people at once, so instead of talking to just one person at a time you had the chance to simultaneously annoy almost everybody.

Before we could travel on the truck there was the task of fitting our rucksacks and holdalls in the lockers beneath the seats. This involved fighting for space in a sea of bodies, bags and flying sleeping bags; side pockets were emptied and goods rearranged until the bags were pushed, pulled and bullied into the holes. Apparently, this chaotic process left one traveller in tears on the last trip but it all seemed good fun to me, my problem of the morning was yet to come.

I thought I'd be sensible before the long bus ride ahead and visit the little boy's room. I found the hotel toilets with a little difficulty. The first door showed a face with long hair so that was obviously the ladies and the second door showed a different face with long hair so that was ... that was confusing. A quick look again revealed neither face had a beard, which would have made it far too simple. This must be where the guides earn their money. I consulted Rob who confirmed that the urinals were contained behind the door with the straight long hair rather than the platted long hair.

The first trip in the truck provided an educational experience for me as I learnt where the good old English two-fingered V-sign allegedly originated. Apparently, when the French caught our archers in 1415 they used to cut those particular two fingers off to stop them firing arrows again. In typical bantering tradition the fully fingered English bowmen would stick their respective two fingers in the air to taunt the French. I raved on about what a fascinating fact it was while everybody else seemed to say '*yeah, I know that*'. But did they know what long platted hair meant on a Peruvian toilet door?

The truck did not have an on-board toilet instead it had a buzzer. When you pressed the button it buzzed in the driving cab. One buzz for a photo stop, two for a toilet stop, three for the bus to start again after a stop and one long buzz for an emergency. James had the first bladder to crack and asked for the buzzer to be pressed which caused the expected derisory comments before nearly everyone followed him out the door. When people headed back to the truck all that could be seen were 15 sets of footprints into the dunes which each led to a wet patch of desert. The rules were simple; find a suitable location, check the wind to ensure no embarrassing blowback and stand or squat until your deed is complete. If it is to be a solid release the trowel should be utilised to ensure an underground resting place for the disposal of the product of your labour. When you return to the truck there is some detergent to spray on to your hands. The detergent is used strictly because germs can spread like wildfire on a little truck like ours. Job complete, return to seat and engage satisfied smile.

Lunch approached along with the town of Seca. As we trooped off the truck it became apparent that we were the only gringos in town. The group were sufficiently strange to attract stares but it was very much curiosity and not malicious so I enjoyed the new found star status. A suitable restaurant was located as I performed a wonderful sheep impression by following the main crowd. The food was fine, and the people were kind and helpful especially the old lady serving the food who had blood dripping from a finger bandage. They even tried to welcome us by stopping the palatable Peruvian music on the stereo and replacing it with some dodgy pop music of the early eighties. The old lady brought us some cups of coffee, which caused some confusion because instead of being brown it was a hot white liquid that just looked like a milky substance. A couple of people tasted it and then she brought out the coffee powder, enlightened faces spooned the coffee into the hot milk and hey presto a cup of coffee.

In the late afternoon the truck reached the Paracas Nature Reserve where we jumped out in a quest to photograph some pelicans. This necessitated traipsing across sandy surfaces and unfortunately for Phil, wet sandy surfaces. The new found shine of his shoes quickly became dull mucky brown.

The hotel was nearby and I shared a room with Russell. Again Russell was unsure as to whether he would join the rest of us at a restaurant and I was concerned about our door lock hanging perilously by a screw. I managed to solve both problems by mentioning, to the security conscious Russell, about how easy it would be to kick the door down, thus he was happy to stay in the room all night and I was happy to go out all night.

As we were by the coast the night was spent at a seafood restaurant and I enjoyed a plate of scallops and rice. I'm sure the sound of purring taste buds could be heard a mile away as it is probably the most delicious meal I have ever had. The food glided down to my stomach on the back of a couple of wine size bottles of beer, which left me as a contented man. Jenny the guide provided a bit of recent Peruvian history to set the scene for modern Peru. The Shining Path was the main terrorist force from the 1970s through to the 1990s. Their ideas were based on Marxist ideals and its members were mainly from the poorest areas of the country. The eighties seemed to be a depressing time because the Shining Path would turn up in villages suspected of government collaboration and slaughter the village, then blame it on the government troops. At the same time, the government troops would arrive in villages, suspected of sympathising with the Shining Path, and slaughter the village then blame it on the Shining Path. The situation reached such a low that many villagers deserted their homes for the safety of the cities. It is only now that people are returning to the villages. Executions by the terrorists were common and foreigners were by no means off the target list.

In the early 1990s the leader of the Shining Path was caught and the organisation crumbled so most attacks are now limited to the odd car bomb. In remote areas vehicles can be stopped and asked for a 'donation', but not with the violent intent of previous years. So, in summary, I could still rest easy in my bed.

Day 4 - Tuesday 13ᵗʰ July - Hot, Wet and Stupid

The 7.30am breakfast consisted of the practical and the Paddington, with a diet of marmalade sandwiches and malaria tablets. I don't know whether it is coincidence or not that marmalade sandwiches are available for breakfast in Peru but I am slightly bemused.

After my stomach accepted the early morning concoction we headed down to the little port where a speedboat would take us to the Ballestas Islands. I had never been in a speedboat. Although my excitement took a knock when Rob's first warning was that the boat would normally go out when other vessels were around in case there is a problem i.e. it capsizes and you could get picked up by the other boats, cue the putting on of life jackets. His second warning was that you needed a waterproof jacket, not just for the sea, but the vast number of birds on the islands meant that there would be an awfully large number of bowels releasing contents in every direction.

The speedboat finally set off and entertainment was soon forthcoming when the first proper wave crashed against the side of the boat sending water over my new Irish friends, TC and Jill. I sat snugly on the opposite side of the boat content in the knowledge that I should stay dry on the outward journey but the return trip may require a change of seat.

The boat sped by a 100 metre high candelabra shape carved into the side of a hill. The reasons as to why and who created it are unknown but the most famous theory comes from a book by Eric Von Daniken. He believed that it was an ancient sign for alien spaceships that pointed them in the direction of the equally mysterious Nasca Lines. The fact that it doesn't actually point towards the Nasca Lines did not seem to have a bearing on his conclusions.

On the first island we approached a sea lion which lay some 30 feet away, and everyone scrambled for the best position to take a picture. Frustratingly I could not get a good shot but managed a couple of attempts on the basis that I may not receive a better opportunity. Five minutes later there were three sea lions that lay before us so I grabbed the chance of a decent photograph. A further five minutes passed by and there were 10 sea lions around the next corner on another side of the island, which was just too good an opportunity to miss so I took some more photographs. It was just a shame I had seemingly wasted the pictures from my first two efforts. Around the corner, there were about 50 covering some rocks so I sighed then took some more photographs convinced they were mocking the stupid humans.

Other rocks were a mass of terns, cormorants and various other feathered friends which prompted our local guide to announce '*it is the local tradition at this point to close your eyes lay your head back and receive a gift from the heavens*'. However, Rob's warning remained fresh in our minds so instead of 20 gaping mouths facing skywards, it was 20 hats and hoods that went on as everyone awaited the stealth shitters first raid.

After we moved out of the danger zone I readied myself for the return journey, all too aware that my seat may be a prime target for the waves. It was even more concerning in that TC and Jill had a plastic covering which could be pulled up from the edge of the boat which after a bit of manoeuvring could keep them dry. Our side had no such luxury.

The first wave arrived, TC and Jill got wet. I could not work out why it was their side of the boat that always received gifts from the sea but I didn't like to complain. Obviously, the luck of the Irish doesn't work in South America.

The time had only reached 9.30am when the boat returned to port and we were soon heading south in the truck. We stopped for lunch after three hours travelling and started the search for a restaurant. The group again utilised the sheep-like strategy to flock together and by the time we found a place to eat required a table for 12. Phil and I were both keen to try the traditional Peruvian dish of ceviche which consists of marinated fish, hot peppers, corn, onions and potatoes. It was a bit too spicy for me but Phil gleefully tucked in, until that is he came across the mother of all chillies which he thought was an ordinary pepper. Now Phil could handle his hot food and the slice of ordinary looking red pepper was quickly bitten into and swallowed. His face didn't mess about with different shades of red, it headed straight to scarlet as various words of advice were cast his way, *'eat some more food'*, *'try to bring it back up'*, *'drink some water'*, *'don't drink any water'*.

I carefully found my red chilli pepper then kindly offered it around. James volunteered to see how hot it really was. First with the toilet buzzer and now this, did the man know no fear or was he just stupid? As his audience waited with bated breath James picked up the chilli and brought it up to his mouth. He then proceeded to stick his tongue out, lick the pepper and agree it was very hot. Thus in answer to my own question, I'm not sure about the brave but definitely not stupid. Meanwhile, it took about 15 minutes for Phil to recover and another minute or so to tell people it wasn't that bad and they should try it! The excitement surrounding the pepper was only interrupted by the interest in the men's toilet. There was only one door to the toilet, which enclosed a gutter type of urinal, but the door was only three feet tall. Granted it started a couple of feet off the floor in order to hide the main event but males and females in the restaurant could happily chat away to the pisser in occupation. Meals never seem this interesting in England.

The afternoon continued on the truck where a game of musical chairs seemed to have developed. Every time we returned to the truck people would have swapped places so you had someone new to chat with, which meant the hours spent on the truck would pass merrily by. Then, from a good idea of playing a game, my torture began. I had missed the first minute of the game's explanation but grasped that it was called 'The Emperor Likes …'. One person would start the game off by saying something that the emperor liked, then individually each person would ask 'does the emperor like' and guess what they thought the emperor would like. The original person would then say whether the emperor did actually like it or not. In summary, I was totally confused. However, there was a common thread to the things the emperor liked and the aim of the game was to work out what they had in common so, on your guess, the originator would hopefully confirm that the emperor liked it.

As rounds of guesses passed by people began to figure out the pattern and could give further examples of what the emperor liked. Apparently, the emperor liked tights but not cheese, he liked Pat but did not like Helen, he liked Scotland but didn't like England or hardly any of my guesses come to that. The times I was getting a *'yes the emperor likes that Jeff'* confused me even more because I didn't know why I had just got the answer right. 10 rounds of guesses had passed, by which time there were eight people constantly having confirmation that the emperor did like their guess and two people becoming intensely frustrated by either *'no Jen, the emperor does not like that'* or *'no Jeff, the emperor does not like that'*. The emperor likes treacle, the emperor likes lightening, the emperor likes computers etc. etc. Another couple of rounds passed by as eight happy faces relayed correct answers and two people provided more wrong answers. How could everyone else find this game so easy but me and Jen, who sat next to each other, feel equally stupid? Our pleads to end the game were unanimously dismissed by the others as we re-named 'The Emperor Likes ... ' as 'The Smug Bastards Game'. Just when I didn't think things could get worse they did, with an *'oh I get it'* Jen deserted me and it became nine smug bastards and one Mr Thicko. Another round passed and the only thing I realised was that an alternative to the normal ending of the game, which is where everybody realises the answer, would be for me to jump out the window under the tyres of an oncoming car and end my misery. Jen and Jill tried to help me, think Jeff, he likes treacle, he likes ports, he likes trains, he loves a good titter. Belatedly the penny finally dropped, it's the letter T, he likes anything with the letter T in, alleluia.

My joy was short lived as the second game of 'The Emperor Likes ...' began. This time I came in about ninth place and Jen in tenth as we pieced together the emperor's liking for Australia, snakes, America, sausages, Abba to be words that ended with the same letter that they began. A couple more games provided a bit more suffering but at least we began to beat the odd smug bastard, however, we agreed that we didn't want to play the game again until our shredded intellectual prowess had recovered.

As darkness fell, the truck reached a hotel in the small town of Nasca. The day was far from over though, as we were not allowed the luxury of actually staying in the hotel but were camping in the grounds. Jenny the guide said that she would demonstrate how to put up a tent. The words were hardly out her mouth when Fiona kindly offered her and Jen's as the demonstration tent. Thus whilst everyone else hammered around in the dark, Fiona and Jen visited the bar to sample the traditional Peruvian drink called Pisco Sour, a powerful brandy combined with egg whites and lemon. It seemed a strange concoction but tasted okay and provided the necessary fuel for Fiona to celebrate her birthday.

The group had been split into three cooking teams that each had to produce three meals over the next couple of weeks. Therefore as the first group slaved away to produce a chicken curry, Jen and I decided to teach some of the others a new game. The others consisted of people who had not played 'The Emperor Likes …' on the bus. We taught them the rules and played the exact four games that were played earlier. The difference was that we knew the answers and it was other people's turn to squirm. This cast a whole new light on a fine game.

My mood was so good I even offered to buy Fiona a birthday drink but the bar said that they had run out of lemons so could not make any more Pisco Sours. Five minutes later and after a trip to the truck, Fiona was at the bar again asking for a Pisco Sour. As the lady explained there were no lemons, Fiona produced a couple on the bar. The barmaid took the lemons and trudged away to make yet another batch of Pisco Sour. I enjoyed a couple of beers and a Pisco Sour then stopped drinking because I had been warned, before I left England, that Nasca was not the place to be nursing a hangover.

DAY 5 - WEDNESDAY 14ᵗʰ JULY - A FLIGHT OF FANTASY

The time was 7.30am as I opened the tent flaps to peer upwards. The sight brought an early morning smile crashing down as mist and cloud obscured my view of the heavens. I had travelled halfway around the world to see one of the great mysteries of South America but the weather seemed intent on spoiling the day.

Our group were meant to spend just the morning in Nasca before enduring a seven-hour drive to Puerto Inca. Unless the sky cleared then Peru's Nasca Lines would remain an even greater mystery to me. The Lines are made up of animal figures, shapes and straight lines drawn in a 525 square kilometre section of the desolate Pampa de San Jose plain. Despite some of the shapes being 200 metres in length, they are not noticeable on the ground. It was only the advent of flying that brought about the reports of strange shapes in the desert. Rather than being cut or built most of the shapes were created by clearing the top surface of the plain, but what makes them incredible is how they could be drawn without seeing them from above. Hence one idea is that they were built by aliens rather than an ancient Peruvian culture.

Other more feasible theories involve the lines being paths to sacred sites or astronomical calendars and that the architects may even have invented a primitive method of flight. The truth though is that no one is quite sure how, why, when and by whom they were created. That morning I was not so interested in the thinking behind them, all I wanted to do was board the plane and see them with my own eyes.

Breakfast passed but the clouds and mist remained. The time had edged past 9.30am, but the only change was that the weather had become darker and duller, which seemed to match the mood. Rob announced that as the weather was unfit for flying, a video about the Lines would be shown in the hotel complex and that the clouds may lift a bit later. I trudged towards the hotel, realising in my heart of hearts, I would not be able to see the Lines for myself. Mark talked of missing out on other trips, for example, Lake Titicaca, so we could stay in Nasca for another day. It made sense, although our hotels are booked for the next few days so it would take a notoriously difficult unanimous decision before the plan could be actioned. The video provided little consolation. In fact, it served only to increase my desire to see the mysterious shapes in the desert.

The documentary had ticked on for three-quarters of an hour when a beam of light shone through from a skylight. Could the sun really be making an appearance? Dare we dream of blue skies? The beam metamorphisised to a stream and amazingly a blue sky greeted us.

The group headed back to the campsite and were greeted with the news 'you can fly'. 'I can fly! I can fly!' I excitedly thought whilst turning into a character from Peter Pan. Rob told us 'okay, there is one plane available at the moment, so the first 12 ready, need to get across the road quick before the weather changes'. A Second World War airfield scene developed as people scrambled in all directions, it was just cameras rather than goggles that eager hands were searching out.

Never mind the first 12, I was in the first three as our little plane filled up. I had never been in a small plane before so I was excited about that, excited about seeing the Lines, excited that after my hopes had been dashed they had risen in a phoenix-like style and generally excited about being excited.

The first shape appeared in the form of a whale. The chatter started, it's a whale? Where? Oh yeah! I see it? 'Brilliant!' Although the whale was on our right-hand side the pilot ensured that everybody could see it, without leaning over, by banking the plane at a 45 degree angle then went back again so it was on our left-hand side and again banked at a 45 degree angle. The banking just increased the fun as the plane tilted one way and another. Next, it was the triangles, then the trapezoid, astronaut (well a strange humanish shape), and duck. It was one of the best experiences of my life as we flew above this historic sight and I enjoyed the twirling movements of the plane. We continued to see one shape after another, hands, dog, monkey, condor, tree.

Gradually the happy chatter died out and was replaced by a deathly silence, the banking plane was no longer fun but pure torture as 12 stomachs desperately clung to their contents. I feared the consequences of peering out the window to the right and only dared to look out the window six inches from my left side. I directed the air vent straight down and did not move my head from the glorious stream of cold air.

The animals kept coming, parrot, yes, spider, yes (the spider looked good but I was slightly distracted by checking for the whereabouts of the sick bag), hummingbird. Although no one mentioned feeling bad everyone realised the situation and that if just one person was actually sick it would set off everybody else. This was a real team effort. In front of me, both Andrea and Paula eyed up the one sick bag between their two seats as things threatened to get a bit messy. The last shape, called alcatraz, eventually appeared and the final banking to the left and right was endured before the plane took a nice straight path back to the airport.

A very pale group left the plane and spent the next hour clinging to the ground but it was worth the agony because I had seen the Nasca Lines with my very own eyes. Luckily as I was in the first plane it gave me two hours to recover before we had to be driven on the truck. Although the group's first thought was about our stomachs, the second thought was that we should be feeling better by the time the others return and would be ideally placed to laugh at them (obviously in a sympathetic manner).

After their flight, the second group, who had flown in a smaller plane, were looking far too healthy for our liking but Fiona confirmed that it may be the fact that she had already filled a sick bag on the plane.

After two hours TC, who had flown with another group, finally appeared and happily jumped straight on the truck to ride into town. I don't think he has an iron constitution rather a black box constitution because he looked healthier after the flight than before it.

In the town, we went to a pottery where a local showed us the fine art of making Inca pots. His ancestors were not a family of potters it just so happened that his father was a grave robber who found some original Inca moulds which allowed them the chance to re-enact the ancient methods. The main problem they had was how to produce the sheen that the Incas managed. After a number of attempts the best method they found, that was also available hundreds of years ago, was to use sweat and grease. Not any sweat and grease, but after trying various parts of the body, nose grease (outside rather than inside) was found to provide the best shine. In fact, the pots were so authentic looking that 'REPLICA' had to be written on the bottom.

At lunchtime the group spread their wings. After yesterday's events, Phil and I found ourselves a nice sedate little restaurant and enjoyed a couple of nice plain omelettes, which were noticeably devoid of mysterious looking peppers. I had to answer a call of nature and a friendly couple ushered me to a bathroom in the restaurant. In fact, it turned out to be the family bathroom. There was a curtain for a door, a bath full of water from a dripping ceiling and an unhygienic but usable toilet in the corner. Whatever, I was grateful that they were kind enough to allow me to use their facilities.

We left Nasca and headed south before turning off on to a dirt road. The sight awaiting us was quite incredible. The sun shone down on the desert whose surface was littered with human bones, skulls, bits of pottery and pieces of clothing. Welcome to the Chauchilla Cemetery.

The cemetery would have been home for the dead of the Nasca culture some 1,000 or so years ago. The various paths around the site were marked out by stones but the sheer size of the place meant that we would only see part of it. I could not get over the fact that in Britain you may be able to creep close to this sort of history under close supervision. But here we were left to our own devices and could easily pick up ancient pottery or fabric. In fact, Jenny told us that on the last trip a couple of girls approached her to air their suspicions that an eccentric old lady had something mysterious in her truck locker. Jenny had a quiet word with her and they took the human bones out the locker before returning them to their grave.

As well as its incredible history the Chauchilla Cemetery possessed what Jenny and Rob referred to as '*the best toilet in Peru*'. As the group queued up to sample the facilities I cursed my luck that I did not need to go. Oh yes, I'd be bursting 20 kilometres from the nearest toilet but a lovely big throne, with padded toilet paper, and neither the bowels or bladder were interested.

In order to counter my disappointment, I thought that I'd try one of the four seats at the top of the bus, which provide a great view of the landscape.

Paula and Phil were already seated as I walked up the steps to join them. I sat next to Phil the amiable Canadian who slowly looked up and said '*I don't want you to sit there Jeff*'. I looked at him taken aback. Phil then explained that he felt sick and unless I was a bucket he didn't want me to sit beside him. I sat down by Paula who informed me that she was feeling rough as well. Unsurprisingly the fourth seat remained empty.

10 minutes later there was a big heave and the contents of Phil's stomach switched its allegiance to the bucket. Poor old Phil looked terrible but my concern was also with Paula and the one bloke who had shared lunch with Phil. The omelettes we had eaten looked fine, tasted okay but the image of the bathroom at the restaurant began to enter my thoughts. Had the kitchen shared the same hygiene standards of the toilet? Should I ask for a bucket now or later?

Phil still had to endure another three hours travelling and Paula still had to endure another three hours of me talking before we turned off the main highway and on to a track. I was glad it was pitch black because the track twisted and turned down the cliff side with what seemed to be sheer drops waiting for any driver that drifted a foot off course. One corner needed us to mount the bank to make the bend but 100 yards further on lay the town of Puerto Inca.

There may not have been much of the day remaining but we still had to put up our tents and it was my cooking group's turn as we organised a barbecue. In the nearest bar enjoying a beer were the Explore group who had arrived hours before, enjoyed a good meal in the restaurant and were about to leave for their comfortable hotel beds. I, on the other hand, would spend midnight doing the washing up.

The dog from the hotel sniffed around for scraps from our barbecue, and had such a successful time he ran across to one of the tents to test its water resistance. I was fairly certain that it hadn't been mine but thought it would be prudent to check the number of the tent so I could try and steer clear of the dog stained tent next time they had to be erected.

The positive side to not enjoying a comfortable bed was the warmth of the campfire, the softness of the sand, the sound of the Pacific Ocean, the bright stars of the southern hemisphere and the companionship of my new found friends. It never had been an ambition of mine to camp on a Peruvian beach but maybe it should have been. After sharing a nip of whisky with Pete and Rob I headed off to my tent. I fell asleep barely 20 yards away from the sea feeling very mellow thanks to the beautiful sound of the lapping waves.

Day 6 - Thursday 15ᵀᴴ July 1999 - The Vomit Sweepstake

I woke up to find that my surroundings were just as serene in the morning light as they had seemed under the stars. The apparent town of Puerto Inca had shrunk to become a village which was basically a hotel complex. However, just a stroll along the beach stood the impressive Inca ruins which had been a major port in bygone times.

The extra time to explore had been due to the late nature of Wednesday night. It meant that we would not be making the early start needed to beat the nearby roadworks. Peruvian roadworks are a bit different from their British counterparts. Many of the roads seem to be on the sides of cliffs so to lessen the effects of the inevitable mudslides they use explosives at the side of the road. They then create their own controlled mudslide and subsequently delay all the traffic. By setting off at lunchtime it was hoped the disruptions would have ceased.

The truck journey was a long haul and caused us deep delving into our heads to create some entertainment. My own contribution was the vomit sweepstake. After Phil had been sick a comment was made that he would be far from the last. Cue my quip that we should have a sweepstake. Jen provided the little bit of encouragement I needed and within a couple of hours, we were drawing names out of a bag. The British eagerly accepted the concept but I had to explain to Morgan and Anne-Sophie that you won if the person you had drawn out the bag was the next to be sick. It took a little while for the Swedes to decide I was actually being serious and then they were happy to play, in fact, everyone seemed happy to play; so many warped minds in one truck!

It was decided that the winner would receive the equivalent of £16 and the person that was actually sick would reap a £4 cash sum. The image of some poor soul puking their guts up while somebody happily danced around them celebrating a forthcoming windfall was an interesting one. In all fairness to my 'runner', I had pulled out a donkey in the shape of TC, the man whose stomach was totally unperturbed by the gut-wrenching Nasca flight.

We reached a town seemingly in the middle of nowhere and successfully squeezed the truck through the narrow streets until there was a scraping and dragging sound. I was fairly certain that the car attached to our bumper had not been there back at Puerto Inca. Jenny and Rob jumped out the cab, decided they hadn't caused any real damage and made a sharp exit. Apparently, if you stand about too long then the 'rich' gringos will soon receive a lot of local abuse thus it is better to make a strategic retreat. The truck headed to the town square and was greeted by a red laser light shining through our windows. As they can cause temporary blindness I was none too impressed with the friendliness of the little town and just wanted to nip to a shop, buy some food and get the hell out again.

I bought a few items, paid my money and hurried away. Then I heard a Peruvian voice shouting at me. I know it was in Spanish but somehow you realise it is directed at you. I turned around wondering what to expect and was greeted with a smile and the change I had left accidentally on the counter.

The journey re-started and the road finally finished in the city of Arequipa at 11.00pm. Our hotel was a fine old colonial building with an outside wall topped with barbed wire and a locked gate controlled from within the hotel. I soon settled down in the grand old lounge next to a cold beer listening to Rob's stories. The strange mixed with the bizarre as Rob finished with '*I'd just moved into new lodgings where I lived by myself in the house. I started frying some chips, but the phone rang and it was my girlfriend. She kept me talking but on seeing smoke drifting out from under the kitchen door I realised the chips would be a little overcooked. I calmly told her I would have to ring her back and made my way out the back of the house via the patio doors. Luckily there were some sheets on the line and I soaked them in the pond. Quite proud of my initiative I made my way to the kitchen door ready to tackle the fire. As the kitchen door opened thick smoke billowed out, but although I couldn't see anything I knew exactly where the oven was positioned. Ready for my big moment I took a deep breath, ran in, and bumped into someone. I shouted 'Who the hell are you?' 'I'm a fireman' he said. Apparently, the fire had been going on so long that a neighbour had phoned the fire brigade.*

This was the man that was looking after us for three weeks.

I headed off to bed but was disconcerted to feel cramps starting in my stomach. Was this the shape of things to come?

Day 7 - Friday 16th July - Nuns, Pizza and the Snoring Englishman

After constant travelling, it was a relief that the whole of day 7 would be spent in Arequipa. This provided us with our first taste of high altitude because the city is about 2,500 metres above sea level. Although the appearance of the hotel looked relatively luxurious I was crammed in a room with Pete, Phil and Russell. Despite the lack of space it felt good to lie in a bed again. Sleep was intermittent but it gave me a chance to hear the odd gunshot in the night.

The sweepstake was progressing with people spending parts of the last two days journey encouraging their 'runner' to try that strange piece of meat on the dirty little stand, a drop of the local liquor or how about a few more malaria tablets. Mark superbly adopted the right spirit by relentlessly providing inducements to help Mary share the contents of her stomach with everyone. He constantly checked whether she felt ill, was always there to shut a window to make it a bit more stuffy and was the first to offer an equal split of the prize money. Meanwhile, the competition started to hot up with James suffering from bad stomach cramps. This caused Mark to increase his encouragement towards Mary. TC was still looking far too healthy and my best chance of any money would be to puke up to claim the £4. Poor Ann-Sophie had been feeling progressively worse for a few days so she and Morgan headed to the local hospital. I hoped to see them again later.

Reports had filtered through from Mark of a strange figure in the night. Originally he dismissed what he thought his eyes told him as a hallucination from the Larium malaria tablets but no, it was true. On this roughtie-toughtie trek across Peru, where people had packed the essentials in their rucksacks and then re-packed leaving a few of those behind, Andrea was walking about in a dressing gown and slippers. The civilisation brought by the British Empire continues, although she did admit to not packing any walking boots, which could be why the extra space in her bag appeared.

The group were left to their own devices for the day but Jenny advised us not to wear a day bag because they have a nasty habit of dropping their contents on the floor when local thieves slash the bottom. A normal plastic bag would be preferable because it is less obvious and people are unlikely to draw a knife for stealing potential groceries. A few of us wandered into the city, passed the bank with the armed security guards on their doors. I would not have been bothered but they held pistols in their hands rather than in the holsters.

The main sight in Arequipa is the Santa Catalina Monastery, which is basically a separate village within the city. The outside walls used to keep the nuns inside the complex away from any prying eyes. There are still nuns living in a large section of it, but the numerous rooms, courtyards and streets took us a couple of hours to look around. One of the more bizarre rooms had paintings of past nuns but they only used to be painted when they were dead so the portraits showed them with their eyes closed.

By late afternoon the casualty list was updated with news of Jen suffering diarrhoea and headaches. On the way back from the market a dog tried to add the name of Jeff Brown to the list when it decided that my ankle would look good in its mouth, but a quick shimmy took my legs to safety. On the positive side, I was pleased to see Ann-Sophie back from the hospital although she had been prescribed some antibiotics to fight her throat infection.

The sick list meant a depleted crowd headed to Restaurant Monza. I thought the Motor Racing theme would help provide a speedy service, and sure enough, different dishes started to appear as I waited for my food. There were pizzas and pasta dishes in all directions except directly below me where there was a distinct space, in fact quite quickly everyone had a dish in front of them except me. Time passed by and not only did everyone have a dish in front of them they soon had an empty plate in front of them. Eventually, when everybody else had finished, my pizza arrived, but even after the long wait I wasn't very hungry and could only eat half of it. Apparently, the high altitude can reduce your appetite but I was quite happy because it did not seem to have much of an effect on my body. I had been concerned that it would set off my asthma but whilst others mentioned a slight shortness of breath my chest felt fine.

Rather than the altitude being of any immediate danger, it was the Peruvian road safety that posed more of a threat. Although cramming six people into a taxi (with Mark and I on the front seat) may not have helped. I preferred my position on the edge rather than Mark's in the middle because a bump and a nasty bend could have meant that before the next change of gear, a surgeon and tub of vaseline would be required.

We arrived safely back at the hotel where a flower arrangement appeared outside everybody's room courtesy of Roger and Anna. Jolly civilised. The stomach cramps and I went to bed together but I struggled to sleep, thanks to Russell's snoring which became progressively louder. I thought I could sleep through most things but the decibels were too great so a cunning plan was hatched. Russell's bed was little more than an arms-length away so I could give a quick tug on his sheets, disturb him without waking him. Thus stop him snoring for enough time for me to start sleeping. I gingerly leaned across, gave his sheet a quick tug and made a lightening retreat to a sleeping pose. The snoring did not break its rhythm. What was needed was a bigger pull, so I leaned right across for a better grip of his undersheet, realising that if he awoke at that precise moment it would look a little odd. Tug, retreat, fast asleep position. The snoring stopped, the rhythm had been disrupted and I could sleep.

The peace lasted ten seconds before the snoring found its beat at a lower level and built up again. I leaned across at full stretch, with everything above the waist outside my bed and my balance being kept by holding on to the edge of Russell's bed. The plan was a bloody good tug, which would not only disturb Russell's snoring but also give me the momentum to get back into bed. Insufficient momentum or gripping the sheets too long and I would fall out of bed, however, the clunk of body meeting floor might wake everybody up so at least the snoring would stop. I gripped, pulled, let go, hit the pillow, closed my eyes and the only sound I could hear was a disturbed Russell moving around in his bed. Behind my eyelids, it was recognised Russell's disturbance was my peace, and sleep would be mine.

Day 8 - Saturday 17ᵗʰ July - The Road Too High

The truck was due to leave at 8.00am, which meant getting up far too early for a shower and the push clothes into rucksack routine. The destination of Chivay lay some 150 kilometres away over many a dirt road. The journey started bumpily as the truck climbed up and up and up but I felt fine if not a little tired from a lack of sleep. The highest point we were due to reach was 4,800 metres (14,600 feet) which is over three times higher than Ben Nevis.

The journey continued, interrupted only by cooking lunch and the now normal toilet stops. However my tiredness grew in the afternoon, then I got a headache, I never get headaches, what was happening? But I didn't worry much about it because I was too busy going hot and cold. I experienced half an hour of hot, cold, headache, hot, cold, headache, hot, cold, headache, hot, cold, headache. I was pleased when someone pressed the buzzer for a toilet stop so I could stretch my legs. I got up, thought 'I feel so tired' then lay down across a couple of seats. I heard the others trudge back on to the truck then the ever caring Mary came across and tucked me up in a blanket. The altitude was having a bad effect on me. The drive continued and I felt worse, my little headache had developed into a pounding monstrosity as I tried to sleep. I even felt a bit sick but had no intention of losing my own sweepstake.

A couple of hours later the truck pulled up at La Calera where you could relax in the hot springs. Unfortunately, all I wanted was to sleep. The words *'those of you who don't want to go to the springs can go straight to the hostel'* was music to my tortured head. Minutes later and the vomit sweepstake threw up a winner.

My ears had picked up that other people also felt rough, although unfortunately TC's name had not been mentioned. Sympathetic excitement, if that is possible, swept the hot springs as Helen re-produced her last meal to net Paula an unpleasant victory.

Luckily our accommodation wasn't far away from the springs and the truck soon pulled up at the hostel. I staggered to my feet and wearily tried to pull my rucksack from its locker and find my sleeping bag. It all seemed far too much effort but Roger came to the rescue by grabbing my bags and making sure I made it safely to my room rather than curling up in some corridor of the hotel dreaming about sea level. I was being claimed by altitude sickness.

I reached the room and immediately crashed out in the bed. Sleep was periodic and every time I woke my body would quickly remember how terrible it felt. The pounding in my head was relentless; I could feel the pressure inside it building up with no sign of release. Hot, cold, hot, cold, hot, cold, all I wanted was to sleep in my own bed in little old Frisby-On-The-Wreake not putting myself through hell in some corner of Peru. I shared a room with Russell who seemed oblivious to my suffering he just carried on writing his diary, day after day, night after night he compulsively recorded every single detail of each day. As I tossed and turned, slipping in and out of consciousness, he sat at the desk in front of me like some sort of guardian angel.

DAY 9 - SUNDAY 18TH JULY - BIG BIRD

At 4.00am I woke up and was surprised to find that my head hadn't actually been placed in a tightened vice, it just felt like it. Add to that my sweat-soaked T-shirt, stomach cramps, feeling of dehydration without a drop of water in sight and it was no wonder that the pillow had my head buried in it. It was awful.

At 6.00am my health situation improved marginally although I was wondering why someone hadn't had the decency to have persuaded me that a beach holiday would be far healthier, Skegness now sounded like paradise. Candy floss, donkey rides, helter-skelter, dodgems, who needs Peru when you have all that?

I should have got up at 6.30am to join my cook group, shopping for food, but felt lousy. I tried to console myself by reflecting that I had not taken my weekly or daily malaria tablet yesterday else I may have felt even worse. I knew that my tablets were meant to have milder side effects, than the alternative of Larium, but they are not the body's best friend.

After another hour in bed, the body felt much better, despite a rush to the toilet for a very loose release. I collected my gear and claimed a place on the truck ready for the next journey. The morning's destination was Colca

Canyon, which stakes a claim to be the deepest canyon in the world with a depth of 1,200 metres in places.

The canyon was spectacular with amazing drops and stunning scenery, but our main aim was to see a condor. They are notoriously difficult to spot, despite their three-metre wingspan, but Rob and Jenny were confident that condors would be seen rising up the canyon on the morning thermals. The despair of the altitude sickness seemed like an old nightmare, as I felt almost normal again with a little help from drinking a litre of water and taking the local medicine. The natives swear by the coca leaf tea, which is simply boiling water tipped into a cup of coca leaves. The most famous constituent in a coca leaf is cocaine which when isolated becomes the notorious white powder. Outside of the altitude sickness, my stomach cramps had worsened so Jenny produced some tablets to make me better. I hate taking any pills but I had complete faith in Jenny and if she told me I should take them then who was I to argue with our very own Florence Nightingale. Just make me better.

I was not the only one in need of a cure because Fiona had been sick several times in the night. Jen and Fiona's room must have been busy. If it wasn't Jen running to the bathroom to sit on the throne for brown liquid releases then Fiona was sticking her head down the pan to throw up.

The serenity of Colca Canyon seemed a world away from our health problems and all the suffering seemed worthwhile as we sat near the edge awaiting our condor. The peace was only interrupted when poor old Russell stumbled into a cactus whose spikes drew blood from his leg. We were unsure what type of cactus had attacked him but kept an eye on Russell to see if it was the hallucinogenic San Pedro cactus. The theory put forward by Pat was that if we spotted a bearded middle-aged Englishman running naked along the cliff top, flapping his arms and shouting '*I'm Colin the Condor, I'm Colin the Condor*' then it would have been the San Pedro cactus.

Then from the depths of the canyon, a small bird began to move upwards and started to grow. As it flew closer the chatter started, 'It's a condor,' 'Is it?' 'Think so.' Our resident ornithological expert, Phil, confirmed the now soaring bird was indeed a magnificent condor. I was a happy man.

Although the group sat on the edge of the canyon for another hour the condors proved elusive. So we headed towards the truck where Rob and Jenny were taking their turn to provide breakfast. Everybody descended on the food and were busily tucking in when Jenny glanced up, '*condor everyone*'. I'm not quite sure how the condor had sneaked up to us but it was an incredible sight and amazingly close. They are remarkable creatures. According to legend when a condor reaches old age (about 100 years old would not be unusual) and they recognise that their days are numbered they fly as high as they can, then dive to the ground and certain death.

My stomach still felt very unhappy but I managed a cheese toastie and a couple of cups of Coca Leaf tea before the pots were cleared away. Then it was back in the truck for the long journey to the remote town of Yauri.

The views outside the windows were full of stunning landscapes with amazing terraces, but as the long journey dragged on the scenery became bleak.

Although my health had improved significantly at Colca Canyon it began to deteriorate just as quickly. The altitude sickness slowly but relentlessly took a hold on my body as our altitude gradually increased.

At 7.30pm we reached Yauri which I am convinced is Peruvian for Hell.

Rob told us that we had purposefully arrived in Yauri at night-time and would leave in the darkness of early morning because that was the best way to see the town. Apparently there were several restaurants in town but basically, all they served was chicken and chips or the vegetarian alternative of chips and chips. The appeal of the town did not increase when Rob and Jenny announced that they would be sleeping on the truck rather than in the hotel to ensure that it would still be there for us in the morning.

The hotel was a shabby little place that had a courtyard in the back. The courtyard was surrounded by the rooms on the ground floor and first floor (with rickety wooden steps and a wooden balcony leading around to all the upstairs doorways). My main tactic before traversing the gangway was to make sure that Phil was not walking along it because the wooden planks seemed to be struggling to hold his frame. The two available toilets were in the courtyard and needless to say, did not have any running water; with about five people suffering either diarrhoea or sickness this was not ideal. The task of flushing encompassed leaving the toilet to grab a bucket of water from the hollowed out tyres in the middle of the courtyard, you were then in a position to wash away your surplus substances. If the toilets did not seem enticing their attraction was not helped by the plummeting temperatures, which had to be met on the 50 yard trek from room to throne. I waited until most people had headed into town for their chicken and chips feast before enjoying the relief of a brown liquid release. It did not bode well for a fun night.

I felt sorry for myself but knew that my misery would be shared by the others on the casualty list. Jen had worse diarrhoea than me, Fiona was still feeling terrible and a fever had begun to get a grip on Pat.

After disposing of the evil contents of my bowels I returned to my room for another early night. I went straight to bed which not only meant getting under the sheets but also my sleeping bag as I desperately clung to any warmth. The warmth I didn't need came from my temperature but it was the return of the booming headache, which led me to wonder why I was putting myself through this trip. Hot, cold, hot, cold, boom, boom, the only way I knew to stop the torture was to try and sleep.

Day 10 - Monday 19th July - The Cold Flush

I surfaced from my misery at 6.00am and headed straight for the toilet. After ejecting the evil contents of my bowels, I picked up a bucket and moved across to the hollowed out tyres. I peered over the edge, which revealed a thick layer of ice over the water. So there I stood trying to break some ice so I could reach the freezing water below. Then I could use a bucket full of the stuff to flush away the diarrhoea filled toilet. This was never in the brochure. I felt a bit better despite everything and at 7.00am we fled from Yauri hoping life would improve.

The roads were incredibly bumpy but the compensation came from the Andes, which provided us with stunning view after stunning view. A journey of 10 hours took us to the city of Puno, which lies on the shore of Lake Titicaca, the biggest high altitude lake in the world. Puno is situated at over 12,000 feet but the good news is that the highest altitudes are behind me.

The rooms in the hotel were assigned and to my delight, I got a single room with an en suite toilet, for a man with diarrhoea this was music to the ears. 10 seconds after opening the door to my room, trousers and boxers were keeping my ankles warm as I thoroughly enjoyed a 10 minute solid (probably not the most appropriate word) sit down on the toilet, my toilet, heaven.

The room even had a television but not a lot interested me. Eventually, I found Baywatch with Spanish subtitles so I watched that because it would be useful in learning some more Spanish words. It also had an intriguing storyline, something about running up and down the beach a lot.

10 of the group left the hotel for an Italian restaurant; however, our numbers were soon down to nine as Ann-Sophie returned to the hotel feeling ill. Meanwhile, I waited for my meal. Whilst other pizzas arrived and were consumed around me, my health gradually deteriorated, alongside my expectation of seeing my ordered pizza. I gave up on my pizza and collected slices from Jenny and Pete. Jen was feeling equally bad and mentioned

walking back so I decided to join her. The only problem was that neither of us could remember the route and we shared a terrible sense of direction. Jenny provided us with directions whilst Fiona looked on, unsure whether she would ever see us again. I was all for dropping bread crumbs along our path so at least we could find our way back to the restaurant, but Jen had a leap of faith so off we trooped.

Right out the restaurant, diagonally across the square, down the little road on to the main road and left towards our hotel. Our confidence was increased when we passed a red painted wall, which James had brushed earlier in the day. Unfortunately for James, it was a freshly painted red wall and his jacket had the addition of a red stripe. This meant we weren't far from the hotel. All those jibes about us not making it to the hotel and we were on target. We carried on walking and carried on walking and carried on walking until we realised that we did not know this part of town and must have missed the hotel. Jen and I headed into a café, to ask directions, but weren't sure of the name of our hotel. We attempted about 12 different pronunciations of various names we thought the hotel may be called, but to no avail.

We gave up and walked back up the path both feeling physically drained but still smiling. Although it was an effort to be cheerful when your head's going hot, cold, boom, hot, cold, boom. Then the stars aligned and our hotel appeared. It turned out that we had somehow walked by it just before reaching the café. I went to bed wishing I was fit enough to be at the salsa bar where the others would be dancing the night away. Instead, I went to sleep with my altitude headache under the sheets and my sleeping bag on top of me. Oh for good health.

Day 11 - Tuesday 20th July - Living With A God

At 2.00am I was genuinely worried because only five days remained before the start of the four-day Inca Trail trek. The main reason I had travelled to Peru was for the walk to Machu Picchu but there I lay with a booming headache, switching between hot and cold, suffering from diarrhoea and possessing little energy because I'd hardly eaten anything in the previous three days. The thought of not making the trek hurt more than the stomach and head put together. I was determined to make the walk but decided the best course of immediate action would be to sleep.

In the morning I felt a bit better again and much more positive. I had not taken a Malaria tablet since Friday and decided that I would not take any more. The argument went something like; I'm sure they upset my system, I have only one mosquito bite on my entire body, no mosquito in its right mind would spend any time at altitude and I don't like the taste of the tablets. Instead, I took a diarrhoea tablet to provide a cork effect and hopefully stop food passing straight out my other end. I celebrated at breakfast by eating three slices of toast.

A bus with our group covering its seats left the hotel for an early morning boat trip on Lake Titicaca. On board, Pete claimed he may well be a local Peruvian god. The god he'd found out about is small, round, has a fag in his mouth and is a symbol of good luck. Despite this elevation in status, he allowed us, mere mortals, to share the same bus with him.

Lake Titicaca is some 8,500 kilometres in size and lies between Bolivia and Peru. There are many islands on it, including the remarkable floating islands lived on by the Uros Indians. The islands are made of reeds, which require continued maintenance to ensure they do not sink. In the rainy season, a new layer of reeds is put down almost every day.

The first island we stopped at seemed fairly solid and linked to a section of land. Nearly everything the Indians possessed seemed to be woven out of reeds, even the toilets. As I stood in the reed toilet hut peeing into the damp hole, trying to ignore the stench around me, I felt lucky to be born a boy. I would be full of respect for anyone that could squat above the hole and go about their business. That said the choice was fairly limited because there would not be another toilet for three hours. On the one hand, I needed to drink to stave off the dehydration caused by the altitude but on the flip side, my bladder would not contemplate the pain that a drink could cause without a toilet in sight.

I'm glad to say the bladder was not on my mind (else I would be a strange beast) because my interest was vested in the three reed boats on the island. They were the type used in the ancient world and I desperately fancied a ride on one. When you have a local god in your group such wishes are not a problem and within minutes we were sailing in our reed boat to a fully blown floating reed island. Bizarrely, the previous month the island had been anchored two kilometres away but in a move designed to entice more tourists, they sailed it to a more accessible location. Although it seemed amusing, it also provided testimony to the way 'civilisation' had affected them and that we were diluting the very culture we came to experience.

We were reunited with our motorboat for the journey to Tequile Island. Several eyes lit up at the announcement of our destination but it is pronounced

Tequilee rather than Tequila. When the island looked to be 15 minutes away I took the opportunity of quenching my thirst safe in the knowledge that the toilets could not be far away. Within five minutes the engine cut out. The driver decided the boat had run out of fuel. After another examination, he looked confused which didn't help my attempts to relax and stop any bladder control problems. The thought that we might have to swim to Tequile crossed my mind but I had overlooked that Pete the god was on board and within another minute the engine was miraculously working again. Knowing Pete he had already planned to spend tonight, using his new godly powers, trying to turn water into wine.

The boat finally docked and I eagerly walked to the toilet, banging my head on the doorframe, before ducking to enter the hut. A strange phenomenon had developed because the smaller people among our party were constantly hitting their heads on the small Peruvian buildings, but the taller people, who were used to ducking at home, were bump-less. As a smaller person this was not helping my nightly altitude headache, but for the time being my health seemed to be on an upward curve.

Unfortunately, my whole body had to face an upward slope in the shape of 525 large stone steps up to the top of the island. I thanked small mercies that the toilet was at the bottom of the hill. The walk would not have been easy at the best of times but the altitude had cut the normal level of oxygen to half that at sea level. I took the walk slowly and tagged on to the pace being set by Mark and Paula which included numerous breaks to admire the stunning view of Lake Titicaca.

At the end of the steps was the main village and more importantly a restaurant which had hot soup waiting for us. I tentatively ate some of the food on offer eager to build my strength up gradually and strike my name off the casualty list. The list now included Anna who had hardly eaten any food in the previous two days and only managed to eat a carrot on Monday. Also, Morgan began to feel increasingly worse and had developed a fever.

Tequile is renowned for its hand-made woollen clothes and interestingly it is often the men who knit. They make special gnome-like hats whose colour reflects your marital status. Red means you're married and white shows you're available, although married men are known to keep a white hat in reserve. Pat purchased a red hat and stood proudly next to his wife Helen who looked suitably embarrassed. This was a good sign though as it showed Pat was feeling a lot better after suffering a horrendous night in Yauri where his altitude sickness caused the tips of his fingers to turn blue.

The boat ride back to Puno was a slow and arduous journey as I concentrated on telling my bladder there was no liquid inside it. The only other item worthy of note was Pete walking out of the sheltered area of the boat and cracking his head so hard on the low roof that he got knocked to the floor. I started to suspect he may not be a god after all.

My recuperation program continued when I headed to a restaurant with a few others. Not only did my food actually arrive but I managed to eat half a lasagne, which seemed quite an achievement.

Day 12 - Wednesday 21ST July - The Magic Touch

I woke up with my usual headache so slept in until 8.30am, which meant I missed breakfast. I arrived in the truck to see that the four seats set above the cab had been turned into a sick bay with Morgan and Helen occupying the patient's position by lying across two seats each.

After a couple of hours, we reached Sillustani where an ancient cemetery with accompanying temple lay. The hill where the temples were built was set between two blue lakes surrounded by a distant rugged landscape. It had originally been a burial site and as a resting place for eternity, I can recommend it.

A circular stone site was said to produce energy, the idea being that you hold your hands over the centre-point and then place them on a part of your body that has been unwell or needs improving. Although several hands slipped down to respective groins I placed my palms on the top of my head and hoped that the Incas amazing knowledge of nature would remove the headache.

The long journey continued as we were taken to a height of over 4,200 metres. The truck stopped at 4.00pm for a late lunch, which was the last of 10 meals cooked by the group. Although it was the job of one of the six-person cook group to buy the food and make it edible there were usually helping hands available. My role within the last meal was to stand by the truck keeping the door open, which may sound an unskilled and futile operation but I was a vital cog in the cookery wheel. Four gas rings could be pulled out from underneath the truck which when lit provided the essential energy to heat the food and thus concoct a feast. The breeze happened to be quite strong so the only way for the gas rings to remain alight was for someone to keep the door at the required 80 degree angle.

After the meal, all the pots were washed up before they each underwent a condor impression. Tea towels were not practical. So to dry items they were placed in the palms of outstretched arms which then flapped away until the worst of the water had dripped off.

Our journey continued until a landslide covered the road in front of us. It all seemed quite exciting as we went up for a closer look at the digger trying to clear the mound of earth off the road. As I mentioned previously, the Peruvian roads seem to be typically on the side of hills or mountains, so landslides across them are quite common. It is just a case of not being in the wrong place at the wrong time. With such thoughts floating around, it was mentioned we were standing 20 foot away from a landslide which was alongside steep hills that had already proved to be unstable. It seemed sensible to take shelter back in the truck. Well, after a couple more pictures anyway.

The truck was due to reach what the Incas referred to as the Naval of the Universe. The destination was Cuzco the sacred capital of the Inca Empire. At 7.00pm we entered the outskirts of a place that was full of light not just on the ground but also up in the hills. This was Cuzco and it had a good feeling to it or maybe I felt better having descended to 3,500 metres.

At 7.30pm we arrived in the main plaza which was overflowing with life. After being the only gringos in practically every town it seemed strange to arrive in Cuzco which was full of backpackers. The truck stopped in the square whereupon Rob and Jenny nipped out to try and organise the hotel. It took some time, but finally we could walk around the corner and take our stuff to the hotel. The usual scrum of people and bags formed so I grabbed my main backpack before walking the 100 yards up the narrow street. The hotel door was small but after going through the narrow entrance a large and spacious reception room formed in front of me. I was suitably impressed, as I walked up the stairs to find the room to be shared with Russell.

I walked back through reception on a truck bound trip to claim my smaller bag when I bumped into the mortal again Pete who provided me with words of wisdom *'I'd hurry up Jeff, the police are by the truck telling Rob and Jenny to move on'*. I considered his words carefully before sprinting out of the reception, down the road and to the truck where the police were indeed telling Rob to move on. To the disgust of the police, I jumped on the truck grabbed my bag and made a quick getaway while Rob kept them talking.

I joined a few others at the restaurant around the corner and proudly made good headway through some fettuccini. I felt a lot better but as most of the others headed for the pub next door I sadly opted for a return to my room. I thought that one more early-ish night (well, before midnight) and I would be well on my way back to full fitness.

I returned to my room and went to bed. Meanwhile, Russell carried on writing.

DAY 13 - THURSDAY 22ND JULY - BURNING THE MIDNIGHT OIL

After a good night's sleep, I made my way down to breakfast. I'd got as far as the reception when there was a shout from the balcony. Rob stood up there with a smile on his face. *'Jeff!' 'Hey, Jeff!' 'I snogged Fiona!'* - next to him Jen wore a 'that's what Fiona was keeping under wraps' look, before a snigger escaped.

Apparently, half the group had met up at the Cross Keys pub then carried on to the Ukuku's club before the bodies gradually dwindled down to Jen, Fiona and Rob. Jen thought she would be subtle and left the club for the hostel. However, subtlety counts for little when you have Jen's sense of direction and she returned to the club 15 minutes later for help in finding the hotel, so she was duly escorted to her room at about 4.00am.

I would have been comatosed at that time but it proved beneficial because I woke up feeling strangely healthy. The signs of improvement had been there for a couple of days. Although it was slightly odd that a day after trying the Inca healing hands my health had improved remarkably well.

The first task of the morning was to congratulate Russell on staying alive for exactly 60 years. I had to admire the fact that he was still travelling around the world and surviving places like Yauri. He had constantly travelled from 1963 through to 1975, during which time he briefly settled in several countries. Russell had even become a pathologist in Australia. He had no medical experience before he started the job, it was just a case of watching the main practitioner and learning from him. He is fairly certain you have to be more qualified these days, even in Australia.

After returning to England his travels became more sporadic but he has kept a journal of his adventures from 1963 up to the present trip. The pen and hand are hardly ever parted throughout the day as every detail seems to be recorded for what I presume would either be thrown away on his death or become a treasured family heirloom of Great Uncle Russell the eccentric ancestor. As he spent most nights copying up a neat version of his journal he hardly ever went out, but obviously that would not be acceptable on his birthday. I mean was he 60 years old or 60 years young?

Breakfast in the hotel was an experience. It seemed very organised and civil when a form was ticked to state what you required. There were even different boxes as to whether you wanted a four-minute boiled egg or an eight-minute boiled egg. The fact that Ann-Sophie's four-minute egg and Debbie's eight-minute egg were of the same constituency led to the conclusion that the detail was not at the cook's request.

The satellite news channel on the hotel television brought us up-to-date information about the political situation in Colombia. Apparently, some of the guerrilla forces had been forced down into the south of the country. They had started crossing the Peruvian border to re-group, killing any Peruvian security forces in their way. Overall the guerrillas are almost equal in strength to the Colombian government but they are due to have peace talks. If the peace talks break down (which Jenny said that they regularly do) then it could mean civil war. Well, there is still a week before we return to Columbia. Gulp.

On my way out the hotel, the receptionist mentioned that they may need to change our room from 217 to 218. It was not a problem, but as Russell had already ventured out we would need to organise it later. With that, I was off to explore Cuzco which seemed a city full of life. It had been the capital of a great empire which in its pomp stretched some 5,500 kilometres from Southern Colombia to Northern Chile and was the largest in the world at the time. When the Spanish conquerors settled in Cuzco they built on top of the Inca buildings foundations and it quickly became a colonial city.

I happily wandered around by myself and got my bearings from the large plaza which is where everything seemed to originate. At the top of the plaza stood the cathedral and whilst wandering up to it I bumped into Phil who joined me on the religious traipse. The cathedral was built by the Spanish on the site of an Inca palace and seemed to be a typically impressive catholic masterpiece.

I moved on to the Inca Temple of the Sun whose remains are within the Church of Santa Domingo. It was a showcase for the brilliant masonry work of which the Incas were famous, they didn't even use any mortar just tightly-interlocking blocks of stone. Allegedly, when the Spanish reached Cuzco they could not believe the beauty of the city and that the stonework was superior to their own.

I returned to the hotel and went to the room, which to my astonishment was completely empty of any belongings. I would have panicked but remembered the receptionist's words about moving rooms so I returned to reception for the key to room 218. In room 218 were my backpack and a neat pile of clothes, which had originally been scattered about 217.

Everything seemed to be there so I went back out on to the streets of Cuzco to heal my chapped lips. A chemist was found but due to a distinct lack of Spanish vocabulary, I just pointed at my lips. Luckily this didn't prompt him to kiss me but provide me with some desperately needed cream. I happily left the shop and immediately broke into the tube of cream so I could smother it on to my lips. 10 seconds later I realised that my pointing in the chemists may not have translated perfectly and it would be wise to find out exactly what the instructions were on the tube.

I was lucky enough to bump into Mary with her fluent Spanish tongue. Among other things, the instructions stated that the cream was good for herpes and for providing succulent lips, which seemed more than good enough for my requirements.

I walked along with my fast developing succulent lips until I met Fiona and Jen who had recovered from their monster hangovers. I joined them for a lasagne and for the first time for a while ate all the food that was put in front of me. We then had a good bitch about everyone, well it was more of a reverse bitch where you say how nice everyone is, although we had to stop because it sounded like a sickly sweet American Sitcom.

We left the café because we were due back at the hotel for our official Inca Trail meeting at 8.30pm. The local guide called Freddie talked us through the conditions to be expected and what equipment we needed. Although there would be the 20 of us plus Rob and Freddie walking, there would be a team of 35 porters carrying our equipment such as tents and rucksacks. It seemed an amazing number of porters but the idea was that it would be preferable to have too many rather than an overloaded 20. Anything we didn't need for the walk would be left in one hotel room, while our required clothing, sleeping bags etc. would be fitted into shared rucksacks plus there was your day bag which you would carry around. There was the threat of rain, so along with a waterproof coat, clothes needed to be wrapped in bin liners and I took a pair of shorts that would be worn if it was hot or wet. I also included a large stash of chocolate for energy, a torch for finding the toilet at night, the essential wet wipes and numerous layers of clothing.

After the meeting finished, I gathered everything together, managed to photocopy my passport (in case we got stopped by petulant officials) and finally packed, by which time it was 10.30pm. That was a shame because Rob had recommended seeing a band at Ukukus nightclub at 10.30pm, his description being it was Peruvian music without all the bollocks. However, I was fit, I was healthy and I spotted Mark and Paula also heading in an Ukukus direction. The club was situated off the main square, along a short alley into a small courtyard then up some stairs. On the stage, at the back of the club, were the band, sending across a modern day sound of Peru with all manner of traditional and modern instruments.

The sound was brilliant, the candlelit club provided an incredible atmosphere and I was healthy. About eight of the others were spotted sitting at a table by the stage, with the presence of Russell's trilby hat (still on his head) providing a clue to their whereabouts.

Everyone thought the band were superb and Phil, who is a music teacher, was particularly in his element. Just an hour before he had been thoroughly exasperated because the clothes he'd sent away to be washed had been returned minus a shirt. He tried to sort it out without any success as a wall of denial built up but a man arrived and was really helpful before announcing he had to go because he was due on stage. It turned out that he was the lead singer.

The live music eventually stopped and the recorded music started up with a real flavour of quality British pop.

I'm sure it was TC that first noticed the lonely stage, which the band had played on. It did seem somewhat under-utilised after the band finished. Well, until TC leapt on it to show off his dancing prowess. He was soon followed by Jill, Mary, Paula, Debbie, James, Mark, Pete, Phil, Jen, Fiona, Rob, Russell and me. The only problem we had was with fire and our repeated attempts to accidentally burn down the club. A couple of times the very drunk, but happy, Russell knocked his jacket into the path of a candle; luckily it smothered the flame rather than set the jacket alight. The other danger came in the shape of Mark who always seemed to end up dancing on the edge of the stage. This would routinely see him falling off and plunging into the tables below, that is the tables with candles on them.

We eventually called it a night at 3.00am by which time I worked out that the altitude sickness was no longer a problem. In the rush to reach Ukukus I'd not removed my new walking boots but hopefully, the dancing had worn them in for the forthcoming trek. Russell and I reached our room and discovered that as per earlier in the evening there was no running water so our bathroom had a less than pleasant aroma. It would have been nice to have peacefully collapsed into my bed but it wasn't to be the case. Immediately after opening the bedroom door I could hear music. Initially, it seemed that Ukukus had not left my head but it soon became apparent our room all but backed on to a dance club. Nevertheless, I wearily scrambled into bed in the vain hope of gaining some sleep. One minute later there was an almighty crash and I positively shot out of bed worried about the stumbling Russell.

He had walked into a table and fallen to the floor but was unperturbed as I helped him to his feet, replying to my question about whether he was okay by telling me how much he enjoyed the club. Russell safely reached his bed and despite the music was happily snoring away within seconds. I lay there listening to the music and accompanying snoring, wondering whether I would ever enjoy any peace when I realised I was not alone in being unable to sleep because a baby started to cry from the room below.

Day 14 - Friday 23ʳᴰ July - The Mystery Of The Magic Circle

I had drunk so much water over the last few days, to counteract the altitude sickness, that my head was clear from the effects of the previous night's alcohol. The truck left Cuzco at 9.30am, but I had enjoyed my four hours sleep. Although we were leaving Cuzco, there was still one more day before the Inca trail started so everything seemed an anti-climax. The good news was that hangovers permitting only Morgan's name was still etched on the casualty list and the hope was that the extra day would provide the time he needed to recover.

The truck rose into the hills overlooking the city and on to the Inca fortress of Sacsayhuaman. As soon as Freddie, our guide for the next five days, mentioned Sacsayhuaman he grabbed our attention. That may have had more to do with the pronunciation being 'Sexy Woman' than to any historical detail. Unlike the grid plan of Milton Keynes, the city layout of Cuzco was in the shape of a Puma with Sacsayhuaman representing the head.

Part of the defensive wall stood in a zig-zag pattern that not only represented the teeth of the puma but meant it was easier to repel attackers. Several of the stones were enormous, with one reputedly weighing 300 tonnes and another allegedly costing 3,000 lives as it was dragged to the fortress. Much of the force for the dragging came from the Incas tall and well-built frames which is strange because most Peruvians are about five foot (and a little bit) in height but possess a strong, stocky frame.

One spot in Sacsayhuaman was very special, it could be described as magical but I'm sure with the Inca's knowledge of the land they may well have been able to provide an explanation. There was a circle marked out with a little stone wall around the outside. Freddie stood in the middle of it and said that when he spoke there was an echo, but we couldn't hear anything. Russell was one of the first to take the stage and was quickly followed by Debbie as we took turns in the centre. The person would stand in the middle talking and then shuffle around until they reached a point and claimed that they could hear a sort of echo. I was still sceptical when I headed for the centre. 21 pairs of eyes focused on me. It is always a quandary what to talk about in these circumstances especially after Russell had quoted Shakespeare with what seemed to be a new found confidence (or he could still have been drunk). I decided to stick with my strong point and talk rubbish, saying whatever came into my mind. There really was a distinct echo, except it seemed to be inside my head, it was amazing. There was no echo when someone else spoke, I could only hear it with the sound of my own voice. Wow. The phenomenon was nothing to do with the wall because Freddie confirmed the echo had been discovered before it had been rebuilt. Strangely there did not seem to be a precise spot for the echo it varied slightly from person to person.

Our group were then driven to the Sacred Valley, which is a beautiful area of terraced slopes and Inca ruins built into the landscape. I passed my pre-walk fitness test by not only eating all my lunch but also finishing the leftovers from Pete's plate, which was an amazing turnaround. The truck then dropped us off at the top of the hill and left us with a two-hour walk along the winding paths to Pisac. The trek proved impressive with stunning views of the valley and relatively well preserved Inca buildings. After two hours we reached Pisac market square where the truck was expected to meet us. However, Rob, Jenny and the truck were still halfway up the slope, apparently waiting for us at the end of another walk. As we settled into the nearest cafe a worried Freddie sent a taxi up the hill to recall our truck.

Re-united, the truck bumped its way along the roads to the small town of Ollantaytambo. Our Ollantaytambo hostel had basic facilities but by the time we arrived the main chore was to find a place to eat. The dark road into the town square was unlit but Pat said he'd got a very powerful torch and had just bought some new batteries. He confirmed it was the brightest torch he had ever seen so there was no need for anyone else to bring their pale imitation of torches. When we reached the darkened street Pat moved his finger to switch on this beacon of light and as we prepared to be bathed in light there was a flicker and then a dull glow. Pat let out an '*oh*' and then a chuckle. I am not sure what batteries he had bought but they needed some Viagra. Instead of Pat showing us the way with his softly lit torch, the stars and moon provided the light to the town square. The restaurant was very friendly, especially the local who seemed to have had one too many coca leaves but he seemed happy with life.

I sat opposite dim Pat (but dim only in the torch sense). We had both suffered from Peruvian ailments, but were so happy to be healthy, it was now an effort to keep the smile off our faces. It was agreed that anything above good health was a bonus and what a bonus lay ahead of us, the Inca Trail.

Pat regaled many a fine travelling tale from around the world as I tried to figure out a country that he and Helen hadn't visited. He has even got a brother who is a diplomat and had enjoyed the pleasures of a land called Eritrea. I had never heard of the country but Pat confirmed it was located just north of Ethiopia, with which it had fought a long war of independence. The Ethiopians had been financially backed by the Russians, then by the Americans, but they could not break the Eritreans down. What the Eritreans lacked in finance they made up for with ingenuity; any Ethiopian weaponry captured or dumped were quickly mended and pressed into service on the Eritrean side. Finally in about 1993 Ethiopia (with about 15 times the population and 12 times the land size) gave up trying to fight them. Eritrea then prospered and developed one of the strongest African economies, all with no thanks to the West. They refused any aid because they had not received any during their long struggle with Ethiopia and relied on the determination that had already served them so well.

I mentioned to Pat that the ancient history of Ethiopia made it an enticing country to explore. He agreed but warned about the serious crime problem they suffer from in the cities. His brother and Eritrean wife were in Ethiopia when they ordered a taxi. They jumped into the back of a taxi and were driving along when the driver quietly locked the doors. Pat's sister-in-law calmly took off her scarf and looped it firmly around the driver's neck. She then told him that unless he stopped and unlocked the doors immediately she would strangle him. The doors were unlocked and they were let out. Apparently, it is common practice for taxi drivers to lock all the doors and drive you to their friends who will beat the living daylights out of you (if you're lucky) before helping themselves to any possessions. If Pat was working for the Eritrean Tourist Board, he was doing a brilliant job.

After the meal, we returned to the hostel with Pat's torch dimming the way.

Day 15 - Saturday 24ᵀᴴ July - Death On The Trail

When I went to bed I had been very excited (in the Inca Trail sense) but surprisingly enjoyed a good night's sleep. The sleep was just the first part of preparing my body for a battle with the mountains. I stuck plasters on my ankles and feet, where my boots were likely to catch after several hours in the shoe. Also a thick pair of socks which are reinforced with high technology walking over-socks that are specially designed to stop blisters; well that's what the packet said anyway.

The morning was spent walking around the imposing fortress at Ollantaytambo. The fortress was very impressive and had been the only Inca stronghold to have ever thwarted persistent Spanish attacks but all I wanted to hear was a few selected words in a specific order.

The long awaited '*and now we are going to start the Inca Trail*' finally arrived. The group clambered into a cramped Peruvian bus where the aisle disappeared as more seats unfolded to leave no space uncovered. The roads were practically dirt tracks with one side providing a 20 foot drop on to a railway track. If other vehicles came the other way the speed was reduced to snail pace as they tried to nudge by without sending one of them careering down the hill. Finally but, more importantly, safely, we reached the two platform railway station where we were to gather for our walk. As we sat by the side of the track, James began to chew on a bit of food, he suddenly looked a bit uncomfortable and began to choke. Then he collapsed on to the ground, dead.

The group looked on interested but not too concerned, this was the start of the murder game. The basic idea was that everybody would draw a card from Mark the organiser-in-chief. The one who drew the Queen of Spades would be the murderer and everybody else, the potential victims. The murderer would go round telling selected people that he was the killer, how they were going to die and when they would die. It is the victim's job to die in the most hammed up way they can muster. The winner is the person who guesses the identity of the murderer, with only one guess allowed per live person. If the guess is wrong a forfeit has to be performed.

James re-emerged from death to the sound of thought as people worked out their theory on who had spoken to him in the last hour.

Our attention returned to the walk as we actually set off. The trail itself was a dirt track, two to three people wide, with steep drops on one side, it twisted continuously upwards with a roaring river down below and snow-capped mountains in the distance. Well that was what I saw in the first 10 minutes.

After about two hours walking we rounded a corner to see many a backpacker sat on a grassy bank munching away on their food. Across the other side, a long row of self-important tables were laid out with cups and plates. All I could think was what sort of people have forced their porters to have carried all that furniture and equipment up the mountain for them. Personally,

I would have preferred to have sat on the grass and munched away on some food rather than make our porters do such a thing. Before I could start on any remarks about the self-centred people who made their poor porters suffer I cringed with embarrassment. It was our table, our plates, our knives, our forks and our porters. The only straw that I could clutch for was that at least it had provided more locals with work. So there we sat like some remnant from the days of the British Empire. If only we could have drunk from china cups; drinking tea from plastic beakers just wasn't the British thing to do.

At the end of our self-conscious lunch, we sat and relaxed at the side of the tables. All seemed peaceful, then there was a gasp and Mary who had been sitting beside me was sprawled out on the ground. She had been murdered!

The question was who had the opportunity to speak with Mary and James? Everybody had spread along the trail on the way up but Paula had been walking with Mary, she could have spoken to her without anybody hearing. Yes, Paula was the prime suspect. What I did know was that the field had narrowed. Pete, Andrea, Russell, Roger and Anna were not playing, so with Mary and James dead that left 12 suspects outside of my good self. When would the killer strike again?

Mary brushed herself down and started to pick up her life again, seemingly unaffected by being dead.

The walking continued on for another hour until we reached a tiny camp-site where our porters had set up the two-person tents. After claiming my main rucksack from the pile brought up by the porters (wonderful fellows) I sank my feet into a bowl of hot water (obviously brought to my tent by the porters) and placed a big smile across my face (managed to achieve this without the help of a porter). 3,000 metres up in the Andes, a nice little campsite beside a stream and my feet soaking in warm water, miles away from so-called civilisation, what more could a man ask for? Then Pete walked by with a bottle of beer.

Miles from anywhere and Pete manages to find a bottle of beer, maybe he is a god after all. Apparently, there were slightly larger campsites up the track and one housed a reducing pile of beer bottles. I adjourned to the meal tent, which included a long table and small stools where we enjoyed afternoon tea. As night had begun to cast its shadow over the Andes I decided to stay in the meal tent for a bit longer. The tent had become a relative hive of activity with card games and Yahtzee being fought out. Dinner was served at 7.00pm which started with soup. The main meal involved meat and vegetables, with the vegetarian option of vegetables and vegetables (with fruit for the fruities), then rice pudding to finish off. All fairly basic but surprisingly tasty, even on the plastic plates.

The dinner talk surrounded the identity of the murderer amongst us with TC, Pat and Paula amongst the main suspects. My money was still on Paula but I didn't fancy making a guess yet, because of the threat of a forfeit. That did not stop Debbie who declared her intent in a beautiful English rose accent. Everybody stopped with bated breath. '*The murderer is ….. Pat*'.

Everyone turned to Pat who confessed that he was innocent and that Debbie would be facing a forfeit tomorrow. The floor was laid open to suggestions and it was decided that she would have to wear her underwear on the outside, Superman style, whilst walking on the trail. Her pleas for sympathy fell on deaf ears and smiling faces.

Day 16 – Sunday 25ᵀᴴ July – Died And Gone To Heaven (Or At Least Part Of The Way)

The time must have been around an unsociable 3.00am but my bladder did not care, it wanted to get up. I was warm and snug in my sleeping bag, but it was cold outside so I tried to regain my unconscious state. At 4.00am the bladder could not be ignored any longer. I cursed that no one had invented a device that I could simply attach down below and hey presto have a wee without leaving the warmth of my sleeping bag (sorry, maybe that thought should never have left my head).

Under the circumstances, if I stayed in my sleeping bag for much longer I would receive a short-lived warm sensation followed by a damp feeling and then a whiff of an unpleasant smell. A visit to the toilet tent seemed to be both the sensible and dry option. The toilet tent was a cubicle shape with no material on the floor. A hole had been dug in the ground, which acted as the toilet. The advantage of visiting at 4.00am was that it hadn't been popular in the last few hours so it wasn't on the verge of breaking its banks. I was quickly back to my sleeping bag for a little more sleep.

The day had been billed as the hardest of the trip with a long slog up to a pass and then a steep descent. At 4,150 metres high the pass would be offering a variety of altitude effects. As we were already acclimatised to high altitude the most likely effect would be the shortness of breath caused by exercising at a ridiculous height.

The earlier we start the better because there are about 1,000 people a day walking along the trail so unless you can beat the majority out of their tents it can become very crowded. At 5.30am a porter knocked on the tent flaps and brought me a much-appreciated cup of coffee. I sat and listened to Russell complaining that it was too early, too dark, he wished he'd stayed in Cuzco etc. before reaching the meal tent for breakfast. It took another hour of eating, packing and re-packing before we were ready for the trek to Dead Woman's Pass.

In the early stages of the trek everyone stayed together, but gradually we started to string out and I took up a space near the back of our bunch. Despite watching years of Dr Who and thrillers, I'd forgotten the golden rule of never, under any circumstances, be the one at the back of the group. I'd made a fatal mistake. The next person to me was a few yards in front but Morgan dropped back to me. '*Jeff, I'm the murderer you will die after Debbie at lunch*'. 'What?' I couldn't believe my ears; Morgan was far too nice to be a murderer. Then off went the Swedish assassin to talk with someone else and not be seen walking near me, well it was either that or I smelled. Despite my impending death, I re-focused back on the walk.

I wanted a nice steady pace for what had been estimated by Rob would be a four and a half hour walk. The initial group had splintered into subgroups but Phil seemed to be setting a sensible speed so I tagged on to him. In fact, Team Phil developed into a group of six. Our leader led the way, followed by Anna, Roger, Pat, Helen and me. The journey was relentlessly upwards as we had to make up 3,500 feet just in terms of height (the equivalent of Snowdon) from the camp to the top of Dead Woman's Pass. The scenery of valleys and white capped mountains was stunning. However, as the trail was basically a narrow dirt track with patches of stones and a sheer drop on one side, it was almost impossible to walk and admire the view at the same time. Therefore, I had my eyes firmly clamped on to the back of Helen's shoes.

Phil maintained our slow but remorseless pace and it was noticeable that people who flew by us were often passed about 10 minutes later when they were resting. The slow speed seemed to pay dividends and the initial plan was to carry on right up to the pass without a break because everyone felt comfortable. After little more than an hour, we were passed by a couple of girls going down the mountain because they couldn't face going up any further. Life was not destined to be easy.

Meanwhile, porters loaded with bags would surge past us. They seemed to be the ultimate mountain men with the short bulky Peruvian build proving ideal. The porters had the ultimate respect of seemingly everyone on the trail and whenever one was behind you, you'd move aside to let them pass.

The walk became harder and harder so my imminent death didn't seem so bad. In fact, I spent quite a lot of time planning exactly how to die. The idea was to wait for Debbie to keel over, then I'd become hysterical before staggering around in the manner of a dying baddie and collapsing in a motionless heap. It would be a masterpiece!

Back in the real world the altitude started to take its toll and our slow pace started to drop until after two hours of solid walking we ground to a halt. Following a much-needed five-minute break we were refreshed, half an hour later we were shattered, another break, another walk, another break. We started to recognise people, especially a group of four American girls who we would pass as they rested and they would return the compliment as our limbs recuperated. The breaks were kept to a few minutes but the walking time between them shrunk and my legs became very heavy. The snow-white mountain tops may have been level with us but the sun and exertion kept us warm.

The numerous chocolate bars I'd brought for the trek were a godsend for providing valuable energy but we desperately wanted to see the pass. Walking seems so much easier when you can see your target. It finally appeared in front of us with a long winding path leading up to it but with less oxygen, the further up you walked. The group chugged along and as we neared the top, cheers rang out from a few of the 200 sitting on the pass.

TC had managed to reach the top at 9.40am, followed by Rob, Mark, Jill, Jen and Pete, so at 11.20am when we reached Dead Woman's Pass, they were our cheerleaders. It felt superb to finally reach the top, not only for a sit-down but to gaze upon the mountain valley below with ant-sized people struggling up the trail. In the distance were more rugged snow-capped peaks topped by a glorious blue sky. The pass was flanked by two grass banks. Due to the lack of facilities, and length of the grass, it also acted as an area of 'relief' or a 'run-off area'. One girl was spotted squatting for about 10 minutes up on the bank little more than 50 feet above us. Poor girl, you have been dying to go for the last hour but then with an audience of hundreds below that constipated feeling suddenly sets in. It became a surreal sight as people started to glance up to check whether she was still squatting. Had she got a grimaced face? Had she been frozen in a squat? If her face changed from grimace to glee, should we be aware of a log flume heading down the pass?

Back on the trail, the binoculars picked up Paula and Fiona trudging along, followed by James and Debbie. James walked painfully slowly and was in obvious distress as Debbie helped him along. Every few yards were punctuated with a rest and a disconsolate dropped head. We willed him on and shouted encouragement as he battled against the altitude. It was painful for us to watch but that obviously paled into insignificance compared to how he felt.

Eventually, to what must have been the loudest cheer of the day, they made it to the top. James finally sat down with Rob's fleece draped around him to try and keep his body warm in the chilly temperatures. James quietly recovered, with his distress being put down to a mixture of the altitude and a general lack of fitness although he admitted the fag breaks on the way up may not have helped.

Morgan, Anne-Sophie and Mary all gradually trekked up to the pass but at 1.00pm there was still no sign of Andrea, Russell and Freddie, so we walked on to where the porters had set out our dinner tables. The meal began peacefully enough although I kept a watchful right eye on Debbie, ready for my moment of thespian inspiration. The soup passed by and Debbie hadn't made a deathly movement. Then lunch was watchfully eaten and Debbie was still very much alive. I was tempted to break Morgan's orders and just die.

Then from my left came an anguished sound and Jen collapsed backwards. Jen had been murdered! I decided to die when everyone had settled down from Jen's death but my thought pattern was interrupted by Fiona. '*I want to make a guess*'. She couldn't do this to me I wanted my moment. I willed Fiona to guess wrongly, how could she do this to me? '*The murderer is Morgan*'. And with that, his reign of terror came to an abrupt end.

The meal had finished when the familiar features of Russell, Andrea and Freddie appeared. They had reached the top of the Pass over four hours after TC but looked in fine fettle and settled down for some food. The remaining trek for the day was a fairly steep descent down to the valley of the Pacayamo river, which was easier in terms of energy but meant the knees suffered a continual pounding on the stone surface.

The campsite, we eventually reached, is much larger than last night's and has a stream running through the middle of it. What happens during the day is that porters from all the various trips forage onwards in front of the groups and claim the best areas of the campsites. As we had a relatively high number of porters this provided a distinct advantage. Meanwhile, the porters themselves were in high spirits after seeing Debbie completing the descent under forfeit conditions with underwear becoming over-wear.

Darkness fell over the valley and everybody descended on the meal tent. Well with the exception of Mary. After resting in her tent she had warmed up nicely and had no intention of venturing out into the cold night air as she had paid good money for her sleeping bag and was determined to receive her money's worth.

During the meal, Pat and Helen re-iterated their need for a torch, due to the lack of light shining from their bulb, at which point Ann-Sophie mentioned she had a spare one. At the end of the meal, Ann-Sophie announced '*you come to my tent now Pat*'. Pat eagerly responded '*Well I'll take up your offer but in England, we don't normally say that in front of the wife*'. After an excursion, Pat returned to the meal tent, not with Ann-Sophie's torch but clasping his excuse for a torch which had started to shine brightly. The question was asked how this miracle was achieved and it turned out Morgan had fixed it as Ann-Sophie proudly said '*Morgan has magic hands*'. Amid much tittering Morgan was re-named Magic.

DAY 17 - MONDAY 26TH JULY - ON TOP OF THE WORLD

Coffee arrived at 5.00am along with Russell's moaning about it being too early. I was in need of a trip across the stream to the toilet in the still dim light. I nipped down the bank of the stream and then had the matter of jumping along on the four stepping stones before hopping up the opposite bank. The way was blocked by porters washing but I already had two successful forays under my belt so I was confident of handling the obstacles. I perched on the edge of the bank then performed a hop-skip and a slip as my left foot slid down the side of the second stone. There may not have been any showers at the last two campsites but I still wasn't keen on getting my feet wet.

The facilities were housed inside a hut, with a row of basins and four cubicles. There was water across the damp stone floor with no locks on the toilet doors and nothing in the way of public toilet paper. I half sat, half squatted on the seat-less toilet, it was quite a technical operation as I also tried to stretch my right leg against the door to stop people barging in. All this was successfully performed practically in the dark as there were no lights. On the way out I met Fiona and wished her luck.

I had run out of bottled water so relied on the purified water provided by the porters, presumably fresh from the streams. We had been warned not to piss in the river and that seemed sensible advice when it was realised what was contained in your water bottle.

The start of today's walk provided a one-hour uphill trek. It proved all the more rewarding for beating many of the others up (in the getting up sense) because, at least to begin with, we had the path to ourselves. The second pass of Abra de Runkuracay was spectacular with an incredible range of brown, green and grey. They may not sound the most amazing of colours but when the forest and mountains are added in, they looked stunning. Especially with the touch of white sprinkled on top of the distant mountains and a little puff of smoke escaping from a distant volcano.

Another hour's walk, thankfully at a relatively gentle downhill angle, brought some Inca steps that led to the ruins of Sacyacmarca. The remains of the town were impressive but the cloud forest that awaited us on the trail was simply unbelievable. I had never been in a cloud forest before but I think it is basically a rainforest that is high in the sky. The density of the plants and trees amazed me plus every time you glanced up there was another stupendous (and I'm not using the word lightly) mountain view. The trail which had become a finally worn path even entered a tunnel which had been carved out the rock by the Incas. I had to insert yet another film into my camera as I entered a photograph frenzy. This gave enough time for the group of Americans who we met yesterday to catch up. 1,000 people on the trail and they appeared behind us again. After finally shaking them off (or them shaking us off) we passed Freddie who was perched 20 feet above the trail creating haunting music from his Peruvian flute.

The third pass was reached and after relaxing at the top for a little while there was a distinctly steep descent to the next campsite. This meant tackling the two kilometre Inca stairway built of large stones where you had to step come jump down the trail. One wrong move could easily send a body crashing down the steps and breaking a few bones, but the porters relentlessly carried on speeding past us with no care for their own health. In some ways, I found the descent more difficult than ever because at least on the ascent falling up did not hold the same fear of falling down.

Freddie had instructed us to make our way down the path ensuring we took the correct turn off the trail else we would miss the campsite completely. A disaster nearly struck half an hour later when Jen and I found ourselves together at the fork in the path. Surely somebody with a sense of direction should have been by our side and not left us to our own devices. The right side was chosen as the path descended along the mountainside, fingers crossed we hoped that it was the correct trail. We struck gold! For there at the campsite was a young girl selling beer with a gold label. I may be a bitter drinker, the liquid may have been lager, but after such a long trek it seemed like the best beer I had ever drunk and among the most well deserved. After the beer had been consumed, the legs had just about enough energy to find my tent and collapse within its walls.

The campsite actually included a hostel, bar and showers. As 'shower' had become a foreign word for the last few days, it was a luxury that could not be overlooked. After purchasing a token, I found myself lapping up the warm water to become refreshingly clean.

I realised that 'clean' would only be a temporary state of affairs, but my chance for a more natural smell arrived all too quickly as Freddie offered to take us down to the old Inca citadel of Winay Wayna in the evening. There were only 10 bodies willing to once more exert their weary limbs for the 15 minute walk.

The town had only been re-discovered 15 years ago but was situated on the side of a mountain, in the thick of the cloud forest. Freddie explained all about Winay Wayna, speaking passionately about the Incas. He must have noticed our wide-eyed enthusiasm and said he would speak of things that he would not tell other groups. A short enthralling history lesson of the Incas began. Apparently, the Incas aren't the Incas they are the Quechua, it was only the emperor who was the Inca. There were only 13 Incas crowned plus one uncrowned, but the ninth ruled during its pomp and may well have started the building of Machu Picchu. There are many theories about Machu Picchu but it is likely to have been built as a religious centre with the aim of taking over from the idol crammed Sun Temple in Cuzco. At that moment the brightest full moon I'd ever seen appeared and shone down on us. I'm not quite sure how Freddie managed to control the moon but we were mightily impressed. The Spanish invaded the Inca Empire just after it had suffered a civil war and mounted an incredibly successful invasion. However, they couldn't understand the Incas and even decided that they must be Sun Worshippers. The Spanish seemed to be confused because the Incas believed that the gods were some-thing unseen that couldn't be recreated via pictures. All too soon the Spanish had colonised Peru and Freddie had told us to return to the campsite.

I started walking back with Pat, Helen and Jen but after a couple of minutes, something made us stop. There was the hauntingly beautiful sound of Freddie playing his flute so we stopped on some steps and sat down.

There we were in an Inca Citadel, lost to the world not more than 15 years ago, which stood on the side of a mountain in the Andes. We were surrounded by dense cloud forest but the mountainside cut away sharply to reveal the valley and river thousands of feet below, with snow-capped moun-tains in the distance. I sat there with three people I didn't know a few weeks ago but would now trust with my life (unless it involved Jen in an orienteer-ing competition) as we bathed in the amazingly bright moonlight and the music from Freddie's flute. I was wondering whether I had ever experienced anything so beautiful, then one by one the stars started to pop out of the sky. It felt as though we had found the ceiling of the world.

This is an amazing and extraordinary world.

After a magical 10 minutes, the music died so we returned to the campsite where James greeted us with '*Do you want to see a baby anaconda?*' I had never been at one with snakes but it's not every day you have such an opportunity so I followed James. Sure enough, there was a snake inside a plastic bottle which hung beside a tent. The porters had found it inside our meal tent and had gingerly caught it using some sticks. Freddie arrived on the scene to confirm that it was a viper rather than the anaconda description provided by the porters. The area we were in was on the edge of the jungle and thus was literally crawling with poisonous snakes, scorpions and tarantulas. I decided a torch and heavy clumping boots would be a good idea as I returned to my tent where Russell was busy writing. It was then I attempted the world record for most 'make sure you zip up the tent' requests in one conversation.

DAY 18 - TUESDAY 25ᵀᴴ JULY - ONE HOUR SHORT

I woke up ready for the short trek to Machu Picchu although a time check revealed it was still only 2.00am. I went back to sleep but excitedly woke up again at 3.00am. It was all a bit frustrating, like the early hours of Christmas when I was a kid. The presents are at the bottom of the bed but I know I'm not allowed to open them until morning. It was tempting to wake Russell up and say 'Russ, Russ, we're going to Machu Picchu in a couple of hours', but something told me he wouldn't appreciate it.

I calmed myself down and once more went back to sleep. Not surprisingly I woke up again at 4.00am wondering where the hell the porters were to wake everybody up and start breakfast. I had only a few minutes to wait before the usual morning sounds and Russell moaning that it was too early and still dark.

Everybody gathered outside bringing with them a mixture of feelings; excitement, tiredness, bewilderment and drunk (the danger of having a bar at the campsite). The time was approaching 5.00am when we set out with Russell still complaining that it was too dark and dangerous. The great advantage of walking at this time in the morning is that most of the campsite is only just getting up. So not only would the paths be relatively empty but also the prime positions could be claimed at the Sun Gate, which overlooks Machu Picchu and is the traditional spot to watch the sunrise.

The walk started and everybody was soon strung out in a line. I drifted near the back with only Russell and Pete in my wake. The path was nice and flat with the usual sheer drop down one side. I'm sure the views would have been stunning but the dark didn't allow us to appreciate them. At that point, an anguished yell rang out from behind me. I spun round to see Pete's right arm down the side of the ravine. I stood frozen as the brain worked out what was going on, the sight of a trilby at path height but on the ravine side provided another clue. Russell had slipped off the path and fallen down the mountainside, only the thick vegetation and Pete's arm had stopped him tumbling hundreds of feet. Pete yelled across for a hand and we helped up a disconcerted but not unduly distressed Russell.

The walk up a relatively deserted path to the Sun Gate took about an hour. I had tried to move from the back of our group to nearer the front, which meant that I had a couple of 10 minute spells totally alone with the trail. It would have been really nice but for nagging thoughts. Where is everyone? Have I taken a wrong turn? There were no turns! I should have seen somebody by now.

The last steep steps were climbed up to the Sun Gate and the first view of Machu Picchu. The legendary Inca Citadel had remained hidden in its own valley of mountains throughout the Inca Trail and it was only in the very last half hour of walking up to the Sun Gate that it became visible. Little wonder the Spanish never found Machu Picchu.

There must have been 200 bodies sprawled across the Sun Gate waiting for sunrise. The valley of mountains was covered in thick green vegetation with the path winding its way to some carefully terraced land, which provided a base for a vast maze of white granite walls. The icy summits in the distance were once again topped by the blue sky. It seemed like a dream but I was fairly certain that it was real and that I wasn't still delirious from altitude sickness in Yauri. The only wart on the landscape was a hotel built part way down the slope below Machu Picchu, but even that was somewhat lost in the vastness of the place. I just hope that it is not the sign of things to come with more hotels warting the area, there is even talk of a cable car up to Machu Picchu from the nearby railway station.

The sun shone as backpackers descended on the sight before the 10.30am train brought carriages of day trip tourists to the village of Aguas Calientes on the valley floor. Freddie took us on a tour of the main sights as our weary limbs willingly traipsed around the beautiful citadel. We entered the temple of the condor where long ago dead bodies would have been laid out awaiting condors to take their spirit away. We left the temple and looked up to see a condor gliding far above us. In all his trips Freddie had only ever once seen a condor at Machu Picchu and never straight after coming out of the temple of the condor. He referred to us as his lucky group, first the full moon and then a condor, we were lucky. In fact, we were lucky to have the endearing Freddie as a guide because he had resigned just three weeks ago. He had been on a trip with the Brazilian ambassador who complained about all the walking and wanted the porters to carry him. Freddie would have none of it but the ambassador complained and Freddie was reprimanded, he considered this to be totally unjust and quit. They accepted his resignation at the time but then pleaded for him to return. His knowledge was impressive but not surprising for someone with a degree in tourism and getting a book published about the flora and fauna on the Inca trail. He was rightfully proud of his heritage and made an eloquent point about history crediting Hiram Bingham with the discovery of Machu Picchu in 1911. How can you discover something that was never lost? The locals always knew about the existence of Machu Picchu and showed Hiram Bingham where it lay. What Bingham achieved was to bring this remarkable place to the attention of the world.

I could drivel on for ages about Machu Picchu but I still could not do it justice. After a few hours wandering around, it was time to make our way to Aguas Calientes and catch one of the two daily trains that head in a Cuzco direction. The station did not have any platforms and when the train arrived it managed to separate Fiona on one side of the train from her bag on the other side. The doors were on both sides of the train but scrums formed around the carriages as people fought for space. I put my rucksack on my back and grabbed Fiona's bag as I looked for my allotted seat in carriage number 35. I saw a few of our group jump on a carriage so climbed up the side, which, without the usual four feet high platforms, meant the bottom of the doorway was at head height. The brain then realised it wasn't carriage 35 but I was already struggling to carry two rucksacks and worried that if I jumped off I'd miss the train. Debbie was just in front of me on the train so I gave her a yell to look after Fiona's rucksack, before scurrying off the carriage.

Up and down I trudged looking for the elusive carriage 35. If I didn't find my carriage then there was no way I would get a seat on this packed out train. Each moment I wasted was a second closer to the train departing, where was it? If I missed the train it was a six-hour wait for another and then I still had to find a way back to Cuzco. Where was 35? My usual calm disposition deserted me as I scrambled around in increasing panic. Where the hell was the carriage? My mind had locked on to finding carriage 35 and it took a head stuck out a window with a plain old '*Jeff! What the hell are you doing! Get in here!*' to knock me back to my senses. I jumped into a packed carriage 36, which somehow happened to also be my carriage 35 and thanked Pete for his blunt advice.

I fought my way through the packed carriage to my seat beside Andrea. Opposite me sat two of the American girls who I had continually bumped into on the Inca trail. There may have been about 14 carriages jammed full with people but there they were again.

They had both been conducting research into the spread of Malaria in Northern Peru. Although the results showed only 1 out of 80 people were suffering from Malaria, it had been the dry season. Amazingly it was reported that 1 in 5 contracted Malaria in the wet season and 80% of people in the area had suffered from the disease at some point. Even when they finished their research, ill health followed them with 12 out of 20 from their Machu Picchu group suffering from sickness and diarrhoea during the four-day trek. Apparently due to the unhygienic conditions that isn't unusual, although it had been the only time that our group had all been healthy.

Also in their group were a couple of Brummies who not only provided up to date news of football transfers but information from their guide. He alleged that hundreds of years ago the Incas had become very friendly with the llamas and caught syphilis from them. The Spanish then became very friendly with the Incas and caught syphilis, which they brought back to Europe. Allegedly some of the farmers still carry on this friendship with the llamas. I know they may look strangely attractive with their long eyelashes and big eyes but they still don't do anything for me. Their guide also claimed that the old Inca tradition of sacrificing a child when everything is going wrong (which I think many teachers in Britain would support), still goes on in darkest Peru. Less surprisingly, he told them that he had never seen a condor over Machu Picchu in 100 trips, until today. Although I found the conversations fascinating my mind kept flickering back to Debbie struggling with two rucksacks. We had been warned that the train stops could be very short so to literally barge your way off the train at the right stop else you could end up in the middle of nowhere. Please Debbie, make it off the train.

After several hours, Rob let up a cry to say that we were at the correct station. Luckily this train seemed to be at the end of the line so there was no rush. A truck was organised to transport us from Ollantaytambo to Cuzco. After an interesting trip where the driver happily tried to overtake anything in his path, particularly if we were on a blind bend with the usual 200-foot drop, we safely reached the hostel. Most of the group desperately scrubbed down in their respective showers to extract dirt from places of the body that they didn't realise existed. Then it was on to the Cross Keys pub to meet Freddie. The number of upright bodies startled to dwindle so there seemed to be only one thing for it, go to Ukukus.

The time headed passed midnight as I realised that a 24 hour day from 4.00am to 4.00am was possible. At 1.00am my eyelids were open and my feet were still dancing, just three hours left. Jen desperately started a game to keep us awake, it involved her dropping a contact lens on the dance floor and the rest of us scrambling around the dance floor on hands and knees looking for it. The search ended unsuccessfully so I suppose that meant Jen was blind drunk (well, it seemed funny after a few beers). The eyelids were struggling to stay up an hour later but there were just two hours left so I kept to the dance floor with Freddie, Phil, Jen and Paula for company. The body gradually ground to a halt and the energy for keeping awake, let alone dancing had been exhausted. Phil, Paula and I dragged ourselves out of the club and along the plaza. We had every intention of heading straight back to the hostel but somehow found ourselves sitting on a bench, in the middle of the square, talking to Colombian and Peruvian drunks, who in turn spoke to Canadian and English drunks.

Finally, at 3.00am, my bed and I were one.

Day 19 - Wednesday 28th July - Peruvian Offerings

It was 10.30am before my stomach enjoyed some breakfast and found out about events I missed from the previous night. The absence from Ukukus of our usual dance choreographer, TC, had been due to a four-hour nose-bleed. He never seems to do anything by halves. Apparently, after our bench trio had left Freddie and Jen at Ukukus, Freddie made a pass but Jen had turned him down on the basis that '*I am involved in a 14 year relationship and you're one foot smaller than me*'. Although there were the '*but Freddie seemed so spiritual*' comments, Mark spoke words of wisdom with his '*he may be spiritual but he still wants to reproduce*'.

I wandered around Cuzco for the rest of the morning, which had been marked down as souvenir and present time, but I didn't actually buy anything. This all changed after a cup of coffee with Fiona and Mary, where their need to shop must have contaminated my wallet. In the following two hours, my purchases encompassed two pictures, a mask, a hat, a scarf, three necklaces and a panpipe, as I bartered my way around the shops.

The day wouldn't have been complete unless I'd bumped into at least one of the American girls, but I needn't have feared. I rounded a corner and there one of them stood. She gave me a warning: '*when you eat guinea-pig, stay away from the claws*'. I would have thought she'd been on the coca leaves but for the fact that it was welcomed advice because within a few hours, our group were due to eat a local delicacy. A restaurant had been booked along with 10 guinea pigs for each carnivore that was willing to try the traditional dish.

When we actually reached the restaurant they admitted to having only four guinea pigs available, so it was agreed to share them around and also eat a normal dish. When the cooked specimens arrived they looked like a normal complete guinea pig less the fur. The 10 carnivores immediately fell to eight. My hunger remained part of the pack of eight. There wasn't much meat on them, the skin tasted terrible and the actual meat didn't taste much better, with comparisons being made to a tough rabbit. We barely finished them despite sterling work from TC, who personally despatched one and a half guinea pigs.

The night took on a routine nature as we moved to the Cross Keys pub and then 12 made it to the dance floor at Ukukus. After so many altitude enforced early nights during the trip I was trying to make up for lost time and was proud to be among three survivors of the previous night's Ukukus adventure. The other two being Paula (who was creating a one-woman Peruvian red wine shortage) and Phil (who on the basis of having more nights out than TC must be immortal). At 2.00am I was completely shattered but content in the knowledge that most of the group were about to leave. The cumulative effect of beer, walking, lack of sleep, altitude, dancing and sun had taken its toll. All I wanted was my bed. Please let me have my bed.

I sat for a minute waiting for all the expected departees to congregate when there was a tap on my shoulder. I looked round to see a Peruvian girl '*Do you have a girlfriend?*' 'No'. '*Do you want to dance?*' 'I can't. I'm shattered'. '*I have nowhere to go tonight; maybe I sleep in your bed?*' 'You'll have to fight me for it'. Although I admit the 'you'll have to fight me for it' sounded something like 'you what?' 'no, it's a nice offer but I'm too tired and I've got to get up at 5.00am'. She may have mistaken me for Brad Pitt (in which case I want to drink what she'd been drinking or at least make sure a lot more girls drink it). Although, my strong suspicion was that she was a lady of the night or in this case a lady of the nightclub. It is somewhat confusing to an Englishman but seemingly in South America, they are often trying to subtly sell their wares in nightclubs. Anyway, I didn't have the time or inclination to boost her income and on discussion, with the others, I was the third one in our group offered her companionship.

Day 20 - Thursday 29th July - Lost Luggage

I woke up knowing that the party was breaking up, the goodbyes were all to come, but I was lucky to have seen what I'd seen and met those that I'd met. However, that was my second thought of the morning as my first was that it was bloody early at 5.00am and I wish I could carry on sleeping. The trusty rucksack had already been partially packed in a strange burst of organisation so I just had to finish the stuffing. When I'd got back from Ukukus in the early hours the water again hadn't been working so the outcome of my sit down on the toilet at 2.15am provided a bite to the air as I entered the bathroom. Russell confirmed to me that he realised there was no water when he returned to the hotel, after the meal, so had pissed in the sink instead. This had never been an option for my solid release although it would have been possible during the dark days of Yauri. The water still wasn't working so the teeth were cleaned with the remains of a bottle of mineral water and at a distance from the sink.

Packed and un-showered I met the group down at reception ready for the bus at the appointed time of 6.00am. At 6.15am everyone was gathered except for James and Debbie. Rob phoned them up and received a calm response that they were on their way and would be five minutes. The truth was somewhat different as James and Debbie jumped out their bed to start packing. 10 hectic minutes later they had recorded the fastest time in South America of the Dress & Pack season.

Freddie was meant to have met us for the guinea pig meal but had not appeared. He did leave a message of apology with the hotel reception at 10.30pm and then another note at 5.00am on which only his name was legible. Morgan confirmed that he would have only missed Freddie by an hour because he, Phil the immortal, James and Debbie had returned to the hotel at 4.00am having followed Ukukus with another club. Unlike everyone else Phil could enjoy a lie in because he was staying in Cuzco for a couple of days before venturing on to a jungle trek for a week. Although he did interrupt his sleep to say goodbye. Also leaving the party was Jenny who had to look after another Exodus group in Cuzco.

It was all a bit sad as the bus drove us to the nearby airport where we flew to Lima.

On the sight of my Lima hotel bed, I fell on it with no intention of moving for the next couple of hours. I did surface again at 2.00pm for Paula's goodbye meal at a sort of posh steak house restaurant. It was fine except I got Andrea's food, Jen got meat in her vegetarian dish, Jill's well-done burger was rare so was sent back, Andrea had my dish, Ann-Sophie received Paula's food, Paula got an odd dish, Jen swapped with Mary and then exchanged it again when she found some chicken. That left Morgan, Mark and TC happy. Following the meal, Paula said goodbye.

I then sneaked back to my bed at 6.00pm. The plan was to sleep for about 20 minutes, but it turned into a long 20 minutes because I woke up a couple of hours later. I felt more tired than ever but a shower eased me back into the land of the living, there was even the novelty that when you turned the hot tap, hot water poured out (despite H meaning cold and C meaning hot). Most of the group met up for a drink in a local restaurant with the intention of going to a salsa bar later on. The lack of recent sleep meant that come salsa time the potential number of dancers had reduced to seven.

After grabbing a couple of taxis and getting lost in Lima we eventually reached 'Latino's' at midnight. The dancing had just started, so after drinking a glass of the local brew my two left feet headed for the dance floor. I have never claimed to be John Travolta, as my early movements reflected, but things seemed to improve when I picked up the pace. It was a total revelation that my hips and feet could not only move at the same time but even in different directions. Whilst I discovered a new found agility, Pete guarded the jug of beer and rejected the overtures of two ladies of the night eager to whisk him away.

DAY 21 - FRIDAY 30ᵀᴴ JULY - STUCK IN A BOG

I woke up at 7.00am to extract body from bed, and head downstairs for my last Peruvian breakfast before having to say some sad goodbyes to Jen, Fiona, Mark, Morgan and Ann-Sophie. Ann-Sophie made an appearance despite throwing up throughout the night, hopefully, she will recover for the few days her and Morgan will be spending in Rio.

We reached the airport at 9.20am whereupon Rob said a quick farewell because his plane was due to take off at 9.30am. Rob flew to Quito in Ecuador where he would collect a truck and drive to Cuzco within two days. I don't think it's possible but Rob would be sure to give it a good go.

The Avianca plane that took us to Columbia was so old that the entrance was at the back rather than the sides and there were no television screens inside. Presumably, because television had not been invented when the plane had been built. The pilot started to accelerate and then turned on to the main runway. He just managed to keep the plane upright as it bounced down the flight strip.

However, the take-off was smooth compared to the landing. As Bogota approached the pilot weaved around in the air to such an extent we thought he must be dodging some surface to air missiles (how bad had the civil war become?). He then calmed down when he approached the runway before actually speeding up as we bumped down. The general consensus was that it must have been the pilot's maiden flight, I was just glad it wasn't our last one.

There was a four and a half hour stop off at Bogota airport before the plane was due to leave, so I planned a couple of hours in the shopping area and then into the departure lounge. I looked around the shops in a distant sort of manner i.e. I kept my distance from the goods because of a nagging memory about Bobby Moore being set up for shoplifting in Bogota. The novelty of distance shopping didn't last very long so I enjoyed a coffee with some of the others.

The peace was shattered when a partially deaf lad from the Explore group ran across to some of his colleagues with an expression of sheer panic on his face and a Columbian policeman in tow. He showed his forearms to his friends and was then taken away by the policeman. What had he done? Had he been beaten up?

An hour passed by and his group had still not heard from him so they came across to our table. Apparently, he ate a nutty dessert on the plane and had suffered an allergic reaction, so he and a fellow traveller who was a doctor had been led away by the policeman. Mary and her fluent Spanish went to help them find out where they were in the airport, but try as they might the Colombian security couldn't tell them. The doctor was, in fact, the girl I had sat next to on the flight out from London and as another half-hour past by the worry over her and the lad's whereabouts increased. Had they been taken to a hospital? Would the plane have left by the time they returned? Would he die? Thankfully the answers were no, no and no as they turned up with attached smiles and good health. Then it was back to the dreary task of waiting for our flight.

I tried to break up the boredom of waiting by heading to the departure lounge. It involved walking the gauntlet of security guards, having my bag searched and the standard frisk. It wasn't too bad at all, as they seemed more polite than British security, didn't plant any drugs on me and there was something endearing about the uniformed security girl with her long dark hair and machine gun.

The entertainment in the departure hall was limited to sleep or the television screen. The evening news was on and although I couldn't understand any words, the pictures were showing whereabouts in Colombia today's bombs had exploded. I recognised some cities near the capital but thankfully there were no pictures of Bogota. What did explode in the departure hall were rumours of the plane being delayed by three and a half hours which would mean we would not depart until 10.15pm. The departure boards did not mention any delay and the Avianca staff were vague on the subject. Jill eventually managed to wean out of them confirmation of the delay and that a free burger, chips and cola feast was available from a local fast food joint. It meant passing through the security again to reach the shopping area and then going through the even more stringent security offered by passport control into the public section. On the one hand we were in Bogota, the murder capital of the world, during something of a civil war, with bombs exploding around the country and would have to leave the high-security area to reach the restaurant, but on the other hand, we were hungry.

A burger and chips later, we were returning to the high-security area trying to convince the passport controllers to provide a Columbian stamp for our passports. It was then on to the security around passport control and trying to look a little bit guilty as I passed the pretty security guard, however, she just waved me through.

Roger and Anna had not been impressed with the offer of burger and chips, which had not been prepared with vegetarians in mind, let alone vegans. The lack of fruit in the airport had left them taking part in an involuntary fast. When the plane eventually parked outside our gate, Roger took matters into his own hands by walking onto the plane and asking the stewardesses for some fruit. After the initial shock that Roger had circumvented the allegedly tight security, they said that there was no fruit on the plane and could he leave immediately. Roger found out that the delay was because of problems in Frankfurt, but I was more interested in how he had managed to reach the plane. His explanation was simple '*Well Jeff, I just tried to walk in a very confident manner and went straight by the security, they saw me but never blinked an eyelid*'.

Nine and a half hours in an airport was not my idea of fun. The departure lounge seemed to be full of frustrated faces, with the only escape from boredom being sleep or the bomb updates on the television screens.

Although the plane had arrived, there was a further two-hour delay before we were allowed to board. We were all sat down, belted up and ready when a man on the other side of the plane looked to be suffering a minor heart attack or some sort of fit. A fellow passenger, across the aisle, sprang to his feet and hit him on the chest then called a stewardess. There was a bit of a fuss and the plane remained on the ground for another half an hour before everything settled down. The man looked uncomfortable but alive, so the plane jumped into the Bogota sky.

An hour later I was dozing when another commotion erupted. The man who had seemed seriously ill was in all sorts of trouble and I feared the plane would have to be turned round to land at Bogota. Surely if it had been a heart problem they wouldn't have allowed him to fly, so what was the problem? He quietened down and I hoped for his sake that was a good sign.

A couple of rows in front of me sat Russell with a Columbian lady beside him. She looked to be in her thirties with blonde hair and pretty-ish in a rough sort of way. Strangely she repeatedly left her seat and on her return would clamber all over Russell in a suggestive manner. To begin with he didn't know where to put himself but soon became quite chatty with her.

In fact, Russell seemed to provide more entertainment than Avianca. The one film on our nine-hour flight was 'Shakespeare in Love'. As the story was still fresh in my mind from the outward flight it seemed an apt time to fall asleep.

Day 22 - Saturday 31ST July - The Last Goodbye?

I awoke in the early hours of the morning to hear from James about what had been happening whilst I'd been asleep. Apparently, the Colombian lady had spent part of the night with her head on Russell's lap. James also added that he had been near her in the queue and her eventual destination was Amsterdam. So was it drugs, prostitution or diamond smuggling?

Andrea and Debbie encouraged James to have a man to man talk with Russell, so he could get a blow by blow account of the night's events. If it was drugs would she ask Russell to carry her bags through customs?

I was desperate to find out the answer, not just as a matter of intrigue but because it would mean that we had landed safely. On approaching Heathrow the plane was all over the place as we randomly dropped or gained height. I think if the Columbian pilots pass their exams they enter the military and if they fail its passenger flights for them.

As everyone began to re-examine their religious beliefs the plane bounced on to the runway and touched down in one piece. We were about 10 feet out the plane when Russell's new found friend was stopped by airport security and led away. The mystery deepened.

The remnants of our Peru group collected their bags before wandering off in different directions for various connections. A trip which had started with me knowing no one had become loaded with new friends, but then it was goodbye and, despite everybody's intentions, I wondered whether I'd ever see them again.

DIARY 5

The organised trip to Peru enabled me to see far more of the country than if I had travelled by myself for three weeks. The fact that my fellow truckees had been generally fantastic had also helped. Although, maybe three weeks was a reasonable time because I think people would have started to grate on each other's nerves if we had crept into a fourth week. I'd also not appreciated the number of early morning starts – that was tough going. Overall though, it had been a great success.

The trip to Peru had completely satisfied my thirst for travel. Okay, that is a complete lie, it had just fuelled my wanderlust. This made it a shock to return to my normal life in Frisby-on-the-Wreake.

In the year 2000, I moved out of Frisby to live and work in Northampton. I lived in a house of six people in Semilong road. As the road wasn't long or short, but longer than it was short, then it seemed to be an appropriate name. Northampton was okay, it was a change of scenery and I really liked my housemates. Northampton though wasn't Peru or India or Italy and I longed to go away again.

The group truck trip had been good so 'Oops I did it again' (sorry, but it is the year 2000 so I think I am allowed this song link) and I decided to go on another organised trip. This time it was the wild animals of Africa that enticed me. I'd never been keen on zoos but thought it would be amazing to see lions, elephants, giraffes and rhinos in their natural surroundings. The main destination for safaris seemed to be Kenya but Namibia appealed because it sounded a bit different.

	UK	Namibia	Africa
Population in millions	65.6	2.5	1,203
Projected population in 2050	77	4.7	2,527
Infant mortality per 1000 live births	3.9	39	57
Life expectancy - male	79	62	59
Life expectancy - female	83	67	62
Gross national income in purchasing power parity divided by population (in $)	40,550	10,380	4,802
Area of country (square miles)	93,638	318,261	11,608,000

NOTE: I didn't realise how far below Africa is every other continent on life expectancy and income

You are right though 'Oops I did it again' is not the 2000 vibe I'm looking for at a time when Big Brother was first shown on television, Ken Livingston became mayor of London, Tony Blair had managed to remain as Prime Minister but Kevin Keegan had resigned and we were waiting for Sven-Goran Erikson to take up his new role as England manager. So I'll ease you into the new millennium with Coldplay's 'Yellow' and a trip to the cinema to see 'Gladiator'.

Day 1 –Friday 3rd November 2000 – A Journey To Hell?

Once again the shackles of work can be cast off and I am free. My happy demeanour was not in the least put off by the fact that I was on a train with the devil and there had already been two emergency stops. Satan had taken the form of a youth, but I knew his identity because of the '6 6 6 ' tattooed on the back of his neck. The two emergency stops were the result of an overcrowded train (in which I stood up for two and a half hours). The first person wishing to relieve their bladder had managed to slip through the congested gangways and successfully meet up face-to-face with the toilet door. They spotted a button by the side of the door, arm up, finger stretched out, button pressed, door still closed. That was due to the button's job being 'emergency stop' rather than 'open toilet'. In fact, I think the button was most insulted that, after all that studying and high tech designing, it could be mistaken for a lowly door opener. The train ground to a halt.

After a little investigation the train re-started, 10 minutes later another bladder releaser faced the toilet door. They looked a bit confused, so a friendly voice piped up with '*make sure you get the right button*', arm up, finger outstretched. All I heard was the piper upper saying ' *N, No!*'. The train once more stood still.

The one hour journey was due to take two and a half hours because of the recent train crashes, but I hoped that, emergency stop permitting, I would reach London before my plane left for Paris. That gave me eight hours. Eventually, everyone seemed to understand the difference between emergency stop and toilet door opening, which allowed our journey to head into a smooth phase. Then the devil headed towards the toilet, what mayhem would he create?

The answer was none, in fact, it was all a bit of an anti-climax. He just opened the door and entered the toilet. A few minutes later, the carriage juddered slightly and I felt someone stagger into me; it was the devil. Satan apologised profusely and headed to his seat. He seemed a nice bloke; maybe he has just received bad press coverage over the centuries. I don't know what had happened to his horns but it may be part of his continuing image change. (Sorry to disturb you so early in this diary but I have an editorial edit here. I researched how the image of the devil had arisen when I got home. Apparently, the devil was originally a fallen angel and was blue with a halo. It was only in the middle-ages that he seemed to take the image of the Greek god Pan. Pan was all about natural experiences and instincts, which tended to show us our wild natural side. This didn't go down well with the Christian religion of the middle-ages, which thought these natural urges were evil so the devil adopted Pan's horns and hooves. And another strange fact is that Pan was thought to be the cause of the sudden fear that sometimes comes for no reason and that's why it's called panic. Okay back to the diary).

Despite the presence of the devil, and the emergency stops, I reached Heathrow with plenty of time to spare. It allowed me to check in over two hours before the flight time, so I surveyed the available sunglasses on my way to the restaurant. One pair seemed ideal, if a little expensive at £50. I normally spend £10 each year on a pair that I wear three times before breaking them or realising I can't stand them. The prudent decision was to head off for some much-needed nourishment before parting with any money.

Before my legs could take me to any food, the tannoy sounded: *'could passenger Brown, on his way to Johannesburg via Paris, please go to the departure gate immediately'*.

Had they found something in my bag? Was my flight fully booked and they were going to kick me off? Was a family member ill? What the Pan's going on?

I reached the back of a small queue at the departure gate. At the front, a lad was being sent to one side. He seemed as confused as I felt. I waited for my turn. 'Hi, I'm passenger Brown, on my way to Johannesburg via Paris'. *'Yes, sit down.'* 'But what's happening?' *'Sit down, we will tell you soon'* and with that, the Air France girl turned to the next passenger.

I had little choice but to join the fellow confused lad, who went by the name of Edward. He had also been summoned by Air France and, like me, was due to fly in a couple of hours to Paris. The difference we had was that whilst I was freeing myself of the working shackles to go travelling, he was on his way to get married in Uruguay. Allegedly, in Uruguay, the family members invite all their friends to the reception. Out of 450 wedding guests, only 15 were his family and friends.

The flight attendants finally called us over to explain that we would be travelling on an earlier flight, then gave us tickets for row 9. Row 9, that's near the front and must mean we are in business class. What a start to the trip, I'd never been in Business Class. I assumed they had spotted us when we checked in and thought '*here are two sophisticated gentlemen that should be upgraded*'.

Edward and I (sounds a bit royal) boarded the plane, only to find that we were in the front row of the Economy seats. So close, but alas so far.

The plane arrived in Paris at 9.45pm so there was still one and a half-hours until my flight to Johannesburg. I was organised enough to find gate 53, where my plane would leave from, before joining Edward for a beer to toast his forthcoming marriage. Well, a Friday night is a Friday night.

At 10.30pm I got itchy feet to check-in, whilst Edward calmly supped his beer, but finally, at 10.40pm, we headed to the departure gates. At gate 51 - a plane to Uruguay waiting for passengers and with an appropriate big queue. At gate 53 - there was not a soul or even anything on the screen. What the hell! Merde! Merde! (pardon, my French) I realised that I could be in the wrong terminal. Apparently, I was in terminal 2 but I actually needed terminal 2a and quickly. Merde! The initial enquiries did not go well because 2a was a bus ride away.

I left terminal 2. As I enquired about 'deux A', the bus driver said '*oui, oui*', and then pointed at his empty bus. For five long minutes, I sat there all alone. Then some people filed down a set of nearby stairs, in fact, I recognised them because they had checked in at Heathrow with me. They were passengers from the flight on which I should have arrived in Paris. The only thing was, they were boarding a minibus. Rather than sit on my empty unmoving bus I jumped out and ran towards the minibus. The attendant said '*Johannesburg?*' 'Yes please'.

Day 2 - Saturday 4ᵀᴴ November – 24 Hours

24 hours in Johannesburg.

One of the most dangerous cities in the world - as everyone has kept telling me over the last two weeks. I thought I might just stay at the airport, a bit boring but safe. It would be difficult to sleep, but safe. I might not meet anybody, but I'd be safe. So that was decided, safe but boring Jeff would spend his 24 hours in South Africa at Johannesburg airport.

I was then approached about a hostel. Suddenly safe and boring Jeff became dangerous and on the edge Jeff as I thought 'ah what the hell'. The devil didn't seem such a bad bloke so how bad can Johannesburg be?

A minute later I was on the streets of Johannesburg, in a car driven by a local called Joseph. I asked the obvious question - 'how dangerous is it?' '*Ah just be sensible Jeff, no camera, no obvious wallet, no valuables on display and don't dress too smart*'. Luckily, scruffy is one of my fortes. '*The city centre can be bad at this time of the month as everybody has just been paid*' (more muggings). He went on to explain that often the troublemakers are actually from Mozambique or Zimbabwe. They cross the border, cause trouble and then get deported. They then cross the border, cause trouble and get deported again. Etc. etc.

The hostel was set in a nice neighbourhood and everyone seemed fairly friendly, I just needed some local currency to cover my bill. With my scruffy confidence, I headed off to the nearest cash-point. What a turn around, there I was walking by myself on the streets of Johannesburg. It was all very pleasant in leafy suburbia, despite the security fences around the houses and the signs stating: 'this property is protected by an armed response team'. A simple 'keep off the grass' sign would have been enough to deter me.

The receptionist had told me that 100 rands would be enough for 24 hours in Johannesburg, so that was the value of the notes that the ATM slipped me. I headed back in a hostel direction but got side-tracked by the sight of an Irish Pub. The brain ticked over, it's about half an hour until Liverpool v Leeds kicks off, maybe just maybe.

Yes! They had Sky Sports, but they were showing South Africa v New Zealand at cricket. I thought that the best course of action would be to settle down to a pie and being the sensible lad I am, just a coke. It was bloody hot and I thought a dose of un-alcoholic liquid would do me no harm.

A coke and pie later, one TV was switched to football and I settled down with a Guinness to watch the game. Marvellous. As the game slipped by so did a couple more pints. After the football ended I considered leaving the bar but started talking to Billy, an Indian Glaswegian, which accounted for a couple more beers. It turned out Billy was also staying at the hostel, so just before he headed off I agreed to try and meet up with him later at the hostel. I thought that while I was in the pub I might as well watch a bit more cricket as I finished my remaining half-pint. Then Darren came over. He was one half of a couple of Aussies I had met at the hostel earlier and I decided it would be rude not to buy him a drink. As we chatted about sport a local joined in the conversation.

It was a fairly civilised discussion until another South African wicket fell. The number 10 batsman for South Africa was an Asian lad and the Afrikaans bloke spouted out '*he doesn't count because he's a kaffir*'. These racist scum do really exist. I decided sarcasm was the way forward and slated the previous nine batsmen for not being English before expressing that 'it must be great for the South African team to have such wonderful supporters'.

It wasn't long before Darren and I had left our new found enemy. We joined Darren's mate Scrawny (otherwise known as James) and a couple of friendly locals for a few beers and the odd tequila. The two local Afrikaans lads who drank with us were only 20 years old, but were about six foot three and that was just their width. The waitress also took an interest in our international group and when her shift finished joined us for a beer. In fact, it all seemed to become quite warped when Afrikaans Peter mentioned that as a 16-year-old he had been a stripper. He went on to tell a tale or two including the time he stripped for a brother and sister.

The locals were insistent that we went clubbing and Emma the waitress suggested Tramps. Well, I think she was suggesting a club rather than a description of us (after all, it is still early in the trip so my clothes are clean). However, the 100 rands I had taken out earlier was slipping away quickly so I refreshed my fund level with another 100 rand injection. Then it was back to the hostel for a quick change before Peter and Jon picked up me, Scrawny and Darren from the hostel. I didn't even want to think about the number of beers our driver had consumed.

At 9.00pm we entered Tramps Nightclub. It was very smart but very empty, which meant we easily found Emma. But we wanted somewhere a bit busier. So after a couple of hours, we trundled to Presley's via a cash-point, which gave enough time for Jon to puke up out of the window, oh the joys of youth. Presley's was suitably packed out but we were tired (Darren was already sleeping on a table) and intoxicated so left the locals to it. That did mean that there was an Englishman and a pair of Aussies somewhere in Johannesburg needing to somehow get back to the hostel that was somewhere else in Johannesburg.

Scrawny asked the Greek doorman how far it would be to walk. He took one look at us, shook his head, flipped out his mobile and called a taxi. When the taxi arrived the doorman told the driver that we were his friends and not to mess us about.

Day 3 – Sunday 5ᵗᴴ November – Attack Of The Rock Creature

I woke up at 8.00am, not actually feeling too bad. In the opposite bunk I could see a still fully clothed Darren, in the 'facedown collapsed here' position.

I tried to summon the energy to move because check-in for my flight to Namibia was midday and I didn't have any money left to pay the bill.

A shower and yet another trip to the cash-point later had let the time slip on to 9.30am. I still needed to pay for the bed and organise a lift to the airport. 9.45am and still no one about as I read the sign saying 'Please pay by 8.00pm the day before departure' (oops). I found an unofficial receptionist who was more of a permanent resident and he nipped behind the counter, took my money and gave me a receipt. That was good enough for me.

He told me that all the staff were at the airport picking up backpackers, but their return was imminent. Apparently, the free lift from the airport to the hostel did not work in reverse; there would be a 40 rand charge involved. Anyway, by 10.30am Joseph had safely deposited me at the airport for my British Airways flight to Windhoek. On this occasion, British Airways was in the form of Com Air. I presumed it was some kind of subsidiary but was not entirely sure of the difference. I just knew Com Air were higher up in the Crash Table than British Airways.

After a crash-free flight, Namibia greeted me with a 20 person queue at lost luggage. An ominous sign. I walked across to the carousel and my ruck-sack came straight around the corner (well, at least if it is possible to go straight around a corner). My destination for the day was Dan Vijeons Game Reserve, which would give me plenty of time to consider Namibia and my guide book.

Most European explorers had ignored Namibia because of its inhospitable coastlines, so it wasn't until the end of the 19th century that Namibia was colonised by Germany. However, they were overthrown by South Africa during the First World War and South Africa was given a mandate to rule the country. Internal problems flared up in the 1960s and the United Nations tried to change the mandate so that Namibia would eventually be granted independence, but they could not reach an agreement with South Africa. In the 1970s the International Court of Justice ruled that South Africa's continued 'occupation' of the region was illegal. South Africa then made an offer to grant Namibia its independence, but only if the country was based on apartheid principles. This was rejected and the eighties saw more fighting and the prospect of a peaceful resolution slipping away. Finally, in 1988, an agreement was worked out and in 1990 Namibia became a new country with a democratically elected government. Hooray!

I knew the country was meant to be beautiful but at the same time fairly desolate. I'd heard it was 'the size of Germany and Britain put together but with a population of 1.5 million'. That there was an amazing desert, skeleton coast and as I told the taxi-driver 'the only person I know from Namibia is Frankie Fredericks the great sprinter'. *'Wow, you know Frankie Fredericks?'* 'No, I mean I've seen him on television'. *'Oh'. 'Did you not see him today?'* This was all getting a bit confusing. 'I've only just arrived in Namibia'. *'He was at the airport today; you must have just missed him'.* 'Really, well he was probably a bit too quick for me' I replied, as the Namibians got their first taste of my dodgy jokes.

After a long drive, we reached the game reserve. The first question I was asked on entering the reception was *'are you Jeff Brown?'* Rather than being the leader of the Namibian branch of the hitherto unknown Jeff Brown appreciation society, it was Tracy the trip leader. She confirmed that there was a room shortage so I'd been allocated a VIP chalet. I may have missed out on the business class flight but at last, my quality had begun to tell.

There would be four of us in the hut. Maggie and Chris from Manchester had already arrived in the hut, but not with their bags. Apparently, they had been in the lost luggage queue, which I had seen at the airport. Tracy alleged that it was a popular Namibian airport queue because they are world class in the baggage misplacement department. This means that Maggie and Chris will be in the same clothes throughout the trip unless their bags are found or they buy some new ones.

I enjoyed a shower and generally relaxed before having to walk up to a restaurant for the first group meeting. I had again decided on an organised trip rather than heading off backpacking by myself. The organised trip is more expensive but I can cram more in a limited time and I didn't fancy driving for hours by myself on the deserted Namibian roads.

Tracy had told me not to worry about the walk up to the restaurant because there was nothing in the Game Park that would attack me. Do the Lions know not to come here? As it was warm I decided to enjoy the novelty of sunshine rather than worry about hungry animals. I did have my first brush with the local wildlife when I spotted a lizard just beyond the wall on the side of the path. As the lizard moved I followed it, not realising that another set of eyes were intently watching my every movement from a rock perch just the other side of a bush, not 10 yards up the path. The lizard ran off, so I continued my walk in blissful ignorance. What happened next truly surprised me.

I rounded the bush and suddenly saw the creature crouched on a rock. It was some six-foot in length and just three foot away. Before I could react, the animal let out an *'alright Jeff'*. It was a genuine Pat Gill, survivor of the Peru trip, who was on this Namibian adventure with his wife Helen. It was great to see a familiar face but just a shock to find it on a rock.

The group meeting proved an eye opener because the age range was not what I expected. There were about three of us in our twenties, about four in their thirties, five in their forties and the remaining seven scattered around their fifties, sixties and possibly seventies. The words Helen had spoken to me, before the trip, rang in my mind: '*just don't compare it with the Peru trip*'.

DAY 4 – MONDAY 6ᵀᴴ NOVEMBER – THE QUIVERING COOK

The introduction to our truck was a prolonged journey of 300 miles. There is nothing like getting straight into the swing of things. The truck is a 24 seater so there is plenty of room for our 19 bodies. Its windows are gaping holes with no glass in sight. So despite the temperature being boiling hot outside, when the truck is moving the air blowing in from the holes keeps you cool.

In fact, the nice breeze turned into a cold gale so I moved out of the path of our self-created hurricane and sat next to Alan. Alan was one of our retirees, a very nice bloke but capable of jokes that make my groan-inducing gags look positively cutting, witty and side-splitting. He was very knowledgeable and full of facts but it was a case of picking the bright silver pins from the haystack. I realise that people have different interests to me but I accidentally entered a half hour conversation on bird spotting with no sign of an emergency exit. Indeed in trying to make conversation, I would dig myself into a deeper hole by asking more questions. How could I switch the topic to my interest in sport? The silver pin he produced was about the Egyptian vulture that lives off marrow. To eat, it picks up bones, flies up 200 feet, let's go, the bones smash on the ground, which allows them to get at the marrow. Interesting but there was more hay to come.

The truck was owned and driven by another Alan. He was in the front cab by himself because Tracy had joined the rest of the group in the back. It seemed as though she was making a real effort, especially with one man who I surmised was in his mid-fifties and travelling alone. In fact, wherever he sat Tracy followed. It took me the whole of the seven-hour drive to realise that despite an estimated 20 year age gap they were boyfriend and girlfriend. The truck intermittently rang with the sound of laughter. The source normally stemmed from a couple called Malcolm and Deirdre. I think with Malcolm around we could reach our laughter quota even if the rest of the truck was made up with completely miserable gits. I also decided that if I told any gags then I should make sure Malcolm is around so it's not just me laughing at my own jokes. In front of Malcolm and Deirdre sat Uls and Monica. They were the other twentysomethings. Uls reminded me of a friendly Walrus and Monica reminded me of a 25-year-old Swiss girl (not that surprising as she is a 25-year-old Swiss girl). They both sported mischievous smiles that suggested they knew something I didn't (other than the French and German language).

After a full day's worth of travelling, we arrived at the eerie quiver tree forest. Amazingly, soon after arriving, a courier turned up for Maggie and Chris. He had driven directly from Windhoek airport with their missing luggage. Apparently, a consequence of the booming tourist industry is a booming lost luggage tracking industry. I always assumed you had to keep going back to the airport to find your missing belongings but apparently not. Anyway, after that interesting diversion, it was back to the quiver trees. The quiver tree forest sounds straight out of *The Hobbit* and they looked like the living dead of the tree world with their skeleton-like branches and lack of leaves. The 'quiver' name comes from when the local Bushmen used to hollow out the branches to make quivers for their arrows, rather than trees actually quivering.

I tried to prolong my survey of the quiver trees but got called back to help cook. Whenever the tents are pitched we have to cook for ourselves, this takes the form of two volunteered cooks and two helpers. As a cook, you would be on duty for 24 hours to complete an evening meal, breakfast and lunch (for 21 people - made up of two guides and 19 passengers). If this wasn't enough, as a helper you would have to assist for 24 hours with an evening meal, breakfast and lunch. Everyone would have to be both a cook and helper at some point.

This is where it helped to have clever friends. Helen nominated herself and Pat as cooks. Then suggested myself and, her friend, Katherine should be helpers. The cunning plan was that the sooner you cook and help, the sooner it's out of the way.

We had not been provided with a definition of helper and the interpretation varied. As a cook, Pat believed helper meant that I was his personal slave providing him with beers, cleaning his shoes, delivering him cups of coffee to the tent etc. As a helper, I believed it meant I had to hide when meals were being prepared and only when caught would I have to stand around pretending to look busy.

After two hours helping with the barbecue I crawled off to my tent for some precious sleep.

Day 5 – Tuesday 7th November – Fish, Rice & More Rice

'Cockle-doodle-doo!'

What the? Out in the middle of Africa and I'm woken by a bloody cockerel!

'Cockle-doodle-doo!'

'Cockle-doodle-doo!'

The time was 4.00am.

Where is a lion when you need one?

'Cockle-doodle-doo!'

The morning moved on to 5.45am and as a helper, I was despairingly separated from my sleeping bag and forced to assist with breakfast. I shared my tent with Martin, a Swiss lad in his mid-thirties who on the first impression seemed friendly and fluent in English. Unfortunately, he wasn't friendly enough to offer to take my place in cooking breakfast. Instead, all I heard from him was 'zzzzzzzzzzz…'

I started to help with breakfast but noticed that the shower was free, so grabbed my toilet bag and ran to the body cleaner. I managed to have a quick shower and got back just in time to hear Helen saying *'where's Jeff gone?'* So I think that was perfect timing in terms of missing as much of the cooking without being missed too much.

Shortly after breakfast, we were back on the truck, heading towards the second biggest canyon in Africa. The journey was interrupted by a meander around the giant's playground, an ancient mountain range that had crumbled into a bizarre set of rocks.

A further stop was needed at a local town for food shopping because now Katherine and I were the cooks, supported by Don and Clare. The trip was turning into slave labour; up at 5.45am to help with breakfast, then food shopping scheduled for tonight and another three hours cooking tonight. This isn't fun. Tracy, the guide, gave us some money and sent us on our way. As Katherine and I searched for inspiration, Pat and Helen offered to help. Our combined brainpower mustered up fish and rice with a couple of vegetables in between. Anything remaining was invested in cartons of red and white wine. Marvellous.

In the middle of the afternoon, the truck arrived at the campsite near Fish River Canyon. It was well over 30 degrees Celsius. The extreme heat meant I just found some shade and settled down for a couple of hours. When the temperatures began to drop we jumped on the bus again for a ride to the canyon. Bizarrely, Martin had got bored and decided to start walking to the canyon himself. He must have got three miles down the track before we caught him up. You wouldn't catch me moving too far in that heat.

Fish River Canyon claims to be the second biggest canyon in the world. It looked impressively big and desolate from the cliff edge, although it was a bit disappointing in another way. There was this great big canyon below our feet to explore, but we couldn't go down into it and walk around because of the danger of flash floods.

Maybe the pleasure had been dulled by the fact that Katherine and I were on cooking duty when we returned to the campsite. With fish, vegetables and rice at our disposal, we set about our task. At home, I tend to favour the boil in the bag rice rather than risk fluffy rice. However, it was me that was on rice duty with no bags in sight.

In my eagerness to produce perfect rice I forgot about the fish. It wouldn't have been a problem except that the fish hadn't started cooking yet. I spent 10 minutes sieving the water out that I had only just added to the rice and then helped prepare the fish. When that was cooking nicely I returned to my instructions which suggested 20 large spoons of uncooked rice. Even with my limited rice knowledge, when the 10th spoon went in, I thought enough was enough. Out of the chaos came some pristine rice, or to be more precise, bowls and bowls of pristine rice. The 10 spoonfuls had become a mountain range. After three hours of cooking, eating and clearing up I was free to crash out in the tent. I need to review my holiday details to check whether I should be receiving a salary.

Day 6 – Wednesday 8ᵗʰ November 2000 – All The Time In The World

Up, up, had to get up.

The time was 5.30am, I was on holiday, but I still had to get up to cook breakfast. The thought of 'only two meals left to prepare' took me out of my sleeping bag and in front of the gas rings. With the leftovers from last night, everyone would get the chance to enjoy rice pudding for breakfast along with a bit of scrambled egg. After my preparation and serving duties were over I returned to the saucepans for some food. But no rice pudding or scrambled egg remained, so instead, I sat and ate a jam sandwich. A cook's life is a tough one.

We were soon on the move. Tracy passed around some paper on which we had to choose our activities in Swakopmund. The list included quad biking, sandboarding, skydiving, fishing, a balloon ride, wildlife treks and a micro-light flight. I decided on quad biking and sandboarding, but also fancied the skydiving. Skydiving in the desert would be amazing, but the £100 price tag concerned me, as did the fact that I'd have to jump out of an aeroplane. Ummmmmm, decision pending.

The scenery out of the truck consisted of a deserty surface, with the odd bush thrown in amongst rolling hills. It was amazing, but it didn't help me with the decision as to whether to skydive. I let my mind wander. Exciting, incredible, a real high in your life versus expensive and scary. £100 for a once in a lifetime experience isn't so bad. I was severely tempted.

My thought process was shattered when Helen read out a section of her guidebook. '*Skydiving in Swakopmund has had a number of fatal accidents in recent years. If you are experienced then check the equipment*'. My knowledge spanned 'have you got one of those silky things that get big in the wind, oh yeah and some strings attached'. Any doubt vanished from my mind, I would not be skydiving.

The scenery continued to be stunning right up until lunchtime when we stopped at a campsite near the mysterious singing rock. If a local guide appeared then we would be taken to this bizarre rock. No one seemed to have any idea what it actually did but I surmised that it liked rock music, The Rolling Stones, Stone Roses and the soundtrack from the Rocky Horror show. Such contemplation was wasted though as no guide materialised so Katherine and myself had to make lunch. After assisting for three meals and then preparing three meals it would be our culinary swansong. No getting up half an hour before everybody else and no slaving away in the heat when everybody else could peacefully sup on a beer. Singing rock or no singing rock, Katherine and I were blissfully happy.

A couple more hours down the road led us to Duwisib Castle. It was built by a German Baron in 1908 right bang in the middle of nowhere. Rather than a place to store soldiers, it was the family home for the baron and his American heiress. When the First World War started they returned to Germany so he could fight. Or as it turned out, so he could fight and die. After the war, the Baroness went to live in New York and never went back to Duwisb Castle. As a Namibian castle it is quite incredible, but in comparison to its British cousins, I would classify it in the very small stately home category.

Our campsite, for the night, was relatively close to the castle. Martin and I were soon into the normal routine of putting up the tent. Then with no cooking duties, I suddenly had time on my hands. It was all a bit confusing, especially with no bar to settle down in. What should I do? Martin suggested a run in the blistering heat but only a nutter would go for a run in those conditions.

We set off towards the castle at a gentle pace. I had copied Martin in my preparations for the run; first drinking a cup of water, then soaking my cap and wetting my shirt. Martin had suggested sticking to the tracks, rather than running on the smaller paths and surprising some snakes. I quickly agreed. This was Black Mamba country - even the name sounds forbidding. Although in this area the mamba is more of an olive colour. Um….. Olive Mamba …… sounds more like a big friendly African woman rather than a deadly snake.

We reached the castle, and then headed towards a neighbouring farm where we were met by a large barking dog showing its teeth. It ran towards us, so I stopped and stared. It stopped. Then we started running, so the dog started running at us again. We stopped. It stopped. We edged away. It stopped. Martin started jogging and I breathed a sigh of pure relief that the dog wasn't going to maul us.

In the intense heat, my soaking wet shirt and cap had metamorphosised into a dry hot shirt and crispy cap. We ran back past the campsite and Martin offered the options of running on the main road or heading back to camp. Not to be outdone by my Swiss friend I confidently ushered him onwards. Another half mile went by and I decided that the Swiss could happily outdo me.

We returned to the campsite whereupon I collapsed in a heap and Martin found another path to run on. The great thing about not cooking, besides not cooking, was that I could now shower, wash and get changed at my leisure while some other poor souls cooked me a meal. Now I am on holiday. The shower was typically tepid, but when the outside temperature is so hot that isn't a problem. Although there is still something strange when you come out of a shower and you're warmer than when the water was spraying your body.

Darkness began to fall as we huddled around the campfire and Katherine offered everyone some liquid refreshment. She could have offered a nice cold beer or a glass of fine wine, but instead, she had bought some cactus juice from the castle and wanted everybody to have a taste. It was not until after I had drunk the stuff that I became aware that the reason she offered (maybe 'nicely forced on us' is a more accurate description) the juice was that she couldn't stand the taste. It turned out that neither could anyone else. We went on to taste cactus jam, which was okay, but I think I'll stick to the strawberry variety. It seemed the castle offered a full range of cactus products, well maybe with the exception of Uls suggestion of cactus condoms. I mean you couldn't risk having a prick in a condom.

A big bright moon lit up the dark sky. My mind reminisced about sleeping outside in India. I even told John about the beauty of sleeping under the stars, without your view being hindered by a tent. Susannah, one of the Swiss girls, was already sleeping out and I told him at some point on the trip we should do it. '*What about tonight Jeff?*'

John was a down to earth Yorkshireman. About 60 years of age but with a new lust for life. He adored nature; whether it be plants, animals or stars and the thought of sleeping out struck an immediate chord with him.

Tonight seemed a bad idea. The grass around us still spelt snake country to me, and that meant 'Jeff in-tent' country. I slightly dampened John's enthusiasm but it did not deter him. He asked Alan the driver about it. When Alan mentioned the snakes, scorpions and spiders that he could cuddle up with, John became suitably deterred. This didn't put off Susannah who had been introduced to sleeping out whilst in Australia. She had already decided that a few pesky animals would not stop her. The example of Susannah soon relit John's enthusiasm so he decided to give it a try after all. He tried to convince me, but I'm made of much flimsier stuff.

The last conversation I heard that night was of John being told by Alan to sleep away from the trees and grass. I went to bed (or at least my sleeping bag) with the thought that 'if anything happens to John, it was me who planted the sleeping out idea in his head'. John just don't get bitten.

DAY 7 – THURSDAY 9ᵀᴴ NOVEMBER 2000 – THE DUNE AND I

I lay in until 6.00am, it was great. When I did get up I saw John's empty sleeping bag by the ashen campfire, with large snake marks leading away from it. Before I could say 'it wasn't my fault' there was a tap on my shoulder. John's dulcet Yorkshire tone rang out '*I think someone's having a joke with those snake marks*'.

After a big sigh of relief and a hearty breakfast, the truck (with accompanying bodies) set off on the long haul to Sesiem. In three hours of driving through amazing scenery, of anything from white grassy plains to imposing hills, we only met five cars. Each driver we saw gave us a cheerful wave (somehow I can't imagine driver's behaving like this on the M25).

The journey was broken up by a stop at a small canyon. Unlike the giant Fish River Canyon, we actually had the chance to walk inside it. The canyon walls were about 100 feet tall on either side and in between the cliff faces was a narrow rocky route to navigate. There was hardly any vegetation, just a mass of rocks but typically with Namibia, there was a beauty in this desolated and blazing hot canyon. We even found a pterodactyl nest. Well, it looked like it; a strange chamber out in the middle of nowhere, inside a rugged canyon - that must be the start of a horror film.

There was no pterodactyl attack and instead, we safely clambered back on the truck for the journey to Sesiem. On reaching Sesiem there was the usual routine of putting up the tent in the blistering sun. The difference from before was that we were in the Namib Desert, the oldest desert in the world. After lazing around in the sun we headed off to see the world-renowned Sossusvlei sand dunes. I have heard varying reports as to whether they are the biggest in the world, but they stand at about 1,000 feet high. The first views revealed pyramid-like shapes made of sand with beautifully sharp edges carved by the wind. The last five kilometres of the trail, to the main dunes, was along a sandy path (a lot more sand than path) with motor access limited to 4x4 vehicles i.e. not our truck. We grabbed a lift at 4.45pm, but as the last 4x4 trip was at 5.00pm we would have to walk back. Even then the park closes at 8.00pm and it was estimated that it was an hour's journey from the car park to the exit gates. By my reckoning, it would mean leaving the sand dunes at 5.45pm.

I fancied climbing to the top of the largest dune, but would have to get up and back within three-quarters of an hour. It all seemed impossible so I posed for photographs instead. When I turned to face the dune, I saw Martin already halfway to the top, with John and Heather a quarter of the way up. 'Hold on, I'm not being left out'. I announced my intentions, then left Pat and Helen standing at the bottom of the dune.

I started on the dune pyramid; one step forward, then the grains of sand slid me half a step back, one step forward, half back. I soon found out that if you trod in somebody else's footsteps then the sand is more compact, so you don't slip back quite so much. I passed John about halfway up, then soon caught up with Heather, by which time Martin had already reached the top. We were almost three-quarters of the way to the summit when Heather let out an '*oh my god*'. I turned around and was equally gobsmacked. I had been so busy ploughing upwards that it was the first time I had turned around. The view was breathtaking, how could something so desolate be so beautiful? There was a lake below us with a small desert plain and then a mountain range of sand pyramids set against a deep blue sky.

We started on the final quarter and the going got tougher. The angle of the slope seemed to increase and the footprints then disappeared instantaneously. Every step became an effort. With the end in sight, I seemed to be stopping more than I was starting. I yelled at Martin to come down and give me a piggyback. He ran down, said *what did you say?* Laughed, and then ran back up again. I carried on my crawl up the slope.

I reached the top, totally exhilarated. I had conquered the world's most famous sand dune (although I can't name any others, and come to that, I didn't know of this one until a couple of months ago). What a view, what a dune, how lucky am I? I took a couple of deep breaths and tried to take it all in. It was one of those moments that you want to store in your memory in the 'for eternity' file.

A couple of minutes later Heather reached the top. The guidebook had said that the climb was only for the very fit, so I was surprised to see that it had only taken us 20 minutes. Mind you I had age on my side, Heather had run the odd marathon and Martin, well Martin was Martin.

Then, to my surprise and delight, others started to arrive. There was John, Susannah, Alan, Clare, Helen, Don and Janet. I would be full of respect to anyone who climbed up to the top, but the fact that five of those seven would be in or around their sixties left me overflowing with respect.

The descent proved somewhat easier than the ascent because the moving sand took you escalator style down the dune. For every one step forward, the sand added a bonus half step. The easy walking didn't last for long, before you knew it we were on the ground and trudging through the sand in a truck direction. It may only have been five kilometres we needed to walk but the boiling hot sun and a sandy surface, which gives way with every step, were not in our favour. How do these older people manage it? And not only do they manage; they do it without a single word of complaint. The most senior of the group was Don, who seemed to be really suffering, but pride dictated that he wouldn't even let me carry his bag. Instead, we dreamed of a nice cold beer. Hmmm.

The beer incentive worked a treat because we reached the truck in one piece. It turned out that the group were a couple of people light. Uls and Monica had decided to walk to the dune rather than take the lift from the car park. That was at 4.45pm and there had been no confirmed sightings of them in the last one and a half hours. The Park would close at 8.00pm and it would take an hour to drive to the gates. However, the time was only 6.30pm so there was no cause for alarm.

At 7.00pm there was still no sign of them. The sun was quickly drawing in and within another half hour, it would be dark. The middle of the desert is not the best place to get lost (that would be a beer cellar or a Swedish women's beach volleyball training centre or the bar at the Swedish women's beach volleyball training centre with large screens that play non-stop sport. Or maybe I am thinking about this a little too much). Anyway, Martin decided to head off down the track to try and find them. Alan, our driver, seemed completely unruffled and I wasn't bothered about sleeping in the truck, although it would be cold without a sleeping bag. Our truck was not alone because another truck, half full of Aussies, stood alongside us. It was half full because they had lost ten of their group. Their wanderers gradually trickled in, but still there was no sign of Uls and Monica.

Finally, at 7.15pm a Swiss trio were spotted in the distance. They were quickly loaded into the van and Alan sped off. 8.00pm came and went while we were still inside the park. The truck met the gates at 8.10pm. Luckily they were still open, so not only would I enjoy the luxury of my warm sleeping bag but also that nice cold beer of my and Don's dream.

When we reached the tents I immediately looked around to see if anyone wanted to rush to the bar. Heather and the ever-eager John were easily persuaded, so we trooped straight off for a lager. To our amazement, Don and Clare were already sitting outside the bar with beers on the table. I couldn't quite understand how they had beaten us to the bar. The Don I'd been with had been absolutely exhausted. I may have the advantage of youth, but it seems that I still have much to learn from Don and Clare.

The surrounding area was desert, so I decided that there would be fewer snakes around than in most areas that we stay. Therefore, this seemed to be an ideal place to sleep out of the tent. It's amazing how brave you get after a couple of beers. There was even a bench within our huddle of tents, which seemed ideal because it would allow animals to crawl underneath rather than over me. I put my mat on the bench, placed my sleeping bag on top, then drifted off to sleep under the beautiful stars.

Day 8 – Friday 10th November – Dune

At 3.59am I was happily sleeping on my bench in the middle of the Namib Desert. At 4.00am the first alarm went off, feet moved, sleeping bags rustled. No more sleep for me.

My body dug deeply to rise at 4.30am. This is a holiday. This is a holiday. This is a holiday. However many times I repeated the sentence, it took some believing. We left for the dunes at 4.45am. The reason for the inhuman earliness was that the dunes at sunrise are meant to be a sight for sore eyes. I just hoped they were a good sight for tired eyes.

The truck pulled up by a couple of the larger dunes. Off we went again; one step up, slip back, one step up, slip back and repeat several hundred times. I followed Martin to the end of the dune and there we sat surveying the scene. A few minutes later Deirdre joined us. She had left her husband Malcolm part way up because he was suffering from a little vertigo. The good thing about the dunes was that if you did fall off then you would have a soft landing, albeit a long soft landing.

The sun started to rise over the dunes, as they drifted in colour from dull brown to bright orange. Serene, simply serene. On one side you had a small flat plain, followed by dunes, dunes and more dunes. On the other side were sand pyramid after sand pyramid. Golden brown on the sunny side and black on the opposite side. Mother Nature is a beautiful artist. I'd been slightly confused yesterday as to why these massive sand dunes are so big and don't simply blow away. The answer Alan provided was surprisingly simple. The sand dunes normally form around an obstacle like a bush or rock. The wind blows sand around it but when and where the wind speed falls the grains drop down around the obstacle. Eventually, the obstacle is covered in sand and has become a dune. The dune then collects more sand in the same way as the original obstacle.

Although I could have happily sat there for a few days, trying to see if the dunes were growing, we had to head back to the campsite and pack up the tents. Then it was off on a five-hour drive to the old German coastal town of Swakopmund.

The scenery was of the usual stunning standard before it just became sand (it shouldn't be a surprise in a desert). Then after hours of desolate sand scenes, the town of Walvis Bay popped up. When Namibia received its independence in 1990, South Africa refused to return Walvis Bay because it is the only natural harbour for hundreds of miles. The official area of South Africa included Walvis Bay and anything in a 30 kilometre radius. In 1994 the Namibian national debt had mounted up, so under pressure, South Africa agreed to return the town to Namibia.

Soon after Walvis Bay, we arrived at the sleepy seaside resort of Swakopmund. The Germans, who were desperately trying to establish a harbour to compete with the British-controlled Walvis Bay, gave birth to Swakopmund in 1893. Ever since then it has been very much a German Namibian town; although the planned harbour never worked. They even have traditional beer festivals here.

Swakopmund finally gave us the luxury of sleeping in beds rather than tents. The accommodation complex was large, with an electric fence running around the outside and security guards by the entrance. I shared a chalet with John and Martin. Whilst John unpacked, Martin and I headed for our beds. Martin fully believed that an afternoon 'power nap', of 20 minutes or so, does you the world of good and it was a philosophy that I eagerly accepted. Two hours later we got up.

John was most amused that the 'youngsters' needed a sleep in the afternoon, whilst his 60-year-old body continued merrily on its way. They don't make bodies like they used to.

Suitably refreshed we headed into town with the rest of the group to book our Swakopmund pursuits. I booked sandboarding for Sunday morning and quad biking on Sunday afternoon. The only option we were offered for Saturday was a wildlife trip. The wildlife was plants, rather than animals, which didn't really tickle my fancy. I did manage to find out that a different group were sandboarding on Saturday morning, so I persuaded the assistant to let me join them.

After the meal - where I tasted oysters for the first time (libido seemingly unaffected) - Martin, Susannah and I headed for Fagin's bar for a couple of beers. The only others from our group that went for a drink were Maggie and Chris, but apparently, that was just because they followed us thinking we were going back to the chalets. The lack of a ridiculously early start meant we could happily carry on drinking until 2.00am. At that point, it was thought that we had sufficiently boosted the coffers of the local bars and our beds beckoned.

Day 9 – Saturday 11th November – Crashed and Duned

My dehydrated body limped out of bed at 8.45am in desperate need of some water. I had to be outside the complex's entrance at 9.15am. I waited from 9.10am to 9.20am but no van arrived. Had they forgotten about me? I ran down to the adventure office and was happy to see the vans still outside. There were four vans in all, which collected 23 people from various locations. Whilst I nursed a slight hangover, and a big thirst, I considered that the rest of the Exodus group would still be tucked up in bed enjoying a nice gentle morning. Why did I book this? Surely sado-masochism involves a whip rather than a sand dune.

We arrived at the dunes, which were very large and very steep from where I was standing. The first action was to sign a declaration stating that you take full responsibility for your actions. Depending on your perspective this is either slightly disturbing or means that you're about to do something exciting. Something exciting in this case meant throwing yourself off a sand dune and reaching speeds of up to 80 kilometres an hour.

After a safety talk, from an American girl, we grabbed the four-foot long pieces of plywood that are the sandboards and put on the gloves, elbow pads and helmets. I was ready for the off.

The off started with a 20 minute walk up to the training dune. To reach the top you had to run the last bit because if you walked it was one step forward and two steps back. At the top, I was glad to see a couple of three-litre water containers. I gratefully drank the water but unsurprisingly when you're on a dune, my lid holding hand was full of sand, which then infiltrated the water. I passed it on to the next person complaining that there was sand in the container to pre-empt the comment they would surely make.

I thought a training slope was meant to be gentle and innocuous. Steep and intimidating were far better words for the descent that faced me. The first three idiots sped down the dune. Unfortunately for me, the fourth idiot went by the name of Jeff Brown. I could have been in bed enjoying a well-deserved lie in, but no, there I stood like a reluctant lemming.

I put my board down, whereupon one of the assistants held on to it to stop it sliding away. I laid face down on the board and lifted the front corners to ensure it would move freely over the sand. I took the position we were taught in the safety talk and readied myself for the release. The helper took his hands off the board and off I went.

The board picked up speed at a great rate and I sped excitedly down the slope. Bbbbbbbrrrrrrriiiiiiiiiiillllllllllliiiiiiaaaaaaannnnnnnntt! I reached the end of the run, not only in one piece, but also with the board facing the right way. Wow!

The second run was even steeper, but more exhilarating despite a mini wipe-out, involving a 90-degree spin at the end. The third was a 'proper run' in that it was a massive dune and frighteningly steep. Three-quarters of the way down I could feel the back of the board moving to the left so I dropped my right foot into the sand to straighten the board. It began to straighten then the back slipped to the left again and I was out of control. The board performed a 360-degree turn and as I desperately tried to cling on there was a nasty cracking sound. By this time I was eating so much sand that I didn't notice that my board had snapped in two and the back was making its own way down the dune. I finished up in a heap, but nothing was broken except my pride, oh and the board.

Up we clambered again, but this time for a two-person ride. An Aussie, called Rob, teamed up with me. We decided to use his board on the basis that mine was in two pieces. I sat at the front with my knees up, whilst Rob was behind me steering with his hands. I warned him that he was taking his life in his hands, following my last two crashes, but at least the slope was gentle for the tandem. We were safely gliding down, towards the end of the slope, when I triumphantly announced that we hadn't crashed, so Rob promptly swayed to the side and wiped us out. If I am not mistaken that would be the Australian sense of humour.

After the relative calm of the tandem, it was back to business. All the practice runs had gradually built up to the last two slopes. From where I was standing they weren't mere slopes they were cliff faces. I heard a montage of comments from *'80 kilometres an hour'*, *'jumps'* and *'no bloody way'*. They wouldn't let us go straight away because they wanted to grease the boards to make them go quicker. They seemed to think I was joking when I told them my new board would be okay, slow and ungreased. A few people pulled out and opted to sit on top of the dune. The first to go was Beth, our beautiful American instructor. Another of the instructors had been videoing all morning and she sat on top of Beth to video the descent. This included a large bump in the slope that provided the 'jump' that propelled them into the air. Mad. How could I whinge about the slope when two girls go down together? Especially with one sitting on top of the other. Mind you, I think all the lads would have volunteered to go down the slope clinging on to Beth.

All too quickly I found myself at the front of the 'plunging down a cliff face' queue. 'Okay Jeff, now would be a good time for a nice smooth run' I thought to myself. I flew down the cliff face, hit the jump, took off into the air, carried on picking up pace, landed and was chuffed to have survived the jump. I was victoriously gliding down to the bottom when I heard Beth shout *'Jump!'* I thought I'd already done the jump, so had just enough time to think 'eh', when I found myself in the air again. I clung to my board, landed perfectly, even if I say so myself, and smoothly brought the board to a standstill. Wow. Oh big WOW. I'm alive. I tried to act as if I had expected to still be alive, but cool isn't easy when your jaw is still gaping.

Then it was back up the dunes to try the other big slope. Again I flew down the cliff face for another smooth, amazing, but well-executed run. After a dodgy start, I had found a rich vein of form to record the longest run of the day.

The final slope led us back to the trucks for some sandwiches (and I mean SANDwiches) and beer. The group were very friendly and it was good to hear their Namibian stories. A few of them were in the Etosha Game Park following a rhino, in their 20 seater overland truck. The rhino became increasingly frustrated at being followed, so turned and charged at their truck. It hit the side of the vehicle, then fell on to the floor. The truck was unmoved and the rhino retreated, only to take another run at the truck and again land on its backside. All of which was recorded on video by one of the travellers.

After we finished the food, Beth said it would be easiest if I travelled back in her truck because she was returning to the office, near my chalet. It worked out well because the truck I had arrived in had a flat battery. I warned her that I would be back tomorrow. It turned out that she actually owned the sandboarding company and she offered me a 50% discount. Beth also added that she'd bring some extra strong boards for me tomorrow.

Early in the afternoon, I returned to an empty chalet, with my face, hands, coat, feet, hair and even ears full of sand. I had a shower, where I managed to create a mini dune from all the sand that fell off me. Then I slipped under my duvet and happily slept for a couple of hours. Bliss.

John and Martin returned home briefly before I dragged them up to Fagin's Bar, where the video of the sandboarding was due to be shown. After a few beers and a bit of food, the local nightclub beckoned. In all of John's 60 years he'd never been to a nightclub, but in his words '*I'll give it a go*'. He may have been the oldest person in the club by 20 years, but it didn't stop him being the second person on to the dance floor. What a star.

Day 10 – Sunday 12th November 2000 – Sandstorms, Prostitutes And The Death Of A Nation

John was up by 7.00am. Martin and I struggled from our beds at 8.30am for another sandboarding morning. Helen, Martin, John, Alan, Heather, Monica, Malcolm and Katherine were losing their sandboarding cherry today. I felt it my duty to inform them about the three broken legs, four broken arms, one suicide and two people missing in action after yesterday's session. For some reason, they wouldn't believe me.

The dunes greeted me once more, along with Beth. She had been passing through Swakopmund five years ago when the idea of starting a sandboarding company sprang to mind. Five years later, she is still passing through but has a successful business to her name. From Monday to Friday she is stuck in the office, but come the weekend she escapes to the dunes and joins in the fun.

As an experienced campaigner I circumnavigated the safety talk and instead I joined Paulus, the assistant sandboarder, on the walk up the dunes (obviously after I had again signed to say that any injuries would be due to my own dodgy piloting). It was important to keep the right side of this man, for not only does he launch you and your board down the slope (and if he doesn't give you a straight start it could lead to a serious wipe-out), he also serves behind the bar at Fagin's. My safety and beer were in his hands.

The difference from yesterday was that each time we started a new slope, Paulus would laugh and say *'Jeff first'*. In fact, wherever I hid it was *'Jeff first'*. The practice yesterday did not provide me with any additional skills because the only improvement I made was in my mastery of the wipeout. There wasn't the previous thrill because I was happy to plunge down whichever slope Paulus or Beth pointed me down. I'd happily crash anywhere.

A strong wind meant we weren't reaching the high speeds of yesterday, but it didn't stop Helen producing a 15 foot jump that nearly caused a bleep on the Namibian Air traffic control screens. Whilst Helen managed to cling on, at that vital high-speed moment, one lad lost control at the same point and WIPED OUT. He said that he didn't realise there was trouble brewing until he reached the quickest section of the dune and there was no longer a board underneath him. His board snapped and ran down the dune, whilst he crashed down the slope ending up in a breathless heap. He stayed down for a few seconds, before slowly standing up and in his words *'working out where he was'*. Concluding the injury report, Malcolm broke a rib and John jarred his shoulder. Reports of Helen suffering from altitude sickness, during her giant leap, proved unfounded.

Beth said that most of the bad injuries they'd suffered over the years were on the tandem, with a large bloke falling on top of a petite girl (three broken collar bones). This explained why they said that, for the tandem, blokes should be at the front and girls at the back. Although, at the time, they told us speed-demons that it would mean that we would go quicker. Other than that, the worst accident was an almost severed finger. This occurred during the lunch, at the bottom of the dunes, when instead of cutting open a bread roll the victim almost chopped off his finger.

Alas, my sandboarding career ended and I had to bid farewell to Beth, our sandboarding siren.

There was no time for my adrenaline to slow down because we were whisked off for some quad biking. My basic feeling, having tried them once before, was that they are brilliant fun on rough terrain and only really dangerous if you tip them over. I remember, previously being told, that they have an amazing capacity to go up slopes, but the important thing is to go straight up, rather than at an angle. Just don't start mucking about on the side of slopes and you'd be okay.

We mounted our machines and drove round in an increasingly quick circle for five minutes. Everyone seemed fairly comfortable, so the leader suddenly broke the circle and headed off, followed by our group. The ever talented Martin swept in behind him, then Malcolm (speeding tickets in three different countries), Pat, somehow me and then a big gap to Chris, Maggie, Helen, John, Uls, Susannah, Heather, Katherine, Don, Alan, Janet, Clare and another instructor at the back.

My aim to be in the slow pack had somehow failed, but at least I knew Pat was fairly sane. The track bumped along but I hung on tight and started to really enjoy it. Then Pat proved to be too sane when he dropped back to make sure Helen was okay. That left the nutters and me.

Things changed. On the plus side, Uls and John caught up our group, but on the negative side, the wind began to build up. It grew in strength and started to whip the sand up into the air. Luckily, my sunglasses helped to stop the sand going into my eyes but there was so much sand in the air that it was difficult to see 40 yards ahead. I'd never seen anything like it. The wind continued to get stronger and in what had become a sandstorm, my vision blurred to 20 yards. That quickly dropped to 10 yards. That was just enough to see Uls, who was in front of me. The options were to keep in touch with him or risk getting lost in the desert. My helmet and sunglasses provided me with limited protection. The sand constantly whipped up and bit into my face as though someone was sticking pins into me. The fact that I wore a helmet and sunglasses didn't stop the sand hitting my face. All I wanted to do was close my eyes, but that is not one of the recognised techniques for riding a quad bike. I occasionally enjoyed a long blink, just as a brief respite, but there was no hiding place for my face, which was taking a battering.

We eventually crossed a stretch of road and John narrowly avoided being cleaned up by a passing car (because of the storm, John didn't even realise he was on a road). Three minutes later we'd stopped because it was deemed too dangerous to carry on, so we followed one of the instructors back to the base at a very sedate pace.

Then it was back to Fagin's, in the evening, to watch the sandboarding video. The place was shut when Martin, Susannah and I optimistically arrived at 5.00pm. In fact, one of the only places open in town was the supermarket, but that became boring after half an hour, two cups of coffee, a doughnut, a pastry and a yoghurt. After a long search, we found one of the only two bars open in town. It was actually in the reception of a cinema and we were the only customers. The barman was very chatty and told us that although only 40,000 people lived in Swakopmund, during the holiday season the population swells to 140,000. Unfortunately, this was the very quiet period, so nowhere was open. What really amazed me was that although he confirmed that the population in Namibia is about 1.5 million, the predicted population for 2007 is 650,000. It seemed very strange, so I asked why everyone was leaving such a beautiful country. '*They're not leaving they're dying of AIDS. One in five are already infected*'. I sat at the bar stool with my jaw gaping yet again. 1.5 million people down to 650,000. 850,000 dead. Bloody hell. But ...... bloody hell.

Another beer later and Fagin's was not only open but my good friend Paulus was serving the beer. After eating some food, John's enthusiasm took us back to O'Kellys nightclub. It seemed similar to a nightclub in a small English town, the only differences being that it was half the size, even worse music and there was the presence of four prostitutes. One of them called Leki, a small barrel-shaped black girl, seemed determined not to let me, Martin or John be lonely. After puffing away on Martin's cigar (that's not a euphemism), she challenged him to a game of pool. Martin had already rejected my offer of a frame, but had no hesitation in pointing her in my direction. My boredom and competitive spirit overcame any wariness.

On the game she may have been, but she certainly wasn't on her game. I won a poor contest only for her to challenge me to another frame because she wanted revenge. We started the second frame with again me unsurprisingly paying to get the balls out (just to clarify, as in put money into the pool table then the pool balls come out). I stood at the top of the table watching Leki play a shot, suddenly I was grabbed from behind. So there I stood, playing pool against a Namibian prostitute with some blokes arms wrapped around me. John and Martin were on the other side of the club and the rest of the Exodus group were back at the chalets. All I could see was a pair of large black male hands locked around my chest. How did I manage to get into this mess? I considered my options:

- hand my wallet over and hope he goes away

- break down in tears

- soil my pants and hope the unruly smell forces my captor to release me

I was edging towards the latter option when the voice attached to the arms let out an '*alright Jeff*'. It was Paulus. I can't remember being so relieved to see someone in the whole of my life and gave him a big hug.

I finished the frame with Leki, before taking on Paulus. That left Leki free, so she headed back across the nightclub to 'molest' John. I beat Paulus and then we were challenged to a game of doubles by a couple of local Afrikaans. I headed to the bar to purchase some liquid refreshment, but John and Martin decided to head back to the chalet. Instead of that sensible retreat, I stayed on for the pool match and thought I'd just keep a low profile. However, Leki still managed to collar me for a drink at the bar.

We started the game of doubles. Meanwhile, Leki did a circuit of the nightclub before returning to hang around the pool table. The game dragged on until Paulus eventually potted the black. We celebrated and then seeing Leki was looking the other way I darted out the club and back to the chalet.

Day 11 – Monday 13th November – An Adrenalin Rush Too Far

The day started in its normal fashion with John getting up early, then after a long gap, me and Martin struggling out of bed. Following the sandstorm forced curtailment of yesterday, we were due to go quad biking again.

The wind had died down, so the instructors said they would take us into the dunes. The only proviso was that they told us '*the sandstorm means the dunes may have moved, so stay on the tracks else you might fall off the edge*'. How do they mean 'dunes moved'? I guessed that meant the dunes weren't that big, which seemed nice and sensible, but falling off didn't sound so clever. Cue adrenalin.

I found myself in the middle of the pack as we rode out to the dunes. After 10 minutes the dunes were upon us. The first one was steep and at least 15 foot tall. Let the adrenalin flow (well, better than the main alternative options of blood or wee flowing).

I may have been worried but I knew that the safest way was to attack. The faster I went the safer I was, because I would make it up to the peaks rather than running out of speed, part way up. The trick was to leave enough room between you and the rider in front, to ensure that you were accelerating into the start of the dunes. My main fear was that I'd run into someone who either stopped near the top or was crawling up. At least we were going straight up and straight down, rather than mucking about along the side of the dunes.

Then to my horror, we had to drive along the side of the dunes.

This meant the bike would travel in an arc shape whilst clinging to the slope of the dunes. Now I was scared. I could hear the instructor's words from that one time I rode back in England '*If one of these lands on you then it is half a tonne of machinery crushing you*'. If you went too slowly the bike could topple down the slope, all I knew to be safer was to go faster, which scared me more, so I'd go even faster. Another steep incline beckoned as I left a gap between Helen, in front of me, and my bike. Gap organised, I attacked, working up some real pace on the flat, the bike hit the slope and flew up it. As I sped, Helen crawled up towards the top. I sped, Helen crawled. Helen's bike clung near the top fighting to reach the peak, while I headed for a collision with the back of her bike. Ahhhh! I daren't stop because I'd be stranded on the dune and was scared of toppling down backwards. I veered off the track, missed Helen, but headed towards a sheer drop down the side of the dune, veered back on to the track, missed the sheer drop, looked behind to see Helen make it to the top and we both breathed again.

I then got caught behind the ever-slowing Monica and just waited for a chance to overtake. It meant I had to be close behind her to have the opportunity to accelerate passed her, but still ensuring there was a big gap up the slopes. My chance came early and after accelerating quickly down a dune I flew by her on the flat. That left me behind Chris and safety.

Happy to be in one piece, I returned the bike and headed back into Swakopmund for a last look at the friendly old resort. The truck departed for Klein Spitzkoppe or what is often called the 'Matterhorn of Namibia'. The peak rises to 5,669 feet, which apparently consists mainly of 120 million-year-old granite (and to think I believed 80 years was quite old).

The group pitched the tents at the bottom of the mountain, before walking around the base on a well-worn route to climb to the top. The exception to the walk was Martin, who decided he would climb to the peak of Klein Spitzkoppe. There is a significant difference between getting on top of the mountain and climbing to the top. One of them is well marked with a much-welcomed chain to hang on to as you go up or down. The other is an extra 600 feet, with no clear route and apparently there was no evidence of anybody successfully completing the climb until 1947.

Our ascent gave the adrenaline another airing as I clung to the chain, whilst moving steadily onwards and upwards. At the top were a series of caves with ancient rock paintings. Tracy led us to the paintings, but as we took a closer look there was a distinct buzzing in the air. Tracy warned us to *'be careful of the hunting bees'*. I looked up to see about 12 large bees hovering nearby. The paintings looked good, but not good enough for me to hang around. Pat immediately decided to examine what the paintings would look like from 20 feet away. I also thought the paintings would look far better from 20 feet so backed away with him. In fact, I was so excited to look at the ancient markings from 20 feet, it almost looked as though I was running away from the bees.

Several brave souls continued to closely examine the paintings. Moments later the sequence went *'oh watch out, watch out', 'oo'* (flap of arms), *'OW!'* *'Watch out, watch out!' 'OW!'* Both Alan and Janet were stung. Everybody decided the 20-foot view was preferable after all.

We returned to the campsite at 6.30pm, but there was no sign of Martin. He'd gone on his dangerous solo climb and hadn't come back. I'm not one to worry but the sooner he returned the better.

7.00pm – where was Martin? Where the hell had he got to? I mean, we left at 4.00pm, how long would it take to get up and down the peak. John seemed equally edgy as we sat around the campfire, looking up at the mountain, desperately trying to see a sign of movement. Others started to glance up. The comments started: *'Well, if it was anyone except Martin I'd be concerned, but he is an experienced climber'.* They were right although it didn't stop John and I had taking on the worried parent's role.

7.30pm – no sign. I walked around the other side of the truck and saw Tracy looking up at the mountain with her binoculars. 'What are you doing?' *'I'm on Martin watch'.* All we could do was watch because if anyone attempted to follow Martin's trail they would just injure themselves. To make matters worse the light was fading fast. If he didn't return soon he'd have to spend the night wherever he was on the mountain or wherever he had fallen. All I could think was 'just don't die Martin'.

Tracy mentioned that because of the heat Martin had not set off until about 5.00pm and she'd told him to make sure he was back before 8.00pm. That made me feel a lot better, although it didn't change the fact that it was getting dark and if the climb had gone smoothly he would have been back by now.

Finally at 7.45pm and with about 10 minutes until it was dark, a tired looking Martin wandered up to the truck. I breathed a huge sigh of relief. An equally relieved John let out a *'thank god for that, I thought I'd lost a mate'*. Martin looked calm and collected; however, he confessed that it had been far from easy. Even before he had started climbing he found a three-foot snakeskin at the base, which made him think twice before proceeding. Then halfway up the mountain, he was reaching for a hold when a supporting rock gave way. He floundered in the air with a long drop on to rocks waiting below him. Martin hung on, recomposed himself and hauled himself up to safety. His conclusion was *'I was stupid to attempt it by myself'*. But it was another mountain conquered.

The darkness, which we hated when Martin was missing, now seemed a beautiful canvas. The lack of light pollution in Namibia means that it is one of the best places in the world to gaze up at the heavens. The stars were shining brightly. We could clearly see Venus, Saturn and Jupiter, there were three satellites spotted and shooting stars to boot. The highlight came when the late-rising moon started to peak above the horizon. I was about to witness my first moonrise. I didn't even know moonrises existed and if they did then surely it was a case of 'oh and there is the moon', rather than 'let there be light'. The moon gradually started to rise and I was left gaping as bright light started to shine down on us. The moon was genuinely lighting the campsite. The light caused many a star to vanish but the sheer incredulity (I think that's a proper word) of the event had me recoiling in disbelief. John even had his powerful binoculars out to show us the craters in the moon. Wow – I've never seen moon craters before; well that knocks the cheese theory out the window.

Day 12 – Tuesday 14th November – Sex, Violence, Death & Intrigue

The time was 'too early o'clock' when I dragged my weary body on to the seemingly ever-moving truck. I dozed away and when I finally drifted into full consciousness a seal colony had arrived outside my window. A small wall separated us from 80,000 seals lying about on the beach, which provided a prime viewing area for all manner of domestic situations. There were fights between the bull seals, defending their patch of territory and harem of lady friends (violence). There was the odd bit of hanky-panky (sex). The birth of a new baby, together with its exasperated mother (trials of parenthood). A number of seals with the life despairingly crushed out of them (death) and the adventure of one baby that was ever closer to being squashed by his clumsy dad (intrigue - for 10 minutes we watched with bated breath for the baby to get clear of his 10 times bigger father). It was better than any soap opera, except for the pungent smell of seal that filled the air.

Then it was back on to the truck. Martin and I were sitting on the back seat. Well, that isn't entirely accurate because the wind blowing through the truck was so bitter that we took up any position along the back seat to try and stay merely very cold. I eventually settled into a scrunched up ball shape on the floor. There were various attempts at gaining the condition known as warmth. The most successful was when Helen and Katherine slipped inside their sleeping bags whilst retaining a sitting position on their seats. We eventually figured out that the flaps on the outside of the truck could actually be let down to cover the windows. This meant we merely travelled coldly to the Skeleton Coast rather than journeyed 'freezingly' to the Skeleton Coast.

The name evokes images of 18th and 19th-century shipwrecks scattered along an eerie coastline. It wasn't far from the truth. The guidebooks described countless ships which have come to grief along Namibia's dangerous coastline. One of them was the Dunedin Star, which ran aground in 1942 with 21 passengers and 85 crew on board. One of the rescue boats ran on to the rocks and two of its crew drowned. Then a bomber, which was trying to help, nose-dived into the sea. It seems that if old Mother Nature is in a bad mood she goes down to the Skeleton Coast to play with gales, dense sea fogs, heavy swell, deadly currents and sand dunes that stretch into the sea.

As is normal with Namibia, it seemed both a desolate and beautiful place. The pure featurelessness of the beaches provided tranquillity. There weren't any piers, any funfairs, any crazy golf courses, no buildings, no people, just water, sand, rocks and bits of shipwreck. The Skeleton Coast stretches for some 400 miles although the government has cordoned part of it off. There are various theories on why:

- protect its desolate nature

- it is a site for dumping nuclear waste

- to safeguard the diamonds washed up on the beach from Angola

We left the coast to pitch our tents, at yet another campsite, before rounding off the day by examining the bizarre shower. Not only did it produce warm water, but it was also in a tree. So there I stood, inside a tree under a torchlight (no electricity in the tree), butt naked, with ants for company and thoroughly enjoying this unique shower.

Day 13 – Wednesday 15ᵗʰ November – Day of the Stiff Dick

The early mornings lose their appeal after, well in fact just before the first one. I heard movement around us at about 5.00am for the 6.00am breakfast. Martin's alarm rang out at 5.50am, but we both decided there was another five minutes' worth of sleep to be enjoyed. I'm sorry to admit, but that sleep from 5.00am to 5.55am was all the more delicious knowing some of my fellow travellers were having to get up to cook my breakfast.

The day was destined for a long haul on the road. After stopping at the valley of the organ pipes (the name hasn't the intimidation value of Skeleton Coast but when you get there, it's a case of 'well they couldn't really call it anything else'), we travelled across to Twyfelfontein to see some more rock carvings on the side of a mountain. They varied in quality but I loved the explanation for some particularly poor ones: '*we believe these to be the work of young children*'.

Then back in the truck, for another couple of hours, until we reached the Petrified Forest. The time had reached midday and the heat edged past 100 degrees Fahrenheit (or 38 as Celsius calls it). It was the highest recorded temperature in the 'Jeff was there!' record books. I headed straight for the shade and sat down. Only to be told that we would have our guided walk straight away - if only I could have taken my bit of shade with me.

The Petrified Forest is an incredible sight, especially as there are no trees. What there is takes the form of the remnants of 50 logs scattered on the ground. Fairly unremarkable, except that they are fossilised tree trunks that date back to between 240 million years and 300 million years. The fossils are so well preserved that despite being formed of stone, they look precisely like bark. If these trees could talk – they'd tell some amazing tales. Although, as they are Namibian trees they'd probably speak Oshiwambo and being British, I'd only speak English, so it would be useless anyway. Or maybe trees speak but it is just at a different level so we don't understand. Or maybe, just maybe, the sun has got to me and I'm drivelling.

After the adrenalin pumped days, yesterday had seemed relatively mundane - I mean, I didn't feel in danger once. So at least that was going to be rectified because not only did a cheetah farm appear quickly on the horizon, we reached the horizon a little too quickly for my liking.

One of the family, who run the farm, greeted us as we filed off the truck.
'Okay then - safety instructions'.
'Don't wear black, the cheetahs don't like black' (good, I'm not in black).
'They don't like sunglasses either'; cue Malcolm: *'well they shouldn't wear them then'.*
'Don't touch a cheetah unless I'm touching him' (no worries there).
'If the cheetahs are within two metres of you and stare at you, don't stare back because it means you are challenging the cheetah. If you want to challenge a cheetah, that's fine, when you're finished we'll take your remains out the back' (now he was worrying me).

In front of us was a farmhouse with a grassy garden running around it, surrounded by a tall fence and matching gates. Apparently, the gates had been left open twice. Both times by travelling salesmen who headed towards the farmhouse, saw the cheetahs and fled. The cheetahs escaped and killed about five sheep before they were found. There were four cheetahs living in and around the farmhouse, plus two dogs and one cat. One of the dogs once tried to take some of the cheetah's food and was immediately rushed to the vet so he could be sewn back up. He hasn't tried a second time.

The enclosure door opened and Mario the guide entered, followed by Don and then yours truly. I wish I could say it was out of bravery, but the thought process was that the closer I kept to Mario the safer I'd be. There was one cheetah running about the enclosure as we entered, but it was keeping its distance. Mario led us around the side of the house to the relatively small back garden. We turned the corner and there, but a few metres in front of us were three cheetahs laying on the grass. My heart missed a beat as my brain tried to comprehend the situation. The mind ticked over, 'cheetahs dangerous', 'in same garden is bad', 'running away isn't much use', 'conclusion – sit down and mind own business'. 'Don't stare, repeat DON'T STARE'.

Gradually, everyone filtered through to the back garden and sat down on a bench that lay against the back wall of the house. I forgot about being scared because I was too busy enjoying the disbelieving looks on people's faces as they rounded the corner. After everyone had reached the back garden we had the dubious opportunity to pet the cheetahs.

Don went first and wasn't eaten. I took that as a good omen so duly approached one of the cheetahs. 'What a beautiful, athletic creature' the cheetah must of thought as I approached, I shared the same thought about him. I slowly bent down next to Mario and stroked the cheetah, what a stunning animal. I returned to the bench, full of awe and sat down next to Gerald.

After a few minutes the youngest, but still fully-grown cheetah started to wander around. It was okay, until Gerald mentioned that it seemed to be prowling across to us. I laughed off his paranoid suggestion.

Gerald started to provide commentary: *'it's still coming across to us, oh my god it isn't stopping'*. It reached the two-metre zone. If we had been looking the cheetah in the eye we would have looked away at that point. However, the fact was that Gerald and I had been operating a total 'don't stare into the cheetah's eyes' policy ever since we entered the garden, to which we added an involuntary 'don't breathe' policy. The cheetah entered the two-metre zone and came into striking distance (or for Gerald and myself the losing control of the bowels distance). *'Oh Jesus'*. What would the lethal killing machine do next? After a brief silence, Gerald's commentary continued: *'Jeff, it's licking me'*. Sure enough, the cheetah was licking Gerald's leg. *'It's quite nice really'*. After a few licks, it turned and wandered off.

About 12 of the group had their picture taken petting a cheetah, whilst the others hung back nervously. Malcolm was one of those happily keeping his distance on the far side of the bench. The youngest cheetah suddenly looked up and ran at Malcolm, within a couple of yards of him it jumped (as did Malcolm's heart). The cheetah landed on the back of the bench in the small gap between Malcolm and the wall (Malcolm's heart landing firmly in his mouth). For the next couple of minutes (or two days if you speak to Malcolm), it stood behind him peering over his shoulder.

It ran off again when Mario threw his cap, which the cheetah leapt on. He threw it a couple of times and the cheetah would run and pounce on it. The next time Mario thought he'd do something different. The cap flew through the air and landed on my foot; before I could react a cheetah had swooped down, picked up the cap and thankfully left my foot at the end of my leg. If that wasn't enough, when Susannah bent down, Mario put the cap on her head. The cheetah started off as if to snatch it and then sort of turned to Mario with a look that said *'hey I can't get that, it's on somebody's head'*.

Just as we had fallen in love with our new found feline friends we had to leave them and visit the wild cheetahs for feeding time. There were about 25 cheetahs in a large compound. The gist was that three groups, including ours, would enter the compound on the back of three vehicles. The lead vehicle was a tractor with a trailer carrying 30 Aussies – which I assumed was the food for the cheetahs. Behind the Aussies was a van with an open back, followed by a truck with an open back where we stood. There were railings around the sides, but nothing that a cheetah couldn't clamber up. As soon as the trucks entered the compound the cheetahs took an immediate interest, they knew it was feeding time. We drove on another 200 yards, down the side of the compound, then Mario jumped out of the tractor. Four cheetahs started to approach him in a threatening manner. A couple of times the front one hissed and looked as though it was about to pounce on Mario. It was only a few metres away, and despite the fact that you were sure that Mario knew what he was doing, I was worried for him. He then grabbed some meat, yelled '*back one*' and threw the meat to the cheetah at the back. '*Left one*' and the cheetah on the left caught the meat and went running off. It continued until all four of the cheetahs had their fresh meat.

We drove around to the opposite side, where more hungry cheetahs got their dinner, before returning to our tents, which were situated at the side of the enclosure (luckily on the outside rather than the inside of the enclosure).

Mario's family used to suffer, like any other Namibian farmers, when cheetahs killed their livestock. One day his father managed to catch a cheetah and, rather than kill it, decided to keep it. Other farmers, who caught cheetahs, then passed them to him. He eventually had three tame ones living in his house and an enclosure full of wild cheetahs. Against all the expert opinion, a pair of cheetahs successfully bred and a baby was born. That was adopted into the house and was the now grown up cheetah that had licked Gerald's knee. They do face a major problem. They are getting more and more cheetahs but have nowhere to put them. The grand plan had been to release them into the vast parks of Namibia. However, despite a lack of cheetahs in the parks, they won't take them. Thus it would leave cheetahs not being accepted into the farm having to be shot. The choices are limited, but one of them is to turn the whole farm into a cheetah park. One way to help them to finance the park is to spend money at their bar, so we put our good sense aside, sacrificed our livers and drank. Whilst Mario conjured up a spit roast, Alan the driver got everybody started on cocktails.

I was most surprised to see Pat and several others with a 'stiff dick' going down their neck. In fact, I even tried one for the first time. It seems essential for all good cocktails to have a comedy name and it certainly gave us a chuckle as innuendo followed innuendo. Ooohhh matron.

Mario's spit was finally roasted, so he could feed us humans as he had fed the cheetahs. 'Big Aussie at the back', 'English lady at the front', 'big-eared English lad on the left'. I raced off to gobble up my food.

Day 14 – Thursday 16th November – Blown Away

The animal theme continued as we left the farm and headed to the Etosha National Park. It covers an area of 8,600 square miles and is renowned for its wildlife. There are meant to be 114 different types of mammal, including 300 lions, 1,500 elephants and 20,000 springbok. According to my guide book, the big five that everybody hopes to see are elephants, lions, leopards, giraffes and rhinos. Or was it buffalo? And what about my new found friends the cheetahs?

We entered the park and immediately saw zebras, springboks and Oryx. Then we spotted an elephant. As Alan edged the truck closer, it became apparent there were actually eight elephants, all by the side of the road. They were incredible, real live elephants in the wild. We looked out the other side of the truck and there was a giraffe. Wow! Now, this is the Africa of my imagination.

The truck drove on until we were near a waterhole where there were count-less zebra, oryx and springbok. There was a blazing hot sun, animals drinking a bit of water and tourists taking photographs at their leisure. It all seemed fairly sedate. John and his binoculars even spotted a brown sack in some distant bushes.

After a few minutes, the brown sack rose up and slowly started to walk towards the waterhole. Although it was still very distant, the brown sack took a lion shape. As it came within 100 yards of the waterhole, the zebras stopped milling around and nervously looked up. The lion continued to stroll along. Eventually, all the animals were looking at him. When the lion began to get close to the waterhole, all the other animals scattered away. Not in panic, more in reverence. They knew that under the blistering sun he would be more interested in a drink rather than dinner. Whilst the lion drank alone, the animals maintained a 25-yard exclusion zone. When the lion finished drinking, he headed off to again pretend to be a brown sack. Once more the animals slowly returned to their 'as you were' positions.

With the main show over, we retreated to one of Etosha's rest camps - a fenced off area filled with bungalows, a campsite, shops, a restaurant and a swimming pool. The pitching of tents had become an art form. The only difference to normal was that security had approached us to make sure no one was wearing open sandals. They told us to be careful because two guests had just been bitten by scorpions. I thought as a security precaution it would be wise to retreat to the local bar for a nice cold beer. Don and Clare had already settled in at a table, again surpassing the speed with which I found the human waterhole. One day, I would beat them to the bar. Mind you, their ambition may well be to have a quiet beer, '*because every time we settle in at a bar, up pops Jeff*'.

I ventured out of the safe house to see how dinner was progressing. There was half an hour to spare, so I slipped down to see what animals were at the waterhole on the edge of the camp. I could see floodlights, on the fringe of the camp, lighting up a man-made waterhole. The audience was kept apart from the entertainers by a wall with a wire fence that sloped in front of it. The actual water was about 50 yards away, but the floodlights gave the whole scene a twilight atmosphere. There were eight, yes eight rhinos. I stood trans-fixed. It was like your best wildlife programme, multiplied by 10, being played out in front of my eyes. On the television they don't seem real, but there I was 30 yards from an actual wild rhino. If I jumped down from the wall, I could touch their horns, before being gorged to death. In fact, Pat and Malcolm offered me a combined £23 to run down to the waterhole and back. They told me that the rhinos just looked fierce and pretended to be bad-tempered.

Everyone quickly shovelled dinner down their respective throats, so as to get back to the waterhole for the next session. When we returned there were 10 rhinos. Then a few disappeared but were replaced by an elephant and a giraffe. It was amazing but, because the animals were so close, everybody kept their excitement quiet, not wanting to scare them. The action hotted up. One of the rhinos took a dislike to the elephant using the waterhole. He broke into a charge, only for the elephant to give him a disdainful look and blow water in his face. The rhino stopped in his tracks, headed back to where he first charged from and restarted his run up. Only for the elephant to stop him with another water shot. The oh so consciously quiet crowd were now a helplessly giggling mess. Whilst the disconsolate rhino gave up. Life seemed to have moved from David Attenborough to Bedknobs & Broomsticks. I couldn't wait for the football matches. We thought that the giraffes would play a long ball game and defeat the rhinos, who would have two players sent off for violent conduct. The counter-attacking jackals would overcome the buffalo's strategy of charging forward. The powerful elephant team would be undone by the speed of the cheetahs whilst the lions would crush the parrots (lions get through by default after the whole parrot team were sent off for talking back to the ref).

Time moved on and a couple of lions drifted down to the waterhole. For one solitary moment, I could see rhinos, lions, an elephant and a giraffe, all at the same time. Malcolm and Pat were so moved that they generously offered me another chance to win the £23 (cash). Although this time they insisted that I had to run down to the waterhole naked. I thought it would bring an RSPCA action against me and was worried as to where exactly the rhino would stick its horn. I politely declined the offer.

Day 15 – Friday 17ᵗʰ November – Water

After seeing so many wonderful animals yesterday, I wondered how today could ever compete. The best time to see the animals is early in the morning or so we were told. To us, it just meant yet another early start. We had been driving around for a couple of hours when the time struck 8.00am and the bladders hit full. You're in the middle of Africa, in an area full of wild animals, and you need a wee, what do you do?

Alan came across a small fenced compound that housed a couple of toilets, but it still meant somebody had to get out the truck to unlock the compound. Gerald, fresh from taming the cheetahs, jumped out the cab and opened the gate.

Suitably relieved, everyone jumped back on the truck, except for Gerald. He had a good look around, to check for any man-eaters lurking in the bushes, then closed the gate again.

Bladders being bladders they filled up again a couple of hours down the track. The truck stopped at some huts with toilets. However, the huts were not surrounded by any fences and to make matters worse the toilets were locked. We took matters into our own hands (among other things) and headed off into the bushes. I maintained a zebra-like lookout.

The third place we were released from the truck was at the Etosha Pan - meaning the great white place of dry water. November is just at the start of the rainy season but it is yet to fall, so the Pan looks like an endless flat and dry surface covering some 1,900 square kilometres. At least the sheer nothingness of the pan meant we would be able to see any brown sacks approaching from a distance.

Instead of brown sacks, the day was full of zebra, oryx and springbok but it didn't have the excitement or novelty of yesterday. The highlight was seeing a mongoose. Snakes have always been the animal that I fear most and since I was a young child I have marvelled at the way these small animals could kill deadly snakes. They are so fast and agile that they can out-jump a strike from an adder, dodge the poisonous spit of a cobra and bite the snake's throat. So

I was overly excited when I saw the mongoose. I went to shout out to Pat and then spotted another mongoose. '*Pat, look there are some mongooses, um mongeese, um one mongoose and another mongoose.*' (Editorial edit: I looked this up when I got back and the most common description is that everyone gets a bit confused. I am about the billionth person to end up saying one mongoose and another mongoose. However, it seems that it should be mongooses. So I may be a bit late but 'Pat, look at those mongooses by the side of the road on the 18th November 2000').

We reached a different rest camp in the late afternoon. It also had a man-made waterhole on the fringe of the camp. Pat came back from it full of talk about only a small wall dividing the observers and the observed. I decided to check it out for myself. I became slightly disconcerted within 400 yards of it when there were already signs stating that you enter the viewing area at your own risk. There was a fairly high stone wall overlooking the waterhole but it seemed very climbable for leopards, lions and jackals. There had already been rumours circulating that a lion had been found in the camp, just a couple of days ago, but had not caused any harm. I for one will not be going to the toilet in the middle of the night.

When nighttime fell, the temptation of the waterhole called. The five minute walk was along a path with long grass and bushes on both sides. Every crackling sound raised a suspicion that there was a lion in the bush. However, I never looked to the sides because I was too busy scanning for snakes on the footpath. When I safely reached the waterhole, there were a couple of rhinos. In the shadows of the floodlights two lions approached. Just a glimpse of these magnificent big cats sent a shudder of excitement down my spine. The lions were 40 yards away and I was on top of a wall they could easily climb. I countered any nervousness by remembering, from somewhere, that they're not keen on the taste of humans. And I'm all skin and bone, now Pat would be far tastier.

The lions were only allowed a short drink before being chased into the bushes by a rhino. Then a massive bull elephant arrived. He looked 15 feet tall, had fearsome tusks and a face full of character. Every ounce of his eight tonne (ish) frame seemed to say 'warrior'. My jaw had gaped so many times on this trip I was beginning to resemble a goldfish. Even the rhinos decided to retreat to the other side of the waterhole. A couple more elephants turned up, then another, another, a couple of babies, more and more. I strained my eyes trying to see deep into the dark for more elephant silhouettes. All in all there were 19 of these magnificent creatures before my eyes. Cue the goldfish again.

Day 16 – Saturday 18th November –
Morning Of The Jackal

I woke up in the middle of the night to a mixture of crashing and animal calls. It was likely to be jackals knocking over bins to see if there was anything to eat, but I had no plans to investigate anything outside of my sleeping bag until a more civilised time.

Breakfast was not until 6.30am so I enjoyed a virtual lie in before we headed off to see some more zebras, springbok and oryx. Alan the truck driver had proved hawk-like in spotting animals, but even he surprised us when he seemingly stopped in the middle of nowhere (although that narrows it down to almost all of Namibia). Whilst we scanned the horizon, he leaned out the cab to say *'squirrel'.* Sure enough, there were two on the side of the road. As the excitement hit squirrel pitch we left Etosha for the Waterberg Plateau.

The flat-topped Plateau has seemingly vertical sides that rise 200 metres above the plains. It resembles Uluru except it is covered in vegetation and animals. Namibia uses it to help endangered species because there is no way down for the animals and it is possible to offer good protection from poachers. The plateau is 48 km at its longest point and 16 km at its widest, with inhabitants including leopards and buffalos. It proved to be a good climb to the top and I managed to pick up a couple more grazes to add to those of my sandboarding collection.

It was our final night together so we gathered around the campfire and allowed the wine and whisky to flow.

John, who was drinking on an empty stomach, got increasingly drunk and fell off his stool. Luckily he fell back, rather than forward into the fire. He did make a couple of attempts to get up but decided it was quite nice on the ground, looking up at the stars. Walking had become an almost impossible challenge for him, so Martin helped him to his tent. Five minutes later, John was trying to get up again. After a couple of minutes, he found his way out and stood next to Pat and Helen's tent. Martin headed across to him and a staggering John announced he needed the toilet. Pat's voice rang out: *'not on our tent!'*

If I had been thinking straight I would have grabbed a cup of water and started dribbling it on their tent. As it was, half an hour later, I filed it in 'good gags if only I'd thought of it in time', just next to the 'good retorts that I didn't think of in time', unfortunately, a section 100 times bigger than 'good retorts I actually made'.

Day 17 – Sunday 19th November – Moving Into Neutral

Monica was sick during the night and John reproduced last night's intake first thing in the morning, but I guess that is what a proper last night is all about.

After the careful consumption of breakfast, destination Windhoek appeared unremittingly on our horizon. It just left me with the task of trying to keep my eyes open to see the beautiful countryside that is Namibia, rather than relent to my 'oh so heavy' eyelids and close my eyes to the wondrous landscape.

All too soon we were back to concrete and people. We had an hour in the centre of Windhoek before travelling to a hotel for the group's pre-flight preparation. Although the main group were flying out today, my flight is not until tomorrow, but I was in good company. Susannah would be staying at the posh hotel tonight, Uls and Monica had organised an average priced hotel in town, which left just Martin and me. Our standards were slightly lower, a cardboard box would be sufficient. Well, that was the name of the hostel we visited. It seemed very homely, with a small swimming pool, lounge area, bar and dormitories. So basically, most of life's essentials and for just $5 a night. How could we refuse?

My final journey in the truck brought us to the posh safari hotel, where we sat around the pool for three hours enjoying the sunshine and just relaxing. Then it was time to bid goodbye to all the English people. It was all a bit strange as the truck, my truck, with most of my group, left me behind. Martin and I got changed in Susannah's room, before heading into town to meet up with Uls and Monica for a meal.

After a nice meal, Martin and I returned to our hostel eager to sample the contents of the bar. The lad serving was a Danish backpacker who said he would close the bar in another 15 minutes. We successfully kept him talking, which meant another couple of hours drinking and enough time to set the world to rights. He pointed out another couple of staggering AIDS claims. Apparently, people in some parts of Africa believe that if they contract AIDS they can get rid of it by either having sex with a virgin or having sex with a white girl, hence incidents of rape are increasing. Bloody hell! What a mess.

Day 18 – Monday 20th November – No Plane Drifter

I woke up to hear a Swedish girl grumbling to her friend that she struggled to sleep in the night because of the snoring. Well, Martin and I didn't hear anything so it was probably one or both of us. Our version of events may be slightly different. Martin and I agreed to 'I spent last night in a room with a Swedish girl and I kept her up all night, all I heard from her was constant moaning, if you know what I mean'. Although my friends would still probably say '*do you mean that you were snoring in a dormitory and keeping some poor Swedish girl awake*'.

My flight was due out of the airport at 2.50pm. The hostel had lined up a shuttle bus to pick me up at 12.30pm, which would take me on the 40 kilometre journey to the airport. Tracy had phoned up to confirm my bookings for the flights a couple of days ago. She had commented on Air France being very helpful but didn't mention Com Air. The fact she hadn't said anything about Com Air played on my mind, so I finally asked Tracy about it. She replied with a somehow unconvincing '*er yes, they've confirmed*'.

The bus arrived on time so I bid farewell to Martin and was alone in Africa once more. The bus drove the five minutes into the city centre then pulled up and waited. Other passengers gradually boarded, but at 12.45pm there was still no sign of action. Come on. Let's go. I was informed we would be leaving at 1.00pm, the journey would take about 45 minutes. So I'd arrive about an hour before my flight.

Their timings were spot on. I saw the check-in desk so made my way to a quiet corner to re-pack my rucksack. Now had Tracy actually confirmed my booking for the flight to Johannesburg? Before I could find out there was an announcement over the tannoy: '*we regret that the Com Air British Airways flight, scheduled to fly from Johannesburg, has been cancelled and also the 14.50 flight to Johannesburg has been cancelled*'. Thoughts tumbled out of my head: 'what?' 'You've got to be joking!'. 'Can they do that?'

What happens now?

The check-in assistant was besieged by frustrated passengers, but knew as much as us. Finally, a British Airways representative announced that they would try to organise alternative flights for us all. I joined a queue behind a British couple called Meg and Dave.

Whilst other passengers whinged, we selected a laugh and joke strategy. It took me an hour to reach the front of the queue, but at last, I would know my options. They could put me on the 6.50pm flight to Johannesburg, with Namibian Air, but I would miss my connections to Paris and London. They then looked at other ways to drop me in Paris, before I pointed out that London was my final destination and I didn't have to reach Paris. That made life easier and she said that, with a one hour wait in Johannesburg, I could catch the 9.30pm British Airways flight to London, arriving in Heathrow at

6.45am tomorrow. This meant that because of the cancellation and missed connections I should arrive 45 minutes earlier than scheduled. Brilliant! I didn't receive revised tickets, just a print out of the new flight details and told that everything had been sorted.

That sounded good enough for me. I took my free food tokens and deposited myself in the café with a local newspaper as company. The story that grabbed my attention was 'Thai boy wins beauty contest'. Apparently, there was a complaint from all the girls on the basis he was a bloke. A check was made and sure enough, there was a piece of evidence, which showed he was from the male side of the species. He agreed to return the $5,000 first prize but made a request to keep his winner's sash!

I met up again with Meg and Dave, who suggested that the civilised action would be to buy some bottles of beer and sit on the grassy bank outside the airport entrance. Whichever way I looked at the proposition it seemed difficult to mount an effective argument, so I agreed. After all, I reasoned it would be my last glimpse of sunshine for six months.

They told me about witnessing the loose lion in their camp at Etosha. They had woken up to hear a commotion and then everyone was climbing on cars, trees or whatever was handy for a better view of the lion. They didn't hear of anyone being harmed, but no one seemed to know how they got rid of it. The novelty just wore off and people started going about their normal business.

The sun shone, it was a lovely temperature, the company was entertaining and the beer tasted good. All in all, it was about the most relaxed afternoon of the whole trip.

The flights were smooth and before I knew it, I was back in England. Namibia was truly beautiful and for me the thought of it will always conjure up images of stunning landscapes. But I couldn't get out of my mind that a population of 1.5 million could be slashed down to 650,000 people.

(**Editorial edit** – I was interested to see how Namibia had got on and am happy that in 2016 its population had increased to 2.5 million. The 2016 World Population data sheet still shows that in Namibia 11% of males between 15-49 have HIV and 16% of females. This illustrates that although Namibia is still one of the worst affected HIV countries, things have improved thanks to the anti-retroviral therapy and a large fall in mother to child transmission).

Diary 6

The group trips to Peru and Namibia were an effective use of limited time but I wanted a lot more time and less early morning starts. In 2001 the company I was working for had merged. I was shifted around five different offices in the space of six months and thought if I was being moved around that much I might as well take it a step further and go on a world trip. I'd always planned to go on a long trip and this seemed the perfect time. A day after England beat Germany 5-1 at football, my friend Matt and I flew to Turkey. We went on to Syria, Jordan, Egypt, Greece, Italy and India. After six months, I returned for a friend's wedding before setting off to travel around my sixth continent.

	UK	Mexico	Guate-mala	North America
Population in millions	65.6	128.6	16.6	360
Projected population in 2050	77	163.8	27.6	445
Infant mortality per 1000 live births	3.9	13	28	6
Life expectancy - male	79	74	69	77
Life expectancy - female	83	79	76	81
Gross national income in purchasing power parity divided by population (in $)	40,550	17,150	7,510	55,179
Area of country (square miles)	93,638	758,449	107,160	9,365,000

NOTE: Strange how North American's have a higher income but lower life expectancy than the UK. My friend Mike also points out that there is something odd about these figures - seems to be North America is only the USA and Canada in the above figures.

Well, time had moved on to April 2002. The Twin Towers had fallen months before, British and American soldiers were in Afghanistan and David

Beckham had broken his metatarsal as England sweated over his fitness for the Japan and South Korea World Cup.

This is the magical time of Lord of the Rings and Harry Potter at the cinema. In that context, I will lift my wand and play 'Sing' by Travis.

12.45

pm on the 27ᵗʰ March 2002 and I'd managed to keep in step with the latest long haul flight fashion by taking an aspirin. In fact, I saw several boxes floating about the departure gate as everyone battled against the threat of Deep Vein Thrombosis. I wish they'd stop inventing new ways for us to die.

It looked like me and 300 Germans were leaving Frankfurt to clog up the world's most populated city. And although I associate it with crippling poverty, a friend told me that there are more billionaires in Mexico City than in any other city in the world.

The fact that I'm heading to Central America is due to one hot and sultry evening spent with a beautiful blonde in a place of legend. Over the previous three years, I'd dreamed of reaching the red rose city of Petra. Pictures of it evoked images of an incredible lost city in the middle of a great desert. Indiana Jones even found the Holy Grail there in The Last Crusade. That's the trailer anyway, legendary city, beautiful blonde, sunset and me. It sounds like the start of a film but the details are far more mundane.

I was more than a little excited when a bus, with me on board, pulled into the little tourist town near Petra. Matt, my travelling companion, and I stepped out into a mob of enthusiastic hotel touts. We'd already picked our favoured hostel from the guidebook. The first tout approached us and offered a reasonable room price and a lift to his hostel. A couple more quickly put in their pitches but we just made use of our standard excuse that we were meeting some friends at our favoured hostel. This excuse nearly always reduced the interest touts had in us. Then another man appeared who was actually from our hostel of choice. Great that made life easy. I asked him to confirm the price. He started to explain that the rooms had been re-decorated and that the prices had doubled. At which point we performed a 180-degree turn and took up the original touts offer to look at his hostel.

When we arrived at the hostel two New Zealand girls, who we'd originally met in Damascus, were sitting in the courtyard. In the weeks after the 11th September terrorist attack, there hadn't been many tourists in Syria or Jordan so every backpacker seemed to know each other. We greeted them enthusiastically and instantly lost our position of strength in hostel price negotiations. The owner triumphantly sang '*you have friends here, you have friends here*' and we agreed to stay. I thought I was going to explain 'why Central America?' within four lines but I am getting there. Kat and Lou, our Kiwi friends, had visited Petra that day, so I asked the obvious question 'What did you think?' '*Jeff it was incredible, just awesome, nearly as good as Tikal*'. 'What? Where is Tikal?' '*Oh it's in Guatemala, it's an old Maya city in the middle of the jungle and is the most incredible place I've ever seen*'. 'Oh no, now I'll have to go there as well'. Normally I let such thoughts fester for a good couple of years but for some reason I had an urge to get there quickly.

175 days later, give or take a few, I found myself on a Lufthansa flight to Mexico City. This time I am a lone traveller (no friend, no adventure holiday group to meet up with, just me and my ever-reliable rucksack). I wanted to see Tikal, work on an organic farm and develop my terrible Spanish. And because I'd quit work, I had nine weeks to play with.

I had prepared for Mexico City by reading the Foreign and Commonwealth website. It said '*Only use taxis from authorised ranks (Sitios). Passengers using other taxis in Mexico City face a much greater risk of attack and robbery. Care should be taken on the Mexico City Metro where there is a high incidence of pick-pocketing. Incidents of short-term opportunistic kidnapping have increased in urban areas, particularly in Mexico City. Victims holding credit or debit cards are required to withdraw funds at a cash-point to obtain their release. In the case of victims with friends or relatives living locally, accessible sums may be demanded as ransom*'. My nerves weren't helped by the Mexican girl sitting next to me on the plane, who also told me to hire an official taxi rather than running the risk of being attacked. I started to wonder about what sort of godforsaken place I was entering.

When Mexico City reached our plane I steeled myself, ready for action. I sought and found the little fixed price taxi booth, which I hoped would ensure a safe passage to a hostel. I passed the man a crisp new note and received a receipt, which I could pass on to an official taxi driver. I made about 10 paces, in what I hoped was an apprehending taxi direction, when I was stopped by an old man offering me his services as a taxi driver. Was he a sweet old man trying to help me? Or a violent psychopath, ready to lead me away into a dark alley where his psychotic family would leave me bloodied and broke? In these situations, where I have no idea where I'm going or what I'm really up to, I tend to click into British Empire mode. Not the 'I'm going to duff you up and then take your country' type mode but the 'confident, polite, firm and I know my way around the world sort of mode'. Anyway, I'd refused his offer of a taxi but asked him to confirm where the fixed-rate taxis congregated? The sweet old man/violent psychopath pointed in the direction I had been heading.

My main strategy to find a bed for the night was to locate a fixed price taxi driver, waft my guidebook under his nose whilst frantically pointing at the name of a hostel and using the odd Spanish word together with several English words. This seemed to have a mixed level of success in that the first driver I approached understood which hostel I wanted, but seemed to want me to help him with its location. At this point, I spotted a fellow guide book wafter also with bird-like Spanish. So I headed across and we organised an alliance to share a taxi and a prospective couple of beers in a strange city.

We got into a taxi and near the end of the journey, the driver claimed he'd taken us as close as possible to our required hostel. Although to us it seemed like the middle of nowhere, on a dark street, in one of the most dangerous cities in the world. Still, at least I wouldn't be beaten up and bloodied by myself; thanks to our alliance I'd got Jim to get beaten up with.

We wandered around in a taxi driver gesticulated direction but it didn't look very hopeful. I can't believe the slackness these days, surely the driver's family should have been waiting for us. But no, it seemed as though we'd have to go and find them before we could get mugged, in fact, the way things were going I thought we'd have to provide the baseball bats and knives as well.

Our wanderings finally led us to a street of people and, rather than mug us they directed us to our nearby hostel. Before you knew it we were settled down with a couple of beers toasting our first night's survival with a couple of other Englishmen. The strange thing was that the Englishmen in question (who answer to the names of Chris and James) actually sat a couple of places away from me on the plane and turned up at the hostel about 5 minutes after us.

Day 2 - Thursday 28th March - Monty Cortes by the Zumas

The hostel was located in the city's main square, which proved a hive of activity. It had an imposing cathedral in the middle and a massive palace at the side. They were undoubtedly colonial buildings and were evidence of the once mighty Spanish Empire. The Spanish arrived here in the early 16th century in the form of a man called Cortes and an army of a few hundred men. At the time Mexico City (or Mexico as it is confusingly called by its inhabitants) was named Tenochtitlan and was a booming city of some 300,000 Aztecs. The Aztec emperor Montezuma (he of the revenge fame) thought that Cortes might be a light-skinned god and let him into the city. The Spanish returned the favour by taking Montezuma prisoner, destroying temples and killing priests. The Aztecs eventually forced them out of the city, but the Spanish simply formed alliances with other tribes (so my alliance with Jim was following a great tradition) to reinforce their army. The Spanish returned to lay siege and eventually take a city that was being ravaged by the Spanish brought smallpox.

The Mexicans of today seemed very friendly. I had expected to be hassled on every street corner but was surprised to be greeted with the laid-back attitude of vendors. So Jim and I decided to dump the maps and just wander around aimlessly. We ate food off the street stalls, looked in the shops and visited an almighty market. It seemed a fairly modern city with skyscrapers and luxuri-ous looking buildings. I can now believe that this city may well possess the most billionaires in the world. I would have questioned my thought that it was a third world nation but I remember the answer to 'which is the only common border between a third world country and a first world country?' is Mexico and USA.

What shocked both of us, even more, was the bad reputation the city had for being dangerous and polluted. Maybe this was just a good day but it seemed a very pleasant and safe place.

DAY 3 - FRIDAY 29TH MARCH -
JESUS AND THE DORMITORY MIRACLE

Jim confirmed that he was heading down to the south coast, whilst I planned a smaller southern move to Oaxaca. He'd organised his ticket yesterday and found out that the bus would be going through Oaxaca so thought he would stop there for a couple of days. As my only friend in Mexico was travelling in my planned direction I thought I'd try to buy a ticket for his bus.

I placed myself in the ticket-buying queue and practised my Spanish for 'I want', then realised I wasn't quite sure how to pronounce Oaxaca. 'Quero Oaks-aca, um O-axa-ca'. There was something about the assistant's blank look that told me I wasn't quite pronouncing it correctly. So I picked up her pen and wrote 'OAXACA' on a handy piece of paper. Blank expression turned to enlightenment and produced a ticket. I even managed to answer her question about what seat I would like. Somebody actually understood my Spanish. Wow, to me it was still a jumble of letters pronounced strangely, but it actually made sense to these people. My Spanish had been learnt from CDs in my bedroom, so to see people respond to my gobbledegook gave me a wonderful sense of achievement. Already my very limited Spanish had moved above my incomprehensible German and abysmal French to become my second (an incredibly distant second) language. Granted, there is still room for improvement because I'd managed to get a ticket on a bus half an hour earlier than Jim's. But people understood me!

After the bus journey, the Jim/Jeff alliance met up in Oaxaca bus station and planned a route into town. After walking in a couple of circles around Oaxaca we located a hostel. Then disaster struck, the receptionist told us there was no room in the men's dormitory so we'd have to sleep in the women's dormitory. We took this setback like true men (although some would say the high fives and whooping was a little over the top).

We headed on to the streets of Oaxaca, but it was a little odd because Jesus passed us three times within an hour. On each occasion, he wore a crown of thorns with blood dripping from his head. Apparently, the carrying of his effigy through the streets is all part of something called the Semana Santa celebrations. It is Mexico's second most important holiday, behind Christmas, and they celebrate from Palm Sunday to Easter Sunday. No wonder Mexico City seemed laid back, this is a holiday week.

Day 4 - Saturday 30ᵗʰ March - Babel Beer

The real advantage of living in the dormitory is that it is easy to meet people. Or in this case, easy to meet girls. The amazing thing about mixed dormitories are the number of girls that you can have a conversation with whilst they remove their bra, shirt etc in such a smooth way that you never see anything other than stomach flesh and clothing.

After having my morning's ration of stomach flesh (I think Jim showed the most), we headed out in search of breakfast. Oaxaca has a big main square, which is ideal for pottering around. By pottering around I mean we'd slowly walk around some of the old streets before finding ourselves in the main square. The square has a bandstand surrounded by grass and paths. On one side is the cathedral and the other sides are dominated by colonial buildings converted into cafes. It was difficult to resist the cafes, so we ordered some coffee and watched the people go by. There was a lot of police milling around in huddles. This included a high number of female officers, who just seemed to hang around in their uniform gossiping to their friends and looking good. The males, well they didn't behave much differently but in my personal opinion didn't look quite so good. Then you have a large section of American tourists, large often being the operative word because there are some big people waddling around. Not forgetting kids running around with various toys they had been bought from the Easter market, travellers with large rucksacks looking a little lost, your local Casanovas, a large helping of pretty local girls and a big dose of Mexican tourists. Mix them all up, let them play and I am happy to watch the world go by. Therein lies the difference between travelling in a group and travelling by yourself. In one, you travel around at 100mph seeing everything and in the other, you can relax to your heart's content but you miss some sights.

The square was still jam-packed at night. In fact, there were so many people around, Jim and I decided the safest option was to join Bill, a Southampton fan and therapist (I think the two roles complement each other) for a couple of quiet beers.

It is amazing what a few quiet beers can do for your communication skills. Now, I know all the scientific research ever done on the subject may disagree with my findings and conclude alcohol does not improve your command of foreign languages. However, I couldn't really speak more than the odd sentence of Spanish and Jorge the hotel receptionist couldn't speak any English. Now with the assistance of the magic elixir, which they call beer, we managed a hugely entertaining 15 minute conversation about leading figures in Mexican and English society and how they relate to the international community. I admit there were large chunks of the conversation taken up with me shouting excitedly 'Hugo Sanchez!' 'Luiz Hernandez!' 'Muy bueno!' and then Jorge shouting *'David Beckham!' 'Michael Owen!' 'Very good!'* But 15 minutes is 15 minutes.

DAY 5 - SUNDAY 31ST MARCH - THE RINGS OF IRE

I was quite pleased with my performance so far because I had managed to get into my travelling mode very quickly. I had set a frenzied pace of long breakfasts, morning naps, long lunches, afternoon naps, coffee breaks and the odd bottle of beer.

I'd also been very impressed with the high standard of accommodation in Mexico. The only real problem with this hostel is that there are just two bathrooms and one of those only produces cold water (occasionally neither produces any water). Jim saw no one was in the hot water room, so he moved towards it only to find Mad Lucy using the mirror just outside the door. I think the 'Mad' bit of her name is more of an in-hostel nickname, rather than her parents being unerringly accurate in their naming ability. Jim politely asked whether the bathroom was free, to which she turned around and shouted *'I'm doing my make-up, get outta here!'* That was mere smoke compared to her later eruption when she was making coffee on one of the two oven rings. A German girl wanted to make coffee on the second ring. Lucy wasn't too keen on this idea and after a lot of yelling threatened to call the police. I still don't think boiling a pot next to someone else's saucepan is a crime, even in Mexico. It was at this point, Lucy realised that the world was obviously against her and said she needed to change hostel; presumably to one with stricter saucepan boiling rules.

Somehow we overcame the bathroom dispute (Jim by waiting patiently and me by not washing) to head out to the ruins of Monte Alban. Mexico is full of stories about the Maya; this once great civilisation that built grandiose cities over 1,000 years ago. What fascinates me is that the Greeks, Romans, Incas and Egyptians were all conquered and their empires disintegrated while the Maya seemed to just disappear.

I thought Monte Alban would be my first glimpse of a great Mayan city. It is set at the top of a mountain, which the builders levelled off and built colossal step pyramids, astronomical observatories and beautiful palaces. It is all the more amazing in that the stone had to be brought up the mountain and they hadn't even bothered to invent the wheel. What surprised me was that this city is actually the work of the Zapotecs, who were contemporaries of the Maya. So the mysterious Maya still elude me. However, like the Maya in around 700AD, the social structure began to collapse and this once great city was left deserted. It is the equivalent of everybody in Manchester leaving to go and live in the villages of Lancashire. Incredible.

The site was immaculately maintained with a grand plaza in the middle, surrounded by various sized pyramids and temples. There was even a ball court. I know that the Maya were meant to play a ball game where the losers are sacrificed, so I guess that the Zapotecs had a similar tradition. The sacrificing is a bit harsh, but as a Leicester City fan, there have been times I would have seen this as a reasonable option – purely for motivational purposes obviously.

Back in 21st century Oaxaca, I was in a state of limbo. I'm meant to be working on an organic farm but I haven't had a response from my e-mails and they don't have a telephone. 'Can I work on your farm now?' is the question that affects my plans of where to go next.

In the meantime, Bill introduced me and Jim to Mezcal. From what my taste buds made of it, it seems to be some sort of cleaning fluid that the Mexicans drink. Strength wise I think it would get rid of nearly any stain. The story goes that it is made from a local plant which is baked in an oven (Mezcal does have a strange smoky taste). The next stage gives it some flavour and can involve various fruits or even raw chicken breasts. Whatever was in the stuff, we chinked glasses and said goodbye to the Peurto Escondido bound Jim.

Day 6 - Monday 1ST April - Billy Too Many Mates

I'd been impressed with the hostel, but Bill was suffering from choosing an already occupied mattress. No one had complained to him but the bed-bug inhabitants had left their traditional line of bites on his body. Well, that was his excuse to request a move into the girl's dormitory. This had the added advantage of getting him away from Lucy because he felt that it was becoming a busman's holiday (I know the sleeping arrangements are complicated, but somehow Lucy was in the male dormitory).

I have to say when all things are considered, whether funny or mad, you do wonder whether Lucy will get home in one piece. Our resident therapist said she seems to get near people as if she wants to talk, but then doesn't know how to and starts being aggressive. At the moment, the only person she can have a conversation with is herself. Her grip on reality is not very strong and she needs to travel from South Mexico to wherever home is in America. To be honest I'm not sure whether she can make it unassisted but who will help her when she shouts at everyone? I hope she does make it, and soon, because god knows what may happen to her if she stays in Mexico.

I carried on my hectic pace, by getting up at 9.30am and having breakfast with a middle-aged American I'd bumped into at Monte Alban. The day then drifted by in a blur of markets, people watching, sun and e-mailing. Although I did find time to practice the pronunciation of the city, apparently it is O-wack-a ...... I think, or it could be O-hwack-a. I'll carry on practising.

I still haven't heard anything from the farm near Oaxaca, but I had a look on the WWOOF website and there is a ranch in San Cristobal De La Casas which sounds interesting. The brilliantly named WWOOF is an abbreviation of the Worldwide Opportunities on Organic Farms. They give you contact details for organic farms that want volunteers. So you help the organic farm, they get free labour and the world is a better place. Well, provided they return your e-mails.

Day 7 - Tuesday 2ᴺᴰ April - The Rat Pack

With a true lack of imagination, I all but repeated yesterday's schedule. The square just brings out the lazy, relaxed side in me. The only interesting things to note emanated from the hostel. I met an American lad who is here to video the plight of the indigenous people. His story went that Mexico made a trade agreement with the US, which meant a change in Mexico's constitution i.e. indigenous groups no longer have a right to their mineral-rich land. Paramilitary groups, with a government tie in, have then been taking over towns and villages to try and force the locals to move away. Hence the indigenous Indians want it recording and seen by the world. I had no idea there was such a history of internal conflict in Mexico.

A different story had started to spread among the corridors of Mexican hostels. It goes ….. once upon a time in the fair city of Oaxaca were four girls who went to live at the Magic hostel (actual name of the hostel). In the middle of the night, the girls heard some strange scratching sounds from a cupboard. When the door was opened, several large rats ran across the room. There are mixed reports of the actual size of the rats. Apparently last week they were small ones, but after a week of storytelling, they are now six feet tall and three foot wide. Anyway, the girls ran out of the hostel (although next week in the story one of them gets eaten) in the early hours and stayed in the hotel over the road, before living happily ever after. Although maybe with the exception of one of the rat girls called Jo. I met her just before I left my hostel and it turned out that her destiny would be to travel on tonight's bus with me – poor girl. Jo had already suffered so much!

Bill stayed at the same hostel as Jo on the Mexican south coast and it turned out they had met much the same people, including Jim and a lad called Kirk. I think being called Kirk is an unfortunate start in life because as a kid you would surely have endured countless Captain Kirk gags. Even now, at the very mention of the name Kirk all I can think of is William Shatner leaping around plastic rocks on some far off planet. Bill, who seemed to like everyone, couldn't stand the unfortunate Kirk but didn't seem to be able to get away from him. They came from completely different political spectrums so unsurprisingly the straw that broke Bill's back was that Kirk's all-time hero was Maggie Thatcher. He reported the lad just wasn't interested in Mexico and complained about the food, people, accommodation and transport. On the basis that I could count on one hand the number of backpackers I have disliked, I thought he couldn't be that bad, could he? Apparently, I'd be able to recognise him because Bill said that every shirt Kirk possessed was a football shirt.

Day 8 - Wednesday 3rd April - Jeff in Wonderland

The bus seemed to be on a continually winding mountain path as I started to wish the Romans had reached Mexico. I tried to sleep but with every other corner my head would lift off the window, I was leaning against, before gravity sent it back with a thud. I placed a jumper between my head and the window. It dulled the thud, but with every corner and little lift of my head, the jumper would slip a little until it had slipped a lot and I'd feel the solid thud of glass again. My mood didn't improve when the woman in front of me was sick. But neither winding corners nor the aroma of diced carrots sautéed in a light brown sauce could wake up Jo. She had selfishly fallen asleep rather than suffer with me.

As the half time service station approached, at 3.00am, I'd managed a total of 20 minutes sleep compared to Jo's three hours of unconsciousness. Mind you, I then had a rip-roaring second half, sleeping for most of the remaining six hours. Only to be outslept once again by Jo, who was still asleep when everyone was getting off the bus at 9.00am. Myself and Jo had been continually told that if you go to San Cristobal you have to stay at the Magic Hostel (we were assured it was far better than the Oaxaca version). The only problem was that it didn't appear in our guidebooks so we didn't know where it was located. We asked a taxi driver 'Magic?' which didn't get any response, so worked our way through a whole range of pronunciations 'Magecc' 'Majeek' 'Maheeeeek', but they were all met by an increasingly puzzled look.

A similar routine was performed for a second man but it produced no reaction other than slightly worrying the driver. However, the third and final driver said he knew of it, so we put ourselves in his hands.

He pulled up outside a large pale blue garage door. My experienced traveller mind recognised it as a scam. There was no sign of a hostel. 'Where is the hostel?' '*Here*'. On closer inspection, there was a button with 'magic doorbell' written on it. Very strange. My mind moved from scam to Alice in Wonderland. I pressed the button and the door opened to reveal a vibrant brightly painted courtyard full of travellers. That was no ordinary door but the first part of something like a cross between the bat cave and backpacker oasis. Pristine dormitories awaited for just £3 a night. Although I did get the feeling I was the only one over 23 and the music seemed to have a distinct American hip-hop flavour, but it gave off a friendly feeling.

I needed to find an internet café because I had given up on the first farm and wanted to send an e-mail to the farm that is near San Cristobal. I don't know what is up with these farms because the latest one doesn't have a telephone either. My lazy wanderings brought me to a cheap internet café. I sent the e-mail to the farm and chatted on e-mail to friends back in England. This whole e-mail thing is staggering. I am actually keeping in better contact with some friends in England when I'm on holiday than when I am back at home. I checked on the latest sports news before going out into the sunny San Cristobal streets.

I was surprised by the number of indigenous Indians in San Cristobal and how many of them were dressed in the traditional bright clothes. These people were Mayans. It had never occurred to me that the Maya still existed. I'd just sort of assumed that when their empire collapsed they died out. What actually happened was that they moved from the cities to small communities and then just carried on, so some of these people are still pure Maya.

Jo was also wandering aimlessly, so we decided to aim our wanderings into a restaurant. It looked posh and was set in a lovely courtyard with live music but it proved wallet friendly. The music was provided by two grinning middle-aged men who produced a uniquely distorted sound from what I can only describe as a giant electronic glockenspiel. Their music was randomly entwined with the sirens of a kid's toy car, of the variety which you'd normally find outside supermarkets.

A strange opening leading to another world and men grinning like Cheshire cats. Okay, where are the Mad Hatters? And exactly how hard had I hit my head on the bus window? These questions were pushed to the back of my mind as we purchased a bottle of wine from the local supermarket. It turned into the worst tasting alcoholic grape juice I have ever drunk, but it helped me fall into a deep sleep.

Day 9 - Thursday 4ᵀᴴ April - Jeff in Wonderland II

Jo got up at 6.30am to move on to Palenque. We shared the same bunk bed (is that the right term for a different bunk but same bed contraption), which meant that when Jo woke up and moved around on the top bunk, my bottom bunk shook me awake. The day sort of drifted after this, to the point where I have to ask what did I actually do? How productive am I being? It is far too easy to sit around doing nothing. At the same time my Spanish conversation skills must be improving and already I know far more about Mexico than when I started. I do remember talking to a local Mexican for 15 minutes, all in Spanish. This was done without shouting the names of footballers, but with the help of my English/Spanish dictionary and a lot of patience on his part.

My dose of culture for the day came from visiting the Na Bolem museum. It is a cultural centre for indigenous people set up by a Danish archaeologist and his Swiss wife. They were heroes to the local Indians because they fought to maintain their rights and were a pain in the ass to the Mexican government. As seems to be the way with travelling, my group of one became three, with Andrew (been in South & Central America for 3 months and only knows two words in Spanish and one of those is wrong) and Anne (an Armenian clinical psychologist) joining me for dinner. I took them to my courtyard restaurant where the distorted glockenspiel was being played in the corner and the kid's car hooted opposite. It was already fairly surreal and then two clowns walked in. Makeup, wigs, sponge cowboy hats, fully costumed and big red noses. They entered quite normally, sat at a table and ordered some food. The question was when you're having dinner with an Armenian clinical psychologist do you mention you have just seen two clowns walk in and sit down at a table? Luckily, Anne spotted them and said '*look at those clowns*' to which I answered 'I see no clowns'. Anyway, after receiving confirmation that my sanity was still in order and I could still produce the bad gags, I ran over to the clowns to have my picture taken with them.

So, recapping; in one corner distorted glockenspiel, opposite corner the toneless toy car and third corner the clowns. We couldn't wait to see what would happen to the empty corner. Alas, no one came.

It was only after I left that my mind ticked over. Clowns in funny hats, wow the Mad Hatters. What is happening here? How did Alice in Wonderland finish?

I retreated back to the safety of the Magic Hostel and ordered a beer. I tried to join in conversations but for once it seemed hard work. Everybody seemed to be in mid-conversation about things I didn't really feel that interested in such as WWF wrestling and suddenly everyone seemed so much younger than me. I stood at the bar/reception feeling a little lonely. No friends here, strange country, no job back home and while most people my age are settling down I'm spending all my savings. I normally think of all these things as positives but for some reason, they began to seem like problems. Then a lad from another group broke off from his own conversation and came across. I felt a little low and it was one of those occasions that your faith in human nature receives a lift. There was no reason for him to come across except that he felt a little sorry for me. He was Klaus, a Colombian German. Yeah, I know Colombian/German is a strange combination, basically, his parents sent him from Colombia to a German boarding school at the age of 14. He didn't speak a word of German at the time and it took a good couple of months before he could understand anything. I was soon back into the swing of things, chatting to everyone and changing the subject from WWF Wrestling.

Day 10 - Friday 5th April - Posh, Politics and Captain Kirk

Another day, another drift around, what do I do? It's not as if San Cristobal isn't an interesting place. On the contrary, the large indigenous population adds a colourful presence to San Cristobal and their typically short and stocky build reminds me of Peru. They still have an almighty presence in Southern Mexico and have been involved in an area of modern Mexican history that I am only just appreciating. The original constitution of Mexico redistributed land to communal holdings effectively owned by the government. NAFTA (North American Free Trade Agreement) changed this by allowing the sale of the land and threatened the indigenous people's way of life. It proved the final straw for some people and in 1994 an armed guerrilla organisation called the Zapatista briefly took control of San Cristobal. They demanded the upholding of indigenous people's rights, democracy across all levels of Mexican politics, an end to government corruption (a long-held Mexican tradition) and restoration of their land rights. This brought the normal reaction to the Indigenous people. The Mexican army used force to drive them out, bombing civilians and murdering prisoners on the way. The situation rumbled on until a new president of Mexico was elected and in December 2000 the Zapatista again wanted to draw attention to their plight. They began a two-week march to Mexico City, which climaxed with a 100,000 strong crowd. Promises were made and in the last year the Zapatista seem to have mysteriously disappeared. Whether the required changes are made is still an unanswered question.

I can now make much more sense of what the American lad was talking about in Oaxaca. The paramilitary groups are probably land-owners private armies who know that if they can force the locals off the land they stand a much better chance of being able to buy it outright.

One of the farms, I am trying to work on is in the Zapatista heartland so it could be a fascinating place to stay. However, I still haven't been contacted by either of the farms that I e-mailed. If I don't hear anything by tomorrow I'll start to travel south.

As I wondered what to do I began another walk up another hill, to another church. Well, most of the way. The steep steps up were blocked by a pack of six dogs. After one dog pawed my leg yesterday, my bravery was down to chicken level and the thought of retreating to the comfort of the hostel courtyard was too good to turn down.

I sat in my sunny courtyard next to Richard from Hull. He is only in San Cristobal for one night and has to be getting up tomorrow at 6.30am for a bus. We had a quiet meal out, setting the football world to rights, then returned to the hostel and I introduced him to the long-term residents. There were Dan and Suki who are waiting for Dan's stolen credit cards to be replaced. Kari, a Norwegian girl who has been laid up ill for the last week, and her travelling companion Karen who has balanced looking after Kari with partying the nights away. JR, a cocky 24-year-old American pilot, who seems to spend all his time in the courtyard watching videos and chatting. They also had a new friend. Someone in a West Ham shirt. It had to be. *'Jeff, this is Kirk'*. After a split second delay, in which William Shatner leapt over plastic boulders, I managed a 'hello'. Kirk disappeared soon afterwards (in the walked out the door rather than beamed up sense) so I didn't get a chance to find out whether Bill's claims were accurate, but on first impressions, he seemed okay.

Happy hour coincided with Gabriel, the backpacker/ receptionist, insisting that I took advantage of the two for one offer on the 45% vol 'Posh' and suggesting drinking games. You could tell the Posh must be a high-quality drink because it was poured from a plastic water bottle with POSH written on it in pen. As ever, with such games, when one person starts to lose, the only way forward is to lose badly. By the end of the night, Richard's 6.30am start was in serious doubt, as was his ability to string together a coherent sentence.

DAY 11 - SATURDAY 6TH APRIL - A WALK IN THE WOODS

My head stirred with movement from my mattress. I looked up to see Richard stood by my bed. *'Jeff'. 'Jeff'. 'Did I do anything embarrassing last night? I don't remember anything'*. I confirmed he hadn't and made a promise to myself to stay away from these people with 6.30am starts, a man has to have some quality beauty sleep. I can't just rely on my afternoon naps, especially with my looks.

Luckily my head seemed fairly clear because Anne the Armenian psychologist came round to enlist me for a hike around the surrounding hills. She soon took on the role of tour leader and rounded up Kent the New York poet, Megan the Seattleite, Dan II (just to differentiate him from the first Dan) who had only been in the hostel 20 minutes and Jess. In very strange but not really that amazing traveller style, Dan and Jess had accidentally bumped into each other in four Mexican cities. They are still arguing over who is the stalker and who is the stalked.

We wandered along a road and up a mountain track deep into the cloud forest that surrounds San Cristobal. Kent really is a poet, a performing poet at that, who stands on stage and reads aloud. As I walked along with him he read some of his recent Mexican based poems. I'm no poetry fan but found it entertaining. One particular rhyme I found highly amusing, although Kent informed me it was a list rather than an actual poem. I confirmed to him that I had written a number of lists in my time and none were as good as that. His poems not only included the normal problems with relationships but frustration that he is endlessly approached by women who fancy him. His poems referred to himself as the good looking Keanu Reeves lookalike in a strangely disparaging way.

He was entertaining company as we reached the climax of the walk which was meant to be a stunning view of San Cristobal from the top of the hill. Unfortunately, the vast number of trees meant that all we could see from the top were leaves and branches. Never mind, I'm sure the exercise was good for us.

Back at the courtyard, there was good news. Lost wallet Dan had received a package with his new credit card inside, it was a week late but at least it had reached the Magic Hostel. Dan was still concerned. Apparently, there had been a knock at the hostel door from a local; the already opened package had been delivered to the man's garage down the street two days ago. They paid him the requested 'reward money' for passing it to them but were worried whether the card had already been used.

I wished them luck before walking to the end of the ticket-purchasing queue at the bus station. I'd previously been an involuntary witness to Jo and Richard getting up at 6.30am for their 7.30am bus and decided to treat myself to the slightly more expensive but more civilised (in time at least) 8.30am bus.

I returned to the hostel where once more Gabriel tried to force Posh down my throat. Although I did succumb to the Posh I did manage to glean one important piece of information from him; the clocks go forward one hour tomorrow. Bang goes that extra hour in bed but at least I would turn up at the right time to catch my bus. Jess said that if I woke her up she'd probably come with me to see if there were any spare tickets. Feeling one step ahead of the pace (or one hour ahead) I smugly danced the night away at a local club.

DAY 12 - SUNDAY 7ᵀᴴ APRIL - THE SCORPION BLOCKER

'Jeff' 'Jeff'.

'Um, what?'

'You're meant to be up'.

'er'.

'To catch the bus'.

'Um, oh, AY MIERDA!'

Jess had searched around the dormitories for my comatosed body. I had slept clean through my alarm and needed to be dressed and have left the hostel within 10 minutes. In my semi-conscious state, I crawled out of bed, put on last night's crumpled on the floor clothes and did whatever Jess told me to do.

We were joined in a bus station bound taxi by Olge and Sasha. They had already missed their scheduled bus because of the time change. Jess propped me up against a wall in the bus station and joined the others in attempting to buy some tickets. Unfortunately, the four lads in front of them in the queue captured the final tickets (they had also meant to catch the 7.30am bus but hadn't moved their clocks the requisite 60 minutes). I thanked the girls for delivering me to my bus and then waved goodbye. The next bus they could catch was in the afternoon, so they forlornly trooped back to the hostel.

I felt a bit bad because if I had got up earlier we may have reached the bus station at a better time and they may have secured tickets for the early bus. Although Jess did say she would have woken me up earlier but when she first poked her head around the dormitory door, there was a couple in a bottom bunk bed opposite me who were making some sort of rhythmic movements together. Hence she waited another 10 minutes (outside the room, not watching). Also, Olge had entered the dormitory, just before Jess, to wake up the receptionist and get their passports back, but as he was half of the couple, he was all too much awake, so she also turned back.

The bus journey seemed long and drawn out, although I think that had more to do with my delicate state and another continually winding road than anything else. The actual bus was very modern and comfortable, a far cry from any third world bus I've previously taken.

I arrived in Palenque town at about 2.30pm. Gabriel had told me that the town wasn't worth staying in and recommended I made my way to El Panchan, near the ruins of old Palenque. Apparently, all I had to do was cross the main road and wait for a passing colectivo. The colectivos are mini-buses that you can seemingly hail down at any point along a specified route. If the one I took today was typical then they are full of friendly Mexican faces and are dirt-cheap. I reached El Panchan all too easily.

I'd read that El Panchan's founder originally came to Palenque as an archaeologist. He bought this land and named it Panchan, which is Mayan for 'heaven and earth'. Who was I to argue? The five campsites/hostels, which it encompasses, are now run by his children and are set in a wonderfully thick jungle.

I'd never been in a jungle before so most of my images of what it should be like have been built up through television programmes. I was a little disappointed not to see an ape-man swinging from vine to vine calling out 'A-ahahahah'. Instead, I decided that jungle is simply a forest that is hot, wet and slippery.

I had every intention of organising a bed in a dormitory so I could meet other travellers, but tiredness had taken its toll. So when I was offered a spacious wooden cabin to myself it sounded too good to resist. It provided me with a bit of time to myself in a very relaxed setting, where it was basically jungle trails linking cabin-to-cabin and cabin-to-facilities.

My peace and quiet began with a stroll down the path leading to a restaurant. Half an hour passed of food and reading before I heard a Yorkshire accent saying '*Hi Jeff*'. It was Jo with a couple of friends, Mark and Jessie. More people arrived including two lads who went to school together but had met here purely by chance. One of them was scorpion Matt. He'd been swimming in the sea at Puerto Escondido and returned to the sand where his towel lay. He picked up the towel and started to dry himself off not realising that a scorpion had entwined itself in the towel. It bit him. He was unsure of the exact procedure as to what one should do when bitten by a scorpion and returned to his nearby hotel. The owner told him it is like a drug trip and just to lie on his bed and enjoy the ride. Matt got to his room and found his slightly odd Mexican roommate inside, so he explained what had happened. Instead of any sympathy, he said '*Ah, you lucky bastardo!*' it turned out that his roommate sometimes injected himself with a particular scorpion poison just for kicks.

Well, the stories continued and the table to which I had started sitting down at 3.00pm still had me as a tenant at 11.00pm, by which time there were 14 of us. That included Jess who arrived at 9.30pm with Olge, Sasha, Bo and Kennet all fresh from the Magic hostel. The party moved to a room as all 14 of us squeezed into a two-person cabin.

I'd stumbled outside to locate the toilet and was happily tinkering away when a scream shot out from the room. I returned to see everybody in uproar. I'd been sitting by the door and when I left, something decided to keep the numbers of occupants at 14. That something was a scorpion, which crawled underneath the door and took my position. Obviously, my popularity was higher than I thought because the scorpion was forcibly removed and I was nervously reinstated in the door position.

A worry did persist though. I'd hardly been in my own cabin and now my bed lay at the end of some jungle trail. I could remember that I needed to cross a stream, bear right and it was somewhere to the left after a big cabin. Other than that I knew it was near a lot of trees, but when you're in the middle of a jungle this is not very useful. The main tracks were dimly lit but I knew that my cabin was about 20 yards walk from such a track. I'd soon found a path that I was sure was wrong so tried another one. My bed had to be round there somewhere. I found the big cabin then stopped on the path and stared out into the darkness. All I could make out were trees.

I walked another 20 yards up the path and stared out at the darkness once more. Amongst the trees, I thought there was some sort of rectangular shape. I concentrated harder on the object until I became convinced it was a cabin, in fact, I was certain it was my cabin. It just left the matter of making some loud clomping sounds on the path to tell any passing snakes I was coming and then I stomped across the path to my welcoming bed.

Day 13 - Monday 8ᵀᴴ April - Better a Poet than a King

My original plan, for an early start, had predictably faltered but I was still walking up to the main archaeological site by 10.00am. I was told the ruins were a bus ride or 20 minutes' walk away. Walking to old Palenque seemed more attractive than standing at the side of a road waiting for a bus. After 20 minutes I found myself outside the exit to Palenque. Apparently, the entrance was further up the road. Up seemed to be the operative word because all I could see was a road snaking around a steep incline. Maybe I should have taken the bus after all. The idea seems to be that the entrance is at the top of the hill and then you can walk down and through the site to the exit. 40 minutes after I set off from El Panchan I wished somebody had mentioned that to me. The ruins were surrounded by jungle but the pyramids stood impressively strong alongside a large palace complex. There were further tracks into the jungle, which led to more structures, and amazingly 98% of the ruins are allegedly unexcavated.

The Maya do seem such a remarkable civilisation to have built these amazing structures and then to have deserted them. They had an amazingly accurate calendar system that even now is only a few minutes out and created a writing system that is thought to be one of just five that were independently invented in the history of mankind. As the Maya King and Queen were deemed the nearest thing to gods on earth they regularly had to draw blood from their tongue and genitals as a sacrifice to the gods. Sometimes being a peasant has its advantages.

Instead of taking a knife up the pyramids for a little traditional bloodletting, I decided to just seek some shade. I not only found the shade but also Jess at the temple's top. I had decided it was too hot to read my guidebook, but not too hot to gratefully listen to Jess reading my guidebook.

Four hours of traipsing around the Maya site in the heat were perfectly ended by a refreshing dip into a beautiful waterfall. Our wet feet dried as we started to walk back to El Panchan. On one side of the road were the thick trees and bushes of the jungle. So we were a little surprised when a man jumped out of the vegetation shouting 'mush-mush'. We had been warned about the 'mush-mush' man and told that the mush-mush on offer is of the magic fungus variety. It was nice to be greeted so enthusiastically but we passed up on his offer. It was not exactly what Jess needed considering she would be crossing the Belize/Mexican border tonight.

In fact, out of the crowd from yesterday, most people seemed to be on their way today; Jo, Claire, Danielle, Tom, Sasha, Olge, Jessie and Jess to be precise. Which left Matt, Matt, Mark and I around a table plus Kennett and Bo somewhere about. It turned out that scorpion Matt was also credit card Matt. He'd been working for a couple of credit card companies whilst travelling in Australia. He'd seen how their systems worked and realised that if he used the credit up to a set amount and changed countries then they wouldn't bother chasing him. And that is precisely how he has funded the last couple of months. Despite the stories from credit card/ scorpion Matt, it seemed a bit lonely with just four of us. I needn't have worried, Kent the poet turned up with a couple of friends and then three young English girls arrived. 10 of us, that was better.

I hadn't really believed Kent about all those women endlessly fussing over him. I'll tell you what though he wasn't kidding. The three English girls were swooning and all but dribbling with excitement over him. I think he spoke the truth when his poems seemed to reflect his frustration with all these girls. As problems go though, I'd swap it for my smelly feet.

Day 14 - Tuesday 9ᵀᴴ April Too Many Legs in My Bed

I woke up and was shocked to see a pair of foreign legs next to me.

In fact, it wasn't just one pair, there was a whole battalion of bloody ants marching up and down my bedsheets. I'll give them credit though, they had the courtesy not to climb over my body. But it made my mind up, I'd be moving to the cheaper and less legged confines of a dormitory.

After a quick evacuation, I joined Mark, Matt, Bo and Kennett on a mini-bus for a waterfall tour. The first waterfall was a large picturesque specimen, which enjoyed celebrity status because it starred in the Arnie Schwarzenegger film 'Predator'. Whilst Matt was taking pictures, Mark and I made our way under the main waterfall and up the side of the wet rock-face into a cave of knee deep water. We entered on the basis that other people had come and gone so it must be safe and what exactly was in the cave? We went in, me first, then Mark with a torch. There was definitely madness behind our method as I took 10 dark steps and then cried 'shit!' as I unexpectedly plunged down another 50 centimetres, completely soaking my shorts, money belt and wallet. We carried on, the ground got higher and we rounded a corner to see a small waterfall within our cave. Arrrrr........ very pretty. It left us time to turn and hear Matt let out a '*shit!*' Who needs a satellite for pinpointing people, without seeing Matt we knew his exact position within the cave.

The second stop was at Agua Azul where there is seven kilometres of blue water surging through rapids and waterfalls. It was a real show of power on the part of Mother Earth. It is possible to swim in certain areas, but people who have strayed into the sections of dangerously strong currents have sometimes paid for it with their lives. We chose a relatively sedate area to swim in but I still looked like I possessed the pace of an Olympic swimmer downstream and was seemingly on a water treadmill going, or trying to go, upstream.

Matt had heard of an incredible canyon further up the river. His instructions to get there were to go past the sign which says 'don't go past this sign', find the rope bridge, then keep going until you find the canyon. Well, we reached the 'don't go any further serious danger of physical assault' sign, which also had six policemen standing around it. Did we really want to do this? I didn't fancy it and Bo, Kennet and Mark didn't look to be bubbling with enthusiasm.

It was agreed that all valuables would be left in the secure possession of Bo and Kennett, which would leave, well somehow me, a mad keen Matt and an unsure Mark, to locate the amazing canyon. I was sort of working on the basis that we'd probably never get passed the police. Unfortunately, we wandered straight by them and they didn't say a word. 10 minutes passed and we hadn't been assaulted but had found the rope bridge, well what remained of it. Almost half of the wooden planks were missing but at least it was only five metres long. It did mean, that where there were no wooden planks, you would have to balance your feet on the ropes at the bottom and grab hold of the ropes at hand level. I definitely wasn't prepared to do that.

Matt went first and said he would check to see what was on the other side (I get the feeling I have just missed a joke). I waited with Mark for a couple of minutes and then he turned to me, motioned to the flimsy bridge and said *'Are you coming?'* 'No, this is as far as I go'. I waited patiently for a couple of minutes, before realising I was now by myself in the 'risk of serious assault' area. It's amazing how quickly you can get across a flimsy bridge with a little bit of motivation. After the bridge, we caught up with Matt and found a nice little beach, which only had two people on it. We thought of mugging them to teach them a lesson that you should obey signs, but waved at them instead.

The path turned into a vague track and a climb through thick jungle. We rose and rose until Mark and I had reached the 'r' of our collective 'tether'. There did seem to be a canyon down below. However, it was seemingly impenetrable to jump into and possessed seriously dangerous currents so we finally convinced Matt to head back to camp.

Our day of waterfalls ended and then it was Bo, Kennett, Scorpion Matt, Waterfall Matt and Mark's turn to leave El Panchan. Of the 14 from Sunday night only I remained. I, therefore, returned to my little dormitory by myself. However, I must have done something good in a previous life because three beautiful Israeli girls had moved into my four-person dormitory. Well, it was either that or they must have done something really bad to end up having to share a dormitory with me. Anyway, they introduced themselves and were very friendly. Unfortunately, it took five minutes for me to forget their names, so I asked again and forgot again and then was too embarrassed to ask for the third time. I have met so many people in the last two weeks that some names enter one ear, have a cup of tea and leave through the other ear.

Day 15 - Wednesday 10ᵀᴴ April - Booked

Whatever the girl's names, they all managed to get up without waking me, an impressive dormitory feat.

So I got up by myself and had a two-hour breakfast with an English lad who dreams of putting little traveller libraries around the world. Then I headed to the little travel agent corner of reception to make enquiries about the route to Guatemala. The price they'd quoted for 6.00am tomorrow seemed very reasonable and my intention of looking for something cheaper was distracted by an internet café in town. I hadn't checked my e-mail for a while and being an addict it seemed like heaven to spend a couple of hours in front of a screen. I returned to the reception in the afternoon to book on to the trip, but it was closed. I didn't want to wait another day but spoke to a waiter in my broken (or mortally wounded) Spanish. He seemed to say that if I turned up at 6.00am tomorrow and waited outside the office I should be okay. Working on the principle that if you can't trust a waiter (who you don't really share a common language with) for travel information, who can you trust? I decided to start packing.

Day 16 - Thursday 11ᵀᴴ April - The Best of Palenque

I began waiting outside the office at 5.55am. Make that a lonely 5.55am. Just myself, by the reception cabin, in the middle of the jungle. It was difficult enough getting up at such a bloody silly time, but if there was no bus…

6.05am came and went.

GGGRRRRRRR. Was that my bed I could hear calling me? My firm belief was that beds call in a silent way while that sounded more like a wild beast. I knew there weren't lions, tigers or leopards around so maybe a jaguar or puma was lurking in the undergrowth. GGGGGrroooorrrrrr. I realised that rather than a growl, it now sounded different. It sounded like snoring. In fact, it was definitely snoring, someone was sleeping in the locked up reception. It is amazing how fertile your imagination can be at 6.07am in the middle of a jungle. The snoring turned into a cough and then movement. A flap opened and a head popped out. 'Quero Flores auto?' *'Wait over there'*. With that, the flap closed and he once more tried to transform into the beast of the jungle.

A few minutes later, a bus arrived full of passengers who had paid for their tickets yesterday. By this time a Mexican traveller had also turned up. He acted as an interpreter between me and the bus driver. He confirmed that I did need a ticket and that the bus was full. But if I placed an amount equal to the ticket price into the driver's back pocket, one way or another, he'd make sure I reached Guatemala. Luckily the local interpretation of full was in operation. The bus driver found a small free-standing plastic chair, like you may take out into the garden when the sun shines. He placed it in the aisle and hey presto, the bus wasn't full after all.

Two hours down the road we made a stop at a campsite and dropped off a couple of passengers but picked up some more. It turned out that my plastic chair was actually an official seat, so there was now no room for me on the mini-bus. A promise was a promise though and he had a friend driving another mini-bus. I was ushered into the other vehicle and told not to worry about my rucksack, which was still strapped to the original bus. Instead of the luxury of a plastic seat, the new driver ordered the trio on the three-person front seat to make room for a little one. On the seat next to me were two Swiss girls and a German lad. The lad spoke in German to the Swiss girls whilst I spoke in English with the Swiss girls, but strangely I never exchanged any words with him.

The bus dropped us off at a small building that housed the Mexican immigration authorities and I was reunited with my rucksack. Those of us destined for Guatemala, walked along a quiet little road, through a tiny village and onwards to the river. In slightly surreal circumstances my time in Mexico ended on a deserted mud bank. There were about six large motor powered canoes, so we scrambled aboard one and I enjoyed the most amazing border crossing of my life. There was dense jungle on either side interspersed with the odd hut indicating a village. After about half an hour the boat drifted into another mud bank, which turned out to be Guatemala. We scrambled up the bank and then started to look for the shack, which was Guatemalan immigration. Heathrow will never be quite the same.

On the bus to Flores, I found myself side by side with the German lad, there didn't seem to be any escape from each other. As people discussed hotels we gave in to fate and decided to look for a twin room, rather than the more expensive single room option.

Flores is built on a little island and our hotel had a little jetty on to the lake, where you can jump into the water or buy a beer. In fact, as we wandered down to the lakeside there were a couple of Norwegian lads who told us to grab a beer and join them. Two Austrians also joined the Norwegian beer grab plus a couple of English girls and a Dutch couple. After meeting our alcohol requirement we all trooped up the hill for a meal and then trooped down again, ready for an early start.

DAY 17 – FRIDAY 12ᵀᴴ APRIL –
I STARTED WITH A TIKAL AND FINISHED WITH A WIFE

It felt like Christmas Day again, the present was Tikal, the stunning Maya city in the middle of a thick jungle. The day began badly with a 4.30am start (anything before 7.30am I regard as a bad start to the day). There are numerous mini-bus trips to Tikal and they all seem to pick you up from your hotel. It means that from 4.30am to 5.30am little Flores is abuzz with the sound of mini-buses crisscrossing the island. The German lad (or Christian as I now know him) and I were picked up just after 5.00am and then enjoyed a guided tour of the many hotels of Flores until 5.30am. The trip had advertised that we'd see Tikal at sunrise, but judging from the bright yellow shiny thing rising from the east at 6.00am, that was a fib.

We reached Tikal at about 6.30am and as my source had reported the place is absolutely amazing. The first feeling of unwrapping the present is when you enter the gates to Tikal National Park, some 18 kilometres from the main site. On first appearances, Tikal is just a sprawling jungle but 1,200 years ago it covered an urban area of over 100 square kilometres and had a population of 120,000 people. The bus dropped us off by a museum and then Christian and I hurried off into the midst of the jungle. The whole site is a vast warren of small but clearly marked paths.

We strode out in the direction of the Great Plaza. An atmospheric mist hung in the air and the various sounds of the jungle were dominated by the roar of lions. This time it wasn't somebody snoring, nor was it a lion, but it came from the little howler monkeys. It is a great form of defence because if you didn't know what it was you'd run away. Even when you know what it is, it makes you think twice.

Two pyramid temples dominate the plaza. The Jaguar temple was cordoned off from the public, so Christian and I clambered up the side of the second pyramid. The sides were steep and it was a relief to sit down at the top. The view from the top was mystical rather than awe-inspiring. All you could see was the intimidating grey stone pyramid jutting out of the thick morning mist and dense jungle. And to think this would be the area that countless people would have been sacrificed.

I took a step forward to walk down the pyramid and was shocked. It may have seemed steep clambering up but it was 'bloody hell where is my safety rope' steep on the way down. The threat of falling was intensified because the stone steps of the pyramid are big so you are reaching out with your leading leg almost feeling for the step-down. After virtually performing a little jump to reach the next narrow(ish) step you then have the next step and then the next step and again for about 100 steps. No wonder these pyramids have a reputation for fatal accidents. I saw the occasional person bumping down the steps on their bottom. I didn't blame, them but could not bring myself to swallow my pride to bottom bump down. After a careful descent, we continued to explore the jungle paths until we came across the magnificent Temple IV. After you have climbed up, you sit like a god above the jungle canopy, looking down on the tops of temples peeking through the vegetation. Tikal is truly a world-class archaeological site set in a world-class natural park. I didn't want to leave my god-like position but mortality called.

We wandered around the various trails and eventually came across an outlying pyramid. Christian and I were the only people in sight although there was a guard around the corner. They have increased the number of guards in response to a big increase in crime against tourists including armed robberies, rapes, shootings and mini-bus hold-ups. But, as I was about to find out, the guards can't stop everything. I clambered to the top of the pyramid and thought I'd see if I could hold my nerve (not at its strongest 100 feet above the ground) and walk around the narrow ledge which circumnavigates the top of the pyramid. I reached the first corner and was about 30 centimetres from the edge when I was hit on the head. My first reaction was to turn round and find out what the hell Christian was playing at, but it was nothing to do with him. A young vulture had flown into the back of my head. The fact that it had nearly sent me plummeting 100 feet, down the side of a pyramid, was all a little too bemusing to appreciate. So we sat down to take in the view and then carried on with our wanderings.

There must have been hundreds or even thousands of people in Tikal, but because the jungle is so thick you can easily go for 20 minutes without seeing anyone. After nine hours of discovery, we headed back to Flores.

Klaus my German/Colombian friend had turned up at the hotel, along with an Englishman named Paul. They'd been to Tikal last Wednesday, so I could explain to them precisely where and how I'd got hit by the vulture. I was astonished to hear that exactly the same thing had happened to Paul, except that he'd been hit by a fully-grown vulture! A Dutch lad was listening and explained that vultures are useless at killing animals. Apparently, their best tactic, other than scavenging, is to knock animals off high places and to their death. Then they can start to eat their victim. Bloody hell, I was the subject of a murder attempt!

The day hadn't finished yet and my body was to undergo another attack. About seven of us had gone for a meal and a bit of liquid refreshment. There were Einar and Finn, the very friendly 'grab a beer' Norwegians. Einar was a solid six foot three with bleached blonde hair and a wholehearted lust for life. Along with the longhaired Finn, he had decided that travel diaries were okay, but they'd record each day via a bar chart measuring the number of alcohol units they had consumed. Suddenly the name 'bar chart' seemed to be very appropriate and presumably, their food intake is illustrated on 'pie charts' (sorry – couldn't resist).

The United Nations feel was increased by Louis and Caroline from Amsterdam, Renana from Israel and Mark from Australia. The dining party was completed by Christian and myself.

The night seemed to be at an end when we walked out of the restaurant at 11.00pm and past a basketball court. There were a few kids standing around bouncing a ball. Einar headed towards them and 30 seconds later was announcing that he had organised a basketball match. It was four foreigners on each side plus a local 13-year-old each. The action started with our 13-year-old scoring a three-pointer and immediately getting enthusiastically mobbed by his new team-mates. For the next half an hour we tore around the court like mad things. What we lacked in skill we made up for in, um, no actually we just lacked skill.

We carried on playing until someone came up with the better idea of rather than running around like maniacs (and trying to keep the recent meal in the stomach) we should go for a nice cold beer. Good old common sense prevailed.

We headed to a quiet looking bar where the locals made an immediate fuss of the girls. The waiter was pleading for a dance with Caroline to which her boyfriend Louis and I encouraged her to salsa. You weren't allowed to just salsa, you had to salsa on a tabletop. But oh, what did she start. On a balcony was the only local Guatemalan girl in the bar and she started dancing provocatively to much cheering. So provocatively that it made you wonder what her occupation was, although we could make a good guess. The 'foreign girl' dancing on a table had stolen her limelight so she headed for the same table. As I was closest to the table I thought it was a good idea to avoid eye contact, just on the off chance that she was looking for a partner.

I knew I was in trouble when a pair of thighs were thrust into my face. In a remarkably British way, I tried to ignore them and carry on a conversation.

She wasn't having any of it and started to try and convince me to dance. This involved various grabs on my shirt and pushes towards the table. In the ensuing struggle, I suffered my first injury (a broken shirt button). My worry level increased when her continued heavy pushing (not even romantic pushing) almost made me spill some of my beer. The lads all provided me with encouragement in between their bursts of laughter. All I came up with was 'no thanks, no, no, no, no thank you; I don't want to dance, no gracias, no, no'. Mark, who was sitting next to me, proved highly vocal in his support of wanting to see me dance. I thought it only right to offer him the chance of a dance (with her, not me). But it was rebuffed with an *'Obviously I would Jeff, but she wants you'*. The girl had been gripping on to me demanding a dance for a couple of embarrassing minutes. I realised that the only way I was going to bring an end to proceedings was to salsa dance with her, on the table-top, for the amusement of the whole bar. 'Okay, okay' I said whilst clambering up on to the main table. My poor attempts at salsa were overshadowed by her dirty dancing. In fact, my groin seemed to act like some sort of magnet to her arse and thighs. She was a prostitute and I needed to escape. My first attempt at jumping off the table failed as she clung on to my long-suffering shirt. My second attempt involved dropping my shoulder, giving a little shimmy and jumping the other way.

I headed for my crowd and safety. Or so I thought.

She was a professional and she wanted money out of me at whatever cost to my honour. There was no way she was leaving me alone; she came across, wanting to drag me off again. The girl was relentless.

There was no escape …unless.

Within the next four seconds, I had become a married man. I suppose it was unexpected for me, although it came as a bigger shock to my new wife Renana. The ceremony consisted of me grabbing her and telling the Guatemalan girl that Renana was my better half and wouldn't let me do any more dancing with her, whether it be on a stage or under a duvet. This momentarily confused her, but she was back a minute later asking for money or beer for the dance. Luckily, Renana backed up my story and told her that she wouldn't let her husband pay for the dance. I was saved. The locals who had been pestering Renana for a dance also backed off when she showed them a ring she had shrewdly switched to her wedding finger. For the rest of the night, I decided it was safest to cower behind my new wife.

I was very happy to reach my bed and reflected that my body had never been so sought after. That is sought after in a sad sort of way. After Renana had convinced the girl in the bar that she would not be receiving any money from me, she carried on talking to her. She was just 19 years old, from a village outside Flores and had a link up with the bar to try and make some money for food and lodgings. I am sure thrusting herself at me was not what she wanted to do but it was a matter of necessity.

Day 18 - Saturday 13ᵗʰ April - Traveller Unchecked

Right arm? Check. Left arm? Check. Right leg? Check, this is pretty good so far, left leg? Check. Head? Yes and not sore. Third from top button on my shirt? Oh – no, missing in action. I had most of the day to contemplate my loss because all I needed to do was replenish my monetary supplies and catch a night bus. My cash card had been receiving a battering so I decided it was time to use one of two sets of traveller's cheques, both of which were remains from other trips. I reached the bank and pulled out my Thomas Cook dollar traveller's cheques: *'we only accept American Express cheques'*. So I pulled out my American Express cheques and received a nod of approval. I signed and dated the first one, signed the second and was just about to date it when the cashier let out a *'No'*. They didn't accept Sterling traveller's cheques. 'Oh great, I've signed them now, can you give me a letter or something saying I signed in front of you?' This was greeted with a blank *'I don't speak English'* look. I gave up and made a witty put down at her expense in English. Well, I could have done for all she claimed to understand. Instead, I just let out a frustrated 'bloody hell, you've just cost me £40'. To compound my misery the other banks wouldn't touch pounds so I couldn't even use the dated but unsigned traveller's cheque.

Out of despair rose a cunning little plan, I think if I bide my time I can still get my money. Cue mad villain like laugh.

I headed back to the hostel and found out that my marriage to Renana was null and void (apparently saying 'um, she's my wife' does not constitute a legal marriage). Instead of spending the rest of her life with me, she was heading off to Belize. Ah well, who wants a funny, pretty and intelligent spouse?

Day 19 - Sunday 14ᵗʰ April -
The Chicken Bus and The Black Stuff

Christian and myself took the cheaper 100 Quetzales night bus to Guatemala City rather than the 220 Quetzales direct bus to Antigua, which everyone else travelled on (everyone else being Einar and Finn, Dan and David the Austrians, two English girls – um, Leanne I think and, um, her friend - and James and Chris). That's James and Chris who had been two seats away from me on the plane from Frankfurt. They turned up in my Flores hotel on Friday. It also meant Christian and I would have to catch one of the legendary Guatemalan chicken buses from Guatemala City to Antigua. They have chicken in their title because of the number of times locals carry chickens on them. Most of the buses are 25-year-old American school buses with the accompanying legroom for a 12-year-old. They throw your bag on the roof and then cram four bodies on to three-person seats and three bodies on two-person seats. It may not be comfortable but life on a chicken bus is interesting. We safely arrived in Antigua at 7.30am and it took us only 10 minutes to find the others (see previous definition), who were all huddled in a coffee shop.

Antigua quickly impressed me with its magnificent colonial buildings, cobbled streets and picturesque squares. Then, to top that off, there seems to be the ruins of once mighty churches on every corner. They are the remnants of successive earthquakes during Antigua's turbulent past. That's not everything though because most exciting of all is that it is set in a valley surrounded by volcanoes.

We sort of pottered around the cobbled streets for most of the day and broke the afternoon up with a good sleep. In the evening we ate and made merry, especially after Einar negotiated a restaurant's 'meal deal', which had been 'with cola', to being 'with beer'. The furtherment of our merriment brought us to an Irish bar. Oh, what I'd do for a Guinness. After three weeks on gassy lager beer, I definitely deserved a Guinness. However, the price shook me down to my money belt. £3.50 for a pint of the black stuff compared to the normal £1 for the gassy stuff. After one pint the furtherment was curtailed and the budget strings were tightened all the way back to the hotel.

The hotel is a sprawling mass of unclean rooms, but it is cheap and has a rooftop area. The rooftop area is also a mess, although it is fine for playing cards in the sun and lava spotting. I'd heard stories, before I came to Antigua, that at midnight you could gaze up to see lava trickling down the distant Fuego volcano. All the stories were true, it was amazing.

Day 20 - Monday 15ᵗʰ April - Mysterious Girl

The hotel does have another redeeming feature. There is a mysterious and beautiful oriental girl that seems to appear from nowhere and disappear just as quickly. I've even seen her in town a couple of times, 'hello's' are exchanged and boom, she disappears again.

Actually, the biggest redeeming feature of the hotel is that it is in a stunningly picturesque city. We strolled around one ruined church after another. Surely all magnificent in their day but following earthquake after earthquake, roofs fell, walls crumbled and just images of former giants remain. Some are slowly being reconstructed but they must always be wary of future earthquakes. Antigua used to be the capital city and was considered to be the pre-eminent place in Central America. It had a printing press in 1660, a university established in 1676 and a population that included renowned sculptors, painters, writers and craftsmen.

Then a massive earthquake in 1773 convinced people to leave Antigua and they made Guatemala City the new capital. It seems that Antigua was left as a virtual ghost town for a while until eventually, it began to re-populate but even then it has only been the last 30 years where a real effort has been made to preserve and restore a once powerful city. There is still a lot of restoration to be completed, but the place simply has an irresistible aura about it.

Our day of culture ended with a trip to the gringo bar named Riki's. It's a small bar where you literally bump into fellow travellers and the way somebody knows somebody knows somebody should connect everyone in the bar. For a start, there was Jim sitting contentedly at the bar. We'd been keeping track of one another's progress since Oaxaca and he'd finally caught me up for a beer. Then on the next couple of bar stools sat the equally contented Klaus and Paul.

Antigua is beautiful, I can't help saying so, but it is not all sweetness and light. I keep hearing *'don't go here', 'don't go there' and 'bandits everywhere'*. I am finding it a little frustrating. Christian and I simply wanted to walk up to the monument that looks down on the town. We asked tourist information which was the best route to walk. All they would say was that it was not advisable to walk up by ourselves but the next free police escort would be walking up there in 30 minutes. This slightly disconcerted us so we waited for the police escort or rather the armed police escort. Klaus even told us that when four of them walked back to the hostel last night, they went past three dodgy looking characters who started to follow them. Luckily they were close to the hotel and as Klaus got through the door, they passed him with one flashing a gun from underneath his coat. As I say, not all sweetness and light.

Day 21 - Tuesday 16th April - In Love with a Moody Smoker

With so many volcanoes about it was only a matter of time before Christian and I bowed to temptation and set foot on one. The interest from the remaining Flores group, still in Antigua, was limited as Einar and Finn had started language school whilst Dan and David, who have become known as the Austrian party boys, were too busy sleeping in the morning, watching films in the afternoon and drinking at night. So that left Christian and I to just organise ourselves. There were a lot of travel agencies offering a trip to the Pacaya volcano and we spent most of the morning comparing prices and tours. All the guidebooks recommend going with a tour group because of the threat of bandits. Before I came to Central America I thought a bandit was someone from 150 years ago who wore a sombrero, gun belt, the bullet holders that stretch from shoulder to hip and one of those cowboy neckerchiefs that allows them to cover up their mouth and nose. If I do see one, then I'll be disappointed if he doesn't match that exact description. Also if I battle it out with him I know from watching cowboy films that I can shoot and kill a bandit from 100 yards, but he can fire at me as much as he wants because he'll just hit the rock that I'm hiding behind. When I catch him I'll make him dance by shooting at his feet, I've always wanted to do that.

Back in the real world, it turned out that the morning's interviews had been a waste of time. All the tourist agencies were putting everybody on the same decrepit old bus. There were about 30 people in our group, but we still had an armed guard and the guides said that if they let out a whistle then everyone should run to them for safety.

We arrived safely and started to walk the slopes of the volcano. It was a bit frustrating at first because they made us stay in the group and walk at the slowest person's pace. If you have 30 people in a group it means you have plenty of time to enjoy the views, which changed from green and pleasant to black, volcanic and lifeless. After one and a half hours, a sign appeared 'Enter at your own risk - danger of poisonous gases and rocks being thrown out of the crater'. It was another 800 metres to the start of the crater, but we had a good view of this still active volcano that was moodily smoking away. Guatemala isn't like America and Western Europe where there are warning signs just to legally protect an owner from stupid people. It means there is real danger ahead. So that was that, they made us turn back. Well, that was what I expected, but instead it was *everybody up*'. So up the steep sides of the crater we went. I could scarcely believe that I was climbing an active volcano. Every stride up fought against a tide of tiny volcanic rocks that were constantly sliding your feet back to where they came from. It was very much a case of one step up and a half step back.

Finally, we reached the top and we could peer into the crater (after a quick glance over the shoulder to make sure there were no vultures about). I walked across in a state of disbelief that I'd actually be looking into an active crater. I reached the edge and peered down, but I couldn't see whether there was bubbling lava or a James Bond baddie inside, because there was so much smoke billowing out. There was something menacing about knowing that if you took one more step forward into the smoke, you'd fall to your death. But wow! I was on top of a smoking volcano.

We spent about half an hour admiring the view and then set about the descent. The guides picked a much steeper path than the one we clambered up. Everyone started to walk down but the walk turned into a 'walk and slide' as the little rocks beneath your feet slipped downwards. It soon became a jump and surf, with a requisite squeal of excitement as the rocks slid you down the outside of the crater-like some gigantic natural escalator. Nearly everyone fell over at least once but finished the surf with a big child-like smile.

It took another hour to walk down to the decrepit old bus. The bus showed just how decrepit it really was by breaking down on the way back to Antigua. Within half an hour we had an eight-strong police guard around us. It just seemed surreal that I had not seen a hint of any trouble, but there was this huge security presence everywhere I went. I waited next to an American lad and conversation turned to work and the fact that he'd been involved in several environmental projects. At one stage he worked for a company that produced solar panels and a good profit. They were bought out by BP and he was asked to suggest ways of bringing the costs of production down so the panels would be affordable to everyone. In his research, he found that if BP used solar panels in all of their offices, the necessary production levels would enable costs and hence prices to reduce to an easily accessible level. The proposal was rejected but he stands firm on the validity of his research.

He went on to work for the American Government, preparing reports on environmental issues, but was totally ashamed and frustrated when they then pulled out of the Kyoto agreement. I went on to mention the North American Trade Agreement and that the lad in Oaxaca said that the Indians were being forced off their mineral land as a consequence. It turned out that he'd also done work on that and assured me that nothing like that had been envisaged and he'd be amazed if the actions of the paramilitaries were directly related to NAFTA. His work fascinated me and helped pass the time until the replacement bus arrived.

We were eventually reunited with our hotel and I managed to summon up just enough energy to collapse into bed.

Day 22 - Wednesday 17ᵀᴴ April - Back to School

I had one aim for the day; after a 12 years gap, I wanted to go back to school. I needed to find an establishment that matched my intellectual abilities (and even worse than that my typically English proficiency with languages). There are about 70 language schools in Antigua that teach Spanish, so the day promised to be crammed full with inspections. The first two schools I examined were quite impressive, if somewhat empty. By this time the novelty of looking at educational establishments had already subsided and I was ready to relax with a coffee. The third school was scruffy but owned by a real character in the guise of wheelchair-bound Marco and was packed with students including Einar and Finn. A price was set and I agreed to return in the afternoon for lesson one, followed by 8.00am to noon each weekday until a week on Friday.

It was one-on-one teaching, which meant no hiding place from my young tutor Jose. My non-English speaking tutor, Jose. This wasn't too bad for the first lesson because I already knew the basic verbs, but it didn't make life easy.

I completed my first day at school and was going to head home. Just by the stairs was a room where I could hear singing and my friends Einar and Finn with three pretty girls. I thought this deserved further investigation. Little did I know of the danger that lurked within.

They were about to start a salsa class. The teacher hadn't arrived yet so the girls were singing songs. Before I knew it I was dragged into a circle and holding hands with two hairy Norwegians whilst attempting some traditional Israeli dancing. The teacher arrived and said they needed another man, I offered to see if I could find one. Too late, the door was blocked, the windows barred; there was no escape however fast my two left feet could carry me. For the next hour, I salsa danced like I had never salsa'd before i.e. my hips were forced to move in strange directions and my feet in complicated patterns. Despite my advice to my partners (that they should be wearing steel capped boots to dance with me), all feet remained intact and I was released on good behaviour.

Day 23 - Thursday 18ᵀᴴ April - Cheque Mate

The body could not believe the mind had signed up for anything that involved eight starts of 8.00am in the space of 10 days. But despite its disbelief (and disgust), it made its way to school. The lack of English from my teacher became more of a problem as Jose continually reached out for my English/ Spanish dictionary to explain words to me. It was during one of these grab and search routines I looked up to see the beautiful oriental girl standing about five yards away. First at my hotel and then the language school. Who was this mysterious and exotic girl? And then - oh my god, there were two of the beautiful oriental girl standing together. How did she do that? Then she was gone and the other one of her was gone as well. This was a confusing distraction from my Spanish lesson.

What I wasn't distracted from was that today was also traveller's cheque day. I still had those two cheques, which I had signed and even dated one of them but the bank in Flores wouldn't accept. I changed the 13/04/02 on the traveller cheque I had dated five days ago to 18/04/02 and slipped it to the bottom of a pile of traveller's cheques. The signed but undated cheque was just on top of that, then three unsigned and undated £20 traveller's cheques on top of that. The bank confirmed they would accept pounds, so I signed and dated the top one and slipped it to the bottom, then the next one, then the next one and then just dated the next and pretended to sign and hey presto I must be at the first one again because the last one is already signed and dated. Very obligingly they provided me with the money.

After a fairly mind stretching morning of Spanish, mysterious girl and sneaky traveller's cheques it was nice to just have a relaxing chat in English with Einar, Finn, Christian, David, Dan and Richard. It was slightly odd to sit around with all these foreign speaking friends and listen to them all conversing in English. For once I didn't feel too embarrassed because at least I was making an effort to learn Spanish. Richard is interesting, just on the basis of his nationality. He is the first person I have ever met from Liechtenstein and seemingly everybody else's first traveller that they have met from Liechtenstein.

We drifted into what has become our routine of playing cards on the hotel roof, consuming a couple of beers and finishing the night by looking at the larva coming down Fuego. You know that you must be doing something special when an ordinary night is watching lava come down the side of a volcano.

Day 24 - Friday 19ᵗʰ April - No Way Jose

There was no Jose today and as much as I hated myself for doing it, I asked for him to be replaced with a teacher who could speak English. They made it clear that you may change teachers at any time, but I still felt bad. We went on a school trip to a coffee museum in the morning and I took my new teacher Julio. About 30 years of age, perfect English and taking the piss out of me straight away. The only problem is that he is fully booked up for next week so I'll be on to my third teacher by Monday. The mysterious and beautiful oriental girls also went on the museum tour. They turned out to be Karen and Chantel from Watford. Their mystique lay in tatters but they proved to be great company. The oriental looks come from their mum, who was born in Mauritius, and they share an English dad. If all my calculations are correct that makes them sisters.

On returning from the museum there was still enough time for a half-hour lesson from Julio. I also mentioned that all I really needed to learn was how to chat up Guatemalan girls and talk football with the boys. He told me I didn't stand a chance on the first one, but he may be able to help me on the second. Then proceeded to teach me *you have big breasts* and *'I feel horny'*. These are unlikely to help me with the girls and definitely will give me some strange looks on the football pitch. And although Julio can't teach me next week he offered me a lesson tomorrow morning. The Friday night I was looking forward to would suffer because of the early Saturday start but I decided to make the ultimate sacrifice.

I am also moving out of the hotel tomorrow and into a house with a Guatemalan family. I suppose there are three factors at work. First, it should be good for my Spanish. Second, it is cheaper than a hotel and finally, well, just the experience. Part of the reason for the second factor is that Christian is moving on to San Pedro tomorrow, so if I stayed in the hotel I would need to move into a single room and pay more money. This also meant I had to drink a couple of going away beers with Christian.

We headed down to Riki's along with Einar, Finn, David and Dan to toast his farewell. I also met up with Karen and Chantel who wasted no time in mocking the way I seemed to be following them about. First the hotel, so they moved out to live with a Guatemalan family, then the language school and now the bar. I had no defence outside of being innocent, so I chose to moan about having to study on a Saturday morning. This proved effective because they joined in on the whinge as they were also weekend scholars.

Day 25 - Saturday 20th April - The Eternal Circle of Jim

Saturday morning and school, I'm sure I have lost the travelling plot. But the first task of the day was to say goodbye to Christian. After sharing a room and a few beers with him, over the last nine days, I will miss him. But now it is time to move in with my family. I wearily turned up at school and poured a cup of caffeine down my throat. Karen's teacher didn't turn up so she joined me for a lesson with Julio. I couldn't help myself but point out 'hey who's following who now'. Anyway, the joint lesson caused much merriment as we tried to insult each other in Spanish. Julio's philosophy is that he could speak English to us when it is needed, but anything we say has to be in Spanish. Karen and I very quickly learnt the Spanish for 'can you say that again' and 'how do you say …….. in Spanish'. Halfway through the lesson, a woman approached us and Julio introduced her as my new landlady. Karen's gaping mouth pre-emptied a *'that's my house'*. *'First the hotel, then the school and now our house'*. 'Well, you can show me where it is then'. *'Julio, como puedo I need to report a stalker called Jeff?'* Then the three of us carried on giggling like schoolchildren.

The house consisted of a garage like door, then eight rooms which all opened on to a central courtyard. There was Chici the mother, her 16-year-old daughter Andrea, two 15-year-old Guatemalan students, Jana an American student, Karen and her sister Chantel. And last, but by no means least, Bruno the three-year-old son and resident livewire. I was sort of given my own room. Well, it was my own room but the dividing wall was paper-thin and included a six-inch gap at the top. This meant it was very handy for chatting with Jana whilst remaining in our respective rooms.

For the rest of the day, I joined Finn and Einar plus two El Salvadorian girls who had come up from San Salvador for the weekend. The way they talked of El Salvador it still sounds like a relatively dangerous country to visit. Ally mentioned that during the civil war there was fighting outside her house. For six days they were trapped inside as machine guns rattled away. Mind you, it turned out that it was her uncle who was the president. El Salvador has a history of trouble and I was intrigued by the 'football war' they had with Honduras. A disputed decision in a World Cup qualifying game in 1969 escalated into a 13-day war, which killed 2,000 people.

Jim joined us later on and seemed to have trapped himself in the vicious circle of Antigua. In the morning he'd have a lie-in, then he'd watch a film in one of the restaurants or bars in the afternoon, this would build up a thirst so he'd head off to Riki's and before he knew it he was dancing at the Casbah. All of which meant he'd need a lie in the next morning, followed gently by a film in the afternoon, which would build up a thirst ……. I confessed I could see no way out for him.

Day 26 - Sunday 21ˢᵗ April - Dunked

Sunday is the day of rest. In a god-fearing country such as Guatemala, I felt duty-bound to obey this rule. Besides, after playing basketball in the morning, I was knackered.

Day 27 - Monday 22ⁿᵈ April - Becoming a Dad

I woke up at 7.00am to the sound of Jana and Chici's voices. They were speaking in Spanish, but I could pick up that it was something about Jana's boyfriend coming to Antigua, probably. I spoke to Jana a little later and she asked whether I had anyone staying over last night. Apparently, Chici had seen a man leaving the house early this morning and wanted to know whose room he had slept in. I confirmed that it wasn't mine and that I could vouch for Jana because soundwise we are in the same room. Chantel and Karen share a room but had a weekend at the coast and just got home and crashed out, which leaves the young girls. Jana was worried that all hell would break loose if it was one of them and suggested that I could take the blame. I pointed out that if it was a girl leaving the house I didn't mind taking the blame, but as it was a bloke maybe we should wait to see how things pan out.

It was another school day today. I'm now on to my third teacher – but there are still about 20 left. I unwound from school in the usual way, with six of us playing cards on the roof of my old hotel. I'd only been there half an hour and Jess turned up. I explained the game to her and then we all proceeded to lose to Jess. This pattern was then repeated over and over during the next two hours. I told everyone that the only explanation was that I am a lousy player but a brilliant coach.

I'm also using my coaching skills on three-year-old Bruno, in an attempt to make him the first international Guatemalan football star. We have been working on his left foot as I think it is important he is two-footed. When he scored a goal he'd run at me to celebrate, as he hugged me I'd lift him up in mock celebration. I thought we were just playing footie, but Jana was choked and thought he was missing a father figure. Well, as long as it makes him a football star.

Whilst I am writing about domestic matters, it turned out that Chici didn't actually see the man leave the house. The outside door was strangely unlocked and then when she looked out the street someone was leaving our small dead end road so she tried to put two and two together. The lack of evidence and everybody's denial meant the prosecution would not be pressing forward with their enquiries.

DAY 28 - TUESDAY 23ᴿᴰ APRIL - SPRINGS SPRUNG

Chantel and Karen had left for Costa Rica yesterday, so it was just me and Jana who traipsed from the house to school. I was starting to get on really well with Jana and jokingly referred to her as 'sis' or if I was trying to find her at school it was 'anyone seen my sister'. She'd had a full-scale adventure reaching Antigua (incidentally I've now had two e-mails from friends thinking I am on the island of Antigua). Jana had been working as a nanny for an American family. Her last two weeks with them were spent on holiday in Costa Rica, from where she planned to journey northwards. However, she wasn't very well for the last few days so her packing was completed by the mother and then Jana headed up to Nicaragua forgetting what she had in her backpack. She reached the Nicaraguan border and the sniffer dogs started barking. It was then she realised her mistake, thought '*oh my god*', and swiftly found herself in prison for possession of the marijuana that she forgot was in her bag.

Jana shared her cell with three other women. One was a Colombian who hadn't realised she needed a visa to be in Costa Rica and there were two Nicaraguan women. The beds were somewhere between basic and non-existent, just a stone slab. Food was simply non-existent for most of the time but water was provided. After a couple of days, she was allowed to make a phone call. She contacted her Peruvian boyfriend who had a contact in Nicaragua. The contact sorted out a local lawyer and after two more days of prison, she was released and expelled from the country.

Jana has since learnt that most people spend somewhere between 10 days and three months in prison for possession. Anyway, that was last night's chat over the six-inch gap between our rooms; today's chatter was about her going to the hot springs.

She had waited at home for her friend Colin, but he never turned up so off she went. 15 minutes later Colin arrived. I passed on the information that he had just missed her but yes she was going to the hot springs, so off he dashed to try and catch up.

I saw Jana later, who reported that she made her way out the required 10 kilometres or so to the springs, only to find that there was no water in them (they were being cleaned out or something). She turned around and just managed to catch the last bus back to Antigua. In fact, she was amazed that the buses stopped running at such a ridiculously early time and confirmed that she should have checked the details in town before charging off to the springs. *'So it was lucky Colin hadn't turned up ....'* it was at this point I started to try and interrupt*'.......else I would have felt terrible'*. 'Um Jana', *'it would have wasted his whole afternoon and it was my idea, he wasn't keen on going anyway'*. 'Jana, Jana, he turned up. I told him you'd gone and he was going to follow you'. Jana's face dropped because this would mean that by the time he reached the closed springs he would have missed the last bus and would have had to walk the 10 kilometres back to town.

We bumped into Colin later and the wary Jana said *'hey, I didn't see you at the springs.'* Colin apologised for not getting there, but after missing Jana at the house he couldn't be bothered.

Jana also reported to us that she had learnt in class that it was prostitute day today. This meant it was legal to go and see a prostitute (and I assume actually have sex with her). What a strange concept, does it mean that they are taxed on that day's earnings? Is it a saint's day? Maybe Saint Roger? Is it an annual or weekly event? Or is just part of some sort of festival? Jana said she would ask more questions in class tomorrow.

In the meantime, we headed across to Riki's to check on whether Jim had broken out of his vicious circle. He hadn't, but he did plan to head off to San Pedro in the next couple of days. In the meantime he'd watch films, drink, go clubbing and lie in.

I'd also told two friends that if they wanted to meet up with me, then I should be in Riki's at 9.00pm. I say friends but basically I'd known them for two days, about three weeks ago. In San Cristobal I'd got drunk with Karen and we then came back to chat to her poorly friend, Kari, who had chatted away to me as if I wasn't the intoxicated, slurring drunk that I had been. There is something about travelling that actually meant I regarded them as good friends and trusted them implicitly. I'm not sure whether it is because most backpackers are of a like mind, you're thrust together in a strange country or quite what but you seem to get to know people a lot quicker than in normal circumstances. Either way, I was chuffed to see them again.

Day 29 - Wednesday 24th April - Break-in

At morning break, Colin and I questioned Jana. Did she have any more information? *'Yes, every Tuesday Guatemalan prostitutes are free'*. The three-person conversation suddenly gained an extra 30 ears. 'Free?' '*No, I mean legal*'. I'm sure, at that moment, I heard someone crossing out a note that they had only just written in for the 30th April.

So bizarrely Tuesday may be prostitute day in Guatemala but for us Wednesday was football day. It was Man Utd v Bayer Leverkusen in the European Cup semi-final, so a bar with a big screen was hijacked for the afternoon. I don't like Man Utd but I do feel obliged to support any English team in Europe, especially against the Germans. The bar was packed out. There was Einar, Finn, Dan, David, Klaus, Paul, Jess, Tim, Michael, Christoph etc. I could name about 20 people in the bar. Having said that Antigua, has reached the stage where I have more good friends here than in some cities that I have lived in.

The drinking tone for the day was set, despite my better judgement, especially as my last day at school starts at 8.00am tomorrow. After the football, we drifted on to Riki's before I started on my usual excuses about why I wouldn't be going to the Casbah nightclub. My arguments floundered and Casbah appeared around me. I'd never been to a Guatemalan nightclub before but it was certainly intriguing. In the space of three songs, the music switched from Salsa to All Saints to Techno. In that time the locals went from dancing geniuses to rhythm-less oafs, whilst the embarrassingly bad salsa dancers from Europe, North America and Oceania became at one with the music.

My dancing skills are not renowned but Kari and I managed to strut our stuff on the stage. This is a strange habit I've picked up ever since I danced on the stage in Peru. I'm either tucked in at the bar happily sipping a lager or dancing on the stage, with little in between.

By the time all was said and done, Dan, Kari and Karen were locked out of their hotel. The curfew was set at 1.00am which Dan had broken every night but it was the first time he had been locked out. There didn't seem to be any way in and all our door-knocking attempts were ignored. It only succeeded in attracting the attention of the people who owned the house next door and they let us into their courtyard so we could try and climb in. Dan managed to clamber up 10 feet on to a balcony. Then he realised it didn't lead to the hotel, but to a flight of stairs that went straight back down to the courtyard we were standing in. The neighbours pointed to a staff bedroom, which still had a television blaring away. We knocked on the window but our plight was ignored. It took another 20 minutes of examining gaps in the hotel security before we found a door to climb over and a gap to squeeze into. After Tim, a fellow student and I had helped to provide various leg ups, it left us five hours to get home, have some sleep and be ready for school.

Day 30 - Thursday 25ᵀᴴ April - The Cardigan Bandit

It was my final day at school and I had a test on the dreaded irregular verbs. I tried to learn them yesterday, without much success. So what hope did I have this particular morning? My brain limped into school and acknowledged Tim, who looked in a worse state than me. That made me feel better. God knows what happened but I was great at the irregular verbs and then started on my longest and most grammatically correct Spanish conversation yet.

I returned to the house very pleased with myself and planned to reward my hard work with lunch and a long sleep. First things first though, I had to meet our new lodger, Kristine from Switzerland. She'd spent four weeks in Antigua studying Spanish before taking a two-week break. Now Jana was good at Spanish but would normally speak English when her Spanish just brought a blank look on my face. Kristine would just keep speaking Spanish. My speaking is better than my listening, so I had no idea what the lunchtime conversations were about. I liked the good old days with Karen and Chantel, they were worse than me for speaking English all the time. So I bolted my food down and played football with Bruno.

After letting Bruno beat me 10-9, I successfully slept through most of the afternoon but surfaced in time for dinner. I was most impressed that on Kristine's first visit to Antigua she had climbed the Agua Volcano. Agua is only 10 kilometres from Antigua and cuts an imposing shadow over the town. People tend to prefer walking up Pacaya because it is still active but Agua is the big volcano you see every day and is a far more strenuous walk. The group she walked with stretched out during the hike. Part way up, a gun-toting bandit jumped out of a bush to rob her and her friend. It turned out that neither of them had any valuables so the bandit snatched her cardigan and fled. I'm still bewildered by this whole bandit concept.

Day 31 - Friday 26ᵀᴴ April - Face Off

School was out, lie-ins were back. The only problem on the horizon was that mum (aka Chici) wanted me to leave today. I thought I had a full week. She agreed. I pointed out that I arrived on a Saturday. She disagreed. I insisted it was Saturday. She insisted it was Friday. Mothers, who'd have them? She seemed to sort of believe me in the end, but wanted to check with the owner of the school.

I didn't think it was worth worrying about so continued to train Bruno up as the next Ronaldo. Chici cooked me lunch so I guessed I hadn't been thrown out. That was to be my last Chici cooked meal though because Jana had organised a teacher-pupil meal for the evening. This unsurprisingly meant another visit to Riki's and Casbah.

The frustrating thing about Guatemala is that all the bars and nightclubs close at 1.00am. So after Casbah everybody stands on the streets looking for somewhere else to go. Normally this is a futile effort but Jana had been talking to a local called Umberto who had decided to have a party. He drove five of us to his house on the outskirts of town and then left us there whilst he returned to pick up the second group. 10 of the group of 12 were from our language school, then there was an American/Guatemalan painter who actually knew Umberto and another American who used Umberto's internet cafe. Nice house though and it was good of him to invite a bunch of strangers back to his home.

The party rolled on for a couple of hours, which was divided up between listening to music and Umberto making speeches about how happy he was to have us as his guests. It all ended when Umberto looked to be about to make yet another speech about how great we were, but instead said 'you all have to go now'. He offered to give us a lift to the edge of the centre but no more. Umberto couldn't fit us all in his Land Rover so Jana volunteered herself and her brother to walk home. Which would have been fine but the outskirts of Antigua is not a place you want to be in the early hours. What made it worse was that Jana was part of my adopted family and as such, I was the brother in question. We started walking merrily along in the dark Antigua streets. Everything seemed to be going smoothly until we heard a distant voice and then footsteps behind us. My heart raced, my mouth went dry and my bowels fought to keep control – was this bandit time? Okay, what do we do? I was all for turning around. 'We have to face them sometime so let's just turn around and walk confidently at them'. '*Let's do it*'. We turned 180 degrees and started walking towards them. There was only one person visible, so we hoped they didn't have a weapon. 'Actually, the figure looks a bit like Colin'; '*it is Colin*', 'thank god for that'. He'd simply decided to join us for the walk and had been trying to catch up with us.

Day 32 – Saturday 27ᵀᴴ April – Home from Home

I packed my rucksack, said goodbye to my adopted family and headed out to the streets of Antigua. I felt really sad to leave, even though I just walked three minutes around the corner and checked back into my old hotel.

Einar, Finn, Dan, David and Richard had all moved on to San Pedro but I chose to stay on for an extra day. I spent most of the time with Kari and Karen who aren't due to leave Antigua until Monday. They even decided to cook me a meal. Well, they said cook, but I pointed out that boiling some water and giving me a pot noodle did not quite meet my definition of cooking. I left them with strict instructions to find me a good beach and then I'd join up with them. Maybe I should have thought of a better incentive for them.

Day 33 - Sunday 28ᵗʰ April - The Point of Jo Return

6.15am and I needed to get up, ready for the bus. I was still wondering how I managed to be dragged to the Casbah again last night. At least the hotel was still open when I returned at 1.15am. I did have one of my more thought-provoking conversations with a couple of Guatemalan lads in Riki's. They were telling me how corrupt their government has always been and they didn't understand how the UK Government could be stopped from being corrupt. It's something I'd not really thought of before; okay the occasional minister may make the odd indiscretion but nothing to compare with the Guatemalan version of corruption. My main thought was of the press. They won't allow anyone to get away with anything. A lot of the time the tabloids seem to be over the top and contravene peoples' rights to privacy. However, the flip side is that it allows your investigative journalists the freedom to find and report on any corruption. The bus journey passed as I tried to sleep through it, unsure whether it was hunger or queasiness that my stomach felt. But pass it did.

I arrived in the town of Panajachel and walked to the lakeside to negotiate a price for a motorboat ride to San Pedro. The journey was fairly smooth but the highlight was that before we even docked I recognised a friend in a shore-line cafe. I couldn't see her clearly but, from the way the jaw was in perpetual motion, I knew that it was Jo. I think it is the first time that I haven't even reached a town but already recognised somebody in it. Jo confirmed that it was the first time she had received verbal abuse from someone who hadn't even had the decency to reach the town she was in before shouting at her.

San Pedro La Laguna, to give its full title, is meant to be the travellers' hang-out of Guatemala. I wasn't quite sure what this actually meant but was interested to find out. It became apparent very quickly; it seems to be a massively laid back village crawling with travellers.

I took on the required attitude and couldn't be bothered to look around any of the hotels. Instead, I took the spare bed in Jo's room which, in this incestuous like world of backpacking, used to be Jess's bed.

It took another 10 minutes to find my Austrian, Norwegian and Litchenstinian friends after which I retired for an afternoon nap. I was resurrected for dinner by the lake, where it was Sophie, Keira, Georgie and Adrian's turn to arrive by boat and recognise a figure before they stepped on shore. This time it was my curly locks that betrayed my identity. The quartet had been fellow students in Antigua and guests at Umberto's impromptu party. What I found remarkable about them is that they are only 18-years-old. Their tender number of years belies a confidence and maturity that has seen them safely work and travel through Central America. When I was 18 there would have been no way I could have travelled around any third world country, sorting out travel arrangements, knowing who to trust, constantly having to make new friends and handling yourself when you are by yourself in a strange and potentially hazardous environment. I was still struggling to come to terms with the bright lights of Skegness when I was 18.

Their appearance meant that there were more people for Einar and Finn's leaving do. After spending two and a half weeks in and out of their pockets I'm going to really miss my Norwegian drinking buddies.

Day 34 - Monday 29ᵀᴴ April - Fire and Beers Day Off

Antigua had not been beneficial for my liver and San Pedro had begun with Einar and Finn's leaving party where among other things we were drinking fire on top of some spirit or other. I may be wrong but drinking something on fire can't be healthy. Therefore, I announced to Jo that I'd be teetotal for the day. Jo reached out for some water with a hand that vibrated uncontrollably. *'Oh god, I think I should have a day off as well'*.

A teetotal San Pedro is still a lovely little place. It's set at the foot of an extinct volcano looking out on Lake Atitlan, itself covering an area that was the vast crater of an ancient volcano. It also seems to be the centre of activity for amateur scientists judging by the variety of substances that are freely available. I think that comes with the resident hippies – I should have included them in my original definition of a traveller hangout.

The only substances that I was interested in this morning were those that make up a good breakfast. The relevant ingredients were located and I took one and a half hours to slowly eat my food whilst looking out on the lake and chatting to Jo. It is amazing to see Jo in yet another different place. I love seeing the same person in two different places but I have now met 18 people in three different towns on this trip (yes, I calculate such things on those long bus journeys, I have also picked the England world cup football squad about 79 times now), but only one person has been unlucky enough to bump into me in four different towns. That accolade goes to poor old Jo.

According to Jo the normal San Pedro day then took hold. It involved a bit of sunbathing and reading in the afternoon, followed by a meal and video at the local restaurant and then unusually rounded off by an early night. This was interspersed with the usual conversations with new people. Where are you from? Where are you travelling to? When? And then a discussion with Dan about what month we were in. We managed to narrow it down to April or May.

Day 35 - Tuesday 30ᵗʰ April - Woodstock

There was a good reason for yesterday's early night, it was volcano day today. It meant an early start for what we estimated to be a two-hour hike. In our group were Jo, Richard and David and our machete-wielding guide. Dan, the other half of the Austrian party boys, had the good sense to call in sick. The climb was steep but this must have seemed like good exercise to the five dogs that joined our group. I was a little apprehensive about this because I have met four people who have been bitten by dogs in San Pedro. The dogs are so vicious that it is standard practice to carry stones to throw near the ones that start snarling at you. I love dogs but I won't think twice about throwing a stone at the feet of these mongrels. It is not as if it is just the odd one, at night they run round in big packs. Having said that, the five dogs that joined us were friendly and they chased away the mad and bad dogs.

For two hours we slogged our guts out, through coffee plantations, up the base of the volcano and then up the steep path until Jo and I convinced ourselves that we could see the summit about 10 minutes' walk away. Despite being shattered, we could eek out another 10 minutes of effort, after all, that's only 600 seconds worth of sweat. A fellow hiker passed us on the way down and we asked the usual question, 'How much further?' *'One and a half-hours'*. Jo turned to me, *'she was joking wasn't she?'* 'Yeah of course she was'.

She wasn't.

Jo and I regarded ourselves as relatively fit and fairly sporty but we were finding the hike difficult. The path was remorselessly steep. Our legs became heavier and heavier, our protective dogs disappeared and we realised that our legs would be oh-so-stiff tomorrow.

The slope hit a 45-degree angle and our legs changed from flesh to lead as we crawled up to the top of the 3,700 metre summit. The cloud had risen a little so the views were limited but we felt a sense of exhausted achievement. All we needed to do was run down and try to watch Man Utd v. Bayer Leverkusen in the European Cup semi-final second leg. We had one hour until kick off so needed to run as fast as our leads could carry us (as in legs made of lead – oh, you did get it – sorry for ever doubting you).

We made a couple of stops on the way down, which were both too long for my liking. I tried to show enthusiasm during the second stop by standing up and edging down the path. This was the sign for the guide to start charging down the path with us all in hot pursuit, going as fast as our battered legs could carry us. We reached a road, with San Pedro still some distance below us. The guide said *okay, this is the deal; this truck needs to be filled with wood. If we help, everyone can jump in the back and we will get a lift to San Pedro'*. There were three large stacks of wood and it took nine of us a good 15 minutes to bundle them into the truck. When the last log was placed in the truck, we clambered up on to the wood. I tried to find a comfortable position but it's not easy on top of a five-foot deep pile of logs. Especially when each log was laden with splinters and sharp edges. The bumpy road added to our woe but it was still better than walking.

We reached Dino's restaurant in time for the end of the first half, at which point Jo crashed out headfirst on to a settee. It must have been about 20 minutes later when Adrian arrived and asked *'How difficult is the volcano walk?'* I simply pointed at the still collapsed body of Jo and he reached the decision that volcano climbing wasn't for him. We spent the rest of the day recuperating.

I did feel better in the evening, but this was mainly to do with Colin and Miguel (another fellow language student) arriving from Antigua and announcing that they would climb the volcano tomorrow.

Day 36 - Wednesday 1ˢᵀ May - Shake a Leg

Two days ago Jo's hands had the shakes; today she was barely capable of shaking her legs. I'd like to claim that my superior level of fitness meant I bounded out of bed but it seemed as though someone had put an invisible cast on my lower limbs. This hindered my original plan of leaving San Pedro today.

A further nail was hammered into the proverbial coffin when Dan pointed out that I'd been travelling with him and David for three weeks so I couldn't go without a leaving do. I lowered the coffin into the ground and announced 'okay, one more night'. I thought I'd still have time to track down Kari and Karen on whatever beach they were on (although I still haven't heard from them).

All in all, it was an exceptionally lazy day as me and Jo wobbled around on our unbending legs, just having enough energy to whinge to anyone who would listen (and some who wouldn't) about how stiff our legs were. Oooo they are stiff.

Day 37 - Thursday 2nd May - Raul Deal

I slept through my proposed early morning start, but after enjoying my usual one-hour breakfast (it's going to be tough switching back to a grabbed 15 minutes before work) I said adios to Jo. I've decided that the best bits about travelling are seeing incredible places and meeting great people. I think the worst bit is saying goodbye, farewell, and adieu, to your new found friends. Jo headed off to help on a local environmental project and I jumped into a motorboat between two Americans, Tom and Cedar. Tom was not your typical American, he was quiet. Cedar's parents were backpackers many moons ago and actually met in San Pedro, his mum is Peruvian and his dad American. Strangely he is fairly quiet as well.

After a boat to Panachel and two chicken buses, we arrived back in Antigua and selected a hostel near the bus station. It was in a bad area but it was a lovely hostel, run by a Guatemalan named Raul. He'd been ostracised by all his family, bar one sister, just because he wanted to stop working on the family farm. He'd studied as his father wished, fought in the civil war as his father wished (and received a hole where his left knee cap should be) and worked eight years on the farm, until he could stand it no longer. He only opened the hostel in November but it was packed out in what is the low season. The hostel does have a strange name though: 'A Place To Stay'. I didn't know how long I needed 'A Place To Stay', because I still hadn't received any beach surveys from Kari. Therefore, I thought I might travel to Honduras. It was a bit out of the way for getting back to Mexico but it's meant to be nice. However, it would mean a 4.00am bus trip. I checked the e-mail one final time before buying my ticket. There was a message in my mailbox entitled 'beach survey'. *'Jeff, we're still in Antigua and will be for a few more days'.*

I met up with Karen and Kari later when they admitted that they weren't yet on a beach, but they did have a plan and they'd reveal all to me over a drink. That idea seemed to appeal. They explained that they'd only started on their malaria tablets last Monday and didn't want to leave Antigua until the coming Monday, by which time the tablets would have taken effect. However, they'd completed their beach research via the guidebooks and suggested Denny's beach on Lake Izabel.

Day 38 – Friday 3ʳᵈ May – Back Home

Just another day back home in Antigua.

Day 39 – Saturday 4ᵀᴴ May – Sweet FA

I'd never missed an FA Cup Final since I was five years old. Today was FA Cup Final day and I had no idea whether I would get to see it or not. I wished I was back home, just for the afternoon. I could lie down on the settee and watch BBC1. But I knew that wasn't to be.

I had given myself every chance of seeing the match by staying in Antigua rather than moving on to a beach resort. Having said that, I hadn't noticed anywhere advertising the game. The UK is seven hours ahead of Guatemala, which meant that kick off was 8.00am. The hostel had cable television so Plan A was very simple. I'd get up at 8.00am and flick through the channels. I found two football matches. One seemed to be an Argentinean League game and the other was a Manchester United match. It is not often that I think like this, but unfortunately United weren't in the Cup Final. It was just highlights of the European Cup semi-final. I moved on to Plan B, Café 2000, the main sports bar, but they had the same cable channels. Plan C – the world service commentary. I stood on the roof of Kari and Karen's hotel roof desperately trying to establish some sort of radio reception, but to no avail. Suddenly the beautiful valley where Antigua is built didn't seem so pleasant. The whistle sounding the end of the first half had already been blown. At this stage, I'd already missed the first half. So I moved to plan D, the last option. I ended up looking at the text commentary on the internet. No pictures, simply a written update every three minutes. Far from ideal, but I was there in spirit.

The Cup Final quest served to increase my sense of frustration that I hadn't really done anything since Tuesday. I couldn't even let out my frustration with a couple of drinks at Riki's. It was shut for two weeks. The limp reason was that the owners are on holiday. Mad. No FA Cup Final, no Riki's Bar, so many of my friends had moved on. Antigua didn't feel the same any more. I knew I should move on again. I've decided to leave tomorrow for Denny's beach and then hopefully Kari and Karen can catch me up in a couple of days.

I sorted out a bus ticket, which was fairly complicated. The bus would pick me up from my hostel, so the travel agent asked '*Where are you staying?*' 'A Place To Stay' '*Yes, which hotel?*' 'No, it is called A Place To Stay'. '*But what is the name of your hotel?*' The name is 'A Place To Stay'. '*Do you live with a family?*' 'No, I am staying at a hostel and I know it is a strange name, but it is called A Place To Stay'. We got there in the end.

Day 40 - Sunday 5th May - Sliding Windows

I got up early in readiness for my bus. Tom and Cedar were still asleep. Cedar was flying home today after travelling for five months, which has to be a shock to the system. Tom was toying with the Denny's Beach idea so I thought I might see him again. I crept out of the dormitory at 6.30am and left them dreaming.

The bus dropped me off in Guatemala City and then I caught another one to Rio Dulce. Denny's beach is a secluded spot, near the little town of Mariscos. Even if you reach Mariscos it is a boat trip away or a longer boat ride from the larger town of Rio Dulce. I knew that I could get a motorboat from Rio Dulce to Denny's Beach, a secluded little spot by all accounts. However, the bus route went unexpectedly and temporarily south, rather than north around Lake Izabel, and suddenly Mariscos was only 20 kilometres away. If I stayed on the bus for another one and a half hours I'd definitely arrive in Rio Dulce, but I would still need a three-quarters of an hour boat ride to reach Denny's Beach. I figured that I should be able to get to Mariscos if the bus stopped soon and then it would be easier and quicker to get to Denny's Beach. The safe option was to hang on for Rio Dulce but how difficult could it be?

10 kilometres down the road we arrived in a town with a busy, but scruffy, bus station and I got out. I'd decided that there must be a quick way to travel from this town to Mariscos. My attempts to locate the 'must be' led me to confusion rather than Mariscos. The official-looking people kept pointing at the ground. I knew this wasn't Mariscos so surmised that it meant I should sit down. So I sat down for 10 minutes taking in the scene. There must have been 20 rickety buses in a ridiculously small area of dirt. Fumes drifted through the air and bodies scrambled on and off buses. More buses arrived

and I asked the 'Mariscos how?' question again, this time I was pointed towards a bus.

The bus was packed out but I made a point of telling the driver, in my best Spanish, 'I need Mariscos, you say when Mariscos here'. By the time I boarded the bus, it was standing room only and more people kept coming on board. The normal idea is for everyone to keep shuffling further back to make room, but I desperately tried to keep near the front of the bus and in the driver's thoughts. 15 minutes passed and the driver's assistant shouted something at me. I clambered by a few people, trying not to hit them too hard with my rucksack and was let out at a junction in the middle of nowhere. Luckily a few local people were standing around, so when I inquired 'Mariscos?' they pointed at a white mini-bus. I jumped aboard and enjoyed a smug smile.

I sat happily on the back seat with the window open and the air rushing through my hair. The ticket man then gestured for me to shut the window. What? He indicated more urgently for me to shut the window. I thought to myself what a nasty little prick he was being and reluctantly shut the window. A second later some vomit hit the window. A little girl was throwing up out the front of the mini-bus. The person in front of me hadn't shut his window in time and had a splattering of puke on his shirt. I cast a 'mucho gracias' in the ticket collector's direction (what a great bloke for getting me to quickly shut my window).

I reached the tiny coastal town and phoned Denny to pick me up in his motor launch. However, the water was too rough so I was advised to spend the night in one of the two hotels in town. Both were empty but I chose Mirinda hotel/restaurant. I was greeted by a friendly local, at the reception, who asked me my name. 'I'm Jeff'. After a moment of considering how to pronounce Jeff, he replied thoughtfully *'Okay, I shall call you gringo.'* 'Um, okay'.

It soon became apparent that I was the only guest in the hotel. And when I say hotel, well it reminded me of the Skegness beach huts of my youth. The rooms were actually miserable looking wooden huts set around a little courtyard. My hut had enough room for a single camp bed and little else, not even a window. I looked out from the courtyard and over the little wall that separated me from an angry lake. The sky was full of dark clouds and the howling wind did nothing to allay my fears that I'd seen this whole scenario at the start of some horror film.

I figured out that I could either wait in my hut for whatever creature of the deep/psycho/demon/vampire was going to get me or I could try and find some food. Frankly, the food sounded more tempting, so I took a stroll to see what nightlife little Mariscos offered to a paranoid lone traveller. Church singing was about all I could find, plus a little cafe that provided me with a generous helping of greasy chicken with stodgy rice, washed down with a cup of coffee. What seemed obvious was that I was the only outsider in town.

I returned to the solitude of the hotel courtyard and decided to read my book to the backdrop of my horror film conditions. It is a remarkable book in a couple of ways. When I was last in India I read Midnight Children by Salman Rushdie and it seemed to have an uncanny knack of being set in cities where I had just visited. Well, I was so impressed with Mr Rushdie's storytelling abilities that I bought another of his books, off a pavement seller, in India three months ago. I didn't open it up until I reached Mexico and blow me if it didn't begin in Mexico. And the other remarkable feature? Well as you read a page it falls out of the book, which depending on your viewpoint is really frustrating or an ideal lightweight travelling companion of a book.

The howling wind wore me down and I retired to my hut. I proceeded to place a table behind the door and then my bed, just to make it more difficult for the creatures of the deep/psycho/demon/vampire to get me (and the wind to blow the rattling door open).

Day 41 - Monday 6th May - Tranquility

I woke up to the sound of the lake gently lapping against the shore. The wind had died down, a new sunny day had dawned and I was still very much one of the living. The only dark cloud around is that it's my brother's birthday today and I have found myself in the middle of nowhere and unable to speak to him. Although with the wonder of the internet I had managed to send him a present and an electronic e-mail birthday card. Bloody great this internet thing.

Although I couldn't make an international call I managed to phone up Denny who said his motorboat would come to town, in half an hour, to pick me up. After a short boat trip, I could confirm that Denny's beach matched its secluded reputation. Other than the barmaid/cook I was the only one around. Pablo the Argentinean receptionist/barman/traveller had gone to Rio Dulce in search of more guests and Denny was lying down in his house because, in his words, '*I have a painful rash on my balls*'. Therefore, I had little option other than to lie in the hammock and read. I barely saw another human over the next six hours, but managed to fall asleep in my shaded hammock and wake up in what had become a partially shaded hammock. That meant I became the owner of a fetching sun-reddened patch across my stomach.

Denny's Beach consists of a little bit of sand with a wooden pier for jumping in and out of the boat. There are four main wooden buildings, which are two accommodation houses, the restaurant bar and Denny's house. There doesn't seem to be any access for any motor vehicles, but there is a track that is meant to lead to a village. Behind the beach is dense jungle. A lapping lake, sand, sunshine, jungle, a hammock and no one else around but a lady to serve me drinks. I had found tranquillity.

The late afternoon arrived with two boats. The first one brought back Pablo with an American couple and a Dutch girl. Then, in the increasingly choppy water, came a second boat with Karen, Kari, Tom and Sven all clad in life jackets. Everyone settled into my restaurant to watch my sunset before enjoying dinner, cards and a couple of beers.

Day 42 - Tuesday 7ᵗʰ May - Swingers

I thought it would be great to have some company because they could take it in turns to gently swing me as I laid in my hammock. I informed Kari and Karen that they were my first nominated swingers and they seemed strangely enthusiastic. However, they pushed me in a harsh Viking way that left me clinging to a hammock that threatened to do a loop-the-loop. As I pleaded for mercy they chuckled away with a *'but Jeff, we were looking forward to pushing you all day'*.

I kindly gave up the hammock to Karen and staggered off to sit next to Sven. I know most people think of Sweden when they hear the name Sven but he is German. Although my mind works a bit differently because when I lived in Sheffield, Sven's was the name of an infamous sex shop in the centre of Sheffield. After I'd established he wasn't a Sheffield entrepreneur, Sven revealed that he'd been studying Spanish in Antigua for the last few months and was winding his way to San Cristobal for drum lessons.

Sitting the other side of Sven was an American couple who seemed very loud, but nice. The male of the pair was named Dan and had a solid 20 stone frame. We found a football in the afternoon and I started to do keepie-uppies, he came across and I thought he might embarrass himself. He smoothly flipped the ball up, volleyed it a few times and caught it on the back of his neck. He's American and 20 stone; how? What? Where? – I was hugely impressed.

The only other activity I managed in the afternoon was playing in the canoe with the Dutch girl, Nushka. It sounds more exciting than it was.

There was an old canoe on the beach. It wasn't even seaworthy for one person but Nushka and I decided that we'd both get in it and take on the lake. We'd paddle about 20 feet out before the waves would sweep over the canoe and sink us. Then we'd try again and again and again. The two oldest travellers on the beach were also the two biggest kids on the beach. We shouted out our live sinking commentary 'and they went on bravely against the elements, wave after wave' then both fall into three feet of water and be in hysterics again. I think you had to be there.

The only other item of significance was the tarantula in our cabin.

Day 43 - Wednesday 8th May - Willy Won't He

The cabin is an impressive two storey wooden construction with a high thatched roof, which has thick cobwebs along it and at least one tarantula. When I lay on my bed, looking up through the mosquito net, I could sometimes spot its menacing presence on the roof beams. But as long as he stayed up there and I remained down on the bed, I think we were both happy. I'm fine with spiders, it is snakes that worry me. Unfortunately, Denny had mentioned that a python used to live in the roof of the restaurant, so I decided that a tarantula was just fine by me. That morning I took a boat to Rio Dulce and left Kari and Karen for the fourth and possibly last time. I had to start making my way north in a San Cristobal direction because I am finally going to be working on an organic farm. Whilst Kari and Karen have another week planned in Guatemala, who knows if and when we will meet again. I waved goodbye and headed to the bus station.

As the evening drew in, my bus arrived in Flores. The only other backpacker on the bus was Willy so I teamed up with him for the normal hunt for accommodation. He complained that he had not got any sleep last night and wanted to find a single room, rather than share with me. This seemed a real pain because it sent the price rocketing up for each hotel we visited. In the end, I had enough and checked into a double room in my old hotel and told the receptionist that if any other traveller wanted a room they could share with me. About half an hour later, Willy turned up on my doorstep, asking whether he could share the room. I was happy to have the company.

Flores is a place where just three weeks ago I seemed to know so many people but now everyone I knew in Guatemala seems to have headed south. So it was a bit of a shock, half an hour later, to bump into the equally astonished Kira and Georgie. And then Adrian, Sophie and Miguel. After dinner,

I said goodbye to the young English quartet and pointed out to Miguel the bar to stay out of, if you want to keep all your shirt buttons.

DAY 44 – THURSDAY 9TH MAY – SIZZLING DANISH BEER CAN RECORD

I always knew that today was going to be long and drawn out. Basically, I wanted to reach San Cristobal and the only way I could achieve that would be via three buses, a canoe and a whole day.

It started with a 5.00am bus towards the Mexican border. Shortly before the 'canoe village', we reached my image of a border town. It was decidedly scraggy, had a crossroads in the middle with dirt roads unenticingly leading off to back streets. The bus drew up near the crossroads and we were invited out to buy some food from the less than hygienic stands. On the sight of foreign travellers buying food, the inhabitants scrambled across in our direction. I'm sure they would have run, but a few of them were missing legs, others had growths on their heads and they all looked a bit odd. Luckily they were just the canine inhabitants, although the people didn't seem to be that much better off. I'm sure it is someone's treasured hometown and that it has hidden charms but it made me very privileged to come from Melton Mowbray. I selected some fruit that I could peel and some nuts I could crack open, before re-taking my position on the bus.

I'd lost track of time over the last few weeks, but we found out that there is a one-hour time difference between Guatemala and Mexico. Which is fine, I mean most of Guatemala is east of Mexico. But why is it that Guatemala is seven hours behind Britain but Mexico is only six. It's back to front I tell you.

After a tiring journey I arrived in Palenque at 2.30pm, immediately bought another bus ticket and started on a five-hour bus journey at 3.30pm. I picked the England world cup squad again, tried to work out the best way to get a job when I return home, wondered what the farm would be like, dreamed of drinking posh at the Magic Hostel and slept. Finally at 8.35pm, after 10½ hours of travelling, I reached San Cristobal. I thought my legs needed a stretch, so took a brisk 25 minute walk to the bat cave and within one press of the magic doorbell, I was back in the Magic Hostel.

The Mexican receptionist welcomed me back and shouted across to Gabriel that I had returned. '*Hey Jeff, good to see you, it's happy hour on the Posh.*' How could I refuse such hospitality? I'd never quite worked out when the happy hour started or stopped but realised that it seemed to last for three hours. I felt like I had returned home. A group of Danes were particularly chatty. It may have been something to do with a couple of them being on the verge of the hostel drinking record of 22 beers for a single person. There were a couple of reasons why I was so impressed. Firstly, my gassy lager limit is three bottles, after which I become a serial burper, and secondly, they were girls. After a couple more Poshes I wished the Danes good luck and sloped off to bed.

Day 45 - Friday 10ᵗʰ May - Lazy Daze

A lazy time was the order of the day and as that is something I have mastered over the last few weeks, I didn't experience too many problems. Time passed between internet, hostel courtyard and cafes until it was happy hour again. A few of us enjoyed some beers before drifting on to a club. As with most clubs in San Cristobal, there was a live band. I wasn't keen to dance so finished up playing pool against Angus, a bin man from Portsmouth.

Day 46 - Saturday 11ᵗʰ May - Midday Cowboy

My four-week-old farm instructions told me to wait outside the language school and a middle-aged, white-bearded gringo, in a cowboy hat, would meet me at midday. The organic farm, I was meant to work on, was a ranch near a little Mayan village but basically in the back and beyond. I think my job is to shoot bandits and protect the local village from any para-military groups. I have watched all the Magnificent Seven films (and Blazing Saddles), so I thought I'd know far too many tricks for the baddies to handle. My time on the farm had seemed a long time coming and it continued in that vein as 12.30pm came and went. Luckily, they had also provided some instructions on how to make your own way to the farm. It involved a bus to within six miles of the ranch and then trying to hitch a lift. It didn't sound easy so I wandered into the language school. A woman there said she knew the man with the cowboy hat and he would be along shortly. That was good enough for me and I sat back down again.

Another 15 minutes passed by, but sure enough, a middle-aged gringo with a white beard and a cowboy hat appeared. He was called Miles, seemed a very jolly character and welcomed me aboard. Miles picked up a few things in town and then we headed to my new home of Rancho Chichuistan. Halfway there he pulled over in the middle of nowhere and said *'now I have a treat for you'*. The mind raced, I think I'd seen something like this in the twilight zone or is this where he offers to show me his puppies. Instead, he pulled out a bottle of the local rum and poured some in a couple of water bottles, then started driving again as we drank the rum. I got the feeling I'd picked the right farm.

Miles used to be a stressed-out lawyer in America, but a heart attack made him realise that he needed a change of lifestyle. He travelled around Mexico in a campervan for a year before deciding that he should settle down and become an organic farmer. His partner in the venture is fellow American, Sean, who is a former architect. Sean has now spent about 20 years in Mexico, has a Mexican daughter and a Mexican ex-wife.

I also had two fellow workers in the shape of Sarah and Greta. Sarah had meant to stay for a couple of weeks but that was on the 29th March and Greta was also thinking about extending her stay. They work about six hours a day for six days a week, all on a voluntary basis. The ranch house consists of a large lounge with a television, a kitchen full of food plus a few bedrooms. A television and a fridge full of food weren't the only reasons why I was working on an organic farm, but it was a good start.

Day 47 - Sunday 12th May - A Hard Day's Work and a Slobbering From a Dog

The farm is 8,000 feet above sea level and in the middle of rolling tree filled mountains. Every which way you look there are trees and set between some of those trees is a Campervan. This is the home of Bill and Sheila. They are friends of Miles who came to visit and decided to stay.

If you walk past enough trees you will find a little clearing. In the clearing is a garden the size of a football pitch with all manner of vegetables and herbs shooting upwards and outwards. One third is covered with cabbages, beets, rhubarb, carrots and potatoes. Basically, you name it, it seemed to be there. The other two-thirds was a weed-covered mess.

I started work by weeding an unused garden bed, throwing out the solid blocks of clay and breaking up chunks of old dry horse dung into the soil. By the end of the day, Greta and I had regenerated an old garden bed to the extent that it was all but sitting up and begging for seeds. I retired back to the lodge after dispensing a day's worth of weeds to the grateful pigs.

After my first day of work, I returned to the ranch hot, sweaty and clad in mud. It didn't stop two fierce-looking alsatians running towards me and giving me a good slobbering. They guard the farm but seem to know which people to bark at and which ones to slobber over.

Day 48 - Monday 13th May - Dung Another Day

More horse dung spreading, garden weeding, fridge raiding, TV watching and dog slobbering.

Day 49 - Tuesday 14th May - Spit or Swallow

The farm is situated in an area that has a 99% indigenous population. This is the heartland of the Zapatista, as evidenced by the modern army base just half an hour's drive away. The village operates at a subsistence level and homes seem to comprise of wooden huts. It is a world away from Mexico City and even outside the usual laws of Mexico. If there are any problems then the local village elders invite the accused to a meeting. They then decide on guilt or innocence and the necessary punishment. It has taken Sean and Miles a long time to be accepted into the local community. However, now they have been told that if any outsiders threaten the farm then there will be a 100 local people with guns rushing to defend them. So you could say that the local neighbourhood watch scheme is fairly comprehensive.

Sean has even been adopted in an advisory role, for the community, in helping to deal with the outside world. One of their current concerns is to keep a roof above their heads and food on the table. If the harvests aren't good then they really struggle and the only other industry that springs to mind in a forest is logging. This has already been done to some extent, but they know it is unfeasible in the longer term because, as other villages have found to their peril, the trees are a vital cog in the local eco-system. The next area they are looking at is tourism and the first step is to invite outsiders to their annual fiesta. An outsider to them means not only paying tourists but also selected guests from surrounding villages. The tourists will be brought in by Miles and Sean, eight in all, which would be a gentle taster for the villagers. The whole thing brought to mind the strange paradox of travel. I travel to see amazing sites and experience different cultures, but by walking around the sites I erode them and by meeting the people I dilute their culture. On the other hand, I'm sometimes bringing in some much-needed money to help people survive and sites to be restored. So am I destroyer or life giver? Probably a bit of both.

I worked all morning preparing the farm for the tourists and the afternoon heating up the Jacuzzi. Yeah, for some reason Sean and Miles had built a Jacuzzi. The Jacuzzi heating sounded like fun, just start a fire under the metal barrel and keep it going. The first hour was fun (but the water was very cold), the second hour was okay (but the water was still very cold) and the third hour felt like work. By this stage, the water still remained cold and it had started to drizzle. Sean had been busy telling me that the rainy season starts tomorrow. He said he knew this because the local people told him it starts on the 15th May each year. Well, this year it seemed to have started a day early. In the fourth hour, the drizzle stopped and I was hacked off with it all. In the fifth hour, people arrived and were having beers but the water was eventually getting warm. Finally, in the sixth hour, the water was genuinely hot and I answered questions from the tourists about the art of manually heating up a Jacuzzi. A couple of them stripped off and jumped in, but it wasn't for me. After six hours of heating water, all I wanted to do was to scrub myself down in a nice warm shower. A Jeff with a distinctly smoky aroma went under the shower and found cold water. Six hours of heating water and then a cold shower. Sometimes life just isn't fair.

The fiesta was at the main ranch in the village. Three areas dominated proceedings; there was a barn with live music where all the men and children stood. Another corner had all the food, women and babies. Then every so often the bells rang and everybody would go to the church. As parties go it was fairly tame. I think the highlight was listening to music in the church.

I pride myself on the fact that nobody can put me off my food and drink, but my shield of invincibility came clattering to the ground. I took a little sip of a local drink. It had a thick texture but I couldn't really taste it, so I took a large swig. It was at this point that Sarah let out a *'tastes like sperm doesn't it?'* The bowl dropped from my mouth, I closed my lips and was left with a mouth full of the stuff. The mouth had an incredible urge to spit the substance out, but I'm sure that would be a terrible insult to my hosts. As Sarah laughed, I and my puffed out cheeks looked around trying to decide what to do with my mouthful. Slowly and begrudgingly I swallowed, and then passed the bowl on to the next person.

DAY 50 - WEDNESDAY 15TH MAY - RAINSPOTTING

In the morning we walked down to see how the fiesta was progressing. Tame it may be, but I'm not lacking in respect for them because it goes on through the night and lasts a full 24 hours. Sarah was busy organising games for the village children. It seems that in the previous years of the fiesta (anytime between 50 and 500 years) there had never been anything specifically for the children. I can safely guess that it was the first time that this village had seen the sack race and the egg & spoon race. I'm not sure what the villagers made of it, but judging from the children's smiling faces, I guessed they loved it. One of the tourists, who was staying with us, took a couple of photographs to capture the historic moment on film. The next thing you know, a drunken villager came charging over to shout abuse and give the participating children a real dressing down. It seemed he was upset about the pictures being taken. His slurred lecture was particularly directed at one little lad (amid a three-legged race) whose face dropped. He untied the third leg and moved meekly away. I think it must have been his dad having the drunken tirade. A couple of village elders stepped in to try and calm the man down, eventually leading him away. You do have to be careful when you're taking photographs. Some native Mexican Indians believe that the camera steals your soul. There are stories of travellers being beaten up for taking pictures of churches and 'trying to steal god's soul'. In other situations, and today's one, it was a case of thinking that we will sell the pictures for money in Europe. Apparently permission had been given for some pictures, but obviously not by everybody in the village. Soon after that (and nursing two grazed knees from a three-legged demonstration) I made my excuses and slipped off to the ranch for an essential part of my culture. Due to the wonders of modern technology, the European Cup final was live on television.

Before the game had finished, everyone had returned to the house and I was busy explaining why a football team would pay £47 million for one player. The game came and went, as did our visitors, leaving just our strange little family remaining. As I mentioned before, against local predictions the rain began yesterday afternoon. Well, it was what I'd call rain, grey skies and drizzly (I'd also call it British weather), but I have to confess that wasn't rain in the local sense of the word. After the game, after the visitors left, after we sat out on the porch, the sky went dark grey and the heavens opened. It hammered down with rain for about three hours. And not English hammered; treble that and you have Mexican hammered. I stood corrected, as per local predictions, the rains started today.

Day 51 - Thursday 16th May - The Bunny Girl of Chichuistan

I was back among the horse dung and weeds, but there was a difference to normal, for today I was planting. Greta and I had made another enticing garden bed and I had been nominated to place the cabbage seeds in the soil. It may not sound much but I was excited. The open air, hands in the soil and making things grow, it was strangely enjoyable. On the other hand, laying around on a beach in glorious sunshine also appealed. The sloth in me wanted to leave on Saturday so I could enjoy some quality beach time before I returned to England.

Sean and Miles were also on their way. They were driving up to America for a couple of weeks and leaving Sarah in charge. Replacement bodies arrived at the farm in time for dinner, in the form of two Dutch girls who'd stayed at our house for the party, then decided it would be a good idea to come and work on the farm. I didn't quite catch their names originally, then heard their names again but they just seemed a scrambled mess of vowels and consonants. I'm used to this problem when I'm travelling and it becomes surprisingly easy to talk and, in this case, live with a person without recalling their name.

Anyway, Thursday night and as a special welcome, we allowed the Dutch girls to cook. I was sitting comfortably at 8.30pm, the evening's meal digesting peacefully. I still can't quite get my head around what happened next but know that half an hour later I was walking around in a playboy bunny outfit.

For some reason between 8.30pm and 9.00pm, it had been decided we were having a fancy dress party. Miles had a wardrobe full of outfits and I made the mistake of telling Sarah to 'just choose any outfit for me'. On seeing the selection I realised my bravery had wavered and I put a cooking apron on over my skimpy outfit. I looked fairly respectable from the front, but am offering good money for the destruction of any rear pictures.

DAY 52 - FRIDAY 17ᵀᴴ MAY - DAM WATER PROBLEMS

In the morning, Sean and Miles drove off in the Campervan and Land Rover. They'd taken two vehicles because of the steep mountain roads. The idea was that if the Campervan was struggling to get up the mountain, then they could attach the Land Rover to give it a helping tow. It took them half an hour to return to the farm and announce that they needed more help. The road or, more appropriately, a five-mile track that leads to the main road, starts with a steep one and a half mile climb. Even with the Land Rover towing and the Campervan at full throttle they had ground to a halt half a kilometre short of the summit. We headed out to the stationary Campervan in a barely roadworthy jeep. Sarah then tried to drive the jeep, which was towing the Land Rover, which was towing the Campervan. Another 10 minutes of slow but steady progress ended with the Campervan triumphantly perched at the top of the road. We bid farewell to Sean and Miles, then returned to try and run their farm.

Within minutes there was a water problem. A stream runs down the middle of the farm from which a pipe syphons off water for the garden sprinklers. The stream carries on to where local women do their washing and then on to the village. The problem was that the water pressure was not high enough to work the pump that sprinkles the garden. So it came down to me and Sarah's damming abilities. Equipped with a pair of wellies and some muddy hands we dug up a pipe, re-aligned it, and increased the size of the mud dam. And all in all, it increased the water pressure running down the pipe. It took about three minutes for the washerwomen to point out that now only a dribble of water was reaching them. The water was building up again to get over the new dam but hadn't reached them yet. The newly self-qualified engineers made a slight damn reduction adjustment and hey presto, water pressure and water for the villagers.

Later on, I headed across the land to try and create some more fertile soil. The two alsatians bounded along after me. I was working on land that was close to the border of the next ranch. Miles had said that it was owned by an unfriendly German couple who had six nasty dogs. As I started to work away I heard some running from a next ranch direction and then some vicious barking. I could make out about four dogs in the distance speeding towards me. This didn't seem a good situation as there was no one else around. I needn't have worried though as my two dogs raced to head the other dogs off. The other dogs slowed down to a stop and then just barked from a distance. I felt well protected and quickly next door's dogs moved away. That was enough excitement for one day. If next door's dogs had come much closer I may have started producing my own fertiliser for the ranch.

Day 53 - Saturday 18ᵗʰ May - Posh and Backs

I got up at 8.30am, or was that 7.30am. It had all become a bit confusing. The clocks in Mexico had moved forward an hour but here in the local villages, they don't bother with such things. As Sean and Miles worked on local time, they had been pleased to notice I was getting up at 7.30am each morning. Meanwhile big city Jeff was happy not to have to get up until 8.30am each morning.

They had left instructions on the best way to get back to San Cristobal. Just walk down the drive and turn left, then it is another six miles to the bus stop. But don't worry, there are bound to be a couple of cars that drive by, so you can hitch a lift and just pay them about 10 pesos. I left the house and was greeted by two growling Alsatians who were waiting for Sarah to feed them. As ever they started to follow me so I gave the command for them to stay. Off I headed, down the road with my rucksack but I could still hear the pitter patter of paws. I was down to one dog though. Again I turned and sent him back. Half a mile down the road I turned again and 20 metres behind me stood the dog. I turned to act Mr Nasty and shout at him to go back, but he had those large sad dog eyes and pushed his head forlornly to one side. All I wanted to do was pat and hug him, but I steeled myself and shouted at him to go. Finally, he got the message and I trudged uphill by myself.

The first one and a half miles were up the steep slope and I hoped a car would arrive before I completed it. To no avail. I continued to walk on the downslope and built up a good rhythm. I soon came across a village where I exchanged cheery greetings with everyone and anyone. Children would actually run to their garden gates just to wave at me. But still there was no car. A second village, just as cheery as the first came and went. After walking for 50 minutes, with no sign of a car, I thought I might as well walk all the way, which was a good attitude to have, as not a single car passed me. It only took a total of 70 minutes so I am sure the distance was far less than the suggested six miles. I then flagged down a colectivo, which returned me to San Cristobal and the Magic Hostel.

It may have been 11.00am, but I checked with Gabriel just to make sure that happy hour hadn't started yet. Angus the bin man was still around and agreed to help me get re-adjusted into English ways. Well, that was my excuse for playing 21 frames of pool in the afternoon.

He confirmed that Kari and Karen weren't staying at the hostel. In which case I'd have to find a nice beach all by myself. I narrowed my main options down to Tulum on the Caribbean coast or Puerto Escondido on the Pacific coast. I can pick between the Caribbean and the Pacific. It sounds much better than the Atlantic or the North Sea. I favoured Tulum because it has some Mayan ruins spectacularly placed above the sea. However, decisions had to wait because Gabriel had carelessly allowed the levels of Posh to stock up and he thought I might be able to help out.

Day 54 - Sunday 19ᵀᴴ May - Kirk's Enterprise

Oh, where to go? A decision had to be made. Tulum, yeah, that was it in completely the wrong direction for Mexico City but a heady mix of a Caribbean Beach and Mayan ruins. With a decision all but made I busied myself with the task of lazing about in the courtyard. Suddenly the bat cave opened up and in walked Kari, Karen and Sven. Amid the usual stalking accusations I inquired as to where they wanted to follow me next. Puerto Escondido was the answer. So I changed my mind again.

With a decision all but made I busied myself with the task of lazing about in the courtyard (sounds familiar). I must have made it look good because I was joined by the Norwegians and the German. In fact, the number built up to 12 and it had fallen dark before we left the confines of the courtyard.

Angus led the way. He'd been staying in the hostel for seven weeks whilst trying (but not very hard) to sort out a flight back to England. I must have just missed him on my first visit to San Cristobal because he'd met Kari and Karen and the infamous Kirk. Apparently, he enjoyed a full day of drinking with Kirk and Robbie Williams (not the Robbie, although I am sure his mother sees him as the Robbie Williams). Somehow they finished up at a strip joint on the edge of town. It was quite a distance from the hostel so on the way back they managed to flag down a taxi and agree on a price. Halfway home the taxi driver said that the price was going to double. Angus argued that he couldn't just change the price. So the driver stopped the taxi, opened up the boot, pulled something out and returned to his seat. He pointed a gun at them and informed them that the fare was definitely doubling. Angus went very quiet and readied himself to pay whatever was required. The gun wasn't enough to stop Kirk. *'Ah fuck off, you're not going to shoot three tourists in the back of your taxi just to double a fare'.* I think the taxi driver was as shocked as Robbie and Angus. He ordered them out of his taxi and just drove off. He would probably have shot them but was side-tracked with the thought of William Shatner on a far off planet leaping over polystyrene rocks.

Speaking of loose cannons, also in our group of 12 was Paul. On his previous travels, he'd spent nine months in a psychiatric hospital after overdoing the magic mushrooms of Belgium. I didn't know Belgium had a reputation for mushrooms but it helps to explain the smurfs.

There was also Siri who possessed Scandinavian goddess looks and the blondest of blonde hair. This must be a distinct disadvantage when you're travelling around Central America because it guarantees her constant attention.

Day 55 - Monday 20th May - David, King of the Sleepy Soles

I calculated that there are four or possibly five dormitories around the courtyard of which I'd managed to sleep in three. The best thing about my present room is that it is full of other lazy souls. Pride of place goes to Siri who has managed to stay in bed longer than me each morning so far. On the first morning we were the only two left in bed at 10.00am but since then we have recruited wisely to the point that at 10.30am I was the first one up. The new recruits included one of the Israeli girls from my Palenque dormitory. She was meant to be heading to Cuba but had been side-tracked with work in Acapulco. However, within days of turning away the attention of a local crime boss, an official came to visit wanting a look at her non-existent work permit. The local crime boss said he'd have a word to sort it out and the official left. Not only did she believe that it was a set-up, but she also thought he would want the favour returned. So she did a runner and first thing yesterday turned up outside my bed. She looked down at me and said *'David, you're in my bed'*. A strange line to start the day with. But there is an explanation. David, because apparently I look like David of Goliath fame and 'my bed' because on her two previous visits to the Magic hostel this is where she slept.

The main activity for the day was a visit to the Medicine Museum accompanied by Siri and yet another Norwegian girl in the shape of Elizabeth. The Medicine Museum is notoriously difficult to find, but Angus provided me with the best advice. *'When you think you've gone past it, keep going for another half a mile'*. This walk proved to be a good time to reflect on the differences in being a man or woman in Latin America. In fact, quoting my guidebook '... *women can be subject to close scrutiny and exceptional curiosity. Don't be unduly scared – or flattered. Your average Latino would wolf whistle at his own grandmother if she walked past wearing a potato sack for a dress.'* Normally if there was a male in tow the locals stopped their whistles and their hissing. The hissing is a strange one, instead of whistling they let out a *'sssssssssssss'*. I often think that wolf whistles don't always mean a girl will come running over to you begging for a night of passion, but a hiss, how does that work? However, two girls including one with blonde hair meant that they couldn't help but whistle, well either that or they didn't consider me a proper man. The girls ignored the whistles while I enthusiastically waved back. Most of the lads took this in good spirit and were immediately teased by their friends. The only time I failed to wave was when a group of girls whistled at me (in this case the wolf whistle may have stood a chance of working) and I was too busy telling Siri *'that was for me, that was for me'* – well I think it was. We reached a point where we thought that we must have walked by the museum when Siri informed me that there was one man who had walked past us three times. This was some feat considering we had been walking in a straight line. He'd managed to be just behind us again, but on the opposite side of the road. I think I found this more disturbing than the girls. I wasn't sure what to do but as we crossed over, I took the opportunity to give him a big jolly wave. He couldn't have been so keen on me as we didn't see him again.

Day 56 - Tuesday 21st May - Court in San Cristobal

Another courtyard day.

Day 57 - Wednesday 22nd May - Return to the Foetal Position

The days in San Cristobal had become an excuse for marathon pool playing sessions against Angus and doing keepie-uppies in the hostel courtyard. There was the potential for trips to canyons and caves but I just could not motivate myself to visit them.

There was something that still interested me though. San Cristobal was a real mix between the Old Spanish colonialism and the native Indian traditions. This mix was illustrated in the religious practices in some of the surrounding villages. I think the old religions sometimes involved various mind-bending substances which helped people to sort of get in touch with their spiritual side. The imported Spanish Catholicism didn't have this feature, but by the time it had reached some of the villages, a sort of hybrid developed that still exists today. This still involves praying to Jesus but also involves getting steaming drunk. Even stranger, and I'm not sure how this developed, they sometimes drink Coca-Cola so they can burp out the evil spirits. I didn't manage to arrange a visit to one of these villages but Angus did show me an old church. Apparently, they stopped using it because their prayers were not being answered, which seems strangely logical.

We returned to the hostel, whereupon I packed my bag and left San Cristobal for the third time and once more waved goodbye to Kari and Karen. I'd been really impressed with the buses in Mexico so I was surprised to find that my bus was one hour late. The surprises continued when instead of the usual 40 passengers there was just three. A German girl, a Mexican and me. The German girl even approached the driver to ask if he could show a film. She was rewarded with a low budget Sylvester Stallone prison 'thriller'.

After Sylvester had overcome the evil governor, played by Donald Sutherland, I had tried to grab some sleep but buses are never as easy to sleep on as a bouncy king sized bed with fluffy sheets and soft pillows. The bus reached a peak of eight passengers as I tossed and turned on my seat looking for an elusively comfortable position.

I set about solving the bus sleeping riddle i.e. how the hell do I get comfortable enough to sleep on the bus. You have the standard sitting position, which I only fall asleep in if I am absolutely shattered. The Mexican buses do have the chair tilting facility but it just puts me at an angle where I think I might fall asleep but can't quite manage it. Then I moved into a sort of foetal position spread across two seats. It's a really tight squeeze (and about the only time I don't want to be a couple of inches bigger) but at least you get to lie down and I have a reasonable chance of unconsciousness. There were a couple of drawbacks to the foetal position. If the bus suddenly stops, my foetal position and me can get catapulted off the seat and into the leg space. Secondly, I can wake up after three-quarters of an hour and find I have no feeling in either my left arm or left leg. At this point, I normally start going through all the other positions again to make sure I haven't missed that mythical perfect sleeping position.

DAY 58 - THURSDAY 23ʳᵈ MAY - INDIANA BROWN AND THE CRYSTAL SKULL

The bus finally arrived in scorching hot Puerto Escondido. In fact, it was the off-season because of the extreme heat. A friend had recommended the Mayflower hotel, which wasn't difficult to find, and a dormitory bed awaited my weary body. On the sight of a mattress, I could not resist collapsing face first on to it. This is still the best position.

Puerto Escondido used to be a sleepy fishing village in the early eighties but word got out about what a beautiful place it was and it became one of those traveller hangouts. Word got around about the great waves so it became a surfer hangout. Word got around about the travellers and surfers having a great time so it became a developer's hangout. Hotel after hotel shot up. Word got out about all the tourists and crime moved in. Word got out that a member of the Kennedy family was murdered on the beach and a lot of the tourists stopped coming. I was interested to see what remained.

The town seemed to be divided in two by the main road, leaving the resort on one side and a normal town on the other. The main drag was very laid back, but I had arrived during the low season. In fact, most of the bars and restaurants were shut.

The beach called out to me and I answered in the traditional English way. I got sunburnt on the shoulders. Why don't they make suntan cream turn blue after you have put it on so I know which bits I have missed? Of all places the shoulders. It's a really useful sore bit to have when you are carrying a rucksack around.

My wanderings eventually brought me back to the hotel. There was a gathering of bodies around a table outside the dormitory and the discussion was about crystal skulls. This didn't seem your average type of conversation so I listened intently. A Canadian traveller, come documentary maker, was trying to track down some ancient skulls. He said that there is a Native American legend that tells of 13 life-sized crystal skulls, which are said to hold vital information about man's true purpose and future destiny. The book he is basing his research on recalls how the authors try to track down the skulls. It all sounded like an Indiana Jones fantasy but part of their research took in the labs of Hewlett Packard. The skulls are made from the same sort of crystal that today's computers use, so the claim that they may hold crucial information isn't as daft as it sounds. He went on to say that the authors had initially helped him but are now doing research for Hewlett-Packard and will not provide him with any further assistance. Also, the scientists cannot explain how the skulls were created because we do not currently possess the technology to make the required incisions. We decided it would be best to continue discussions over a few beers.

Day 59 - Friday 24ᵗʰ May - Sanday

I woke up at 11.00am, which was a bit of a shame because I planned to be up at the bus station by 9.30am to see Kari, Karen and Sven arrive. The fact that I went to a party on the beach until 5.00am may have had something to do with it. Instead, I just stumbled down to the beach and bumped into them.

Stumbling to the beach is not completely straightforward because there are six within striking distance. We wandered up to Marinero beach for a swim and then on to the long expanse of sand that is Zicatela beach. Zicatela claims to have the fastest breaking waves in the world, which are meant to be a challenge to even the most experienced surfers.

There is an English lad from the hostel called Brian who manages to surf at Zicatela. He has developed residency status after two months in the Mayflower. Brian had planned to move on but his passport got stolen so he thought he'd try to organise a new one from the beach. This meant he knew Jo, Jim, Bill and Kirk. I think every hostel should have a traveller in residence; it makes it sort of homely that they already know your friends.

Day 60 - Saturday 25ᵀᴴ May - Almost Waving Goodbye

Just four days of my trip left and, yes, I am counting. Not that I dislike Mexico, it is just because my departure seems so close. I, therefore, knew I should make the most of the stinking hot temperature before I returned to England. I didn't last too long in the sun though because the burning heat drove me into the shade or the water. The water was both more interesting and more dangerous.

The large waves attracted surfers and made swimming interesting because every now and then the waves would threaten to totally engulf you. Did I mention the rip tides as well? They're fairly strong. In fact, by all accounts, people are regularly pulled out of the water by the lifeguards, but there is something enticing about the waves.

Nearly everyone I knew who had visited Puerto Escondido had got into difficulties at some stage. Either because of being dragged under the water by the waves or the strong undercurrent not allowing you back to the beach. Brian said that Jim literally saved one lad from drowning by keeping his head above the water until a lifeguard rescued both of them.

However, there was something about the waves that just made you want to play in them. As they broke above you, it was great fun to either try to jump over the top or dive underneath. I'd built up my confidence on the smaller waves at Principal beach then moved on to the big ones at Marinero. It was great fun as the water rushed in and I ducked or leapt my way around the wave. I am not the greatest swimmer but still felt confident because I could just about touch the ground.

It came from nowhere (or I was looking the wrong way). I knew it was big but thought I'd just rise, salmon-like, over it. It was the wave that did the rising and I didn't get high enough. It smashed into me, knocked me horizontal and dragged me under the water. The sheer force pinned me down. I remember thinking that this is where I'll be holding my breath then. My 30 seconds under the water (felt like it at the time - but was probably five seconds in real earth time) passed by and I found myself on my knees facing the beach, about 30 feet from where the wave hit me and in two feet of water. I can't say it was anywhere near a drowning experience because it was only ever going to throw me at the beach, but I felt that I'd tasted the essential Puerto Escondido experience and that it had left a sandy/salty taste in my mouth.

Day 61 - Sunday 26ᵀᴴ May - Dying Peacefully

I'd already booked my bus to Mexico City so it was my last chance to try and drown in Puerto Escondido. I've always preferred the idea of dying quietly in a comfortable armchair with a football match on the radio and a glass of red wine in my hand. Drowning and the glass of wine just don't fit comfortably together, well unless I drown in a giant wineglass, which I don't think will happen unless I get kidnapped by a cartoon supervillain.

It felt as though the trip was over, but I suppose that was because I was going to my final destination and saying goodbye to Kari and Karen for the last time. Sven, as had become his tradition, stuck two fingers up at me. He'd been intrigued by the V sign ever since I explained that it allegedly came from the English archers fighting the French. I don't know whether it lost something in the translation because he seemed to use it to me for hello, goodbye, your round and each time find it hilariously funny.

Then I was by myself again, once more searching for that Holy Grail of the perfect bus sleeping position.

Day 62 - Monday 27ᵗʰ May - Friend or Weirdo

I returned to the Cathedral hostel in Mexico City and dropped off my rucksack. Then set about the main priority of the day, to contact Lufthansa. Ever since my India debacle, I have been completely paranoid about confirming flights. This paranoia meant that rather than simply phoning them, like any normal person, I wanted to find the office and receive the confirmation in person. I caught the metro to what was meant to be the nearest station and asked directions for the Lufthansa office at 239 Paseo de las Palmas. I kept asking the way as I walked but there didn't seem to be any sign of Paseo de las Palmas let alone Lufthansa. When I was told three times on the trot that I needed a bus I decided that I needed a bus. The final time was outside a posh hotel and the doorman even waved down the correct bus for me to jump on. I finally found the office and they neatly tucked away my paranoia by confirming that on Wednesday my bottom would have a seat under it and a winged metal box surrounding it.

With my paranoia suitably dispatched I enjoyed the rest of the afternoon walking around the city until a dog attacked me. It made a grab for my leg. I thrust it off by kicking out with my leg and then we stood two yards apart staring at each other. It snarling, me with right foot cocked and ready to blast it into the top corner. For 10 seconds we stood poised. When I felt it wasn't going to attack I slowly backed away. In San Pedro, I would have expected it, but with hundreds of people walking by in Mexico City, why me?

I survived my skirmish and fancied sitting in the hostel with a bottle of beer, reading my book. 370 pages gone and still 300 remaining. 300 sounded a lot so I thought a beer and some company was a better idea. I headed to the bar and spotted a group of traveller type people. 'Hello, can I join you for a beer?' *'Yeah sure, what's your name?'* Then I was part of a group of seven. I have to say that one of my favourite things about travelling is that it is so ridiculously easy to make new friends. If I tried the same thing in England people would think that I was some weirdo.

The hostel bar closed but the Aussies in the group decided that the night was still young, so off we all trooped looking for another beer. Nowhere looked open but a car of four young Mexicans stopped and offered to take us to a bar. This involved the seven of us squeezed onto the backseat and the two tequila soaked local girls sitting on top of the car with their legs dangling down from the sunroof. There were a couple of policemen watching us, although as the locals had confirmed, they weren't interested in us.

They dropped us outside an expensive bar and the friendship ended when they asked for £25 for the ten-minute lift to an area we didn't really want to be in. We did manage to find a relatively cheap bar, but the problem was that the time had crept well past midnight and we had to work out a route home. It was drunkenly decided that we would walk. Those safe and relaxed streets of the daytime had become dark and menacing. I didn't recognise any of the roads and thought it was lucky that I was drunk else I'd be scared. I definitely wouldn't like to have done the walk by myself, or as a couple, or a trio, maybe as a four, I'd be okay as a five and felt safe as a six. The hostel proved to be only a 20 minute walk away and the only items of drunken interest on the way back were our group kicking a can around and some youths swearing at us (I understood what they said so it shows my Spanish has continued to improve).

Day 63 - Tuesday 28th May - The Place of the Gods

I made it downstairs in time for a late breakfast. I was quite excited because I had saved one of the most famous sites in Central America until last. Teotichilan. I'd heard that you could get a public bus out to the site rather than pay treble the amount to use the hostel's tour bus. I caught the underground to the required bus station and then kept stopping official looking people to ask directions. The stop and ask policy led me to the bus and a 50 kilometre journey out to the site. It was a massive site that was befitting of a great city that was once home to 250,000 people. Monte Alban had been impressive and it only had a population of 20,000.

Teotihuacan is thought to have been inhabited between 300 BC and 600 AD but the place is still a mystery. No one knows where the people came from and are still not certain exactly why they disappeared. Even the proper name of the city is unknown. The Aztecs found the city hundreds of years after it had been deserted and named it 'Teotihuacan' which means place of the gods. It is set in a large valley and is dominated by three large pyramids, which are interconnected by a vast avenue of small pyramids. The whole scale of the place is astonishing. Isn't it strange that 1,800 years ago, Rome and Teotihuacan may have been two of the most powerful and impressive cities in the world but neither was aware of the other's existence.

The top of the pyramids made me feel small and somewhat unimportant. I sat down happily lost in my own insignificance, thinking what the city would have looked like in its pomp. After letting my imagination run free I drifted back to the 21st century and the hostel.

The Australians were all set for another big night out but I turned down their offer of sampling a Mexico City nightclub. All I wanted was a couple of quiet beers at the bar. After vultures, the threat of bandits, volcanoes and the magnificence of Tikal I was happy to finish with a whimper rather than a roar.

Day 64 - Wednesday 29th May - Secret Of Life

I packed my rucksack for the last time and deposited it in the luggage room. Then I had breakfast with the de-shrivelled wrecks of four Australians before visiting the Museum of Anthropology. It would have rounded everything off nicely if I'd found the answer to life, the world and everything in the museum. But they didn't have the answer or if they did, I didn't find it.

I had no time to resolve the issue because a swift return to the hostel was required so I could unpack and re-pack my rucksack a few times. I sent my final e-mails announcing my imminent return and sat down for a coffee.

So, back to England. Back to fridges full of food, pints of bitter, cold mornings, drizzle, cold afternoons, more drizzle, cold nights, good music, working for a living, breakfasts on the run, playing tennis, running in the rain, people moaning how tough life is, green fields, fish and chips, not having to carry a toilet roll, flushing toilet paper down the toilet, a diet without malaria tablets, drinking at the local and sleeping in my own bed.

My world trip had been amazing but I realised I couldn't do it again, well at least for a few years. I needed to start working again to build my savings up and then look at buying a house. I did think though that I should know my capital city better, so I moved to London. I knew it would probably be too hectic for me and only expected to last there a year. It came as a surprise that I absolutely loved living in London. There was great live music, incredible museums, fantastic pubs, brilliant restaurants, world-class sport, a lifetime of historical nooks & crannies to explore and people to meet from all over the world. I felt like a perpetual tourist – it was great!

I did manage some trips away and reached Nepal, Russia, Croatia, Bosnia, Malawi, Zanzibar, Morocco and Norway. Unfortunately, any diaries I attempted to write petered out soon after I started them. A trip to my 7th continent would definitely get me writing again. Antarctica was on my list of potential destinations but hadn't risen to the top because of the high costs, notoriously tough sea crossing and the fact that it looked a bit chilly. I had Brazil, Uzbekistan, Iran, Japan and Ethiopia, ranked ahead of Antarctica. Unbeknown to me, fate was writing a different list which included; stop Jeff Brown backpacking and for his own good he should write one more diary.

DIARY 7

I guess the end for my backpacking days started on the 29th September 2007. It was just that no one told me my world was changing. I was 35 years old, still very single, no mortgage and no ties. I then went to my friend Greg's wedding in Thorpeness and my world started to change. It was a slightly different wedding in that there was no table plan, except for the head table, and the only bridesmaid was a man. Apparently, several months before the wedding, the bride complained that all her female friends were far too slim and pretty to be her bridesmaids. One of her best friends, who happened to be a burly male rugby player, said that if he was her brides-maid then she would definitely look slim and pretty in comparison. Before he had time to withdraw the offer, it was accepted. As Greg was Scottish, the newly appointed bridesmaid was provided with a kilt rather than a nice flowing dress but he gamely took up his duties, including a lovely dance with the father of the bride. Anyway, as is my habit, I am strolling down tangent boulevard. At some point, at the wedding, I had spotted a pretty Indian girl. The flexible seating plan made it simple to sit down and chat at her table. She smiled a wonderful smile and I was eased down a path of no return.

The pretty Indian girl was called Bharathi, but after the wedding, she headed off for a week-long course in America, so we organised meeting up on her return. Unfortunately, I had made a schoolboy error and had arranged our date on the same night that England were in the rugby world cup final. I wondered how I could tactfully re-arrange it. I phoned her up and before I could make any excuses she said '*I know you love your sport. So shall we go out on Sunday, rather than Saturday night, and then you won't miss the rugby world cup final*'. Wow – this is good.

I remember, on the Saturday night, telling a friend that I'd be going out on a date tomorrow but it would not be serious. Bharathi had already told me that she would be returning to India in 6 weeks' time, to look after her terminally ill father, and despite having a UK passport thought she may then settle permanently back in India.

We went on a couple of dates where the only rational explanation is that cupid pulled back an arrow on his strings and struck me squarely between the eyes. I suddenly could not imagine being without her, that smile, that thoughtfulness, that playfulness - she was like no one I had met before. The only odd thing, about her, was that she liked me - how did that happen?

Bharathi returned to India to look after her very sick father, but we spoke every day. She was the only member of her family in England and initially wasn't sure how they'd react to her going out with a white Englishman. When she finally plucked up the courage to tell them, they all seemed delighted that she was happy.

After she spent six months nursing her father, he reached the point where he knew that he was very close to death. Bharathi was his youngest child and the only one who was unmarried. It was his last wish to send her back to the UK to be with me and allow him to speak to us as a couple. So she reluctantly returned to Britain, knowing she would never see her father alive again. We spoke to him together on the phone and then a week later he died. She mourned her father but at least had the knowledge that she had shared his last six months and his last wish had been fulfilled.

14 months after meeting Bharathi, she urinated on a little piece of paper and we waited nervously to see whether a little blue cross appeared. Sure enough, the pregnancy test produced the hoped-for blue cross and blew my mind. 'Wow! Just wow! We are going to have a baby! Brilliant!'

Although her family had been fantastic about her going out with a white Englishman, we had now upped the stakes. This was definitely a trickier one. To Bharathi's delight and surprise, her brother was really happy. She had to check though. '*Are you okay that we are not married?*' '*No problem*' said Ravi. '*I'll just tell everyone you are married to Jeff*'. Brilliant – I hadn't met him but already thought he was fantastic. Besides, her father had symbolically passed her hand to me and in my eyes that was far more important than any religious or legal ceremony.

Life was very good.

And then it got even better when, our son, Jothi Edward Brown arrived on the 3rd June 2009. Amazing!

Jothi would go from lying flat on his stomach to a crouching position, on his knees, with his arms trying to push him up. His arms would then give way, leaving him to crash head first on to the bed. Then he'd try it again – thwack. It seemed desperate. Almost like a plea for help. It seemed like someone in their death throes – but we had only been discharged from the hospital two hours before. Death throes – discharged, death throes – discharged. Death throes – I don't care what they said, this just isn't right. I phoned the hospital and got put through to a nurse at the Children's Accident and Emergency. '*He is probably fine, but if you are really concerned then you can bring him in*'.

We realised we were probably being over-protective, but something didn't feel right.

We grabbed clothes to keep warm and bundled ourselves into the car at 2.00am to head to Stevenage hospital. 10 minutes later we went through to Accident and Emergency, expecting to be told that we were just being daft. Instead, all hell broke loose. The nurse took one look at Jothi and called in help. A doctor rushed across. He laid Jothi on the bed and frantically started working on him – something was wrong – we just didn't know what or how serious it was. Bharathi said '*phone, Prakash*' – 'what do I say?' '*I don't know but just phone him*'. So I phoned her friend Prakash – who was a consultant at the hospital. He seemed fairly bright for 3.00am and I explained what was happening – '*I'll be right down Jeff*'. He arrived about 15 minutes later. Venkat, another of Bharathi's medical friends was on duty and magically appeared. They took charge of the situation and worked on Jothi. I didn't know what was going on. My head felt strange. I'd never fainted before, but could feel myself becoming increasingly light-headed and I had to sit down before I collapsed. Prakash and Venkat then whisked Jothi away, with us in tow – clinging to each other. More familiar Indian medical faces appeared with grave looks – all working hard. Now it was us looking desperate. I was silent, slightly numb; there was nothing I could do. Oh god, Allah, Zeus, Thor, Shiva, Jupiter, anyone, everyone - help my little boy.

Prakash came over and said Jothi had probably contracted Meningitis. They confirmed that they were trying to make him reasonably stable before he could be taken to one of the specialist hospitals in London. They were waiting to hear which one had a spare bed. Venkat explained that it is one of those diseases that an adult can walk into the hospital of their own accord and hours later be dead.

Our little boy – we love him so much – how can this be happening? I needed my brother as I had never needed him before – Graham, come now. I tried to phone him, but there was no answer. I didn't want to worry mum and dad but I really wanted my big brother. So I tried to hold myself together to tell mum the terrible news and ask her to send Graham down to Stevenage immediately. I was that little kid in the playground wanting his big brother. Time passed in a blurry mess of emotion.

I had to phone work as well. The phone rang in the office and my friend Garry picked up, but I broke down in tears as I tried to explain what was happening. As a fellow dad, Garry told me to stop crying and get back in with Jothi and Bharathi. I felt like a boxer getting a pep talk from his corner, before going back into the cauldron of hell again. Although when I was with Bharathi I was controlled, it was only when I was away from her and Jothi that the tears started to flow.

Graham then arrived and I gave him a huge hug. Again I could keep myself together in front of Bharathi, but as soon as she was around the corner I broke down in tears in Graham's arms.

Shortly after, the ambulance from London arrived. The ambulance paramedics took over Jothi's medical care – re-arranging tubes and wires to their preferences. It was confirmed to us that only one parent could sit in the ambulance with Jothi. We both knew that Jothi would want it to be his mummy. She was warned that this would be the worst hour of her life. That at any point on the journey they may have to stop at the side of the road to try and resuscitate him. There was never any doubt in her mind that she was getting in that ambulance - she headed into that ambulance as a mum and my hero. The paramedic told her that whatever happened she would have to remain in her seat - completely helpless. They then all headed into the ambulance and the doors were slammed shut. The last I saw was the ambulance speeding off and the siren sounding. I stood there. My inners felt like a huge bomb had gone off leaving utter desolation. Utter desolation except for a little flower of hope.

My brother and Venkat stood next to me. Graham asked him whether he thought Jothi would survive the journey to London. It was a question I did not want to hear, but an answer I needed to know. Venkat said he would - I hoped he was right, hoped liked I had never hoped before, I begged the universe to let my little boy live.

Venkat headed off to his office to carry on working. However, the emotional strain of working on a friend's child had left him exhausted and his colleagues sent him home. By this time the Indian community were rallying around and two of Bharathi's close friends had also arrived at the hospital. Vasan and Smita joined me in Graham's car to drive down to London. I was in turmoil as my world seemed to be tearing apart at the seams. I desperately wanted to be with Jothi and Bharathi, but there was nothing I could do except sit in the car. There was normal conversation in the car, but it was just background noise to me. I hated doing nothing, hated this situation, how could this happen, for fuck's sake. Fucking car, fucking traffic, fucking meningitis, fucking traffic. I could not just sit there cursing I had to do something but all I came up with was willing Jothi to get better.

Progress in the London traffic was frustratingly slow. Then my phone rang. It was Bharathi. They were at the hospital, but all Jothi's major organs were starting to fail. The next hour would be crucial.

We were in central London and edged closer to the hospital. I was so frustrated and just wanted to be with my son, rather than surrounded by lanes of cars, lorries and buses. I recognised where we were and that it was half a mile to the hospital. It was four lanes of very slow traffic and I'd had enough. I opened the car door and stepped into the traffic, telling the others I would see them at the hospital. I ran between the cars and on to the pavement and sped towards the hospital. I reached the hospital doors breathless, but realised that they were locked. These were the back doors of the Evelina hospital and I needed another sprint round to the front door. I just wanted to get inside. The front doors led to a bright, light and airy hospital. There were six floors, but the airy atrium meant there was nothing between the middle of the ground floor and the roof.

I made my way up in the lift and to the intensive care ward for little children. The doors to the ward were locked and I pressed the button to ask to be let in. The room was large and spacious but had the harrowing sight of babies and toddlers fighting for their lives with connecting tubes and medicine being pumped into them. I wasn't prepared for this.

I made my way to the right-hand side where Jothi lay in bed with Bharathi by his side. He was still alive and still fighting. He lay prostrate with a zoned-out look and a completely limp body. Tubes weaved their way around him and into him, while the beeping machines stood behind him. I took Bharathi in my arms and hugged her like our lives depended on it. I had never felt so utterly helpless.

All we could do was be with him, talk to him and tell him how much we loved him.

Bharathi and I sat side by side, holding hands. What do you say? Nothing really, nothing you say helps and nothing needs to be said to each other. We knew we felt the same pain and anguish. We knew that given the option we would prefer to swap places with him. Just to take the pain away from him and give it to us. I love that little boy so much. '*My little miracle*' my mum calls him. Although I'm not sure whether that refers to the miracle that a girl actually decided to have a baby with me. The brain's thoughts drift and then suddenly reality slaps you across the face and you realise that you are living one of your worst nightmares. Our boy, with organs failing, being pumped full of medicines through tubes, listless on his bed, a mask helping him breathe and desperately trying to keep him alive. The only positive was that if we hadn't returned to the hospital he'd be in the morgue rather than a bed now. The nurse looking after Jothi introduced herself, but I struggled to take in anything she said. Graham, Smita and Vasan arrived at the hospital. But it was just two visitors allowed per patient, so they acquainted themselves with the parent's room opposite PICU (Paediatric Intensive Care Unit).

Jothi had survived the crucial hour, but with no real sign of improvement. The consultant spoke to us and told us that he was a very ill little boy and the next 24 hours would be crucial. The consultant was very good and explained that a sample was taken from Jothi which they would develop in the laboratory back in Stevenage. The sample would be given different antibiotics to see which was the most effective. In the meantime, he would carry on taking the current antibiotics. I knew that meningitis was a killer – the stuff of parent's nightmares, but it was explained to us that there is viral meningitis and bacterial meningitis. Although both are serious, it is bacterial that is worse and that is what they think Jothi has contracted. Even if Jothi survives, then there can be a whole range of after-effects including brain damage, amputated limbs, blindness, deafness, damaged limb growth, depression, cerebral palsy, the list goes on and on.

When Bharathi left Jothi's side for a break, Vasan came into the ward. His son is the same age as Jothi and when he entered the ward his face was aghast at the sight of the first child fighting for its life. He turned his head away, but just towards another baby struggling to survive. Vasan's face reflected the hurt he felt every time he saw one of those poor children attached to tubes, wires and beeping machines. When he saw Jothi his lip wobbled, tears escaped from his eyes and he fought to hold himself together – that already seems a familiar feeling.

After a long period of staring at Jothi, and the machines keeping him alive, I took a break in the parent's room. The parent's room is about 40 feet long with chairs, television, kettle, fridge, microwave, toys – when I saw the toys I thought 'my little boy would like to play with…..' I had to stop myself. He isn't up to playing at the moment. Oh god – is this really happening? The parent's room is really useful as a little refuge to sit down, have a cup of tea and try to absorb what is going on. Then I feel like I'm going back into battle by pressing the buzzer on the door of PICU again, to say 'Hello, I'm Jothi Brown's dad'. '*Okay, come in*'.

The doctors and nurses all seem incredibly professional, caring and patient. We were talked through the practicalities of the situation. Jothi's condition has not seemed to change during the day, but everything seems so finely balanced.

In the evening the nurses presented us with a diary. It was a beautiful dark blue book with coloured stickers of parrots, fish and polar bears on it. It was for us to write in whilst Jothi is in intensive care. The irony. I always had a feeling that part of the reason I kept a travel diary was that when things went wrong I could think 'I'll write about that' - it always was some kind of therapy. So the diary made complete sense to me. So my final travel diary, a trip to the gates of hell, and who knows where? Bloody hell, the rough guide to intensive care would be useful and an itinerary so I know what happens? On second thoughts, I am not sure whether I want to know because it is just hope and love that are sustaining me.

The diary also allows comments from nurses and friends, so I've included them in italics. Here is the first:

'You had been feeling poorly for the last few days. Mummy and daddy had taken you to the hospital yesterday because you had such a high temperature. The doctors at Stevenage hospital had a look at you and then sent you home with antibiotics. During the night though you became really unwell and mummy and daddy had to take you back to the hospital.

When you got to A & E, the doctors and nurses had to do lots to help make you better and they had to call a special team called STRS – the South Thames Retrieval Service who could take you to a children's intensive care unit to be looked after. Before the retrieval team could take you back to the intensive care unit they had to put a breathing tube on your mouth, in order to put you on a ventilator, so we could help you with your breathing.

You had to be given lots and lots of fluid to help bring your heart rate down and your blood pressure up! They also started you on some medicines called Dopamine and Noradrenaline to help your blood pressure.

Once you were more stable they put you in an ambulance. Mummy came with you back to the Forest Ward at the Evelina Children's hospital. (Ed, Suzanne and Marten).'

Ed, Suzanne and Marten were part of the retrieval service. Not only did they seem good at their job but Suzanne even phoned up later to see how Jothi was getting on.

***Nurse Hannah** - I was the nurse who looked after you once you arrived in Forest Ward and you kept me very busy all day! The doctors and nurses were still finding it hard to keep your blood pressure where it should be so they had to give you lots more fluid. They also gave you some blood products like Platelets because your blood wasn't sticking together (clotting) like it should do. Because of that, we found out you are blood group A+.*

I started some more medicines to help your blood pressure called Milrinone and Adrenaline. You were also given lots of antibiotics to fight off whatever infection you have, and because you were still running high temperatures you were wrapped in a special suit to cool you down. You were given lots of sugary fluid as your own sugar levels kept falling. Hannah

Bharathi and I thought we'd stay by Jothi's side throughout the night and try to grab some sleep by his side or in the parent's room. However, we were told that the Evelina had a number of bedrooms, especially for parents with children in PICU, and that we had been assigned a room. The room itself was like a basic hotel room with a small bathroom. It meant that we had one less thing to consider and the bed felt like an unexpected luxury.

It was 9.30pm when we headed to our room and my brother took over sitting next to Jothi. Graham sat there talking about football to him and then read his magazine out loud. I think we all felt a need to talk to Jothi so that he might know we were there.

I laid down on the bed and clung to Bharathi. I was shattered, dazed and frightened, but that little flower of hope had withstood a storm or at least the initial part of the storm. My mind carried on thinking, trying unsuccessfully to process everything.

Thursday 11ᵗʰ November

At midnight, Bharathi went to sit with Jothi, whilst Graham came to the bedroom. I woke just before 2.30am. But come to that, I had also woken up just before 2.20am, 2.05am, 1.45am, 1.30am and 1.10am. Sleep had been difficult to reach and I had closed my eyes more than actually sleep. I was awake at 2.30am but in a daze and sort of numb. Numb, as in I felt so much anguish and worry that my body felt it couldn't take any more. The numbness dulled the pain to a level that I could still operate at, but I was tired, so tired. I got out of bed, miserably put on some clothes and tried to open the bedroom door. It wouldn't open. I remembered that there was a button on the wall to unlock it. So I felt my way around the wall until I found it and pressed it. Then I went down a floor in a lift, out the lift, across the eerily empty atrium, through some doors, round a corner, up two flights of stairs, across a corridor, pressed the intercom button, 'it's Jothi's dad', through the security doors and then round a corner to my little boy and a tired looking Bharathi. I embraced her and we looked at our son. We had a few minutes together before she headed to the parent's room to curl up on a settee. As I sat with Jothi I looked at the ward. As wards go, it is beautiful, all lovely shades of green in a forest theme, but there is no disguising that it is an intensive care unit. Just a brighter and leafier one than normal.

Jothi would normally have loved to have played with all these machines, wires and tubes that covered him. Instead of that I picked up some children's books from a row of shelves and started to read them to him. I must have gone through four books, that were interspersed, with numerous 'I love you Jothi'. I never could get through a day without telling him that I love him. I remember going to a business meeting in about 2001 and the client took a phone call from his daughter. At the end of the call, he said '*I love you*' (not to me, to his daughter, else that would become an entirely different story, although maybe that way I would have got the business). Then he turned to me and said that you should always tell your family that you love them. I thought 'you are right, why don't I do that?' However, I am English so from that point on I would always tell my mum that I loved her, but it was more difficult with my dad and brother. It was far easier to just insult them in a loving way.

Nurses Jane and Ros – *Well Jothi, you have been a star for us overnight. You are still on the ventilator, but we have been able to wean down the amount of oxygen you need.*

We had to give you a bit more fluid, but we have been able to turn off the Dopamine, one of the medicines supporting your heart. All of your gases that we have taken are getting better, so everyone is very pleased with you. We gave you a wash and changed your sheets last night. They are on a special blow up mattress to stop you getting sore.

Mummy, daddy and Uncle Graham have been taking it in turns to sit with you, so somebody has been with you all night. Well done Jothi, keep getting better, love Jane and Ros.

At 6.30am Bharathi came back to Jothi's bedside. I was shattered, in fact, I'd been shattered at 3.00am and had now surpassed shattered. I stayed with Bharathi and Jothi for a little while, gave Jothi a kiss then headed off for a lie-down. I reached our room and lay face down on the bed, hoping sleep would take me for a while. By 10.00am I'd stirred myself and had a refreshing shower. I was going to write enjoyed a shower, but I'm not really enjoying anything. Enjoying seems a long way away. It wasn't long before I headed across a now busy hospital atrium (which had about 60 children and parents spread across it) and was outside the ward. I pressed the buzzer and said 'It's Jothi's dad'. How long will I be able to say that for? What a sad thought. Then I was back into the intensive care ward. I looked at Jothi initially but my eyes quickly moved to the machines and the readings. Heartbeat, blood pressure, oxygen saturation and god knows what else. On each reading, I know what number it has to hit before the machine starts beeping a warning to the nurse. The numbers are mesmerising, I can't look away for more than two minutes before catching myself looking at them again.

In the afternoon I spoke to my mum and wished her a happy birthday but it was the most hollow 'happy birthday' I'd ever said to her. At least I could offer her the information that Jothi had improved slightly. It just felt that the crucial hour had become a crucial 24 hours, which had changed into a crucial 48 hours to who knows how long a crucial time. Bloody hell – every minute feels crucial to me, every second I spend with him could be the last.

Bharathi – *'Kutti, this is from Amma. You gave us all a scare; got daddy, myself, Uncle Graham, Auntie Ramya, Uncle Vasan, Auntie Smita all crying. You were the bravest little boy mummy has ever known. You're mummy and daddy's little soldier. I came with you in the ambulance from Stevenage hospital to St Thomas's and that was the longest hour I have ever lived. I was willing you to be okay all the way and you were amazing. I am so proud of you my Jothi Edward. You are loved by so many people Kuttippa'.*

(I'll give you a little Tamil lesson here: Kutti is little one, Amma is mummy and Kuttippa is, hold on I need to check with Bharathi, well it is also little one but with even more affection).

As soon as Bharathi's brother found out what had happened to Jothi he dropped everything and got the earliest flight from India. He arrived at 4.00pm, straight from Heathrow. Ravi is tall, resolute and has a happy smile. I'm not sure what a sad smile is but Ravi definitely has a happy smile. Although today he was tall, resolute, concerned and tired. He stayed four hours before the tiredness overwhelmed him and Vasan took him to his house to sleep.

Friday 12th November

At 2.40am I successfully remembered the button on the wall and left the bedroom. Then down in a lift, out the lift, across the atrium, through some doors, round a corner, up the stairs, across a corridor, pressed the intercom button, 'it's Jothi's dad', through the doors and round a corner to my little boy and a tired Bharathi. I embraced Bharathi and we looked at our son. We had a few minutes together before she headed back to our room.

I now knew my routine. I would go upstairs desperate to see my boy but with a sense of dread. I'd enter the ward and there would be prostrate children in every direction - except behind me. I would have an urge to turn round and run away from all this pain and misery. But that wasn't an option because the most precious things in the world were waiting for me around the corner and I needed to be with them. To hold Jothi's hand meant everything and everything was hanging by a thread. I would check all the stats on his machines to see whether he had improved and then hold his hand. At some point, that beeping would start and I would be transfixed on the machine until the beeping stopped. Sometimes a nurse would come across and switch off the beeping. They would see the scared look on my face and reassure me. *'Don't worry Jeff, it just beeps to tell me to have a look at him - I rely on what I see, not on when machines beep'.* Those beeps still scare me though. They make me want to run away – but I know that when I am away from Jothi I want to run back twice as quickly. It is emotionally draining but the parent's room is good for re-charging my batteries. I have a cup of tea, talk to the other parents if I feel like it and slowly process what is going on. I don't feel like talking to friends on the phone as that seems tiring. In fact not talking to people outside the hospital seems to help me to conserve my energy for being in PICU.

It was noticeable that, despite being heavily drugged, Jothi had started to move around a little on the bed – he always was a little wriggler. The tube that was in his mouth had been switched to his nose so he was a little more comfortable and I stroked his head affectionately. He seemed to settle into his sleep again but I knew that given half a chance he'd be wriggling. All his figures look steady this morning. I'd like to whisper that in Bharathi's ear as she tries to sleep. Tonight, or is that last night, Graham was with him from 8.30pm to 11.15pm, Bharathi 11.15pm to 2.45am and then Bharathi will be back again at 6.00am. Jothi started wriggling again and my stroking did not calm him down so he received a little extra morphine to help him settle.

Later on, and for the first time since we got to the hospital, the nurse's offered Bharathi the chance to change Jothi's nappy. She enthusiastically agreed and for a couple of minutes, she felt like a normal mum.

Nurse Suzanne

Hello Jothi,

You have been a little superstar today, we have managed to wean down your ventilator, which is your special breathing machine. Great news – well done!

You are still on a few drugs for your heart, to keep your blood pressure up, but they have come down as well – woohoo! You are such a brave little boy.

You have been waking up and moving around today, even though you are on lots of sedation. You are a real fighter - keep it up. Your mummy and daddy have been with you all day and your two uncles, all of them giving you lots of kisses and cuddles and stroking your head, which you like very much.

Have a good night's sleep tonight and build up that strength to get better. Lots of love

Suzanne

You are a little superstar gorgeous boy!

Saturday 13ᵗʰ November

At 2.40am I left the bedroom. Then lift, atrium, doors, round a corner, up the stairs, across a corridor, 'it's Jothi's dad', through the security doors and round a corner to my little boy and a tired Bharathi. I embraced Bharathi and we looked at our son, then she headed back to our room.

Bharathi re-appeared at 6.30am, which is also the time a tea trolley comes round. It is a good opportunity for a little family time. The last couple of days I have sipped my tea and then, at about 7.00am, have gone back to the room to sleep. Sleep continues to be very fitful but for some reason, maybe exhaustion, that 7.00am till 10.00am slot has given me my best bit of sleep. In fact, the sleep was deep enough that when I woke up I had a second of blissful ignorance - before remembering where I was and what was happening.

All I have heard this morning is that Jothi has made good progress over the last 24 hours. The start of the 24 hours seemed to have coincided with when Graham arrived yesterday claiming that he was in his lucky pants and had a really good feeling. I think the pants he had borrowed, from friends he was staying with in London, were a little tight but he maintained he just had a good and lucky feeling.

This afternoon Graham had a headache - I don't think it had been caused by the tight pants, but he was suffering. He had asked a nurse for a tablet and was told that she couldn't give him one because he wasn't a patient. She agreed that it was ridiculous but said she would accidentally leave a paracetamol tablet on the table in one minute. If he picked it up and swallowed it then that was something he had taken of his own accord. With that incredibly sensible bend in the rules, Graham's headache got a lot better.

Later on, Graham came into the parent's room, from PICU, when myself and Bharathi were having a break. '*I have just been speaking to the consultant and was asking whether Jothi will survive*'. 'She said he will - why didn't anyone tell me?' That was amazing news. As good a news as I could hear. But Jothi was still very weak and couldn't breathe by himself. The reason that no one told Graham that he'd survive, or should now survive, was that no one knew. Despite this news, Bharathi and I could not celebrate as there was still a long way to go, but I could raise a smile because we'd taken a big step in the right direction.

Ramya – (Vasan's wife) Hi Jothi, this is Auntie Ramya . I came here to see you with Rishabh, Vasan mama and Ravi mama. When I saw you in the Intensive Care ward I felt like crying aloud. Then I saw your bravery certificate, the way you were fighting and heard the doctors saying you have crossed your critical stage and I got a bit brave coming to see you.

I am praying all the time for your speedy recovery. I am looking forward to playing with you very soon darling.

Get well soon Jothi Kutti.
(a second Tamil lesson here – mama means uncle)

I was in the parents' room in the afternoon when a family with a little boy came in. I continued making my cup of tea and then looked across. I was dumbstruck, because there was Jothi happily playing with a toy. Just for a split second, I'd thought the meningitis had been a vivid nightmare. I had to do a double take because the boy looked just like Jothi. Then reality was back. Shame.

Back in PICU, Jothi was moving around, despite being sedated, which was a very good sign. The extra movement also involved his hands. This was fine until his hand reached up to his face and pulled out the oxygen tube that helped him to breathe. It is not straightforward to put this back and would involve heavily sedating him again, so they decided to leave him and see whether he could breathe for himself.

> **Nurses Katie and Tash** - *Hi Jothi, what an absolute pleasure to meet you, you have been such a good boy and an absolute pleasure to look after. You have done a lot of my work for me today, you have removed your own lines and your catheter. It was very helpful of you I must say, although one of them I actually had not planned on taking out (oops). It doesn't matter though as we have had a nice positive day today, taking out your breathing tube as well as managing to turn off and switch down some of your medicines for your heart. Well done. You are such a fighter. We have admired your lovely long eyelashes and your gorgeous brown eyes. You are now having some milk, which has made you happy. Thanks for such a good day, love Katie and Tash x x*

As the evening wore on, Jothi's breathing became more and more laboured. We really didn't want him to be heavily sedated again, but by sedating him they could re-insert his breathing tube. They tried helping him with an oxygen mask, however, a one-year-old has little interest with putting a mask on and it just agitated him. They didn't seem to be in a particular hurry to put the breathing tube in, but to us, it seemed that no one wanted to make the decision. Well except for us – insert the tube. He was struggling to breathe and they weren't moving quick enough. Time dragged on as we watched him struggle for breath. We asked, we asked again, we told them and implored them. Finally, they sedated him again and put the breathing tube back in.

SUNDAY 14TH NOVEMBER

Yesterday had a distinct high and low feeling.

The low – well the breathing tube had to be put back in, which was disappointing but necessary. But the speed with which it happened was so frustrating at the end of a very long and tiring day. Bharathi works for the NHS and warned me that the standard of care can slip at the weekend. Quite simply, who wants to work at the weekends? Especially, Saturday nights. So the less experienced doctors and nurses are more likely to be on the frontline. Our nurse simply didn't have the experience to forcibly harass the relevant doctor into a decision. And the less experienced doctor didn't want to make a prompt decision.

The high - at one stage the sedation had worn off enough for Jothi to recognise his 'Spot the Dog' cuddly toy and for him to want to cuddle him. It was a magical moment to see a little glimpse of his personality, but because he needed the breathing tube the heavy sedation took him away from us again.

Today is Remembrance Day, when we salute so many heroes. Both yesterday and this morning, Bharathi was my hero again. She put in a 23 hour day, eventually joining me in bed at 5.00am this morning, when she was satisfied that Jothi's breathing was okay. At that point, Ravi got out of bed to keep Jothi company. I had gone to bed at 3.00am and didn't realise that Bharathi had replaced Ravi in bed. When I woke up I knew I was cuddled up to someone, but it took me a couple of confused seconds to work out that it was Bharathi.

My close friends Matt Billings, Matt Barton and Dana Morgan travelled down from Leicester to provide me with some support. I'd known Billings, well, forever, we were brought up three doors apart and I was born a year after him. He is, without doubt, the most stubborn person I know. In fact, the stubbornness is hereditary. His parents told me that one of Matt's ancestors was caught by the French in the Napoleonic war. The prisoners of war, including Matt's ancestor, were then paraded in front of Napoleon who went down the line shaking each man's hand. When it came to Matt's ancestor, he refused to shake Napoleon's hand and instead stuck two fingers up to him. The French soldiers grabbed him and asked Napoleon whether he wanted them to shoot him. Napoleon answered *'No, he was very brave to do that to me – I respect that'*. Although along with the stubborn streak the loyalty runs equally deep. If I was being attacked by 10 ninja warriors then Billings would be the one coming charging in, like a steam train, to rescue me. Although to be honest, we don't get too many ninja warriors in Frisby-on-the-Wreake, where Matt and I grew up, so he hasn't been put to the ninja test. It must be a good sign that I can digress so much.

Anyway, Barton reported that the doors of PICU nearly came off their hinges in Billings eagerness to check on Jothi. As for Barton, we'd been at school together and had backpacked together several times, whilst Dana was his girlfriend of a few years. The first time I met Dana, she was holding Matt's hair back whilst he was being sick in a bucket – probably a good indicator that they would be together for a long time.

I felt boosted by their presence and I was happy to answer their questions about Jothi, without crying - although I needed some big hugs. I took them for a coffee in the hospital restaurant. It is a normal cafeteria, just bigger and with a stunning Thames side view of the Houses of Parliament. It seems strange to have such an amazing view while you are in the bowels of an old hospital.

Jothi was sleeping peacefully for much of the day and had quite a good day, although his legs have swollen up and I'll be happy to see them go down. We are just hoping that it is not the infection causing it. I think I'm judging a good day on the basis that the machines didn't beep too many times while I was with him. I hate the beeping – it still makes me want to run away.

Although Ravi had spent his first night at Vasan and Ramya's house he had since remained at the hospital to be with Jothi. He either slept in our room at the hospital or in the parents' room slumped in a chair. Bharathi had tried to send him back to Vasan and Ramya's house so that he would get a proper sleep, but he was adamant that he wasn't going anywhere until Jothi was out of PICU. Yet more stubbornness that I admire. Feel the love Jothi, feel the love.

Nurse Leanne - *Hello Jothi, my name is Leanne and I have been your nurse for tonight and last night. Last night was very busy – you had your breathing tube taken out in the afternoon, but by the evening you were not managing very well.*

We tried giving you a CPAP mask on your face but you didn't like it. You had some medicine to help you sleep and mummy sang to you.

Unfortunately, the CPAP didn't make you better and by 2.00am the doctors had to put your tube back in, which is called re-incubate. You were so brave throughout it all - what a strong boy.

I am so amazed by how many visitors you have – you are never alone. Mummy and daddy have a great system where one of them or your Uncle Graham or Uncle Ravi are always sat at your bedside, you are obviously a very special boy.

Tonight is a much quieter night. You are sleeping peacefully, with your feet up and bunny under your arm. Your chest sounds much better and your blood results are slowly getting better too. Get well soon Jothi.

Leanne XX

Monday 15th November

2.40am, bedroom, lift, atrium, doors, corner, stairs, corridor, 'it's Jothi's dad', doors, corner, my boy, Bharathi, hug, Bharathi to our room. Bharathi re-appeared at 6.30am, we sipped our tea together and then I headed back to our room for a sleep.

This morning I got a feeling that Jothi looked at me. As the day went on his eyes definitely moved around and focused on people. I read a story called Mr McGregor to him and his eyes started to follow the pictures as I read. After having been slumped in the bed for so long, it was fantastic to see Jothi's eyes looking at the pictures. He is coming back to us.

We had been receiving very supportive messages from friends. Bharathi received one such text from her friend Esther. Esther said that she was praying with Archie (her four-year-old son). She was saying '*god, please make Jothi better soon*' and Archie said '*no god, make Jothi better now*'. I'm with Archie on this one and it put a smile on my face.

Inspiration and support were coming from many sources. I was sitting in the parents' room this afternoon when a lady in a burka came in. We started talking and it turned out that her nine-year-old daughter was born with just half a heart. She had undergone several cutting edge operations, including one this week. The lady was used to these terrible situations and told me to stay positive and if you can't be positive then pretend to be positive. '*I was sitting beside my sleeping daughter when she woke up to catch me crying. She asked – mummy, why are you crying? Well, I couldn't tell her I was upset. So I said - one of those doctors just came along and poked me in the eye*'. This put another smile on my face.

> ***Nurse Katie*** - *Well Jothi, what can I say? We are like the terrible two when we get together. Tonight, again, you helped me with my work quite spectacularly. This time you coughed out your breathing tube. Thankfully you were okay, which was the main concern. You have clearly decided enough is enough, you are fed up with me and Tracy suctioning you, so thought you would save us the trouble. You are working a little bit hard with your breathing, but it has not got worse overnight which is very reassuring. We have had to put another cannula in you, as you very helpfully pulled one out earlier and the other one that you had was really sore, so we took it out. Your blood results are slowly improving which, fingers crossed, means you're getting much better. Your feet and legs are still swollen, but they are going down. You also did the biggest wee I have ever seen, me and your mummy were amazed.*

I can't wait to see you when you're better Jothi. Your big beautiful eyes and those lovely eyelashes make me feel so guilty when I have to do horrible things to you. You look so scared, I'm so sorry. It's hard to explain to you that all these horrid things will make you better.

Thanks again for being such a star and keeping me on my toes. I am back Wednesday night, so will come and see you. Keep strong.

Lots of love Katie XX

Yes, Jothi's breathing tube was out again. My eyes spent an inordinate amount of time looking and looking again and again and again at the Oxygen saturation figures. His breathing was not easy but was a definite improvement compared to Saturday night.

TUESDAY 16TH NOVEMBER

2.40am, bedroom, lift, atrium, doors, corner, stairs, corridor, 'it's Jothi's dad', doors, corner, my boy, Bharathi, hug, Bharathi to our room. Bharathi re-appeared at 6.30am, tea, bedroom, sleep.

The day started very well. It was wonderful to see Jothi without the tubes and looking around. His eyes following people and his dry mouth open wide for the water I could give him, which came from him sucking a tiny wet sponge on a little stick. If they aren't already called sponge lollipops they really should be. Jothi was propped up on pillows because he couldn't hold himself up in a sitting position or even support his own head. He had a good morning, but suddenly started shaking uncontrollably and had a seizure. Bharathi noticed first and yelled to the nurse, by which time Jothi had got himself out of it. However, it was a bad sign and could indicate brain damage. The doctors said that he would need a CT scan to make sure nothing was wrong with his brain. Oh to go through all this and then have a chance of brain damage.

It broke our heart to see Jothi sedated again and needing the breathing tube re-inserted so that he could go for the scan. Our poor baby's body had gone through so much in the last week. And just when things seemed to be getting better! Ahhhhhh!

We wheeled his bed, and a sense of dread, to the CT department. I felt physically sick. As we waited, a radio sounded in the background. I could hear Belinda Carlisle singing 'Heaven is a place on earth'. That was the song that I heard when I went to collect my first exam results as a 16-year-old

– they were far better than anyone expected and put me on the unexpected path to university. I clung desperately to the good omen.

We waited for his scan results with a sense of trepidation. Come on Jothi. *'We are glad to tell you his brain seems fine'* – the tension gripping my body was released in a wave of relief. It was fantastic news.

Gena, from the Philippines, was his nurse during his seizure and looked after him during the scan and when he returned to PICU. She refused to take her lunch break until the evening when he was settled back into PICU and his figures had returned to the morning's levels.

Marilyn, our consultant, talked to us about what Jothi had been through and that he was showing that he was a little fighter. As she talked about him her eyes filled up with tears. It amazes me, time and again, how much these wonderful people care about Jothi and all the other children.

In the afternoon I was settled in my seat next to Jothi when suddenly an alarm screeched through PICU. Doctors were scrambling to the source of the alarm, in a bid to resuscitate a child. It sent a shiver down my spine. If there is a car accident, everyone has a look. This was the opposite. I, and every other parent looked in any direction, except for where the alarm rang. It feels as though everyone is in this together and you want everyone to get out of it. Poor child, poor parents, come on you wonderful doctors and nurses – save them.

Wednesday 17th November

2.40am, bedroom, lift, atrium, doors, corner, stairs, corridor, 'it's Jothi's dad', doors, corner, my boy, Bharathi, hug, Bharathi to our room. Bharathi re-appeared at 6.30am, tea, leave, bedroom, sleep.

I am not sure whether to write nice statistics or low heart rate. The figures on Jothi's machines look nicer than before, but that heart rate looks a little too low for my liking. Although, the real story of the day is nice statistics. When Ravi came in to see Jothi this morning, he looked at the screen showing heart rate, oxygen saturation, blood pressure and said *'nice statistics'*. And I chuckled. To tell you the truth, I have normally been keeping such a close eye on the statistics that I have set internal beeps in my head. These go off before the actual beep and I won't turn away until it has got passed my internal reasonable level. Jothi's breathing tube was due out again today. Steve and Martin, the physios, gave him more treatment to bring up the phlegm from his chest and improve his breathing. Then this afternoon his tube came out and slowly our little miracle's character started to emerge from the sedation. Bharathi even sat him on her knee for a cuddle.

He looked so much more like his normal self. I spent time with him reading, but he was very weak and stiff, so the nurse recommended that Jothi returned to bed. I stroked his head and ran my fingers through his hair. However, he wasn't for lying still and seemed to indicate, by hooking his hand into my shirt's top pocket, that he wanted a cuddle or at least get out of bed again. So he sat back on my knee and I gave him a cuddle like the proudest dad in the world. Although it is not surprising as, at that moment, I probably was the proudest dad in the world. When Bharathi came back, he put both arms up for a cuddle with her. I then phoned my mum and dad. I spoke to mum, who relayed to my dad that Jothi was improving. She then went into the kitchen and burst into tears. My worried dad rushed into the kitchen and demanded to know what had happened to Jothi and what wasn't she telling him. She had to reassure him it was tears of relief and that everything was moving in the right direction. Dad adored Jothi and sat in his armchair for many an hour, with a picture of his only grandson fixed on his armrest, willing him to get better.

When Ravi saw me later he said that Jothi was back on the bed, but putting his arms up for Bharathi to pick him up again. When this did not work, he turned to Ravi and lifted up his arms to get picked up by him.

Every day, either Bharathi or I had stayed overnight by Jothi's side (with help from Graham, Ravi and Smita). That was our intention again tonight, but Nurse Mary had other ideas. She was the archetypal large West Indian mum (big-hearted, loving and 'no arguments'). She told us unequivocally that Jothi would be fine with her and that we would need all the sleep we could get, ready for him being moved out of PICU. We were ordered to get a proper night's sleep.

Bharathi - *I'm so glad Ravi and Graham have been here with us. Ravi is looking after all the calls from India, staying with you and sleeping on the floor tonight in our room. He has been a tower of strength to me. Graham has been a tower of strength for daddy and both your uncles love you so much. I can see that in their faces, and their tears and in their smiles.*

No more setbacks okay? I want my Jothi better, I want to see you smile and you calling 'daddy'. We both love you so much chellum. Mary is looking after you. Daddy and I liked her straight away. You are sleeping peacefully, so mummy is going to sleep. Then be ready for you tomorrow when you wake up. You looked so scared yesterday night, watching nurses coming near you. I just want to hold you baby and make you feel safe. Love you.

Thursday 18ᵗʰ November 2010

Nurse Mary - Morning handsome, you have been the most brave boy in the unit tonight. You had your breathing tube taken out yesterday afternoon and you did very well. You have been doing it all yourself and your numbers have been just right. You started drinking and eating banana delight, which you love very much. You slept fairly well and your parents have stayed beside you most of the night because they love you and want you to get better. Well done handsome, your nurse Mary

Nurse Katie - Hey Jothi, I didn't look after you last night as I was not sure anyone else could cope with a terrible two get together. I was looking after a little baby next to you, so I got to see you, and we read a book about a caterpillar and I gave you some lollipops with water on. It is so nice to see how much better you're looking, well done.

I am on holiday from today and am so pleased to know you look so much better. I will be checking up on you though - so keep improving.

It has been a pleasure to look after you Jothi and to meet your lovely family. You are understandably so very loved. Keep fighting and getting stronger, love Katie XX

At 6.00am I left the bedroom with Bharathi. Then went down a floor, in a lift, out the lift, across the atrium, through some doors, round a corner, up two flights of stairs, across a corridor, pressed the intercom button, 'it's Jothi's mum and dad', through the security doors and then round a corner to my wonderful little boy and nurse Mary. I didn't hug Nurse Mary, but I thanked her warmly. Bharathi and I looked at our little boy. My mouth started salivating for the tea round.

Today would be different. Jothi had reached the stage where he is breathing comfortably by himself, his medicines have been drastically reduced and the infection has almost gone. We were, therefore, being moved from PICU to a High Dependency ward. We thanked everyone, from the very bottom of our hearts, for getting us through a traumatic week and then moved to the High Dependency ward.

The new ward was like PICU, in that it was bright and colourful. However, it was set out in more of a traditional ward layout and had the added attraction of special toy rooms. We no longer had a nurse who focussed solely on Jothi. Instead, we had to vie for attention with five other patients. The onus on looking after Jothi's normal needs was now very much on us – and that was what nurse Mary had been trying to tell us. The ward change also meant that we lost our hospital accommodation room. Instead, Bharathi had a bed next to Jothi that pulled down from the wall and I was found a room at Ronald MacDonald house. Yes, that is right, Ronald MacDonald house. I wasn't sure what to expect, but was fairly sure it wouldn't be full of men in red wigs with long red shoes and coated in red and white makeup. It was two miles away, down the Thames, near Guys Hospital. The accommodation had a small reception area and there were corridors of rooms along at least two floors, plus a television and breakfast area. It reminded me of a student's Halls of Residence. Although the main difference was that everybody there had a loved one undergoing serious medical treatment. It was understandably not the most joyful of places, but there was an undercurrent of camaraderie.

An inter-hospital shuttle bus took me to see Jothi each day. I'd arrive at about 8.30am and stay until lunchtime. My employer had been incredibly supportive of me. Although we were a small company, of 16 people, they gave me compassionate leave whilst Jothi was in intensive care, allowed me to work half days while Jothi was in the High Dependency unit and Tony, my boss, even came to visit Jothi in PICU. Their main concern was Jothi. Bharathi worked for the NHS. Whilst Jothi was in his first week in intensive care, Bharathi was receiving calls from them asking curtly when she would be back. It was only when Bharathi told them where they could stick their job, that they changed their attitude and just wanted to be informed of Jothi's progress.

Although Jothi had moved from PICU he was still physically weak and struggled to even hold up his own head. His usual cheekiness wasn't there when we started in the new ward and he was understandably clingy. At times, usually at night, he would cry uncontrollably. They say that adults who have been in an intensive care ward can struggle with nightmares – so god knows what was going through Jothi's head.

Bharathi found it particularly hard at night when she was shattered and he was crying and couldn't sleep. In the end, the nurses gave her a pushchair and she would push him around the ward to lull him to sleep. This had the advantage that occasionally the nurses would take over the pushing without Jothi realising. Then Bharathi could grab a quick nap until the nurse brought him back.

Every morning Bharathi would be shattered. I'd arrive to look after Jothi whilst Bharathi would try to catch up on some sleep. Although quite often, when I arrived, they'd both be asleep. It took several days, and my brother larking about, for Jothi's smile to re-appear. Another three days passed before he started laughing again and then the voice was back 'Daddy!' 'Daddy!'. There was no sweeter sound in the world.

Bharathi and I both found the new routine very tiring, especially on top of the emotional exhaustion of the previous two weeks. I was even a bit jealous of parents who were 'just' in the High Dependency ward for a few days. Although some children had spent months in the hospital. Next to us, was a lady called Iman and her 12-month-old baby. Her baby had significant mental and physical limitations and had spent his whole life in the hospital so far. Iman spent a large chunk of every day in the hospital and her marriage had collapsed under the strain. We had tremendous admiration for her dedication. We were thinking that we were exhausted and here she was living this stressful, worrisome, exhausting hospital life for a year. I told her she was amazing and asked how she managed it. Her answer was simple '*I am inspired by my son*'. She was right, just looking at Jothi gave me the strength to carry on doing whatever I could to help him. I just hadn't realised it until she told me.

We realised that we owed a huge debt to the PICU team. One evening we nipped down to PICU to start trying to pay off that debt in boxes of chocolates - with extra boxes of chocolates and special cards for Gena, Suzanne and Katie. Katie had already phoned up the nurse, looking after Jothi, in High Dependency to see how he was getting on and then came up to see him as well. I thought it was strange that we hardly ever had the same nurse caring for him in PICU, but Bharathi said that this is to stop the nurses getting too attached to the children. I'm not sure whether that worked in Jothi's case. All the nurses seem to be emotionally attached to him, although maybe that is why the PICU in the Evelina Hospital is world class, because they care so much. It was a strange feeling to visit PICU. I got a feeling of dread in the pit of my stomach, but an equal feeling of inspiration.

I continued to stay at Ronald McDonald house and on several occasions spoke to a Scottish family. One morning, I asked the grandmother how her baby granddaughter was doing. She sadly confirmed to me that she had died in the night. There is nothing you can say - just listen. She told me that they had been on a walk that morning, when a little girl, who she had never seen before, picked up a flower and gave it to her. She said it was a beautiful moment, in a sea of desolation, and felt like a message from her granddaughter. It is only now that I remember describing that when Jothi was taken ill, hope seemed like a flower. It seems bizarrely coincidental that for this poor family, the flower was plucked and passed to them.

They were leaving the accommodation that day and would have to start thinking about the funeral. I had thought, on a number of occasions, that I could be organising Jothi's funeral and expressed heartfelt sympathy. I knew that it would be horrific for them. If it had been me I would have bouts of crying for weeks and months. I'm English, so after the first couple of weeks I'd probably cry in the shower to cover up my tears, but life would never be the same. In fact, following this experience, I could never truly be mad with Jothi. It wouldn't stop me telling him off, but I would appreciate the fact that I could still tell him off.

Slowly, day by day, Jothi improved. After two weeks, in the High Dependency unit, we were transferred back to Stevenage hospital. We were there for just one night before being allowed back home, albeit with daily visits to the hospital. Jothi took a further six weeks to regain his strength sufficiently to crawl around and another four weeks to re-learn how to walk. I had suppressed my feelings when I was told he had turned the corner and would survive, I had suppressed my feelings when he'd been allowed to transfer from PICU to High Dependency, I had suppressed my feelings when we were transferred to Stevenage and I had suppressed my feelings when we were finally released home. I expressed satisfaction on each occasion, but there always seemed a long way to go. But when he took those first steps since he'd been ill, the tears rolled down my cheeks – he had made it through.

THE THOUGHTS OF JOTHI

When Jothi started to talk, as with every child, he came out with some beautiful lines. This is the world according to Jothi Brown (age 2 to 3):

Jothi seemed quite interested in tennis from a young age:

During the 2011 Wimbledon ladies final, Jothi woke from his afternoon sleep. I put him on my knee as he slowly woke up. Bharathi returned from completing the weekly shopping. Jothi, immediately looked at Bharathi, pointed at the tv screen and said *'nice ladies'*.

During the 2012 Wimbledon – *'Where is Sharapova?'* It was only then that I realised that Jothi's interest in tennis nearly always coincided with Sharapova playing.

Jothi loved the 2012 Olympics

Jothi was in the midst of watching some gold medal-winning British cyclists blazing around the velodrome. The commentator said '...and the British cyclists are on fire.' *'Oh no'* said a concerned looking Jothi.

On watching basketball - *'Why don't they play tennis instead?'*

After going to the Olympics - *'Can I take the Olympic park home?'*

Just nuts

Whilst complaining about not being offered some cashew nuts. *'I want some'*. 'I didn't think you liked nuts.' *'Yes I do, I like doughnuts'*. (We laughed at this and then thought – what has the childminder been feeding him?)

Probably right

'Did Uncle Graham pick his nose?' (after my brother had a nose bleed soon after Jothi had been warned picking his nose could make it bleed).

On divorce

In response to a friend's parents being divorced. *'If you and mummy ever try to separate I will get some glue and stick you back together.'*

On his future:

'I want to be a footballer when I grow up'

'Do you know Joe Hart?'

'Don't want to be a football man or tennis man, want to get a trailer and attach it to a fire engine with rope and follow the fire engine around all day and invite everyone on to my trailer.'

Epilogue

I am travelling on a plane by myself. Bharathi and Jothi are in India and I am embarking on a short trip. Well, it is a short-big trip. In fact, it is the shortest-biggest trip I've ever been on. The reason for the 'short' in my trip can be traced back to Jothi contracting Meningitis seven years ago.

We thought he had beaten this vicious disease, especially after he started walking again in 2011 and then was quickly running around. He continued having check-ups for a while, which looked for signs of side-effects, but Jothi seemed to be sailing through. At one such check-up, a physio said that it would be a long time before he could hop. The two-year-old Jothi responded to that by jumping up and down on one leg and saying *'like this?'*

Hold on, the flight attendant is approaching with an important question. 'Yes, red wine please'. 'Um, thank you'. Two little bottles of red wine may be more than I was expecting, but it is kind of the steward to put an extra one on my tray. I'm sure it will help me carry on with my explanation. Where was I? Besides 40,000 feet up in the air. Oh yes, Jothi continues to be a positive ball of energy, but he hasn't had an easy time.

He has undergone five painful operations to correct a separate bladder problem. That includes two operations that made the problem worse and for three months left him in screaming agony every time he went for a wee. After a running battle to convince Addenbrooke's hospital that there was a problem, they finally concluded it was a nightmare. As our concern mounted, one of our friend's, Smita, suggested we seek a second opinion. Through Smita, we spoke to an Indian urologist from Kings Lynn who said the man we needed to talk to was Peter from Great Ormond Street hospital. We booked an appointment with him and walked into his office full of anguish. He took one look at us and said *'don't worry, whatever it is I can sort it out for you'*. He undid the previous operations and then, after another procedure, he had Jothi capable of peeing for England (or India).

This may be turning a bit Aesop's fables, but the moral of the story is - 'if you are in any doubt about what you have been told about a health issue then get a second opinion'. I have digressed slightly but a picture is slowly taking shape whilst my wine waits seductively in my glass (the plastic glass is not quite as enticing as its contents). Jothi was four years old when the water-works were finally flowing beautifully. We were so thankful that we seemed to be at the end of all the operations because they were thoroughly unpleasant. Bharathi and I hated hanging around fretting whilst he was undergoing an operation. We equally detested that before every operation he would sit on my knee whilst a mask, filled with smelly gas, would be put on his face to send him off to an unconscious state. After experiencing this once, he knew what was to come and would usually fight, struggle and hit anyone near him. I'd hold his arms and body tight to restrain him while the anaesthetist would keep the mask over his face until he was unconscious. Happily, all of that seemed to be over. He was just a healthy little boy, full of energy, loving tennis, cycling, football and life. This lasted for six months.

Then he started limping. The limp gradually deteriorated until he couldn't walk. It was then that we noticed his right leg was somewhat bent. We took him to the local hospital which after tests referred us to their orthopaedic surgeon. As experienced hospital parents, we also sought a second opinion. The local orthopaedic surgeon said it was 'interesting' and to come back in six months. The second opinion said that it was highly likely that the meningitis had damaged the growth plates in Jothi's knees and ankles. This had resulted in his legs not growing properly and one leg being longer than the other. Bharathi was concerned that he wouldn't be able to play any more sport, but I thought there had been professional sports people that had overcome a significant leg length discrepancy. The first name on an internet search was David Beckham but Usain Bolt got a mention too – that didn't sound too bad. Unfortunately, it soon became apparent that Jothi had the added issue that his legs wouldn't grow properly and would mean that Jothi would need many more operations. Even writing this now has led me to quickly drain the contents of my glass. There are tough times ahead.

The damage to Jothi's growth plates meant that his tibia and fibula were growing at different rates, with his tibia hardly growing at all. Every two to three months he would have a growth spurt and we'd watch his walking grind down to a halt. The 'halt' period would last about a week and then slowly, over about six weeks, he would improve until he could jog again. Well for about four weeks, then the process started again.

I know this context is taking a bit of time, but I am slowly getting to the point. He had an operation to slow the growth in the fibula, it took the pain away but didn't help straighten or lengthen his leg. His left leg has now also started bending due to the same damaged growth plate problem. The only lower leg growth he is now likely to receive sounds like medieval torture. His legs will be broken and metal pins from an external frame are inserted into his tibia and fibula. We will then need to turn screws in the frame to stretch the bone over a 10-week process. Despite all this Jothi is the fastest cyclist in his class and when he is fit plays tennis to a good standard. Where are you going with this? Well, this year he may have his first big leg breaking operation. I'm therefore saving up all my holiday for the big operation and it means that I am on a ridiculously short trip to India to attend my niece's wedding.

My niece, Jane, was brought up in India but lived a large part of the last three years with us in England. Although her name may lead you to think that she is related through my side of the family she is Bharathi's sister's daughter, and I'm not sure how she received such an English sounding name. At the age of 26, and having seen many of her Indian friends getting married, Jane decided that she'd like an arranged marriage. The more modern Indian arranged marriages seem to be similar to normal internet dating but with extra questions about career, education, religion and parents. Although the main difference seems to be that by the second date you decide whether you are going to get married. I found it both fascinating and terrifying.

After several months of this process, Jane hadn't reached the successfully concluded second date stage (or terrifying second date conclusion if you're an uncle not used to things moving so fast). The reasons ranged from '*he sent a message saying I was wonderful but too much of an independent woman for him*', '*I'm not sure I could live with a man that smokes*', '*he seemed nice, but has disappeared*', '*there was no chemistry with him*' and the one that bemused Jane most of all – '*this has been going on for two months now; the parents have been to our house and I've met his brother-in-law, sister-in-law and niece. They have asked for my measurements to work out whether we are physically compatible and whether I would move to Germany (where he is currently working), but I've still not met or even spoken to the boy!*' Jane thought that the arranged marriage process was maybe not for her and decided to bring proceedings to a halt. It was at that point a suitor named Richie phoned Jane's mum saying he would like to meet Jane. Bharathi's sister said '*you live in America but Jane doesn't want to live there*'. Richie confirmed that although he liked living in the States he could move to England if it made sense. To which Jane's mum said '*but she can't cook*'. Richie's response was that he could cook so it was not a problem. His details were then passed on to Jane and they arranged a time to meet up when they were both back in India. They met in Bangalore and got on very well. Jane then visited him in America at which point they decided to get married. I pleaded with Jane that this was emotionally too quick for me and I wasn't ready to become an uncle-in-law. Despite this, a wedding date was set for the 16th July in India and everything seemed to move forward quickly, so I felt the best course of action was to support Jane in her plans to get married, move to America and start a new job. The thought of so much commitment, so quickly, has driven me to the second little bottle of wine.

Very logically I announced that I probably couldn't make the wedding because I may need all my remaining holiday for Jothi's likely operation. Bharathi understood this but a combination of wedding stress, Jothi going to India on crutches, potential Indian social stigma (that meant if I didn't turn up it was a bad sign of our marriage) and just wanting me there, all built up to my Indian princess telling me where I could shove my logic. I really wanted to go to Jane's wedding as she is probably as near to having a daughter as I'll have and I've always wanted to go to an Indian wedding. This meant that the choice became: go with the logic (after I'd retrieved it and given it a good clean) or fly to India for the weekend. Bharathi also said that she could barely put into words how much she wanted me at the wedding, which is a difficult argument to counter.

Bharathi always could run rings around me in arguments. I remember the one time where I was winning an argument. Bharathi was claiming that I always got my own way to which I gave numerous examples of Bharathi getting her wish on a host of important decisions. To which she responded '*Exactly, so what is the point of arguing with me if all that is going to happen is that I get my own way*'. It seemed to be the football equivalent of dribbling past a couple of defenders shooting gloriously into the top corner of the net only to find that I had scored an own goal.

In this wedding quandary, there is sound logic supported by good financial sense on one side. On the other side is a desire to be at Jane's wedding, backed by the wife. Depending on your point of view, I either gave in to the inevitable or (for the romantics out there) love overcame logic and I am on the 1.00pm Saturday flight from London. This arrives at 3.00am on Sunday morning in Chennai, but I will be back in England on Monday.

Despite my complaints, there is the traveller in me that is excited by the whirlwind nature of the trip. I only booked a few days ago, so Jane still doesn't know that I'm coming to the wedding.

Sunday 16th July

I came out of Chennai airport at 4.00am and there waiting for me were a beaming Bharathi and Stu Blood (yes, Stu of my previous India and Australia trips). Stu, his wife and children have all come across to India for the wedding experience. Stu immediately reminded me that it was 20 years since we had last been in India together, but surely I am still young, so how could it be 20 years? Unfortunately, whichever way I did the maths the answer was still 20 years.

We drove back to the hotel and I went to bed for the next seven hours. I quite liked the idea of Jane not realising that I was in India until she gets to the church. However, a wise friend pointed out that she would be emotional enough already and unexpectedly seeing her uncle may tip her over the emotional precipice. Anyway, Jane was tipped off that there was a surprise in Bharathi's room and came in to find a sleeping uncle.

It was great to be there for the wedding and to be part of my Indian family. Who would have thought that 20 years after Stu and I were originally in India we'd be so involved in an Indian wedding. In fact, based on my first backpacking trip I think I've done well to get anywhere outside of Lille. The wedding reception slowly wound down and we returned to our room where I kissed Jothi goodnight and told him I'd see him when he returns to England in a week. He has tough operations ahead but he has a happy knack of making the most of the good times and we try to enjoy the tough times because we are so lucky to still have him.

Monday 17th July

My 25 hours in India was coming to an end at 2.00am when Bharathi and Ravi took me back to the airport. I boarded the plane and was greeted cheerfully by a couple of the stewardesses. They recognised me from the flight from London because it turned out that the same flight crew that flew me to Chennai had enjoyed a good sleep and were flying me back to London.

Hold on the flight attendant is coming across with an important question. 'Thank you, but just tea for me – I am due to be in work at 1.30pm'.

Epilogue of the Epilogue

Oh no, it is the 6th May 2019 and I have still not completed my book. I want to include an update, but the publisher says I need to wrap it up in 14 words. As that is the case, the only appropriate word to finish on is:

'JothiHadTwoBigLegBreakingOperationsIn2018HeIsGettingFitAgainBy CyclingSwimmingSneakingOffToPlayFootballLearningGuitar AndGenerallyGrabbingLifeWithBothHandsSoIBetterFollowHisExample ByGettingThisBookPublishedAndEnjoyThisExtraordinaryWorld'

ACKNOWLEDGEMENTS

Well, we've reached the end of our journey and it is time to go our separate ways. I've put blood, sweat and beers (oh okay, a few tears and some afternoon naps) into the writing of this book but there are many people who have helped along the way. Yes, it is that Oscar type speech time. So thanks mum for always encouraging me to keep a holiday diary (even if the first one was a trip to Wales when I was 8 and it mainly said 'rained') and my late dad for the dubious sense of humour that I inherited. Ironically it is mum that is always late and dad that was early but there we go – that is life and death for you.

Whilst I remember; I better mention books I've used during my trips that were often a source of my historical or local information. There has been Europe by Train, Cheap Sleep Guide, Rough Guides, Lonely Planets and Footprints. I know I read up on things when I returned from trips but never expected my diaries to be published so I didn't keep a note of books and websites. If there is anyone out there thinking that I used their facts and figures – thank you and please get in touch.

I need to give a pat on the back to all those people I pestered into checking a diary or two. Your help, word-changes, commas and enthusiasm have helped me take a breath and keep going. At the last word-count that included Nick, Triggsy, Mark, Tony, Arjun, Ian, Craggy, Jane, Bharathi and my mum. Plus a grateful handshake to everyone I asked 'what do you think to this cover/introduction/website/strange rash?'

A perfectly drawn pair of clapping hands to Emma for her cool illustrations and for stopping me having stick men on the front cover.

High fives (not sure what greetings I have left) to Kim and Sinclair at Indie Authors World for all their support. Once I teamed up with them there was never a day that I doubted that I'd finish the book.

Although Olivia Colman, in her Oscar speech, offered to snog anyone she forgot to mention, I think it is agreed all round that it is best I don't make that

offer. Instead I'll just add a huge thank you to ....
(insert your name here, especially if you helped me and I haven't mentioned you) for being so amazing.

Last but by no means least thanks to Bharathi and Jothi for putting so much effort in to providing me with a final chapter. Although both of you note for future reference, I'd have preferred a boring last chapter about a nice family holiday to Cornwall with plenty of ice cream and crazy golf.

The book is finishing and I'm getting emotional - like any Englishman in such circumstances I'm off to put the kettle on.

Any online book reviews are appreciated.

Visit my website at www.jeffbrownauthor.com

Lightning Source UK Ltd.
Milton Keynes UK
UKHW010605231119
354040UK00002B/70/P